Shojo Beat

Crimson Hero

Story & Art by

MITSUBA TAKANASHI

6

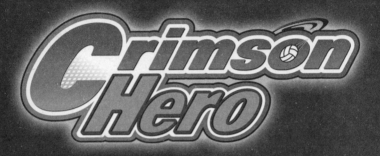

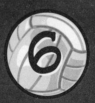

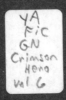

CONTENTS

STORY THUS FAR

Nobara Sumiyoshi is a first-year student in high school who lives for her one passion, volleyball. She's the successor to "Seiryu," the high-class ryotei restaurant her family runs, but she enrolled in Crimson Field High School expressly to play volleyball. When Nobara's mother arranged to have the girls' volleyball team eliminated, an angered Nobara ran away from home, and ended up living and working in the Crimson Dorm, where the boys' volleyball scholarship students live and where she met Yushin. She managed to put together a girls' team, and they went to the Inter-high Preliminaries, but they lost.

Later Nobara went to a game to cheer on the boys' team, and there she realized she had feelings for Yushin. After the game she was with Yushin when he caught his girlfriend Satomi cheating on him. Yushin was crushed and dejected, and a tearful Nobara tried to cheer him up.

During the summer volleyball intensive, newcomer Kanako provoked Nobara to confess her love to Yushin. Now Nobara's private feelings are public knowledge. Yushin rejected her, but Haibuki is pursuing her intensely!

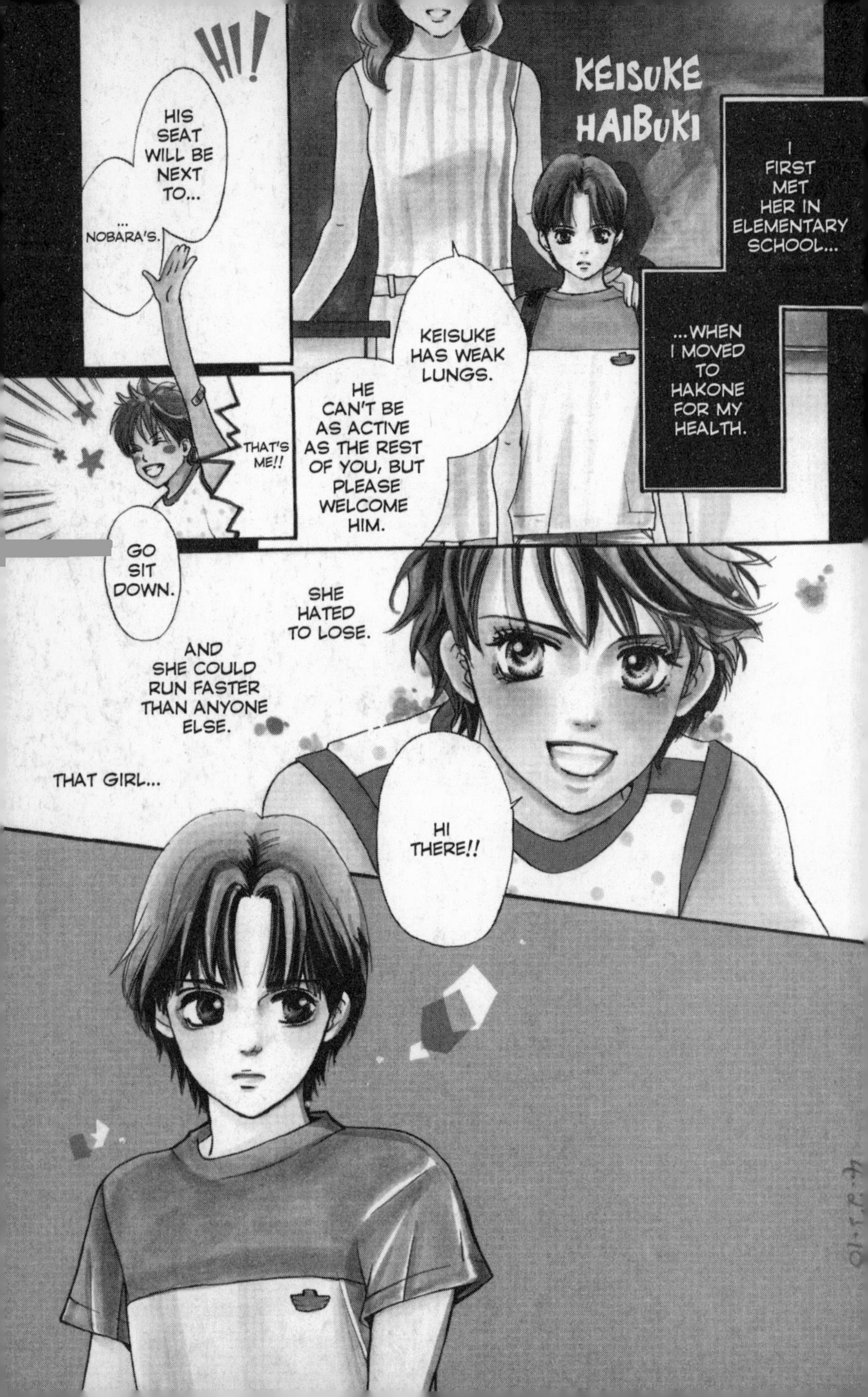
KEISUKE HAIBUKI
I FIRST MET HER IN ELEMENTARY SCHOOL...
...WHEN I MOVED TO HAKONE FOR MY HEALTH.
KEISUKE HAS WEAK LUNGS.
HE CAN'T BE AS ACTIVE AS THE REST OF YOU, BUT PLEASE WELCOME HIM.
HIS SEAT WILL BE NEXT TO...
...NOBARA'S.
HI!!
THAT'S ME!!
GO SIT DOWN.
SHE HATED TO LOSE.
AND SHE COULD RUN FASTER THAN ANYONE ELSE.
THAT GIRL...
HI THERE!!

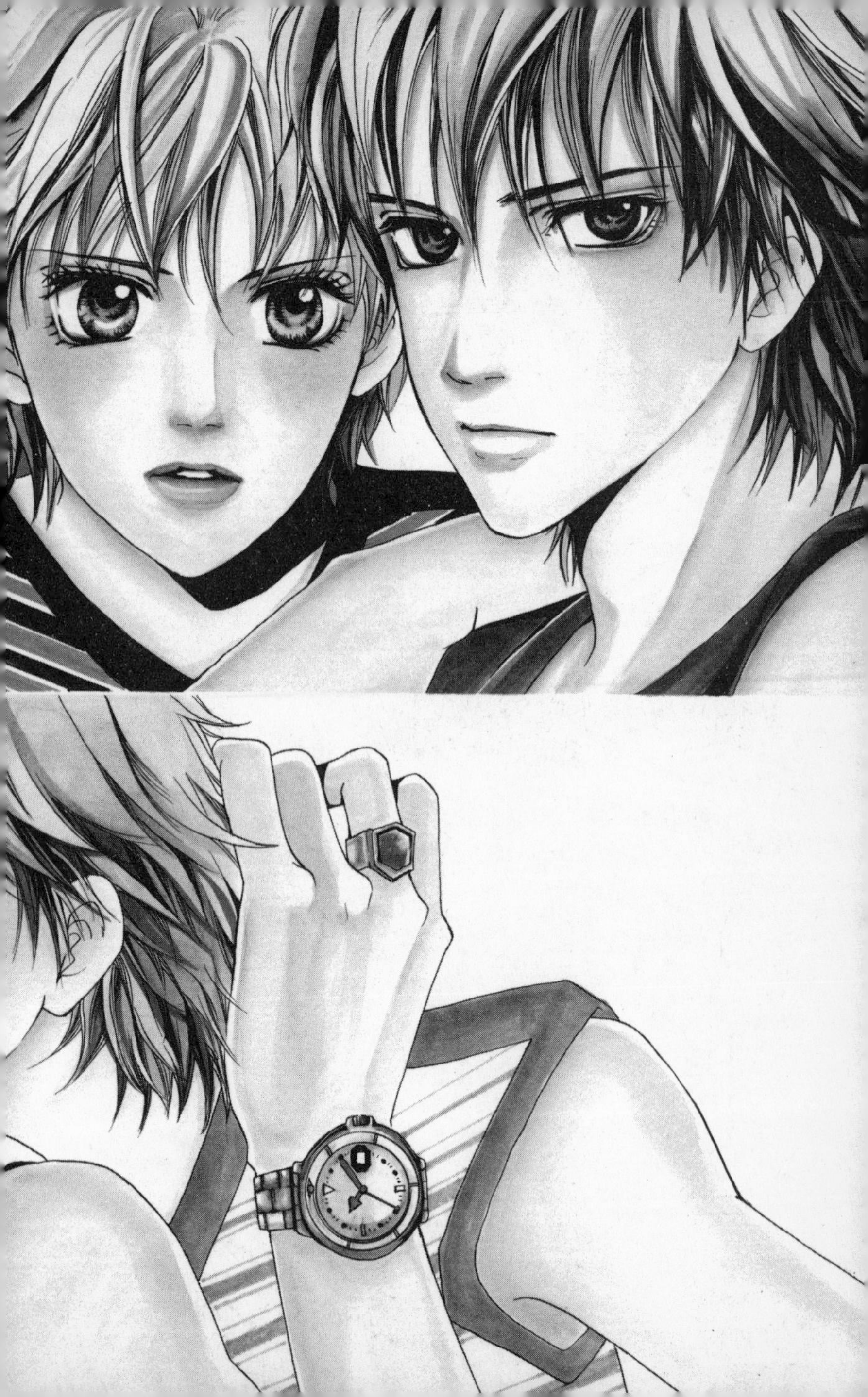

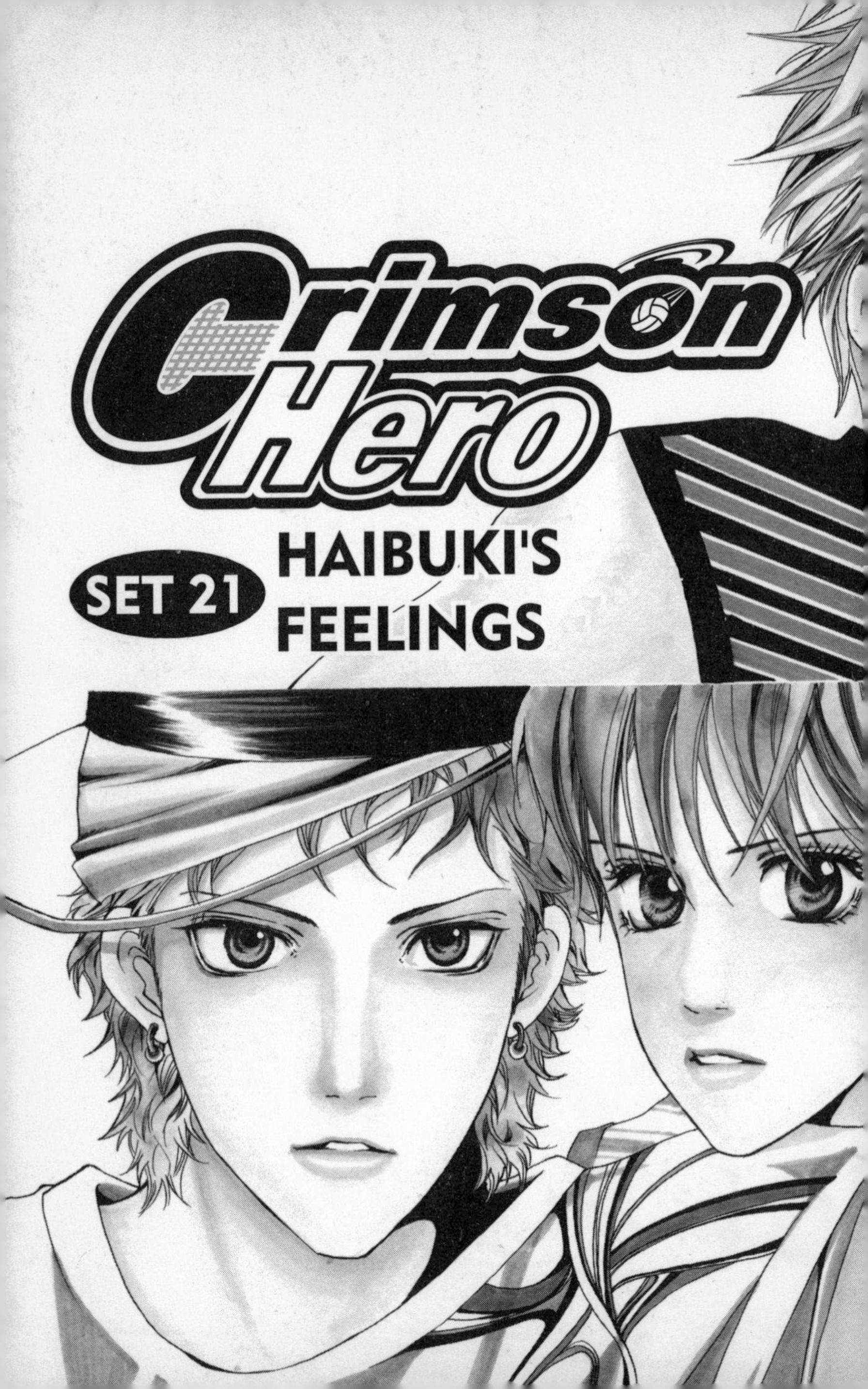
Crimson Hero
SET 21
HAIBUKI'S FEELINGS

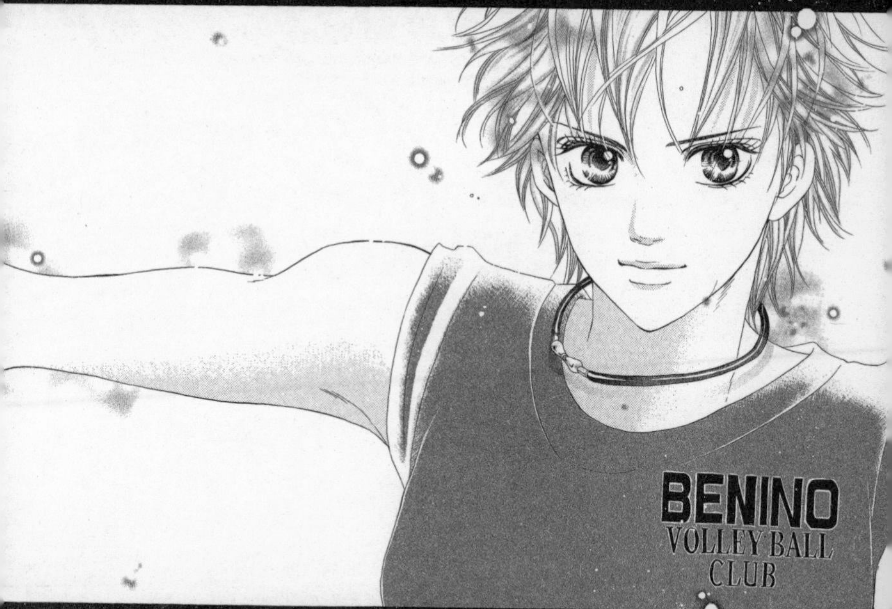
BENINO
VOLLEY BALL
CLUB

Crimson Hero

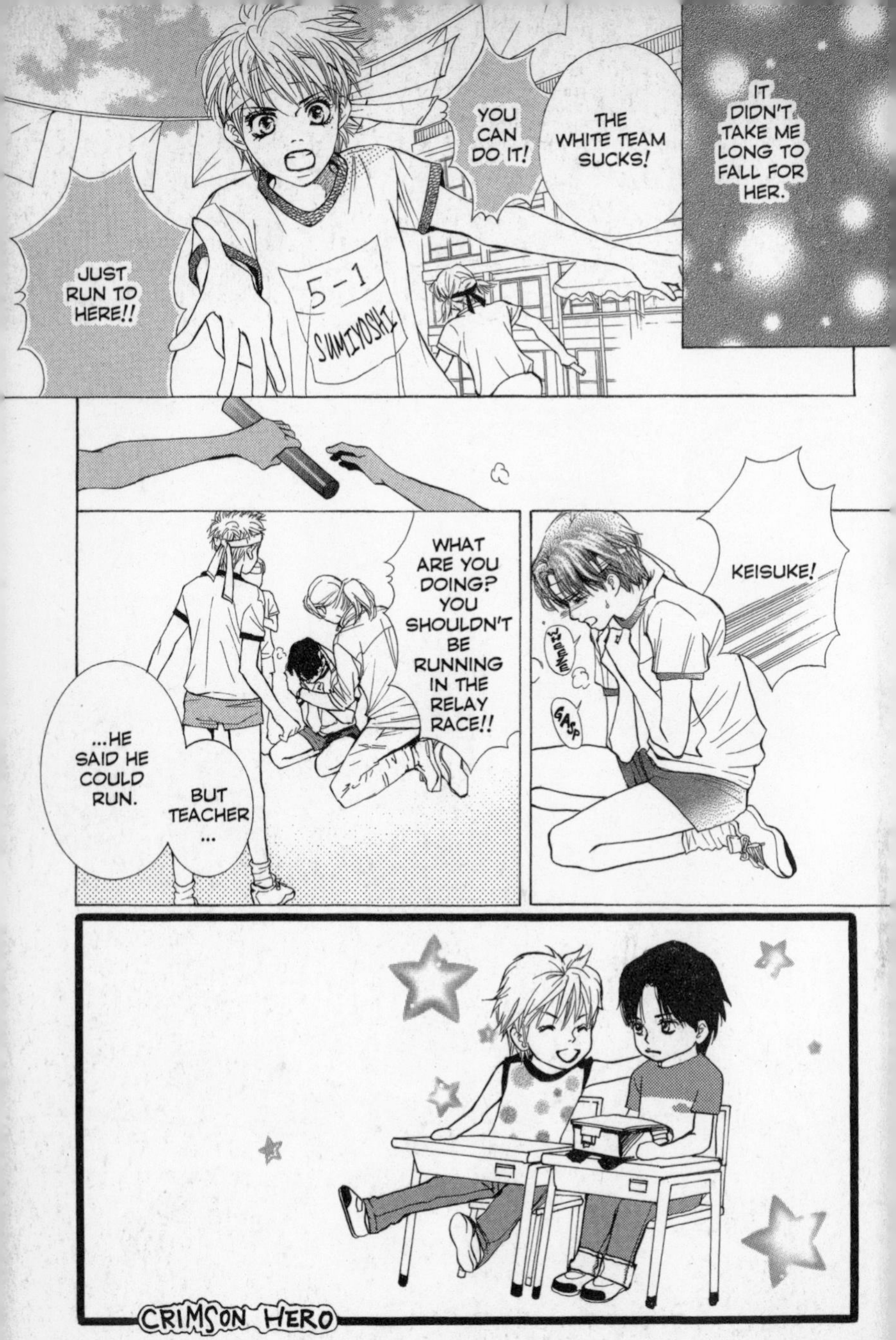

IT DIDN'T TAKE ME LONG TO FALL FOR HER.
THE WHITE TEAM SUCKS!
YOU CAN DO IT!
5-1
SUMIYOSHI
JUST RUN TO HERE!!
KEISUKE!
WHEEZE
GASP
WHAT ARE YOU DOING? YOU SHOULDN'T BE RUNNING IN THE RELAY RACE!!
BUT TEACHER...
...HE SAID HE COULD RUN.
CRIMSON HERO

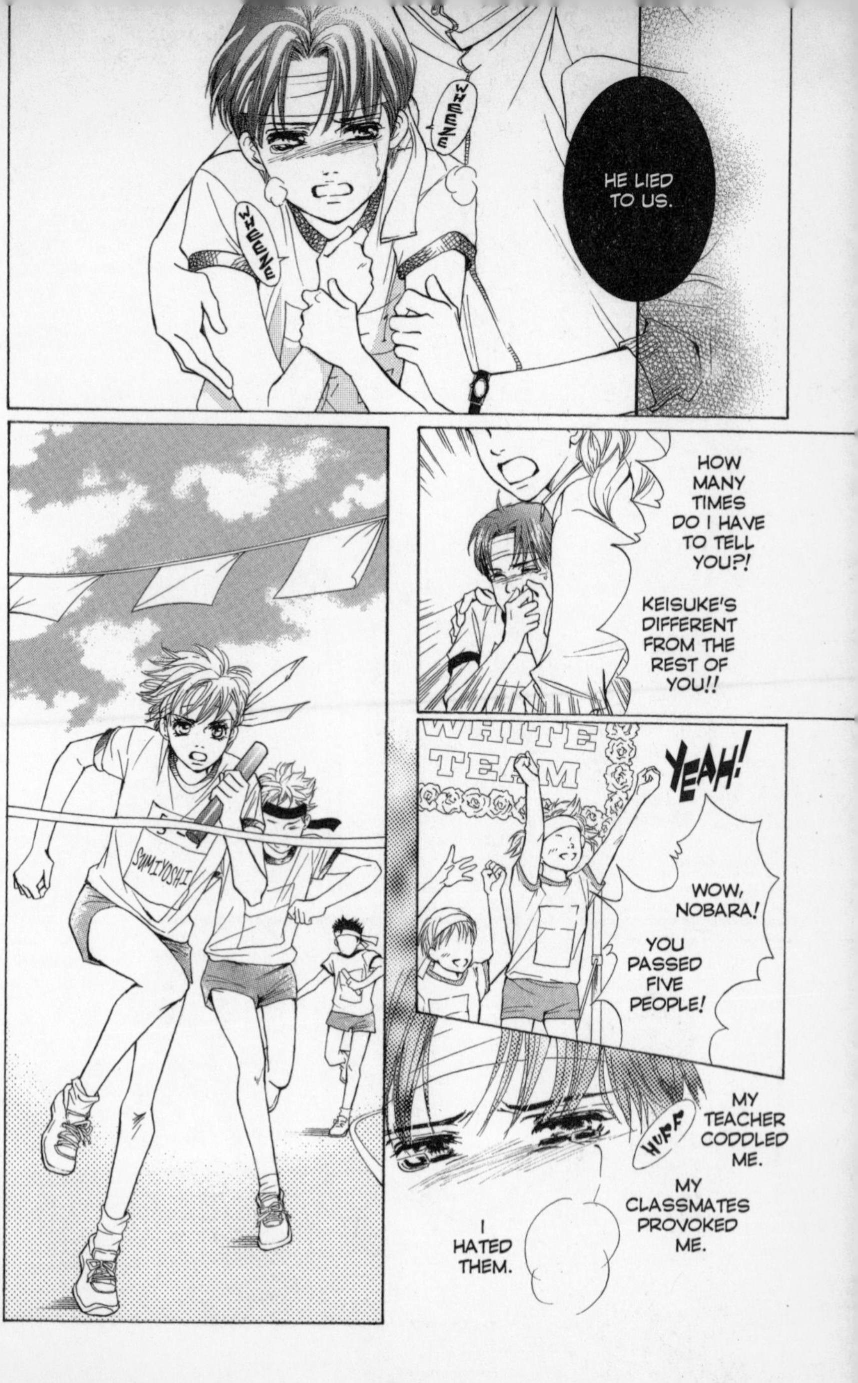
HE LIED TO US.
WHEEZE
WHEEZE
HOW MANY TIMES DO I HAVE TO TELL YOU?!
KEISUKE'S DIFFERENT FROM THE REST OF YOU!!
WHITE TEAM
YEAH!
WOW, NOBARA!
YOU PASSED FIVE PEOPLE!
MY TEACHER CODDLED ME.
HUFF
MY CLASSMATES PROVOKED ME.
I HATED THEM.
SUMIYOSHI

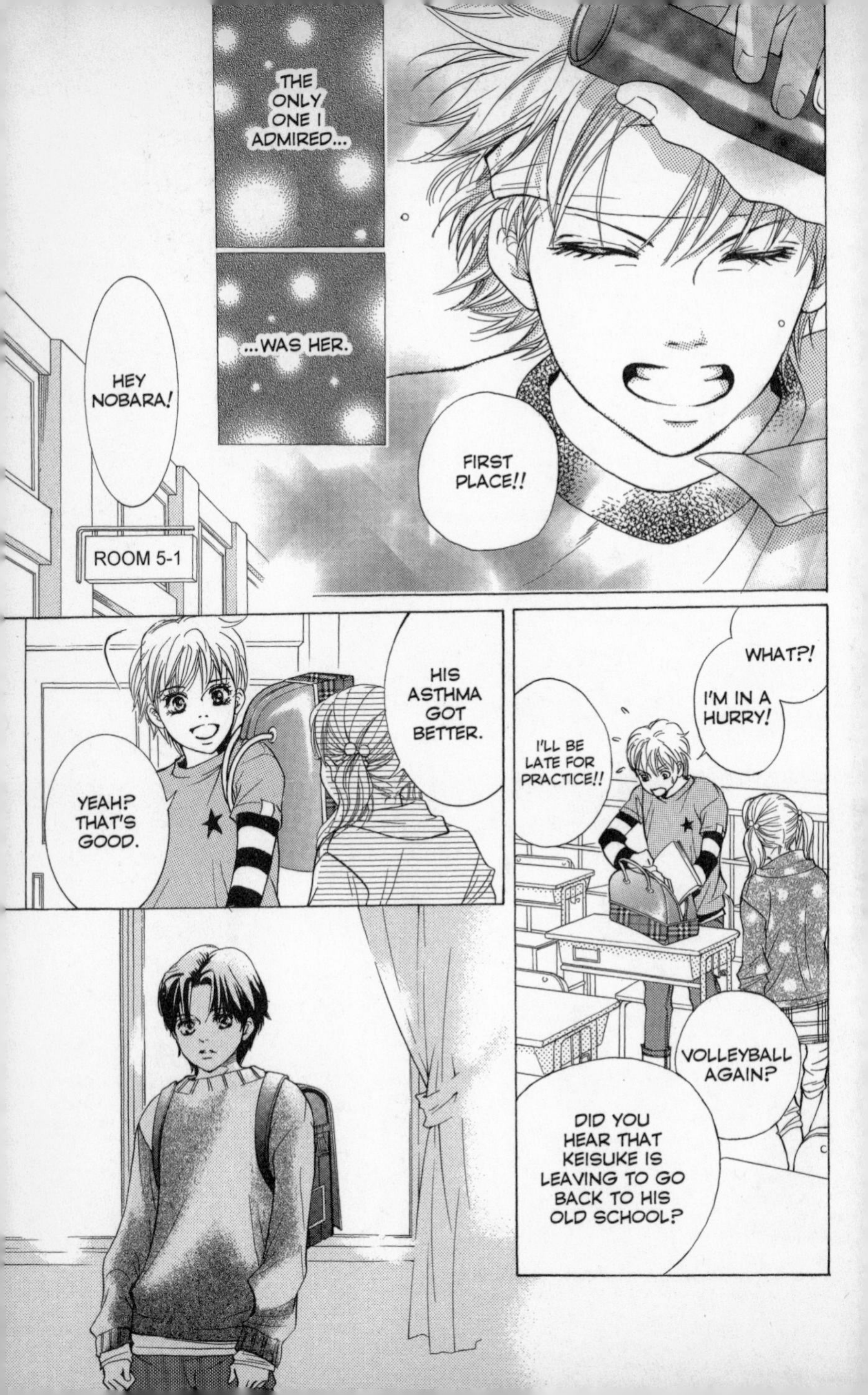
FIRST PLACE!!
THE ONLY ONE I ADMIRED...
...WAS HER.
HEY NOBARA!
ROOM 5-1
WHAT?!
I'M IN A HURRY!
I'LL BE LATE FOR PRACTICE!!
VOLLEYBALL AGAIN?
DID YOU HEAR THAT KEISUKE IS LEAVING TO GO BACK TO HIS OLD SCHOOL?
HIS ASTHMA GOT BETTER.
YEAH? THAT'S GOOD.

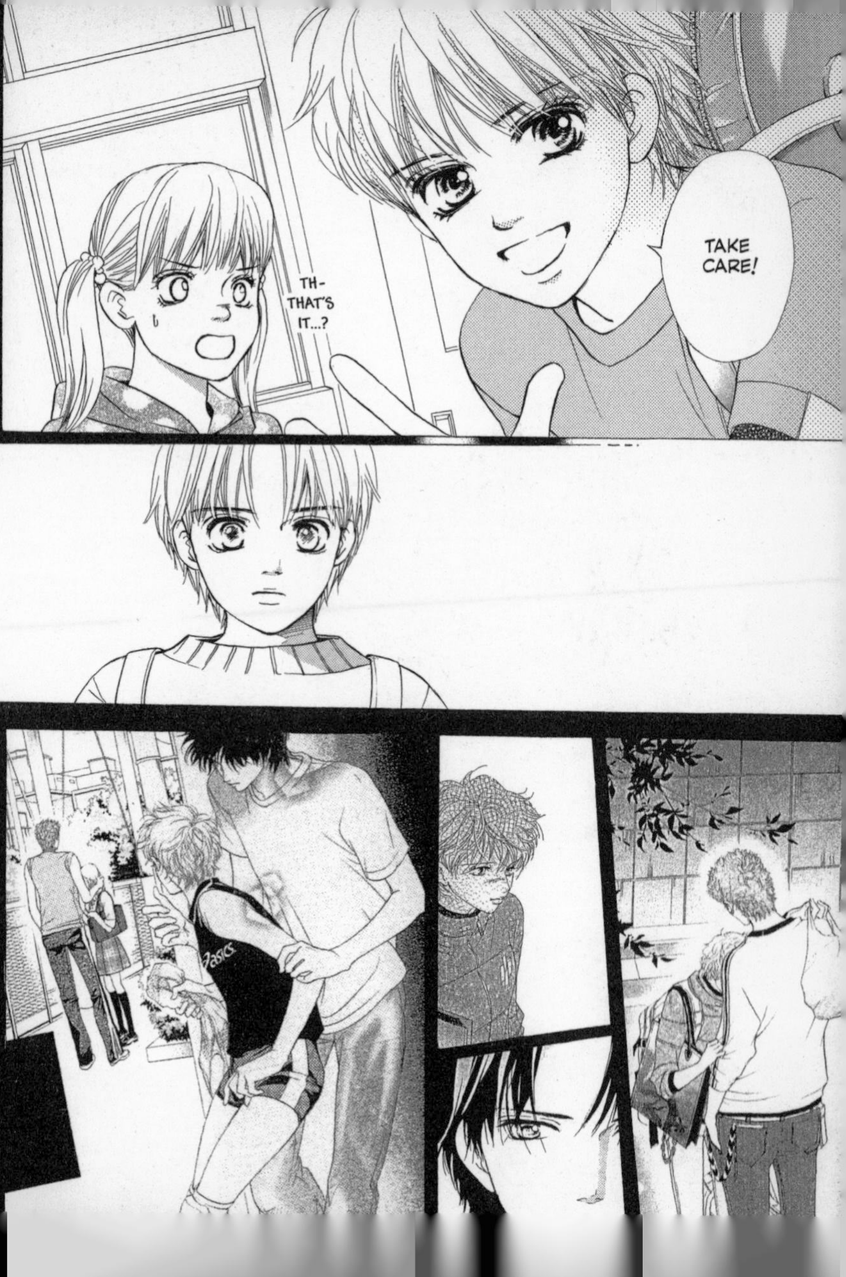
TAKE CARE!
TH- THAT'S IT...?

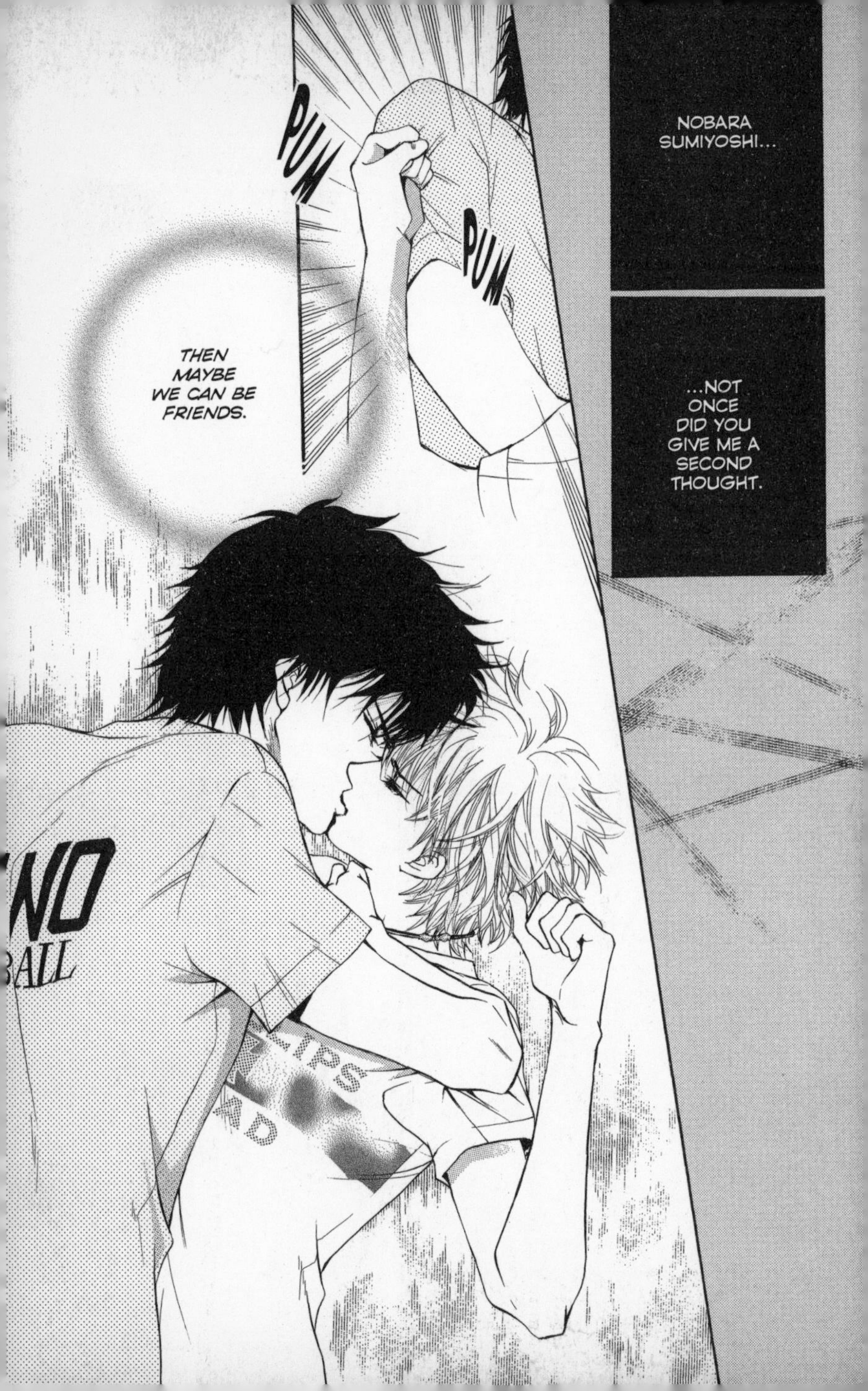
NOBARA SUMIYOSHI...
...NOT ONCE DID YOU GIVE ME A SECOND THOUGHT.
PUM PUM
PUM PUM
THEN MAYBE WE CAN BE FRIENDS.

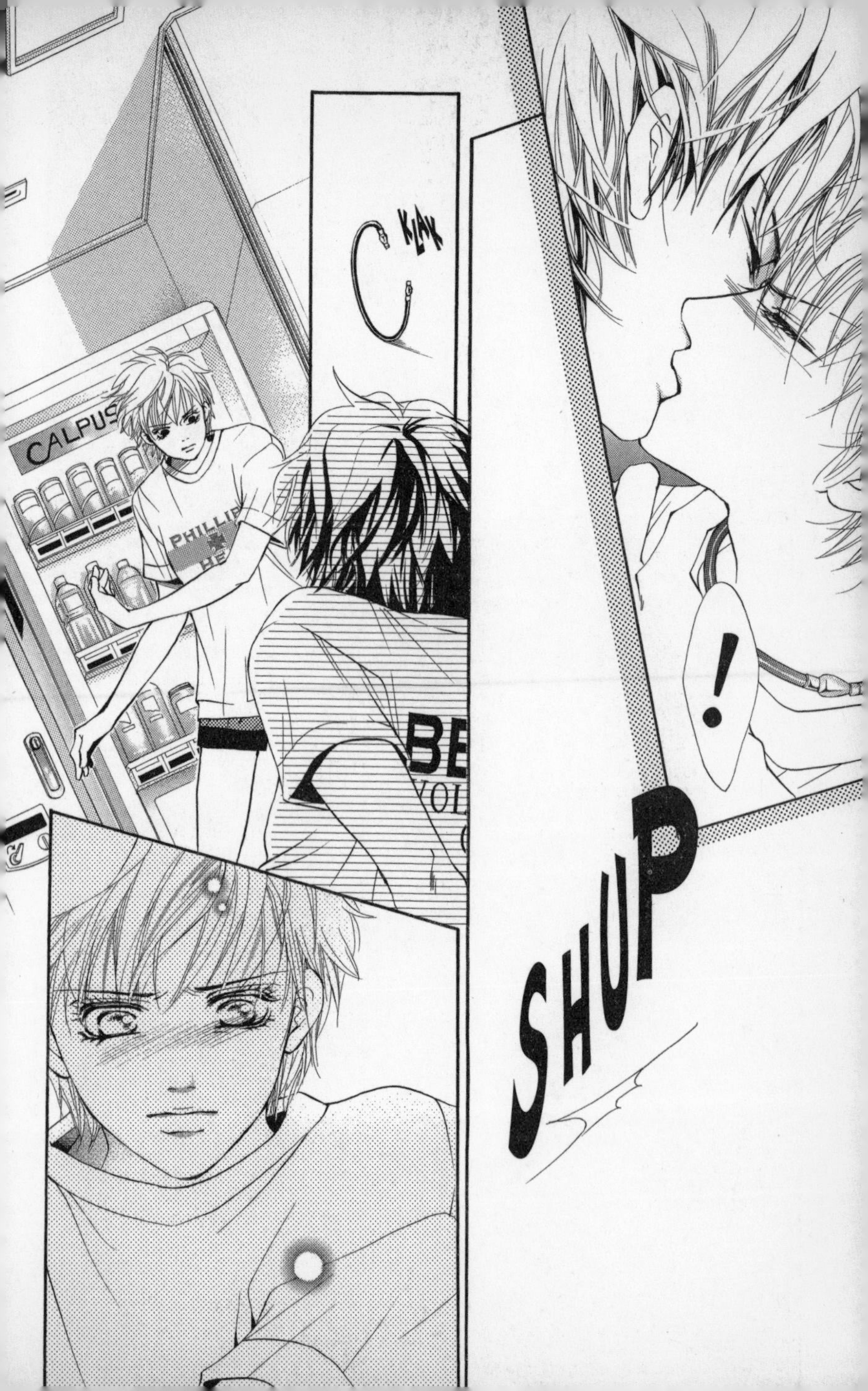
!
SHUP
KLAK
CALPUS
PHILLIP
BE

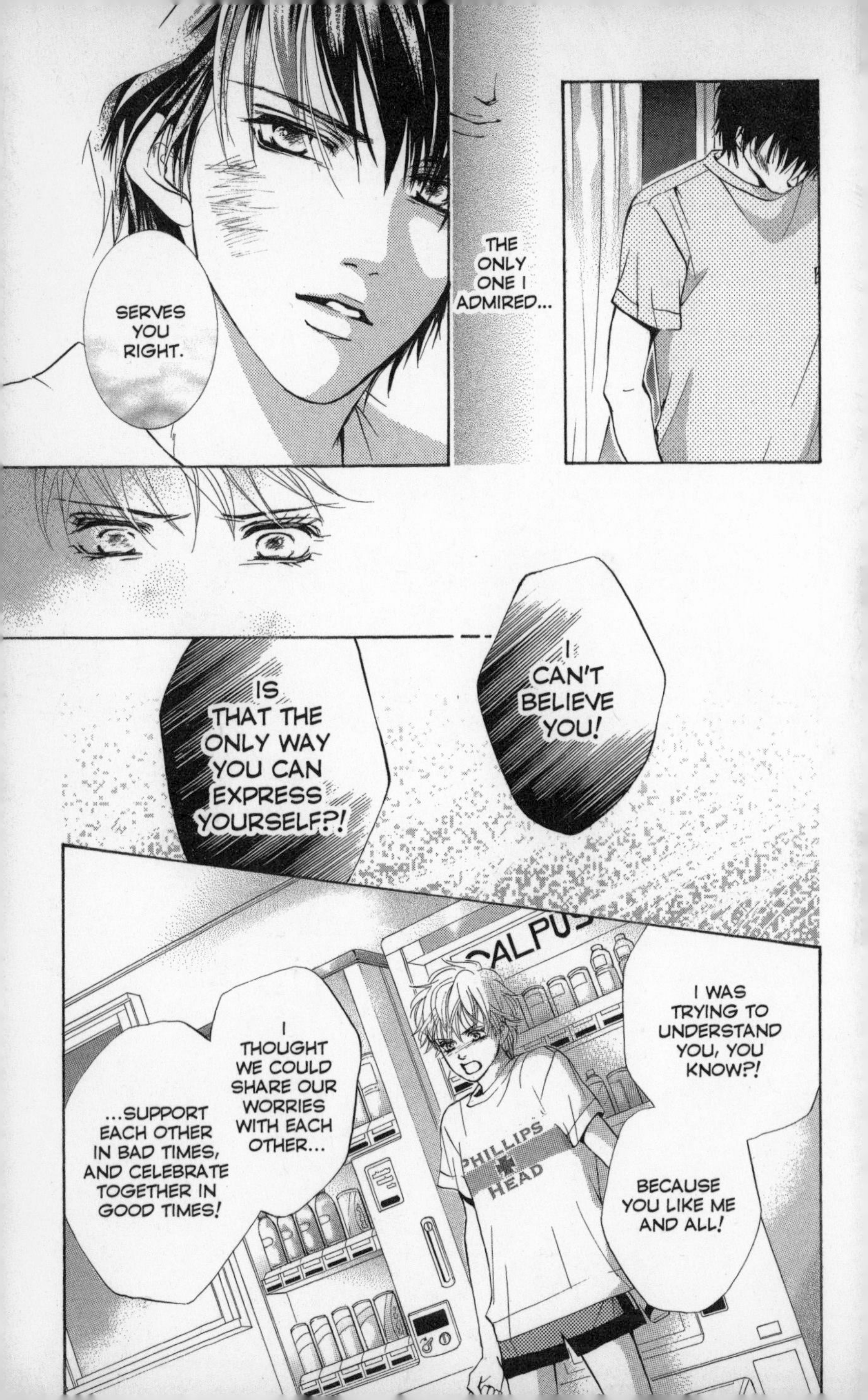
THE ONLY ONE I ADMIRED...
SERVES YOU RIGHT.
I CAN'T BELIEVE YOU!
IS THAT THE ONLY WAY YOU CAN EXPRESS YOURSELF?!
CALPUS
I WAS TRYING TO UNDERSTAND YOU, YOU KNOW?!
BECAUSE YOU LIKE ME AND ALL!
PHILLIPS HEAD
I THOUGHT WE COULD SHARE OUR WORRIES WITH EACH OTHER...
...SUPPORT EACH OTHER IN BAD TIMES, AND CELEBRATE TOGETHER IN GOOD TIMES!

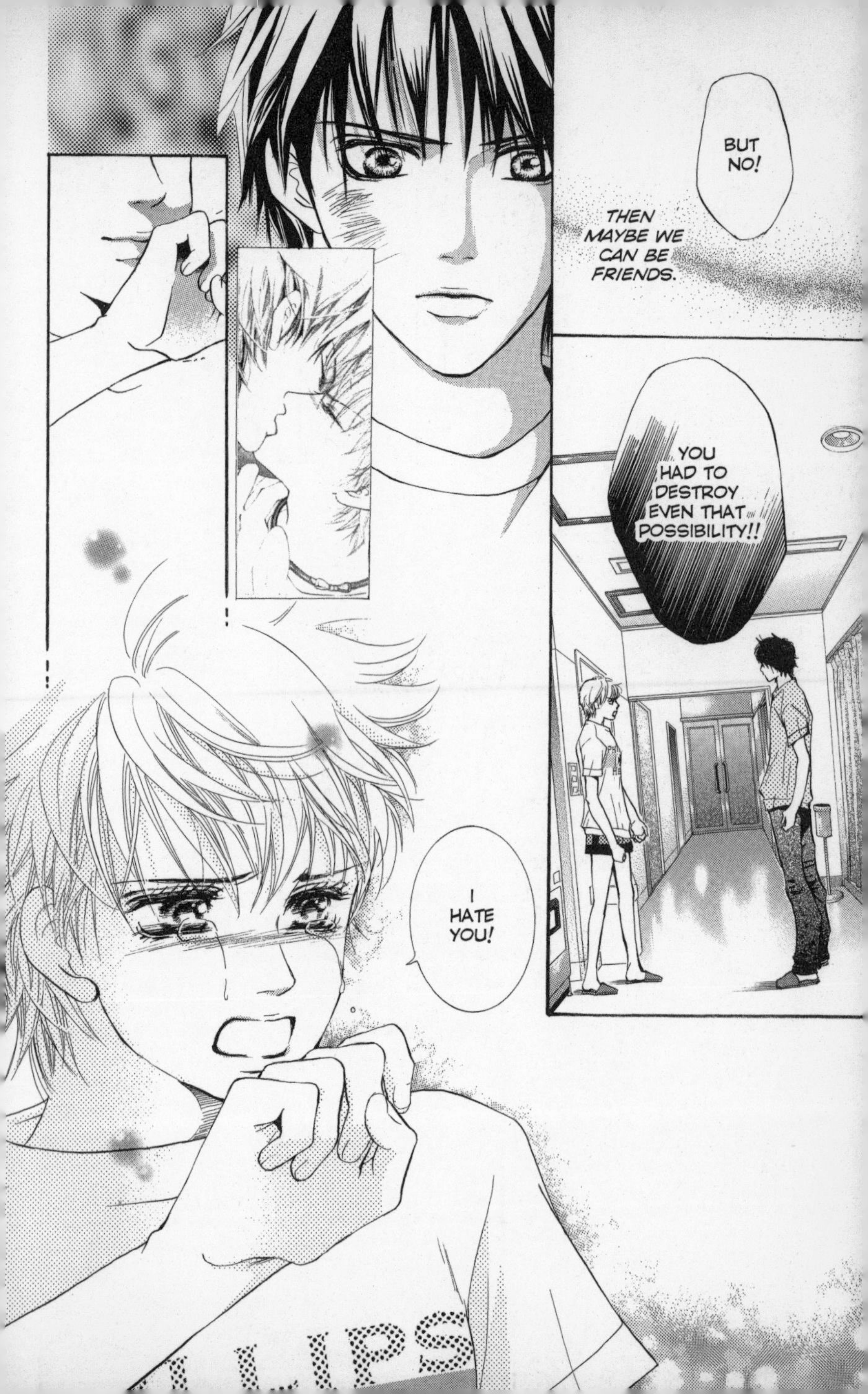
THEN MAYBE WE CAN BE FRIENDS.
BUT NO!
YOU HAD TO DESTROY EVEN THAT POSSIBILITY!!
I HATE YOU!

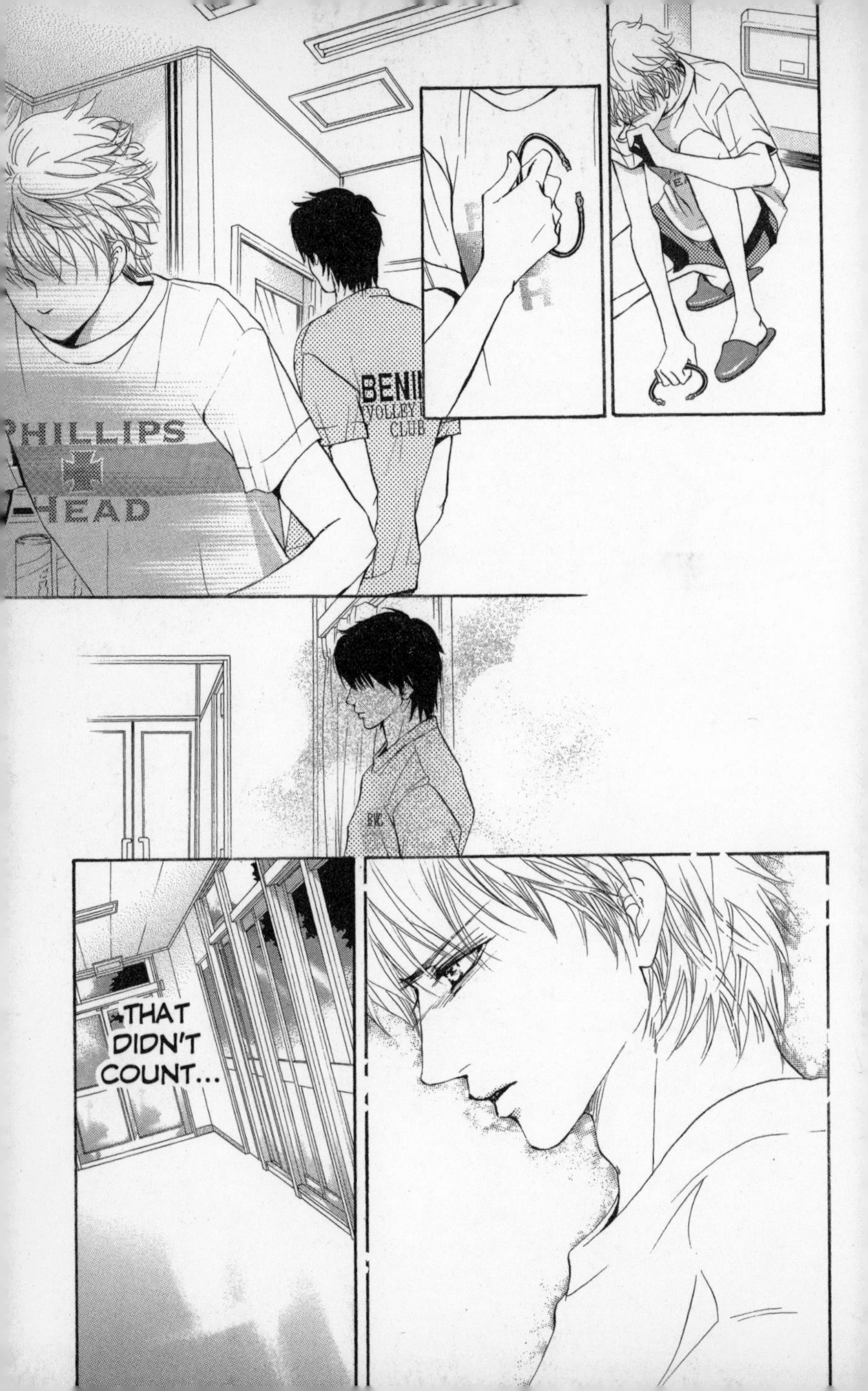
BENI
VOLLEY
CLUB
PHILLIPS
HEAD
…THAT DIDN'T COUNT…

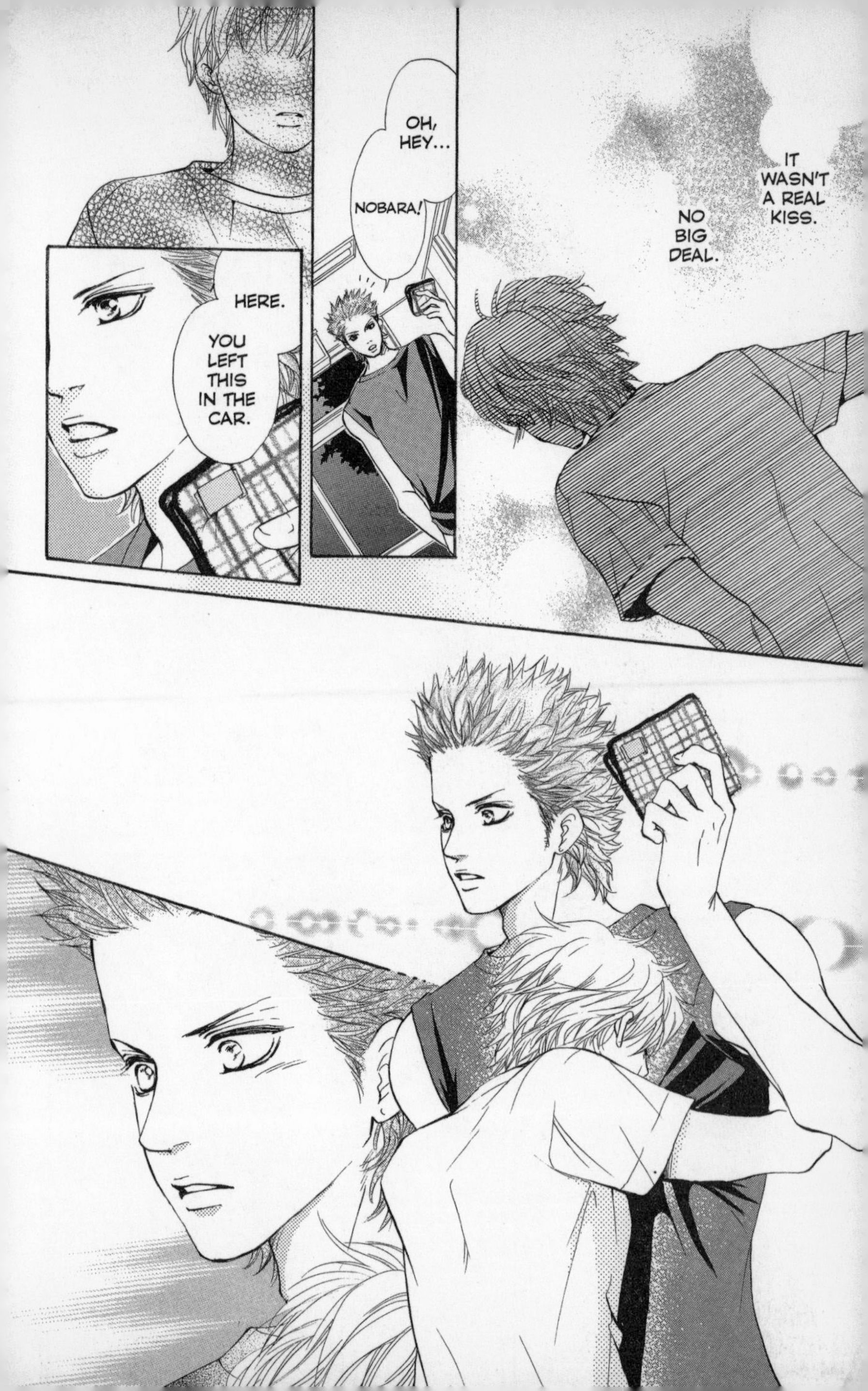
IT WASN'T A REAL KISS.
NO BIG DEAL.
OH, HEY...
NOBARA!
HERE.
YOU LEFT THIS IN THE CAR.

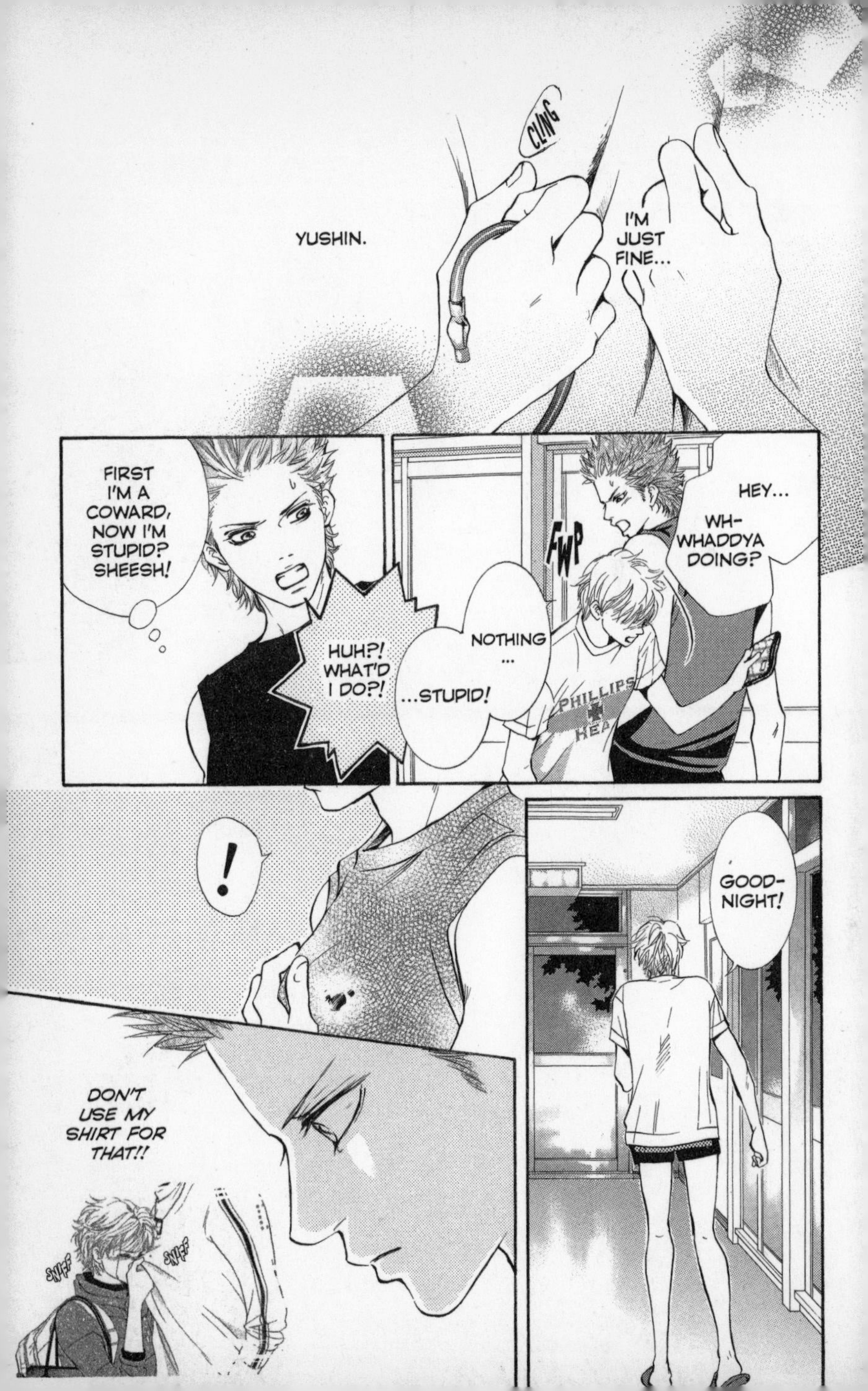

I'M JUST FINE...
CLING
YUSHIN.
HEY...
WH-WHADDYA DOING?
FWP
NOTHING ...
...STUPID!
PHILLIPS HEA
HUH?! WHAT'D I DO?!
FIRST I'M A COWARD, NOW I'M STUPID? SHEESH!
GOOD-NIGHT!
!
DON'T USE MY SHIRT FOR THAT!!
SNIFF
SNIFF

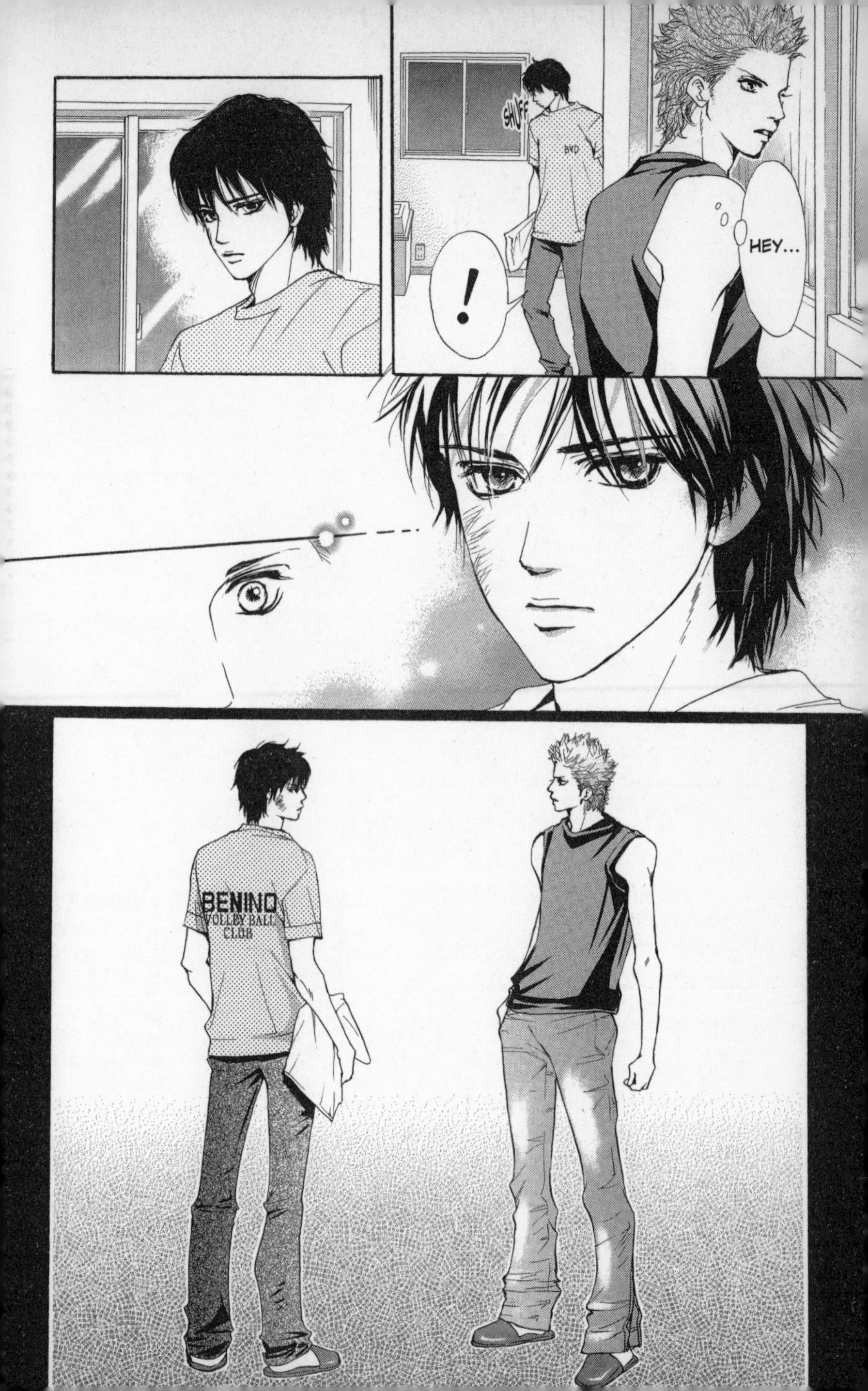
HEY...
SHUFF
!
BENINO
VOLLEY BALL
CLUB

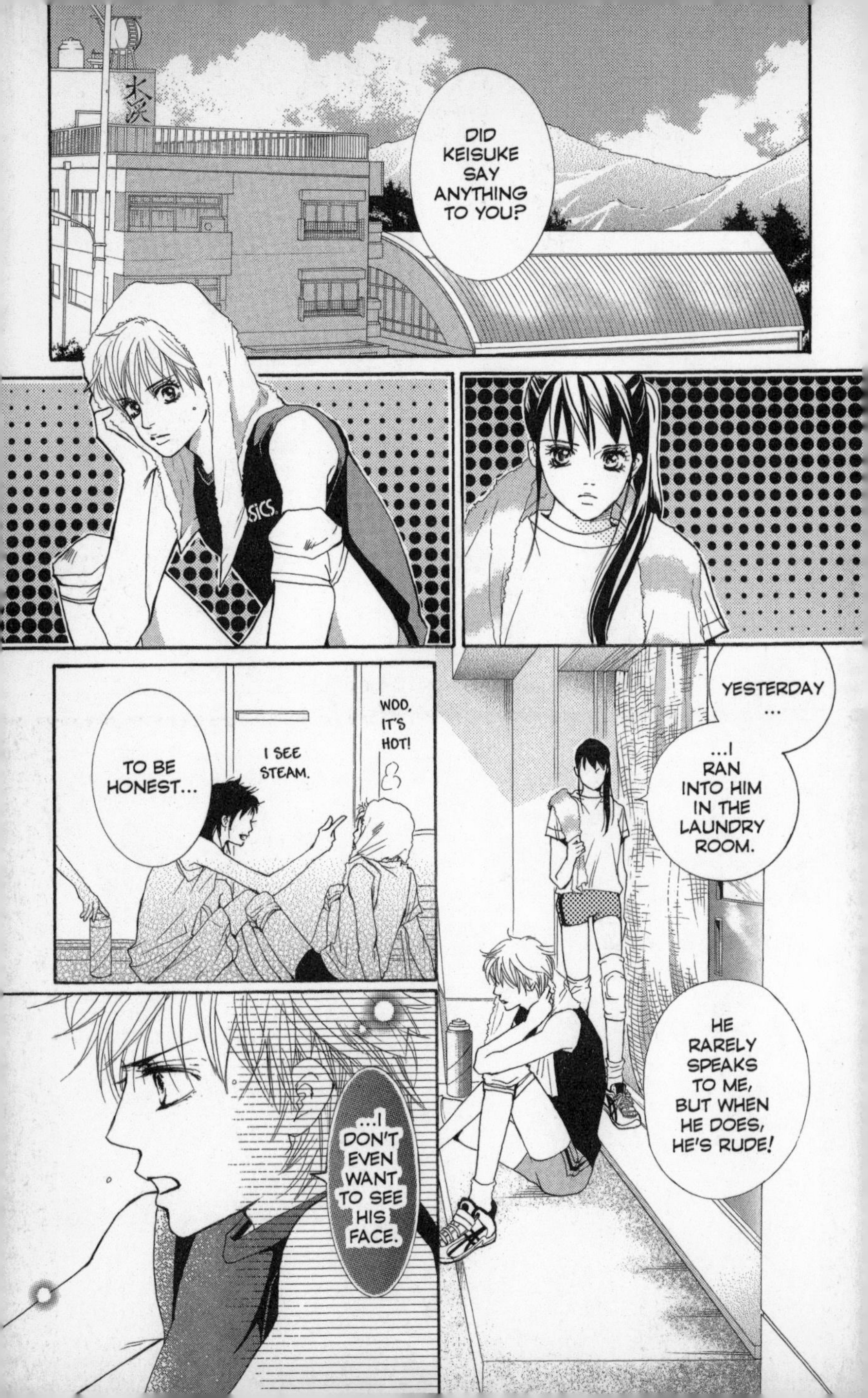
DID KEISUKE SAY ANYTHING TO YOU?
YESTERDAY ...
...I RAN INTO HIM IN THE LAUNDRY ROOM.
HE RARELY SPEAKS TO ME, BUT WHEN HE DOES, HE'S RUDE!
WOO, IT'S HOT!
I SEE STEAM.
TO BE HONEST...
...I DON'T EVEN WANT TO SEE HIS FACE.

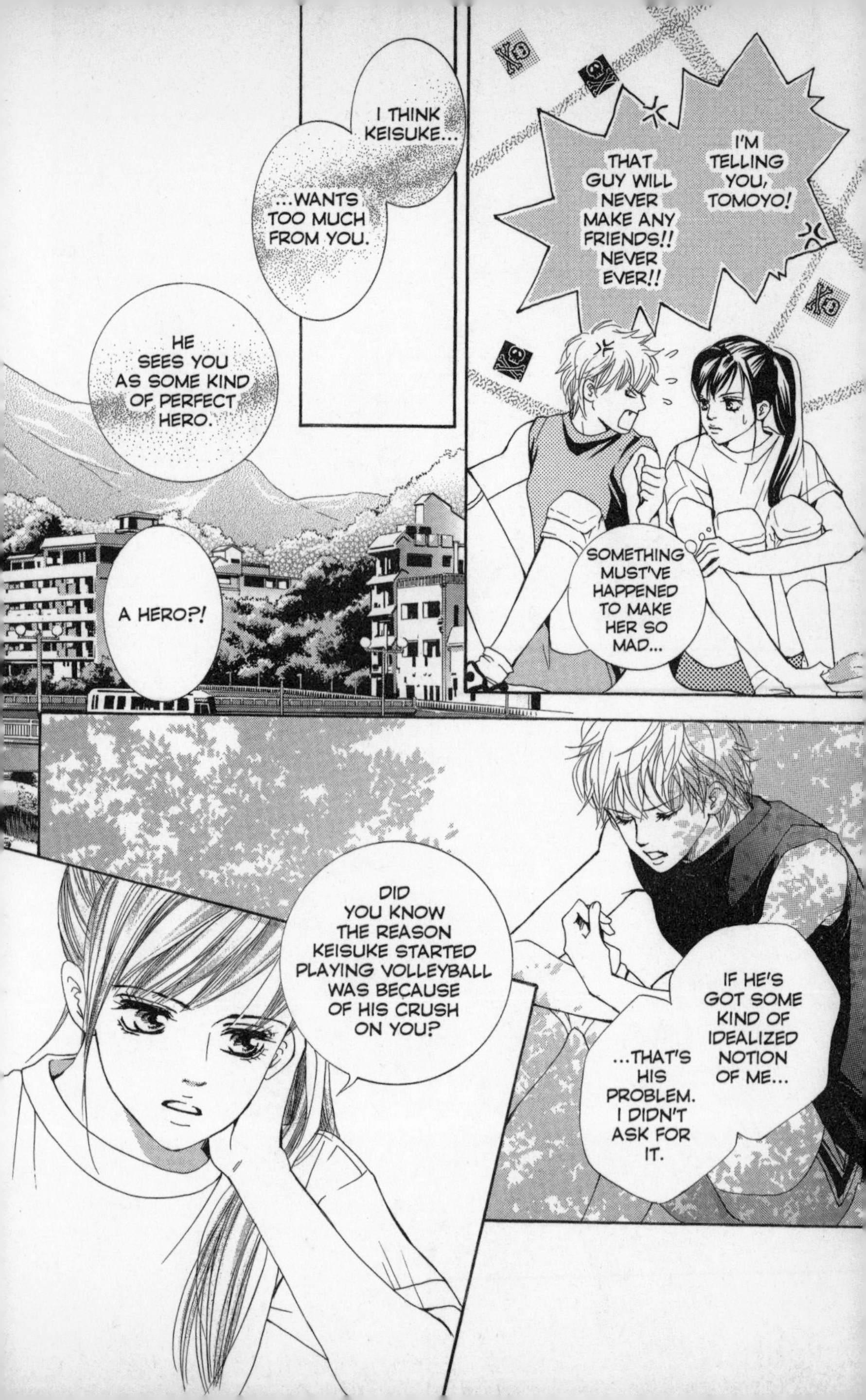
I'M TELLING YOU, TOMOYO!
THAT GUY WILL NEVER MAKE ANY FRIENDS!! NEVER EVER!!
SOMETHING MUST'VE HAPPENED TO MAKE HER SO MAD...
I THINK KEISUKE...
...WANTS TOO MUCH FROM YOU.
HE SEES YOU AS SOME KIND OF PERFECT HERO.
A HERO?!
DID YOU KNOW THE REASON KEISUKE STARTED PLAYING VOLLEYBALL WAS BECAUSE OF HIS CRUSH ON YOU?
IF HE'S GOT SOME KIND OF IDEALIZED NOTION OF ME...
...THAT'S HIS PROBLEM. I DIDN'T ASK FOR IT.

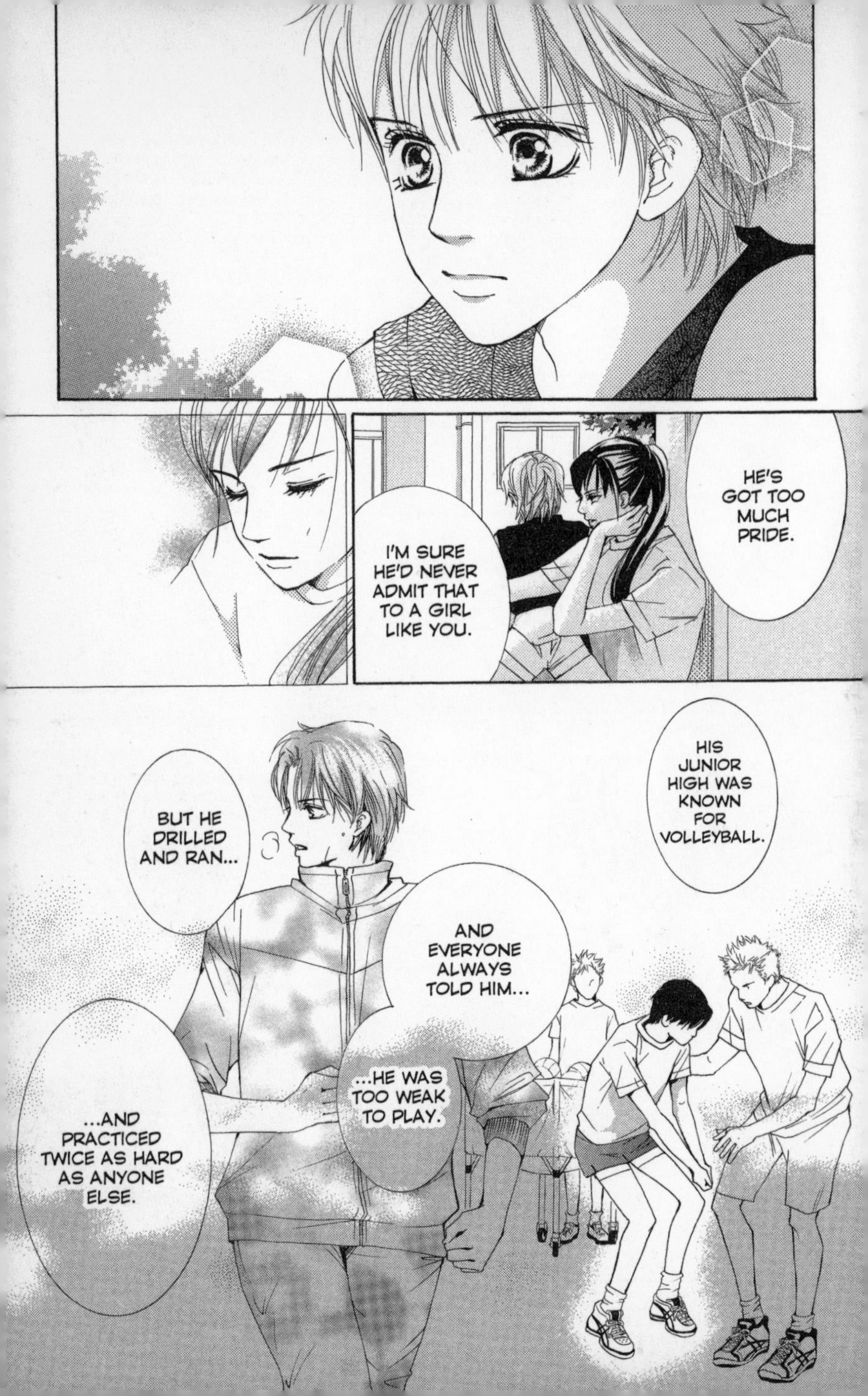
HE'S GOT TOO MUCH PRIDE.
I'M SURE HE'D NEVER ADMIT THAT TO A GIRL LIKE YOU.
HIS JUNIOR HIGH WAS KNOWN FOR VOLLEYBALL.
BUT HE DRILLED AND RAN...
...AND PRACTICED TWICE AS HARD AS ANYONE ELSE.
AND EVERYONE ALWAYS TOLD HIM...
...HE WAS TOO WEAK TO PLAY.

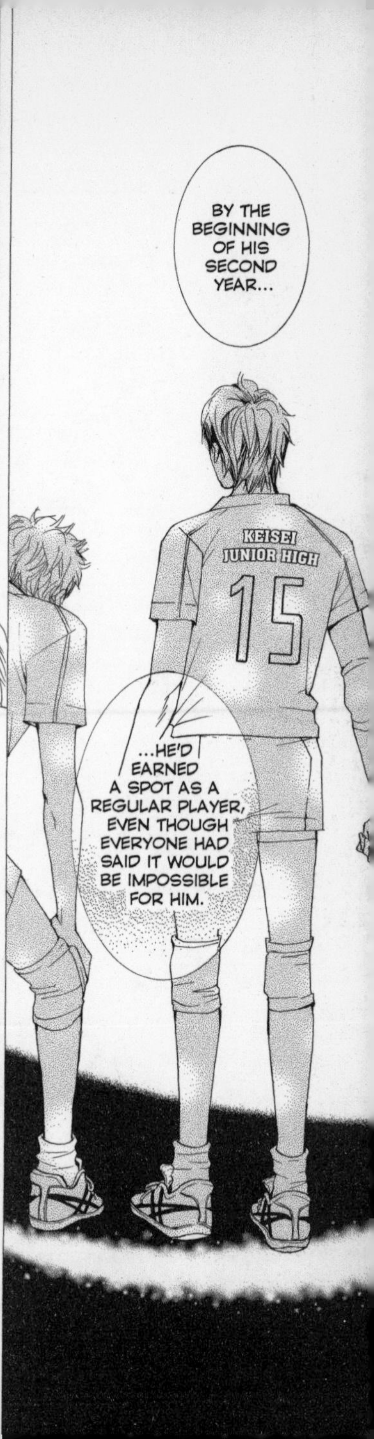
BY THE BEGINNING OF HIS SECOND YEAR...
KEISEI JUNIOR HIGH
15
...HE'D EARNED A SPOT AS A REGULAR PLAYER, EVEN THOUGH EVERYONE HAD SAID IT WOULD BE IMPOSSIBLE FOR HIM.

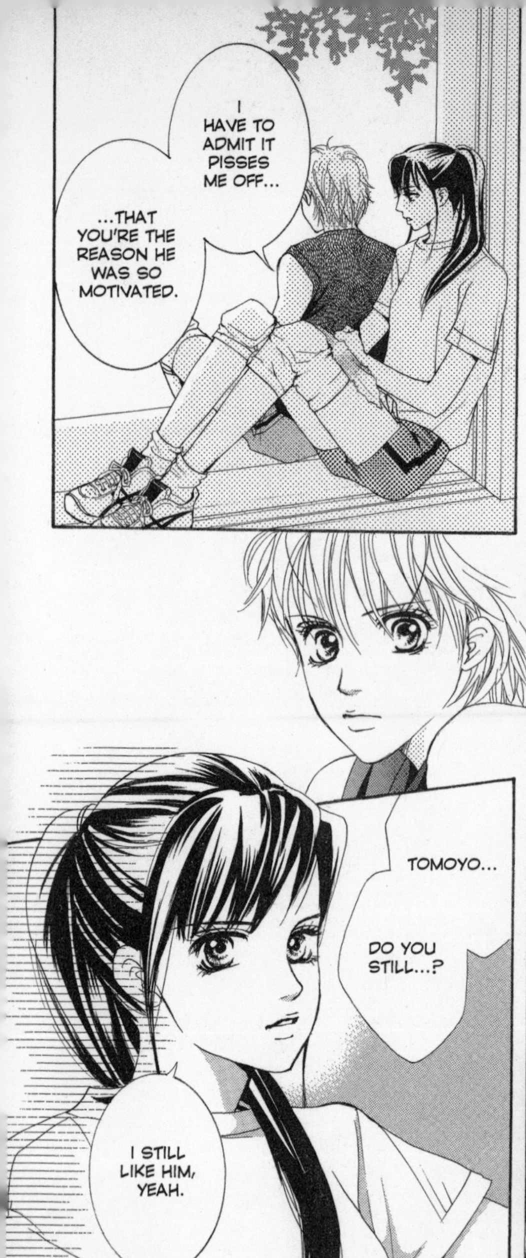
I HAVE TO ADMIT IT PISSES ME OFF...
...THAT YOU'RE THE REASON HE WAS SO MOTIVATED.
TOMOYO...
DO YOU STILL...?
I STILL LIKE HIM, YEAH.

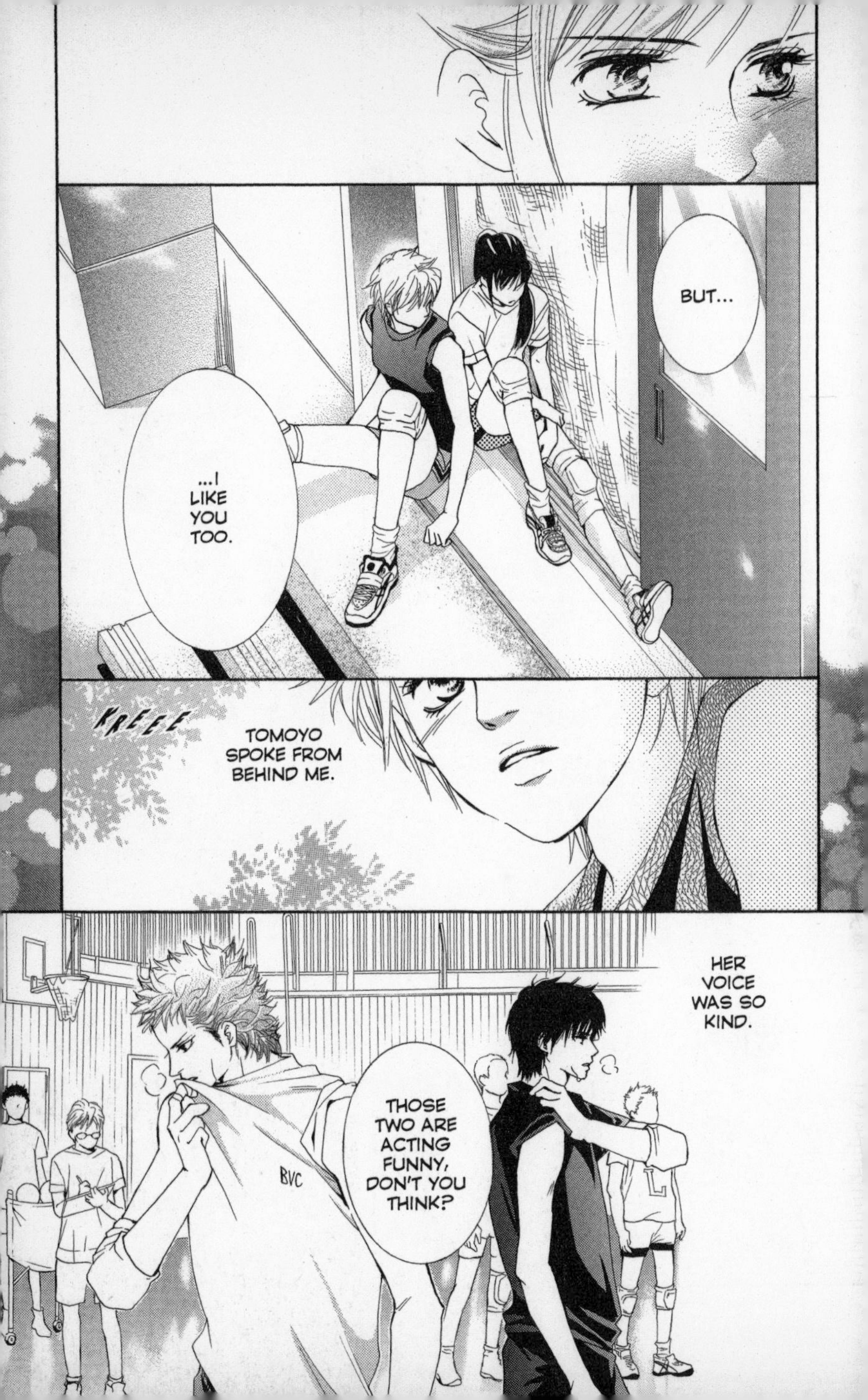
BUT...
...I LIKE YOU TOO.
TOMOYO SPOKE FROM BEHIND ME.
KREEE
HER VOICE WAS SO KIND.
THOSE TWO ARE ACTING FUNNY, DON'T YOU THINK?
BVC

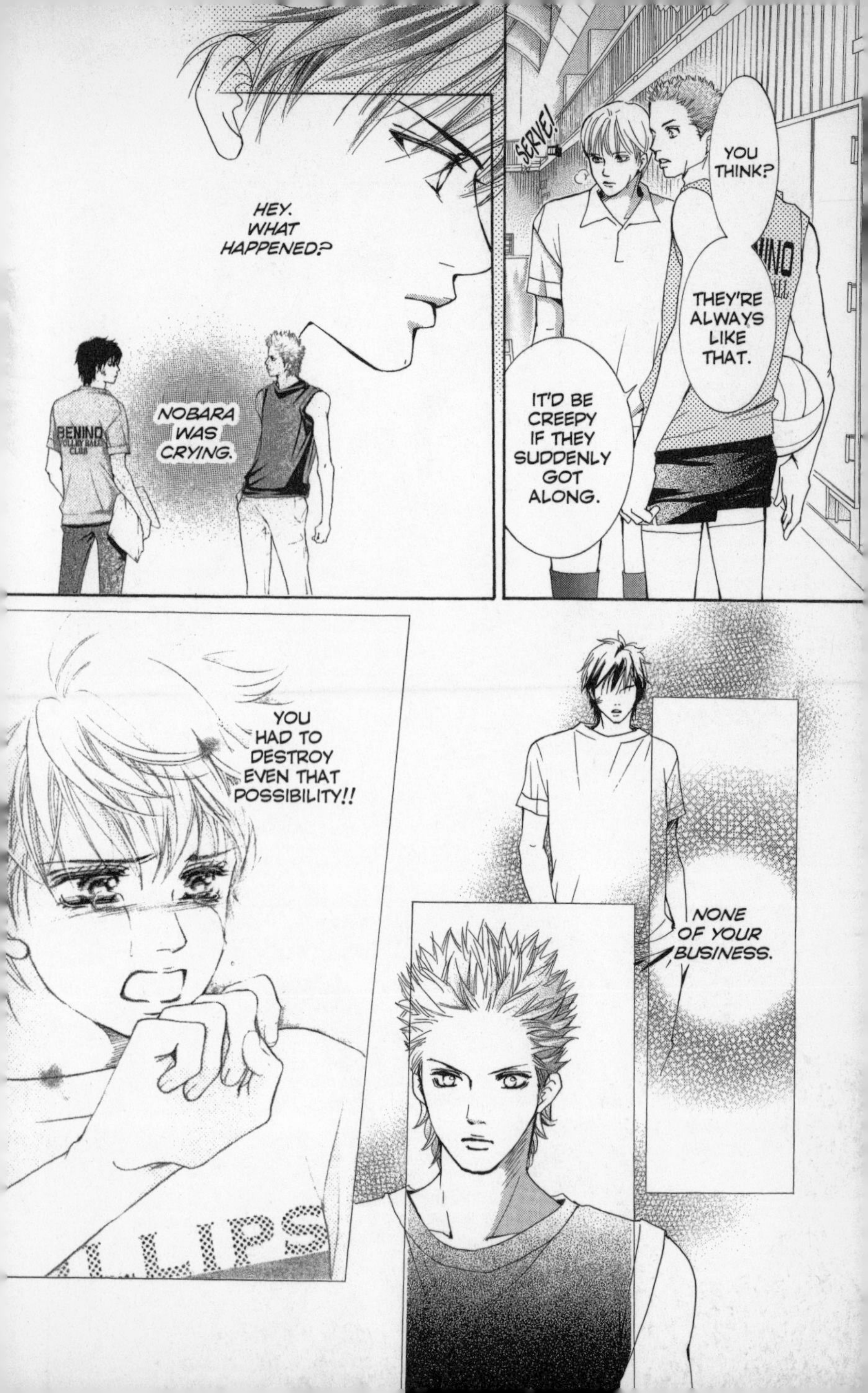
SERVE!
YOU THINK?
THEY'RE ALWAYS LIKE THAT.
IT'D BE CREEPY IF THEY SUDDENLY GOT ALONG.
HEY. WHAT HAPPENED?
NOBARA WAS CRYING.
BENINO
NONE OF YOUR BUSINESS.
YOU HAD TO DESTROY EVEN THAT POSSIBILITY!!

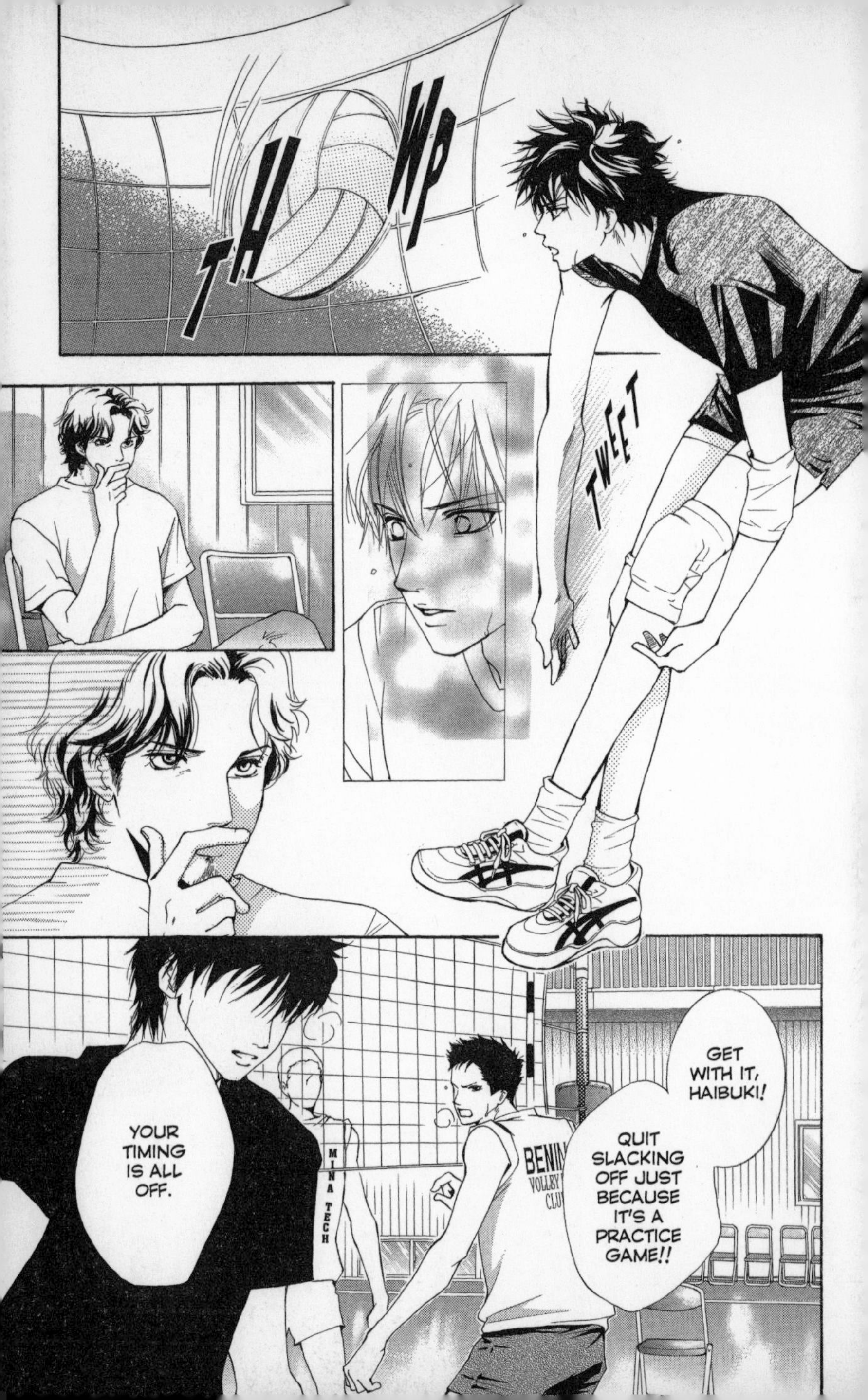
THWP
TWEET
GET WITH IT, HAIBUKI!
QUIT SLACKING OFF JUST BECAUSE IT'S A PRACTICE GAME!!
YOUR TIMING IS ALL OFF.
MINA TECH
BENIN
VOLLEY
CLU

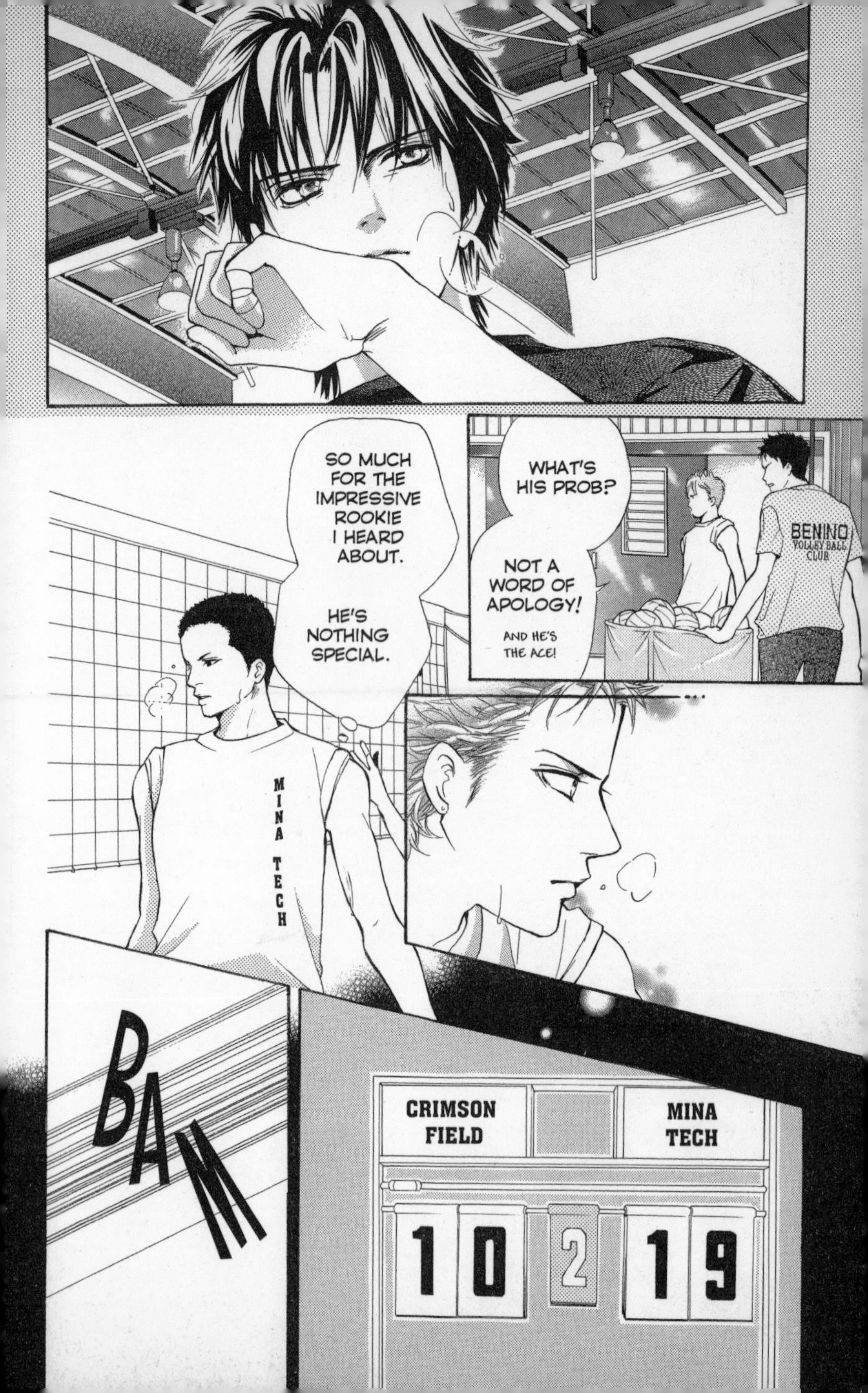
WHAT'S HIS PROB?
NOT A WORD OF APOLOGY!
AND HE'S THE ACE!
BENINO VOLLEY BALL CLUB
SO MUCH FOR THE IMPRESSIVE ROOKIE I HEARD ABOUT.
HE'S NOTHING SPECIAL.
MINA TECH
CRIMSON FIELD
MINA TECH
10
2
19
BAM

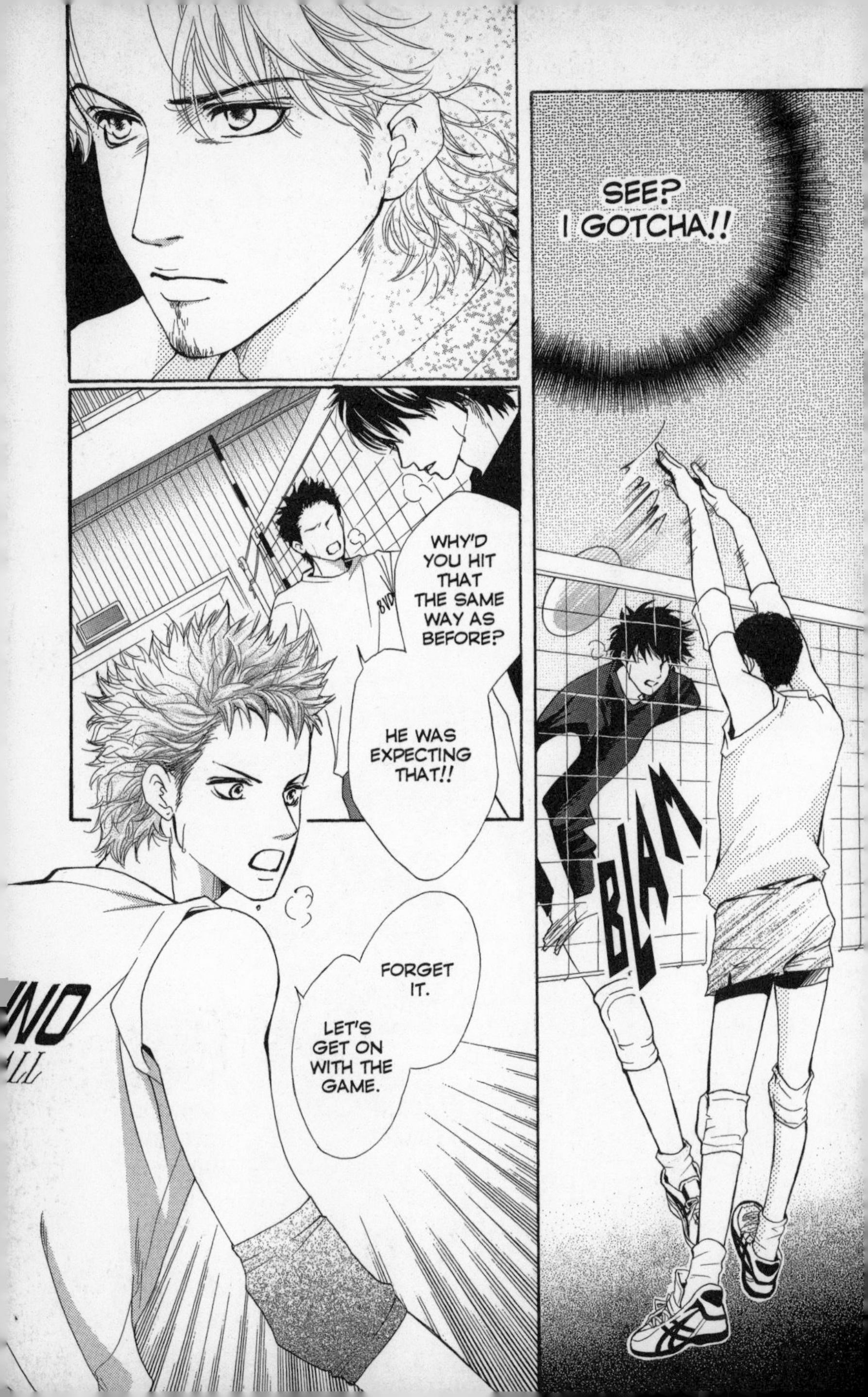
SEE? I GOTCHA!!
BLAM
WHY'D YOU HIT THAT THE SAME WAY AS BEFORE?
HE WAS EXPECTING THAT!!
FORGET IT.
LET'S GET ON WITH THE GAME.

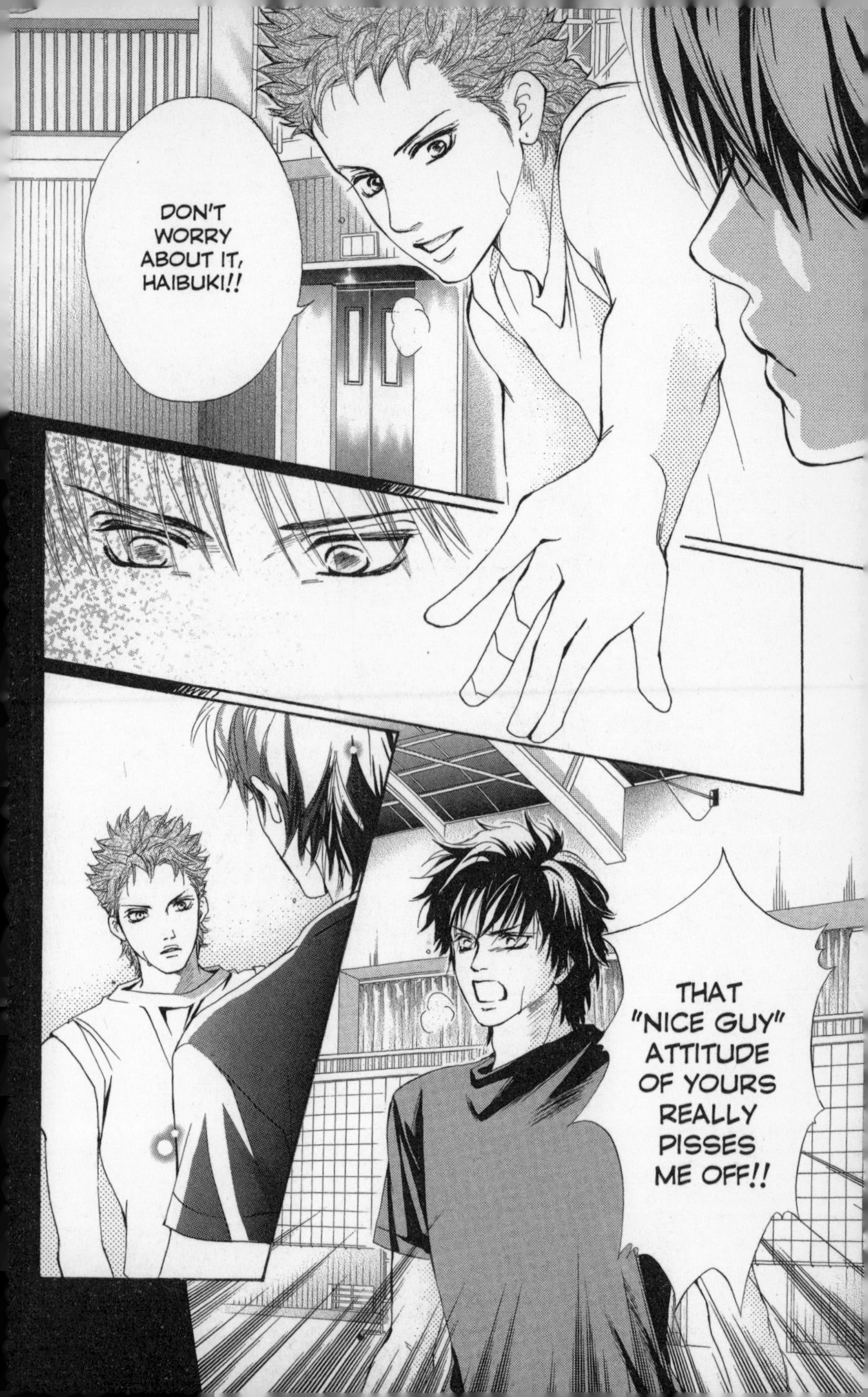
DON'T WORRY ABOUT IT, HAIBUKI!!
THAT "NICE GUY" ATTITUDE OF YOURS REALLY PISSES ME OFF!!

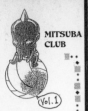

MITSUBA CLUB

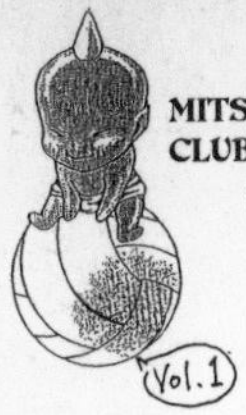
Vol. 1

HI! IT'S BEEN A WHILE. TAKANASHI HERE. SOMEHOW OR OTHER, WE SEEM TO HAVE GOTTEN TO VOLUME 6 OF CRIMSON HERO. IN THE MAGAZINE WE'RE AT THE END OF WHAT WE'RE CALLING PART I, AND NOW I HAVE SOME TIME TO PREPARE FOR THE NEXT PART. THE MONTH AFTER THIS VOLUME IS PUBLISHED, PART II WILL BEGIN. AND IN *BETSUMA* (THE JAPANESE MAGAZINE) I HAVE BOTH *CRIMSON HERO* AND A ONE-SHOT MANGA, SO PLEASE READ THEM BOTH. IT'S BEEN A WHILE SINCE I'VE HAD A CHANCE TO DO A ONE-SHOT. I WORKED HARD TO CREATE SOMETHING WITH A TOTALLY DIFFERENT FEEL FROM *CRIMSON HERO*, BUT WHAT I ENDED UP WITH WAS A TYPICAL HEART-THROBBING SHOJO MANGA. I'M EMBARRASSED FOR MANY REASONS AND I CAN'T BRING MYSELF TO READ THE FINAL COPY.

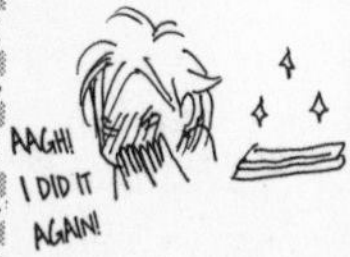
AAGH! I DID IT AGAIN!

BY THE WAY, AS I WAS CREATING THE ONE-SHOT MANGA, I WENT BACK AND RE-READ ALL THE ONE-SHOTS I HAD DONE IN THE PAST. I COULDN'T HELP BLUSHING. THEY'RE ALL HEART-THROBBING SHOJO MANGAS!! AAARGH! ★

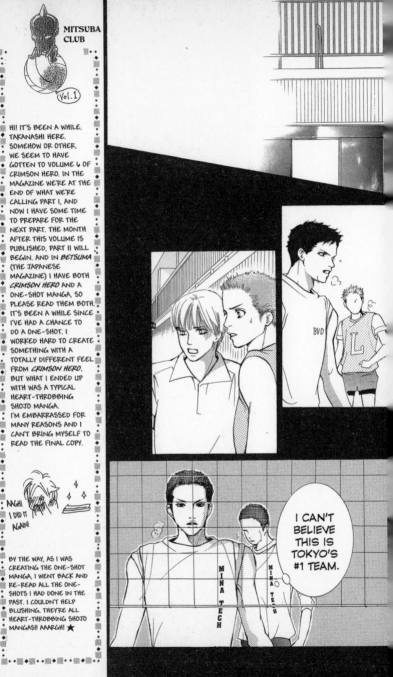

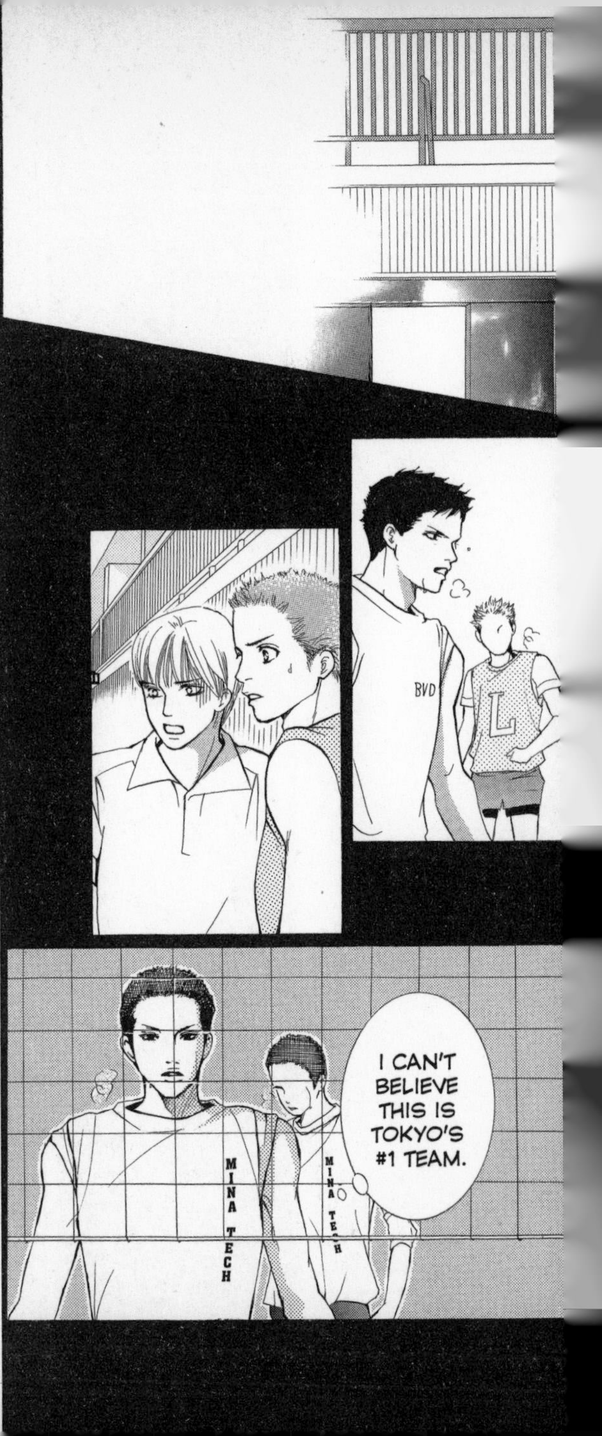
I CAN'T BELIEVE THIS IS TOKYO'S #1 TEAM.

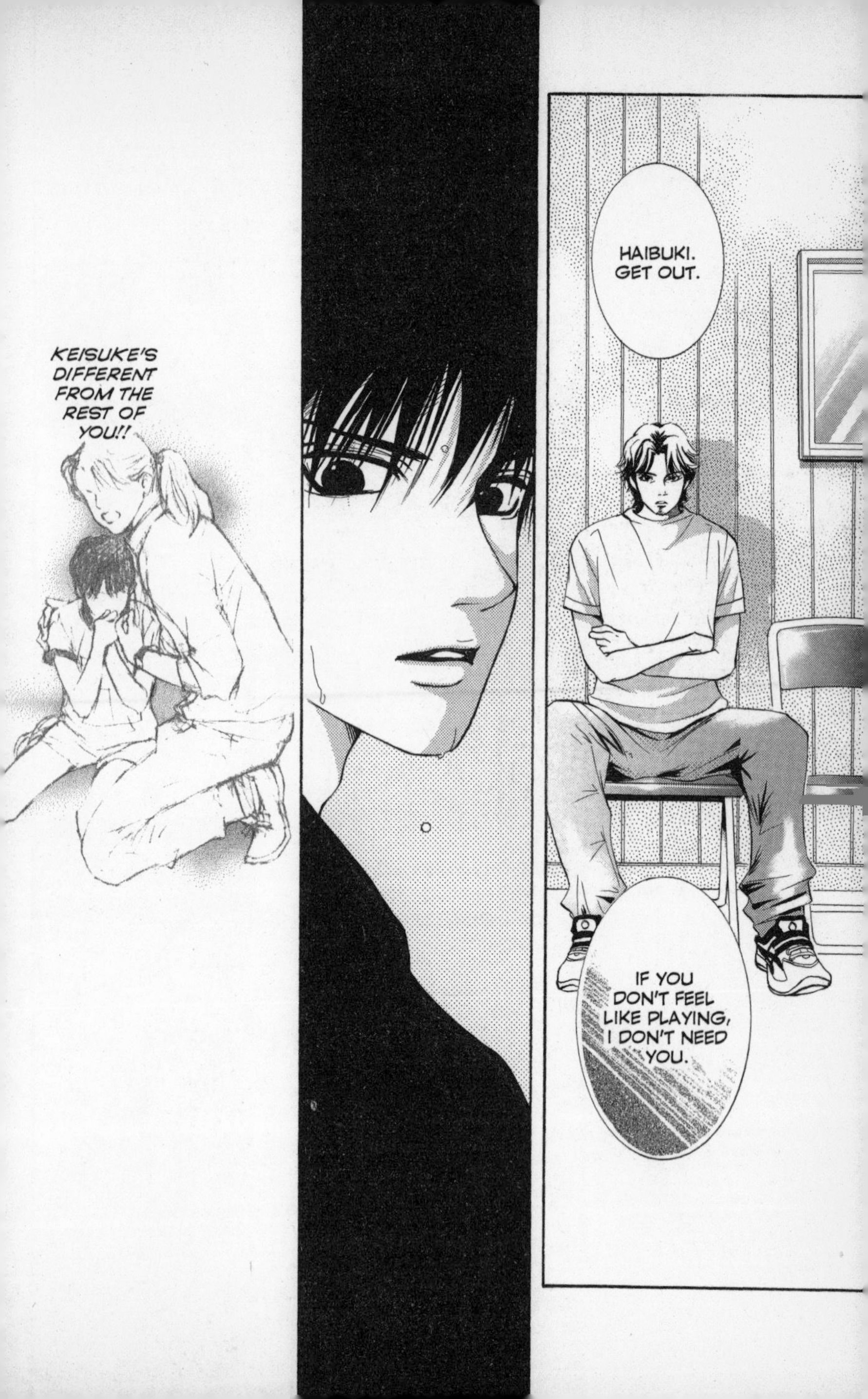
HAIBUKI. GET OUT.
IF YOU DON'T FEEL LIKE PLAYING, I DON'T NEED YOU.
KEISUKE'S DIFFERENT FROM THE REST OF YOU!!

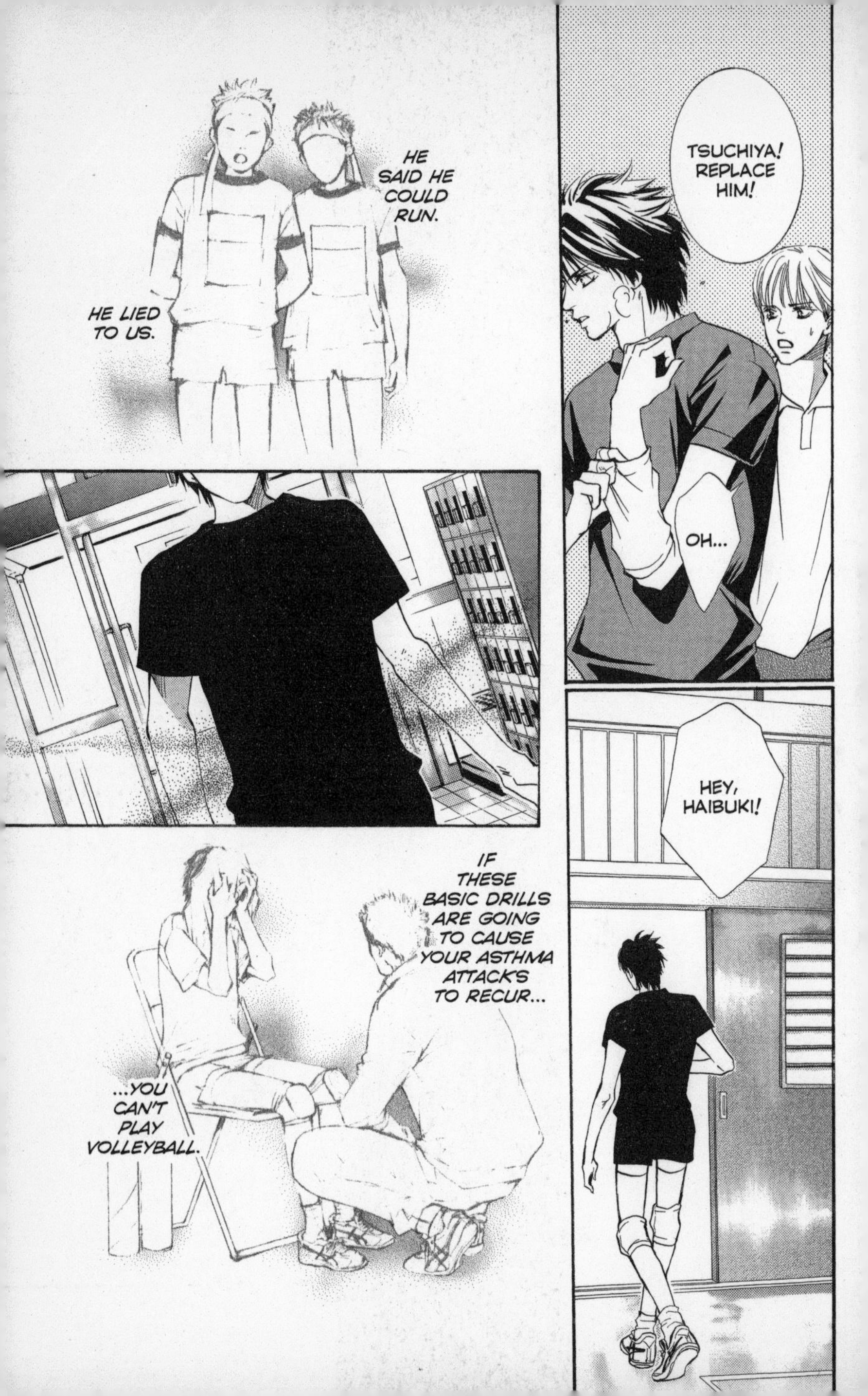
TSUCHIYA! REPLACE HIM!
OH...
HEY, HAIBUKI!
HE SAID HE COULD RUN.
HE LIED TO US.
IF THESE BASIC DRILLS ARE GOING TO CAUSE YOUR ASTHMA ATTACKS TO RECUR...
...YOU CAN'T PLAY VOLLEYBALL.

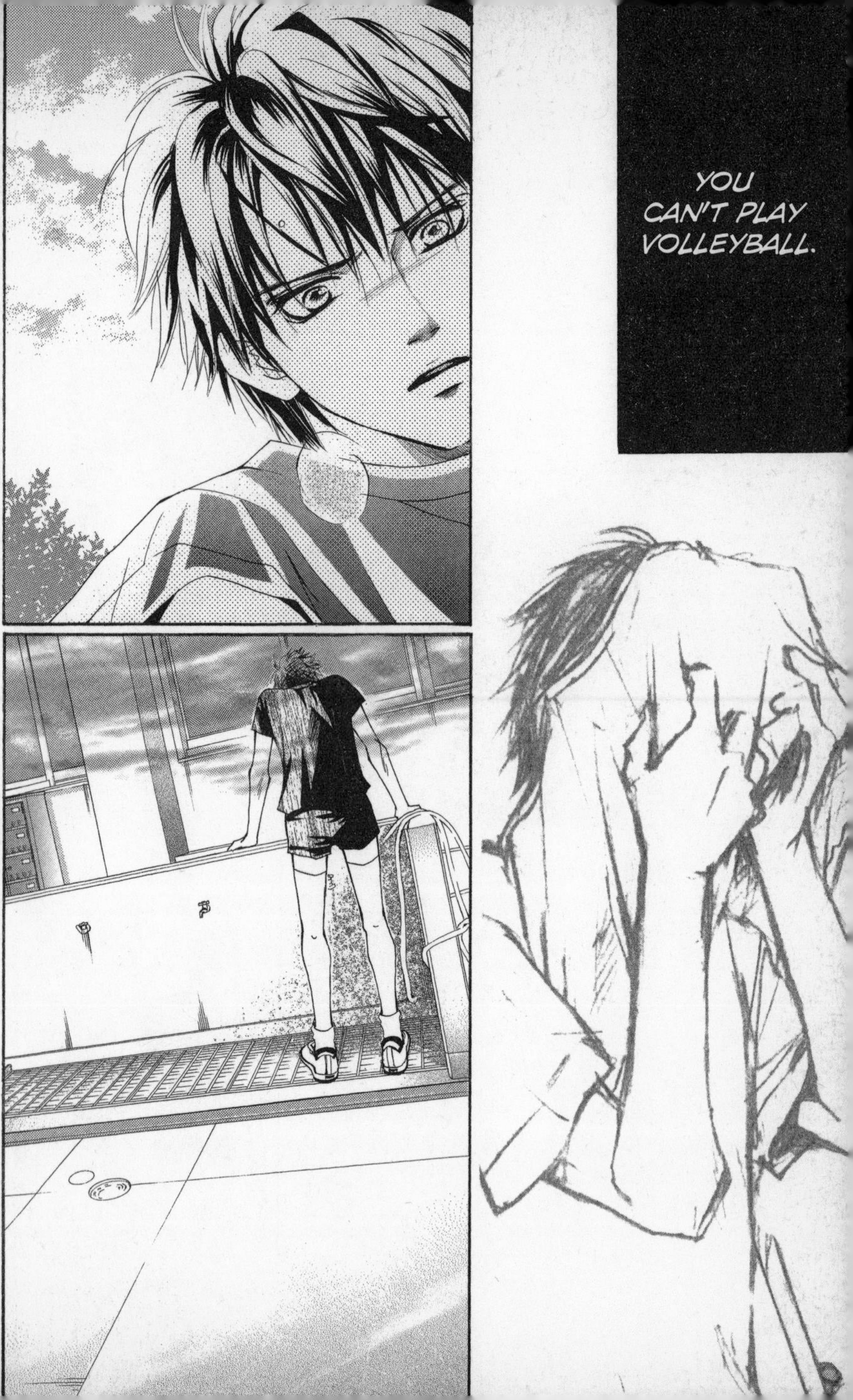
YOU CAN'T PLAY VOLLEYBALL.

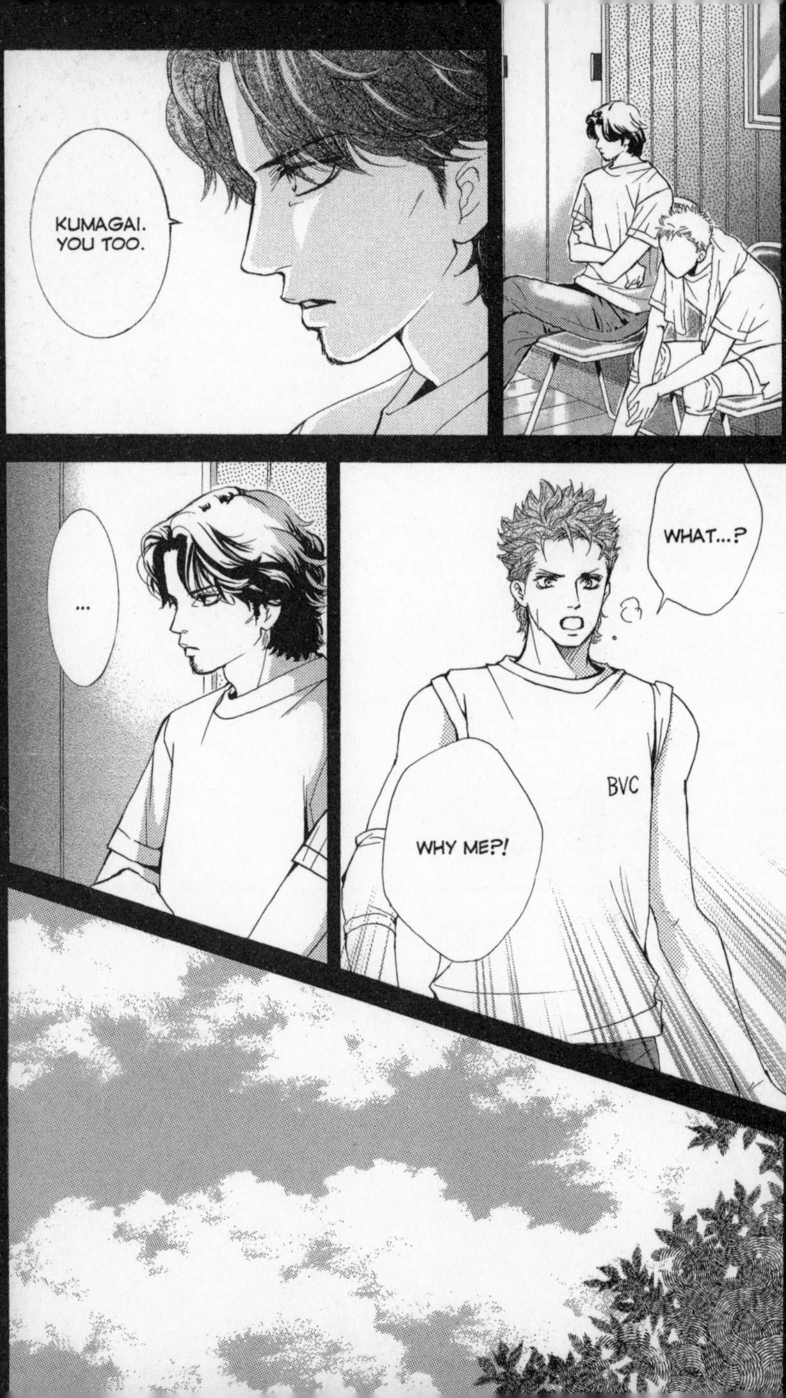
KUMAGAI. YOU TOO.
WHAT...?
WHY ME?!
BVC
...

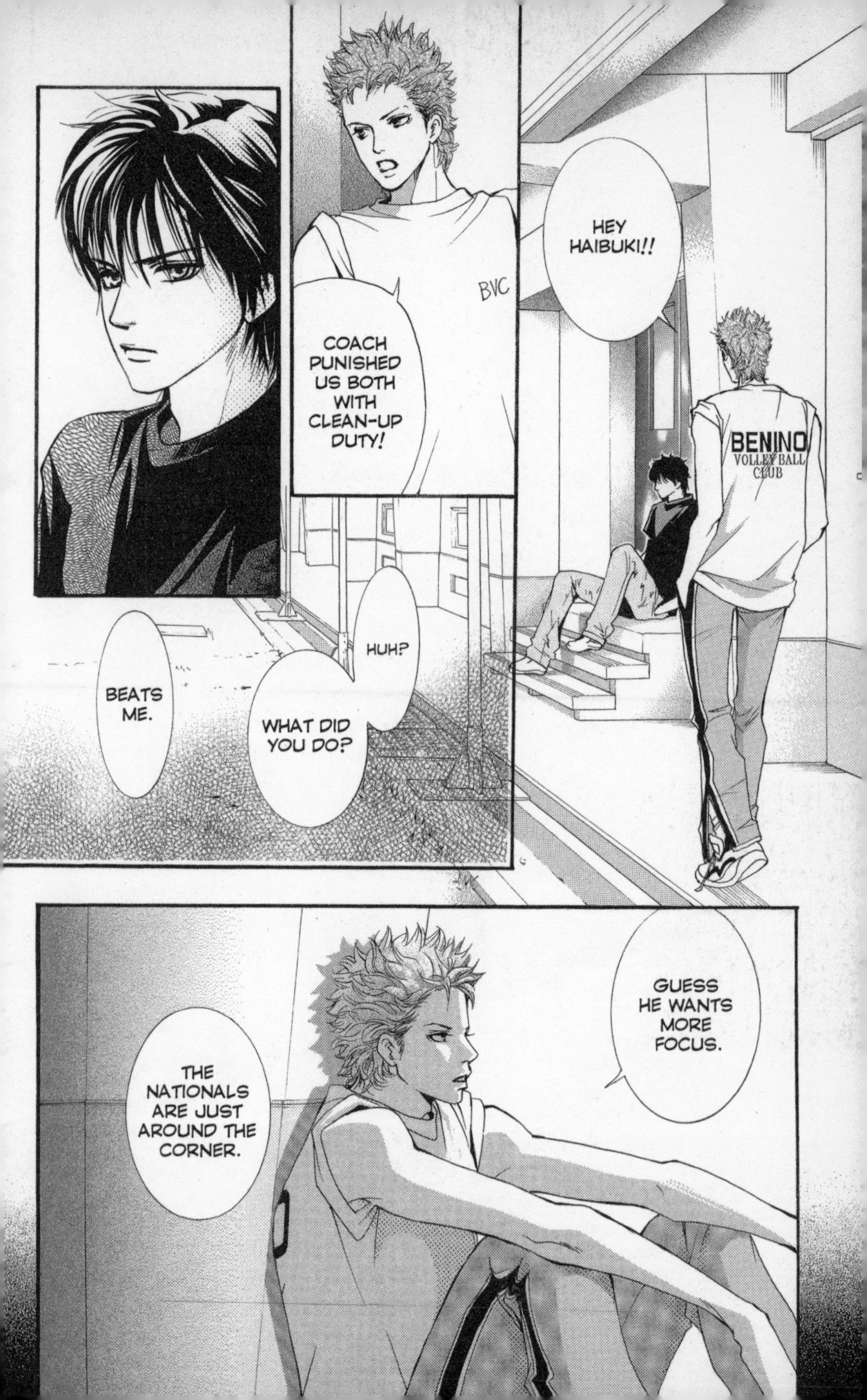
HEY HAIBUKI!!
BENINO VOLLEY BALL CLUB
BVC
COACH PUNISHED US BOTH WITH CLEAN-UP DUTY!
HUH?
WHAT DID YOU DO?
BEATS ME.
GUESS HE WANTS MORE FOCUS.
THE NATIONALS ARE JUST AROUND THE CORNER.

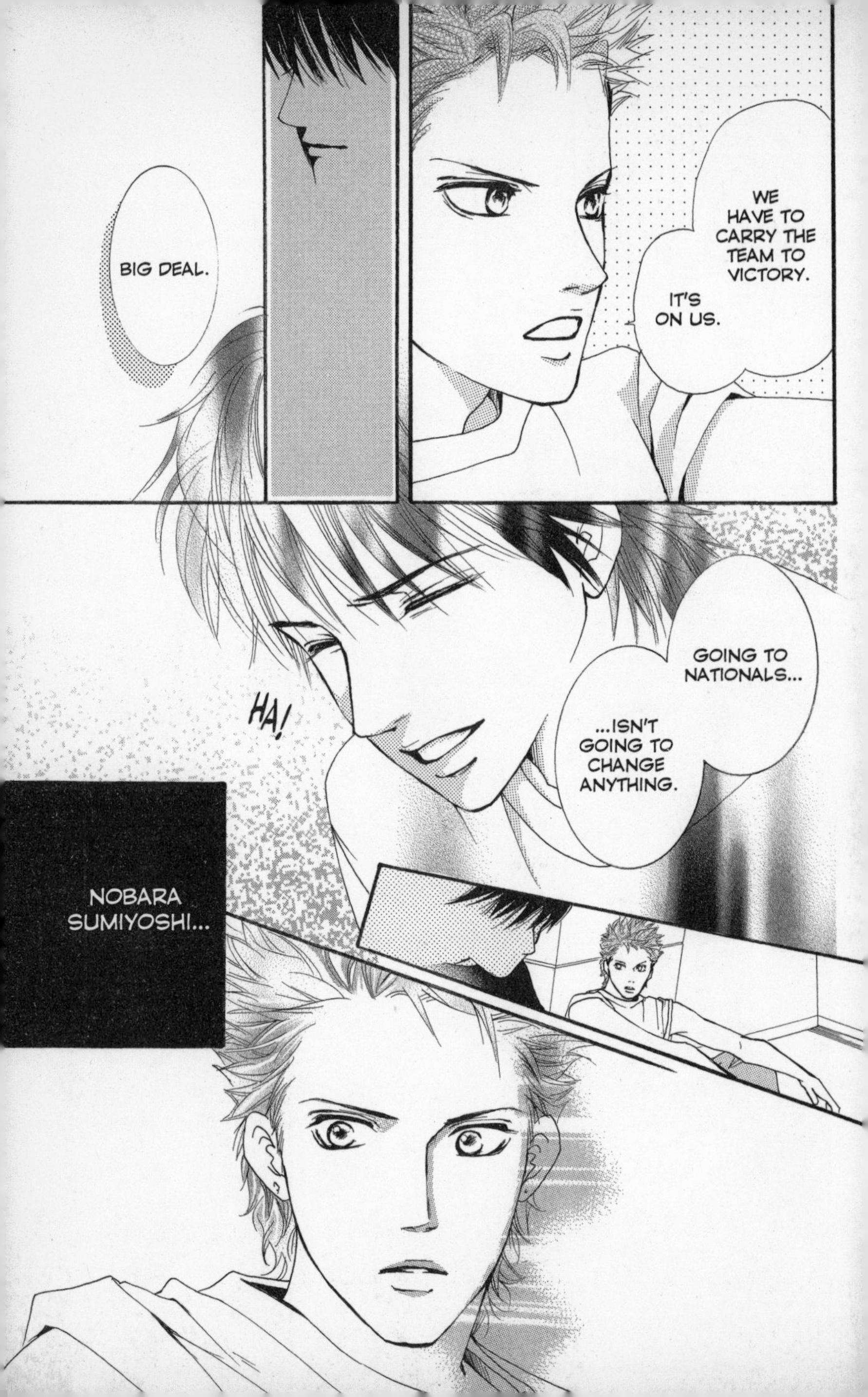
WE HAVE TO CARRY THE TEAM TO VICTORY.
IT'S ON US.
BIG DEAL.
GOING TO NATIONALS...
...ISN'T GOING TO CHANGE ANYTHING.
HA!
NOBARA SUMIYOSHI...

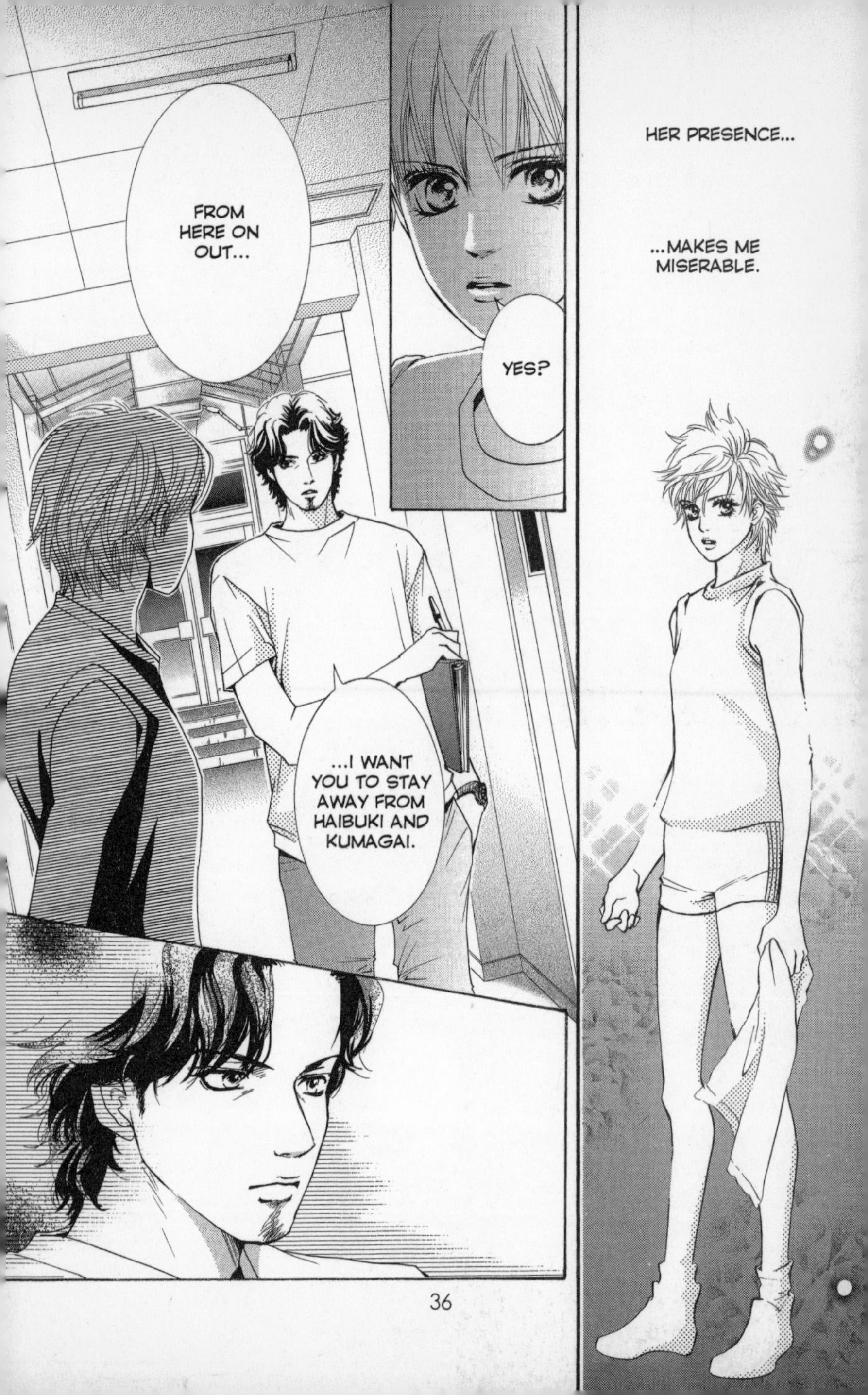

HER PRESENCE...
...MAKES ME MISERABLE.
FROM HERE ON OUT...
YES?
...I WANT YOU TO STAY AWAY FROM HAIBUKI AND KUMAGAI.

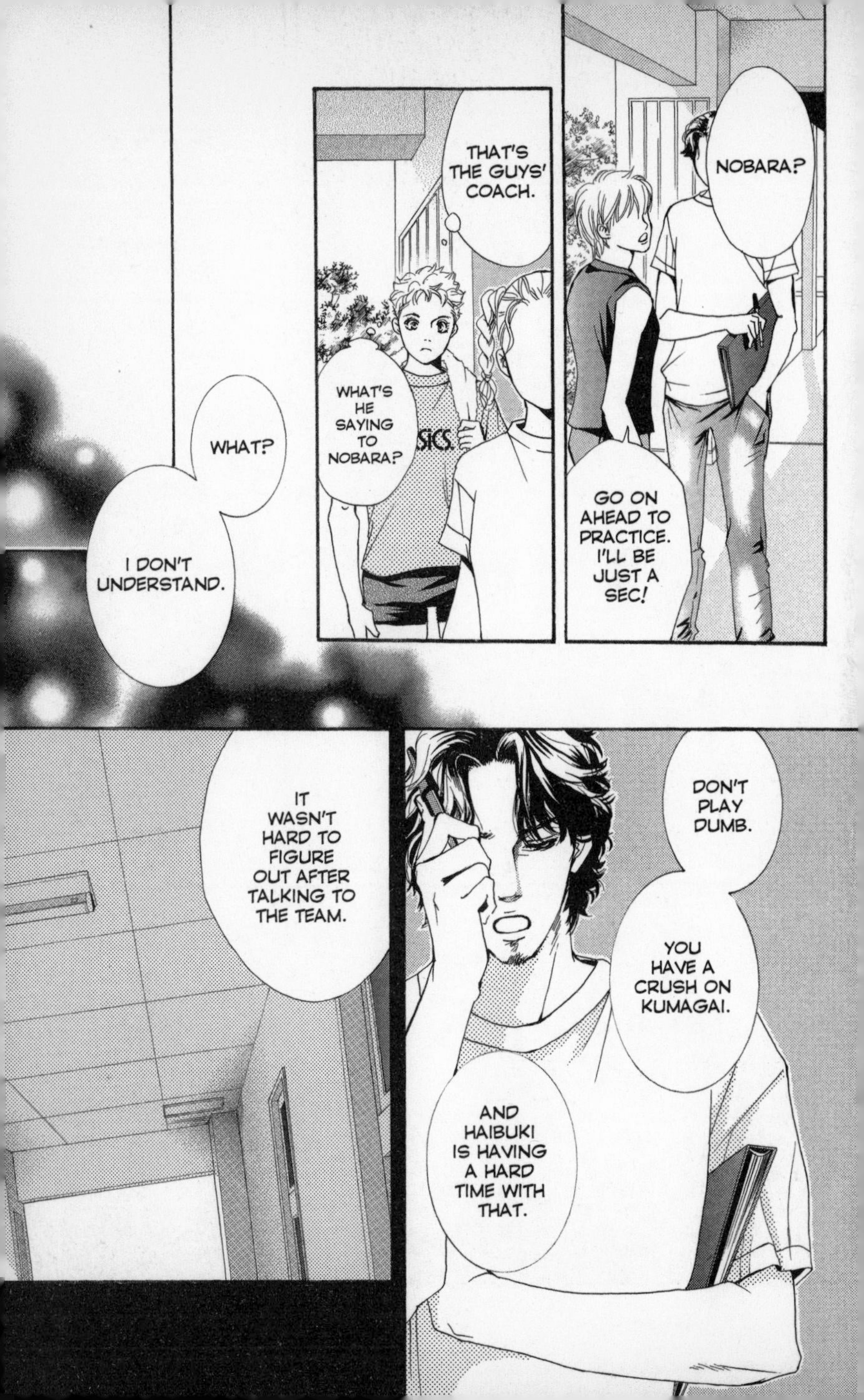
NOBARA?
GO ON AHEAD TO PRACTICE. I'LL BE JUST A SEC!
THAT'S THE GUYS' COACH.
WHAT'S HE SAYING TO NOBARA?
WHAT?
I DON'T UNDERSTAND.
DON'T PLAY DUMB.
YOU HAVE A CRUSH ON KUMAGAI.
AND HAIBUKI IS HAVING A HARD TIME WITH THAT.
IT WASN'T HARD TO FIGURE OUT AFTER TALKING TO THE TEAM.

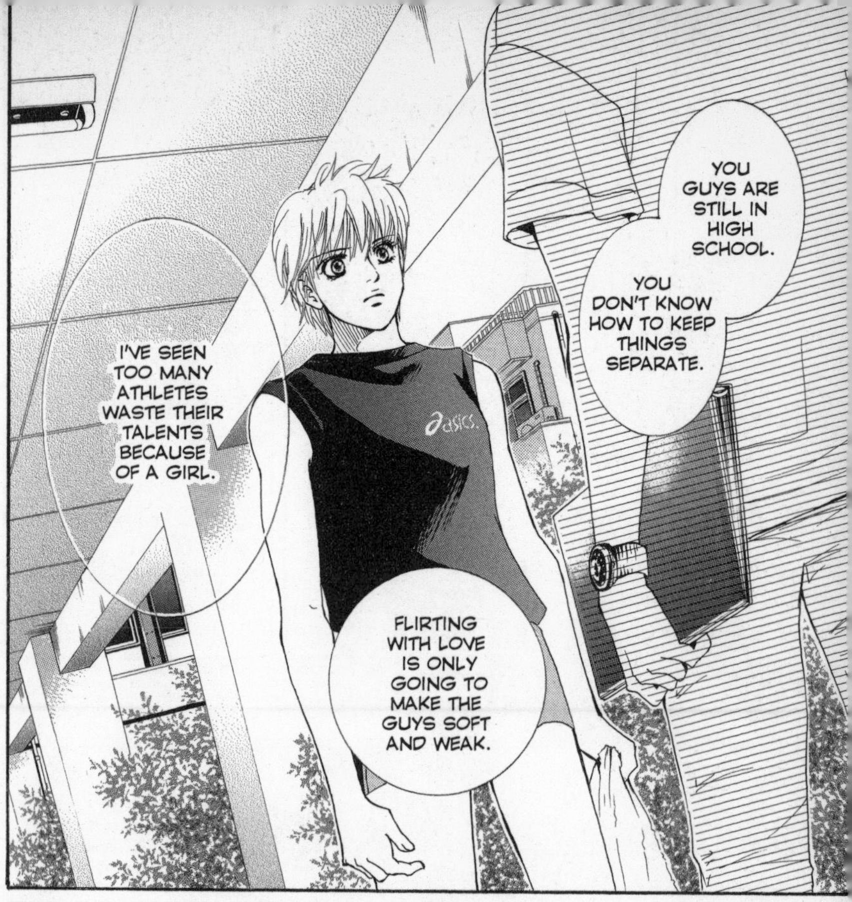
YOU GUYS ARE STILL IN HIGH SCHOOL.
YOU DON'T KNOW HOW TO KEEP THINGS SEPARATE.
I'VE SEEN TOO MANY ATHLETES WASTE THEIR TALENTS BECAUSE OF A GIRL.
FLIRTING WITH LOVE IS ONLY GOING TO MAKE THE GUYS SOFT AND WEAK.
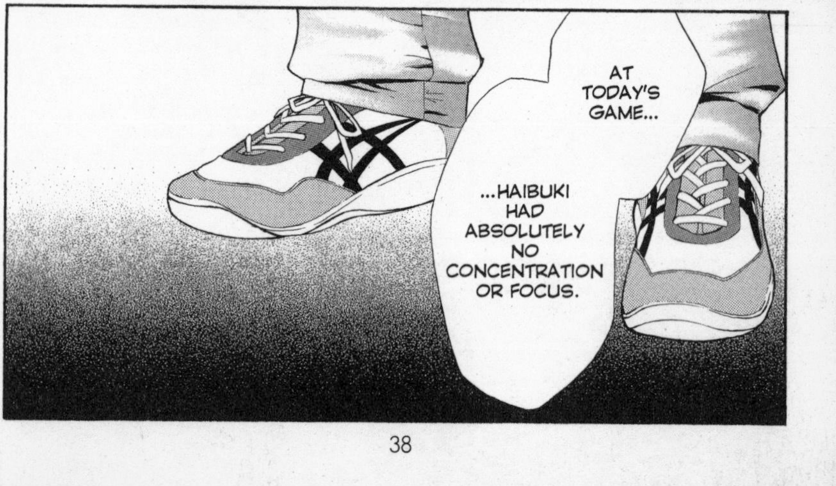
AT TODAY'S GAME...
...HAIBUKI HAD ABSOLUTELY NO CONCENTRATION OR FOCUS.

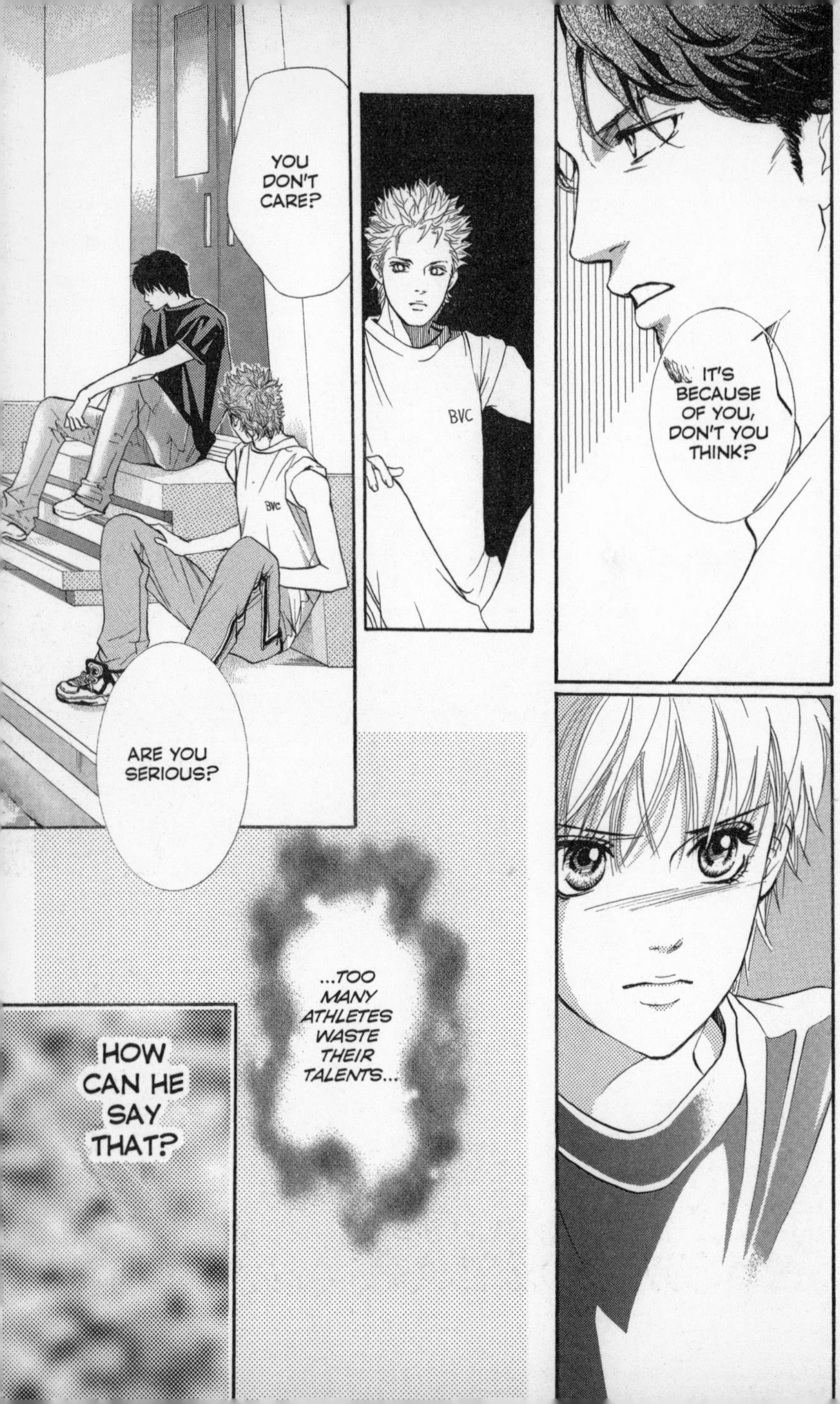
IT'S BECAUSE OF YOU, DON'T YOU THINK?
YOU DON'T CARE?
ARE YOU SERIOUS?
...TOO MANY ATHLETES WASTE THEIR TALENTS...
HOW CAN HE SAY THAT?

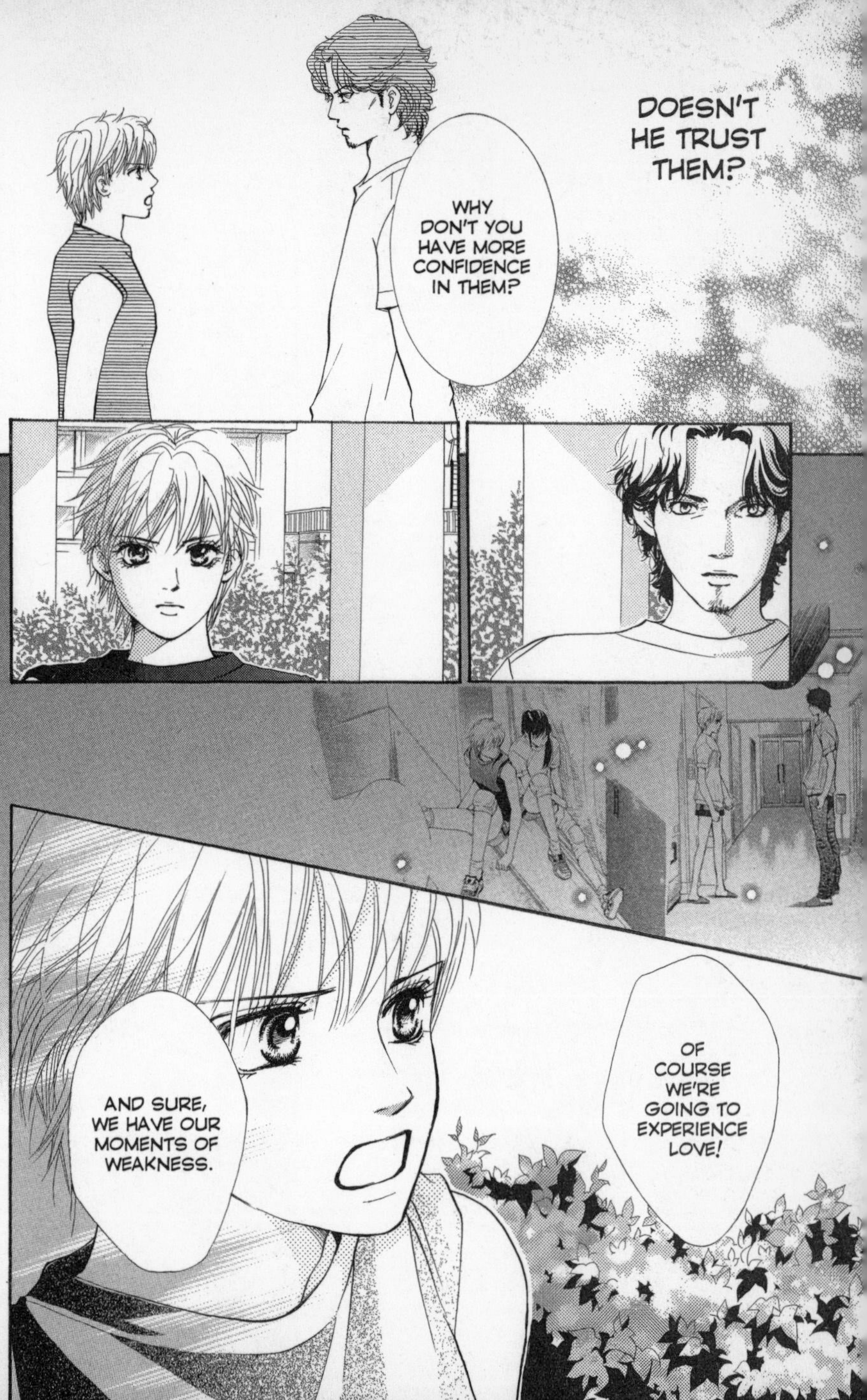
DOESN'T HE TRUST THEM?
WHY DON'T YOU HAVE MORE CONFIDENCE IN THEM?
OF COURSE WE'RE GOING TO EXPERIENCE LOVE!
AND SURE, WE HAVE OUR MOMENTS OF WEAKNESS.

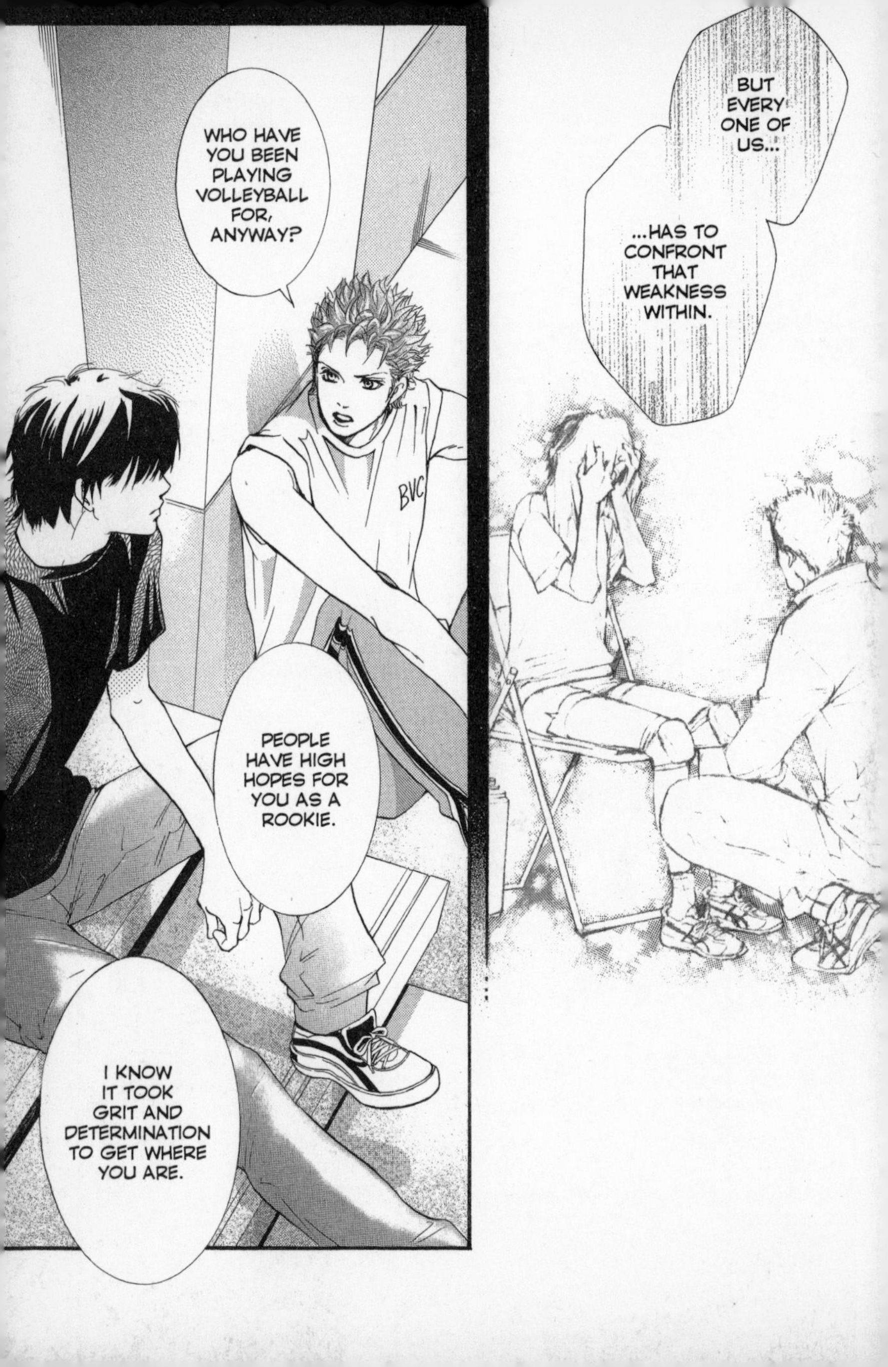
BUT EVERY ONE OF US...
...HAS TO CONFRONT THAT WEAKNESS WITHIN.
WHO HAVE YOU BEEN PLAYING VOLLEYBALL FOR, ANYWAY?
PEOPLE HAVE HIGH HOPES FOR YOU AS A ROOKIE.
I KNOW IT TOOK GRIT AND DETERMINATION TO GET WHERE YOU ARE.

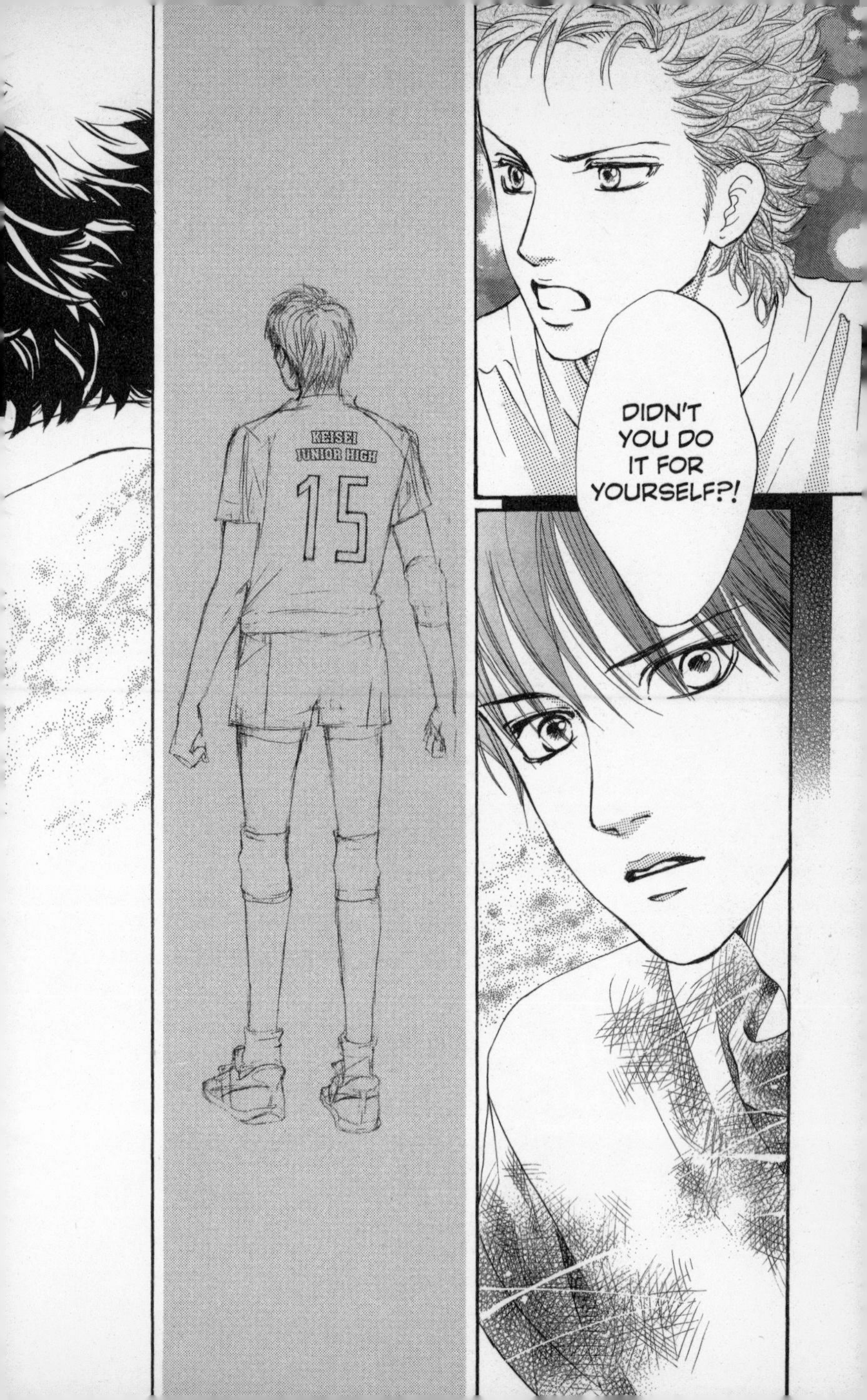
DIDN'T YOU DO IT FOR YOURSELF?!
KEISEI JUNIOR HIGH
15

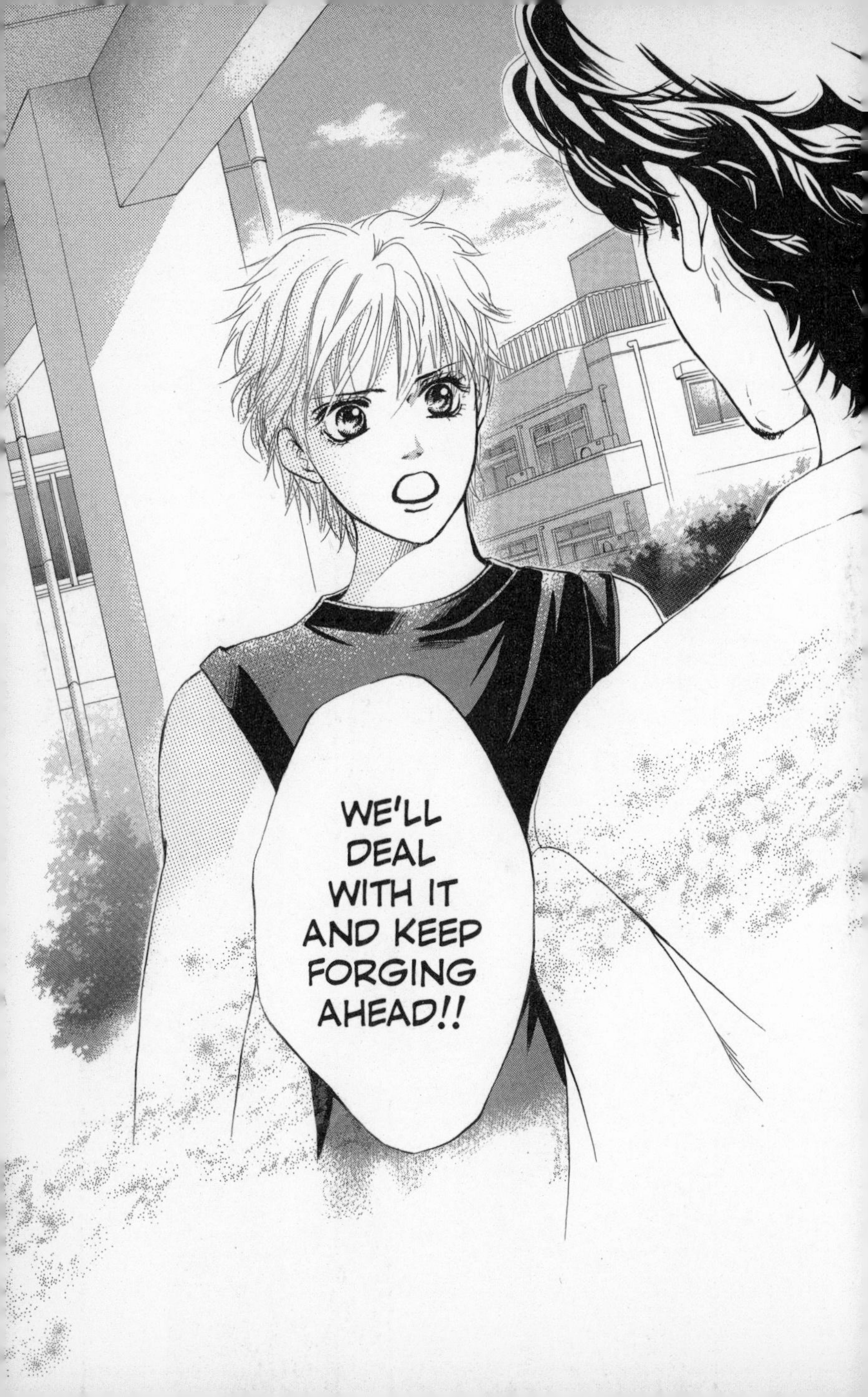
WE'LL DEAL WITH IT AND KEEP FORGING AHEAD!!

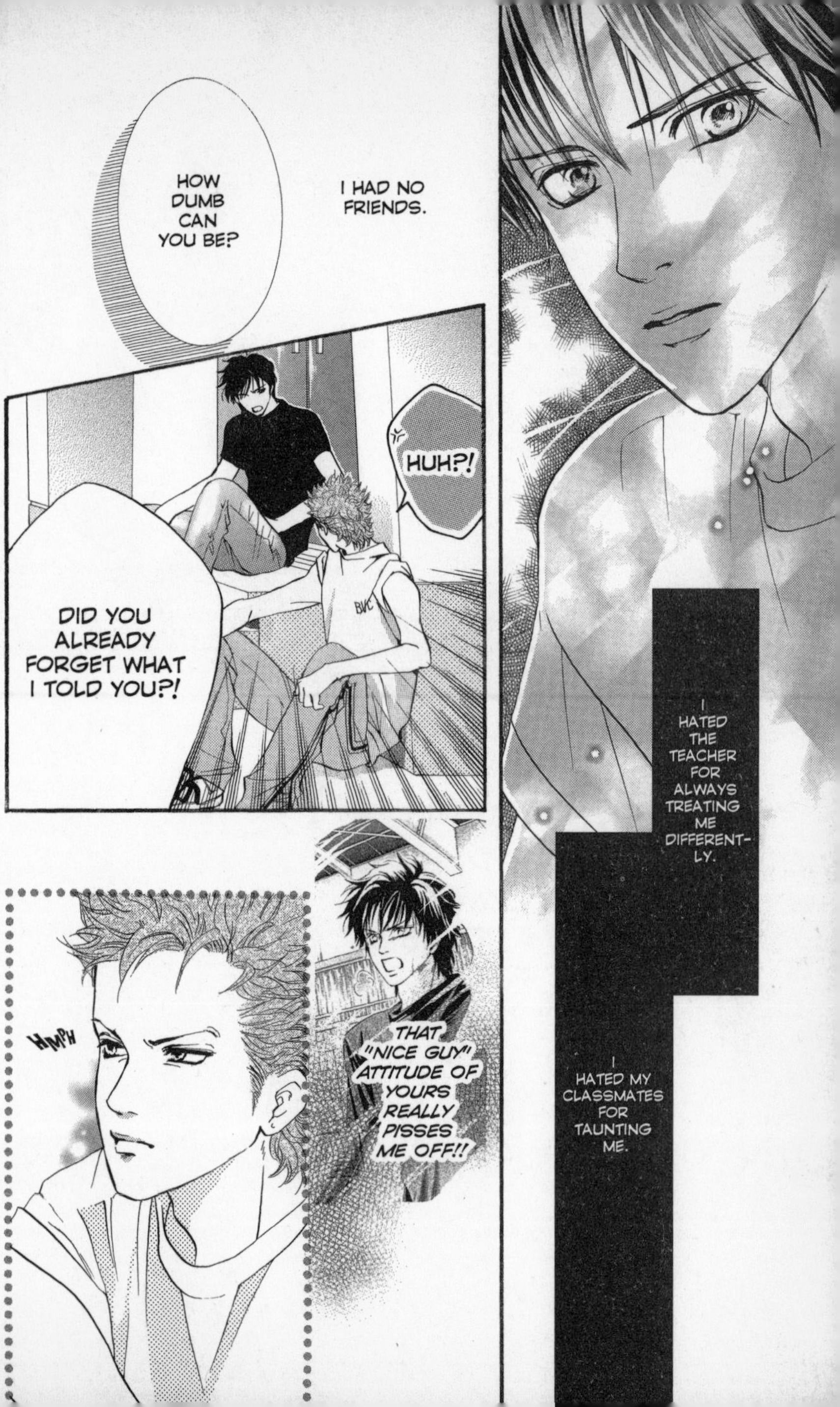
I HATED THE TEACHER FOR ALWAYS TREATING ME DIFFERENT-LY.
I HATED MY CLASSMATES FOR TAUNTING ME.
I HAD NO FRIENDS.
HOW DUMB CAN YOU BE?
HUH?!
DID YOU ALREADY FORGET WHAT I TOLD YOU?!
THAT "NICE GUY" ATTITUDE OF YOURS REALLY PISSES ME OFF!!
HMPH

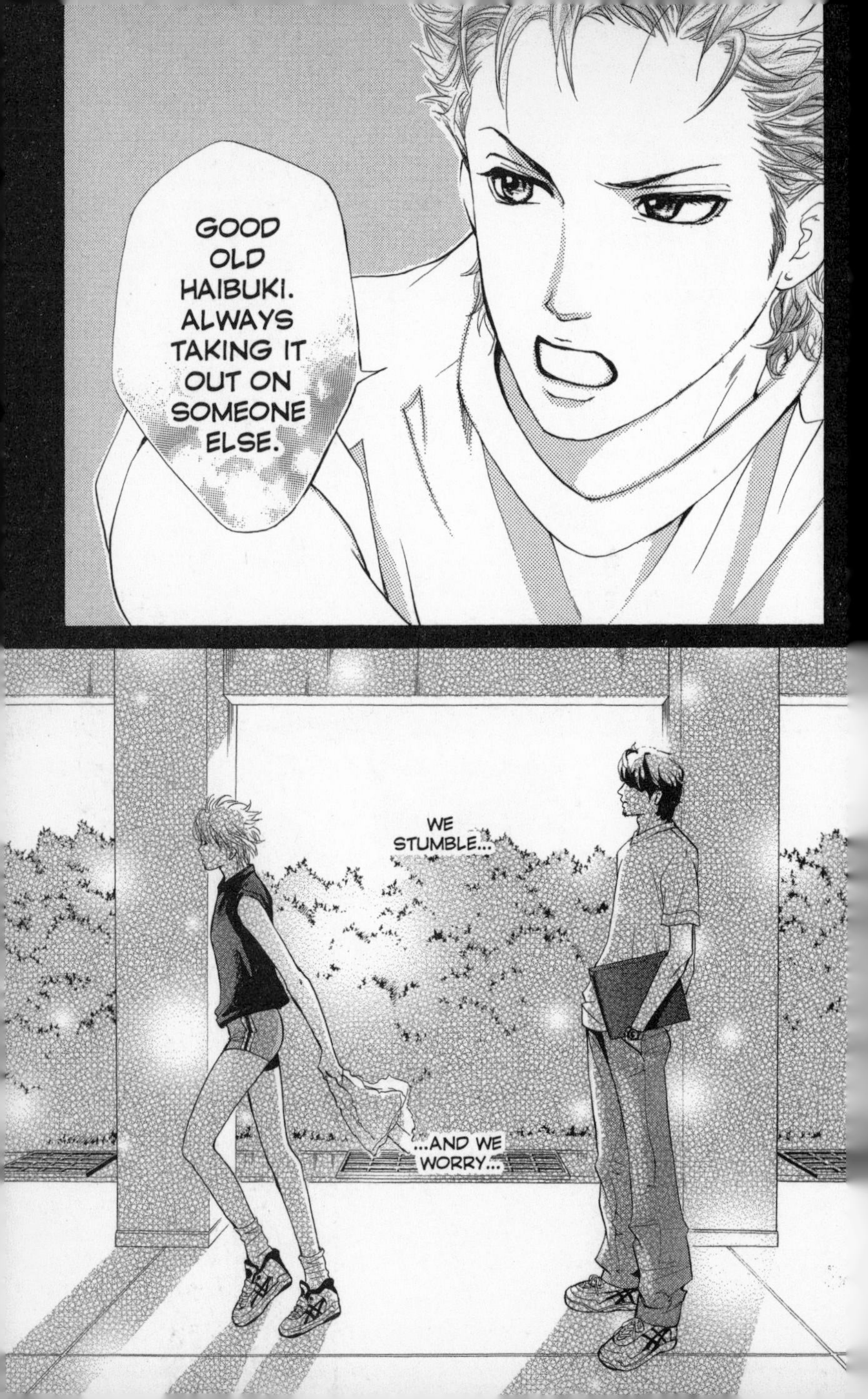
GOOD OLD HAIBUKI. ALWAYS TAKING IT OUT ON SOMEONE ELSE.
WE STUMBLE...
...AND WE WORRY...

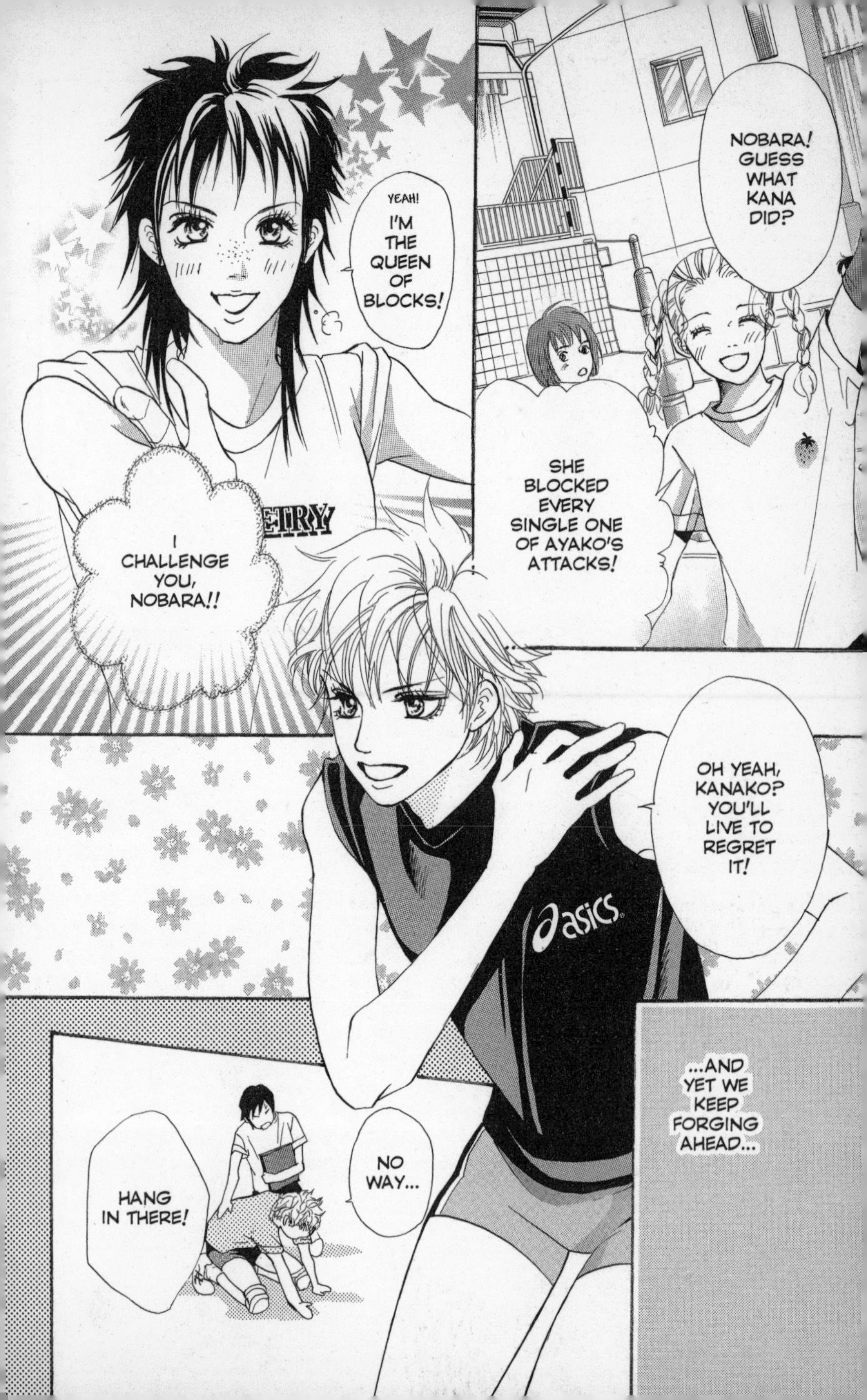
NOBARA! GUESS WHAT KANA DID?
SHE BLOCKED EVERY SINGLE ONE OF AYAKO'S ATTACKS!
YEAH! I'M THE QUEEN OF BLOCKS!
I CHALLENGE YOU, NOBARA!!
OH YEAH, KANAKO? YOU'LL LIVE TO REGRET IT!
...AND YET WE KEEP FORGING AHEAD...
NO WAY...
HANG IN THERE!

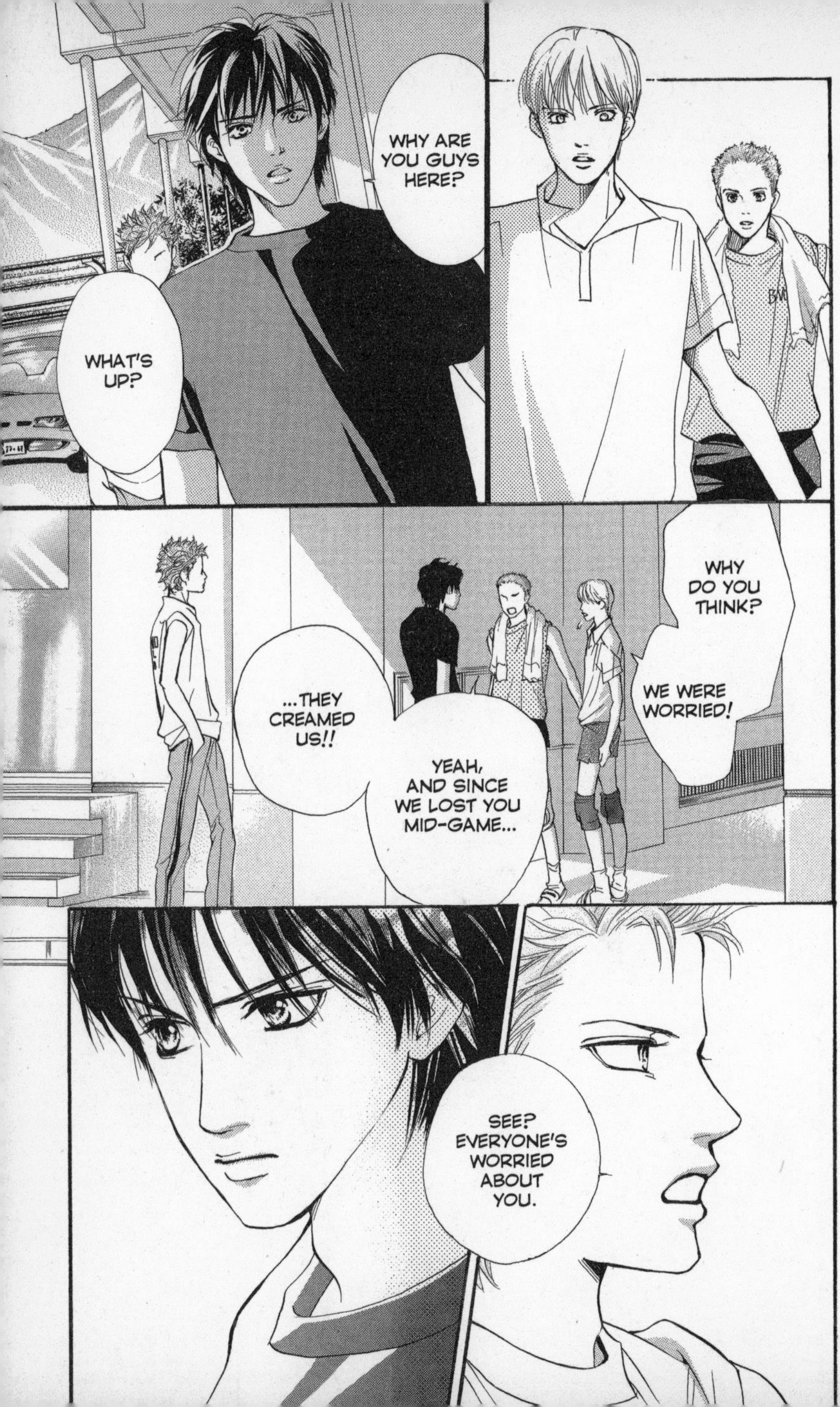
WHY ARE YOU GUYS HERE?
WHAT'S UP?
WHY DO YOU THINK?
WE WERE WORRIED!
YEAH, AND SINCE WE LOST YOU MID-GAME...
...THEY CREAMED US!!
SEE? EVERYONE'S WORRIED ABOUT YOU.

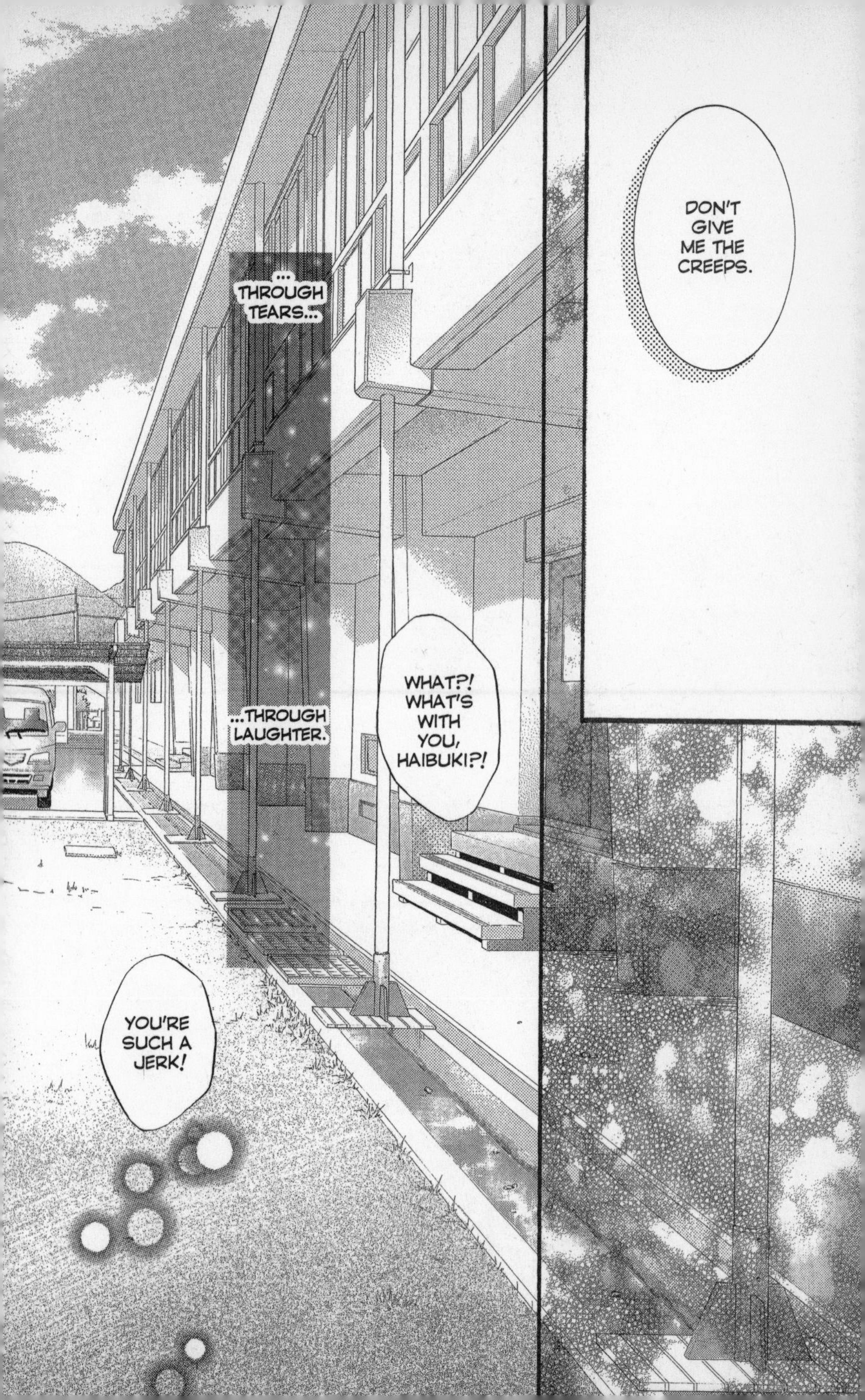
DON'T GIVE ME THE CREEPS.
...THROUGH TEARS...
...THROUGH LAUGHTER.
WHAT?! WHAT'S WITH YOU, HAIBUKI?!
YOU'RE SUCH A JERK!

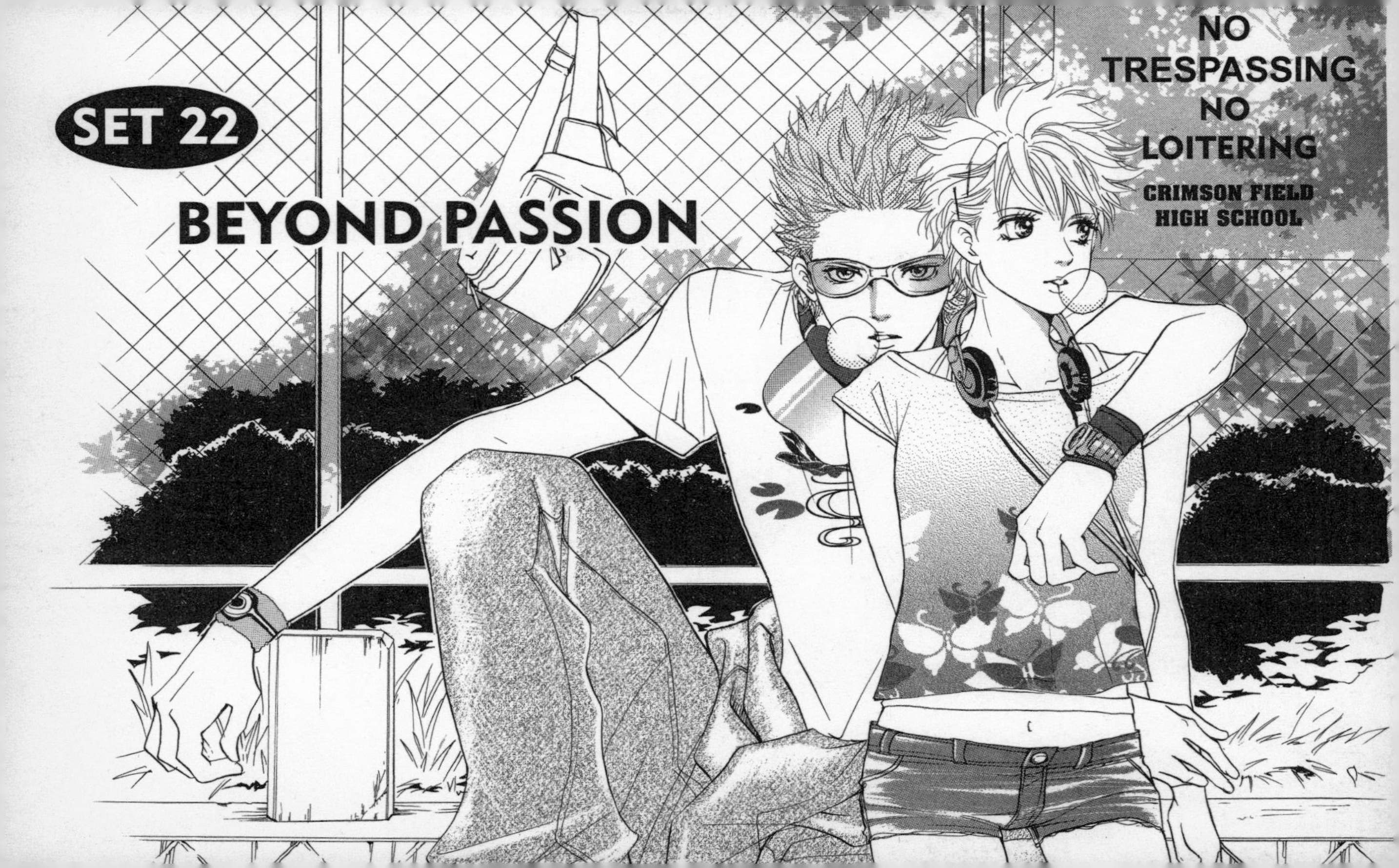
SET 22
BEYOND PASSION
NO TRESPASSING NO LOITERING
CRIMSON FIELD HIGH SCHOOL

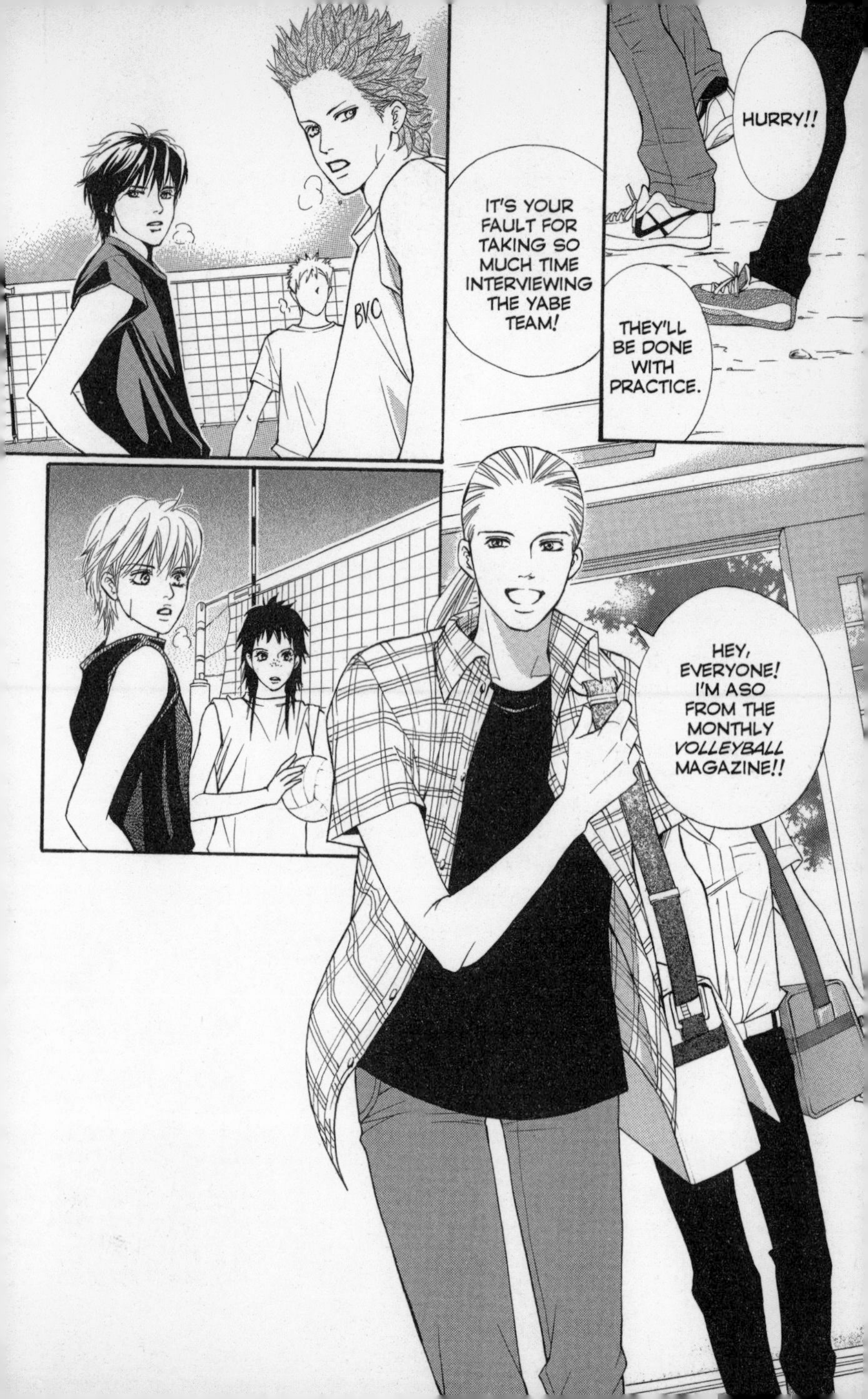
HURRY!!
IT'S YOUR FAULT FOR TAKING SO MUCH TIME INTERVIEWING THE YABE TEAM!
THEY'LL BE DONE WITH PRACTICE.
HEY, EVERYONE! I'M ASO FROM THE MONTHLY *VOLLEYBALL* MAGAZINE!!

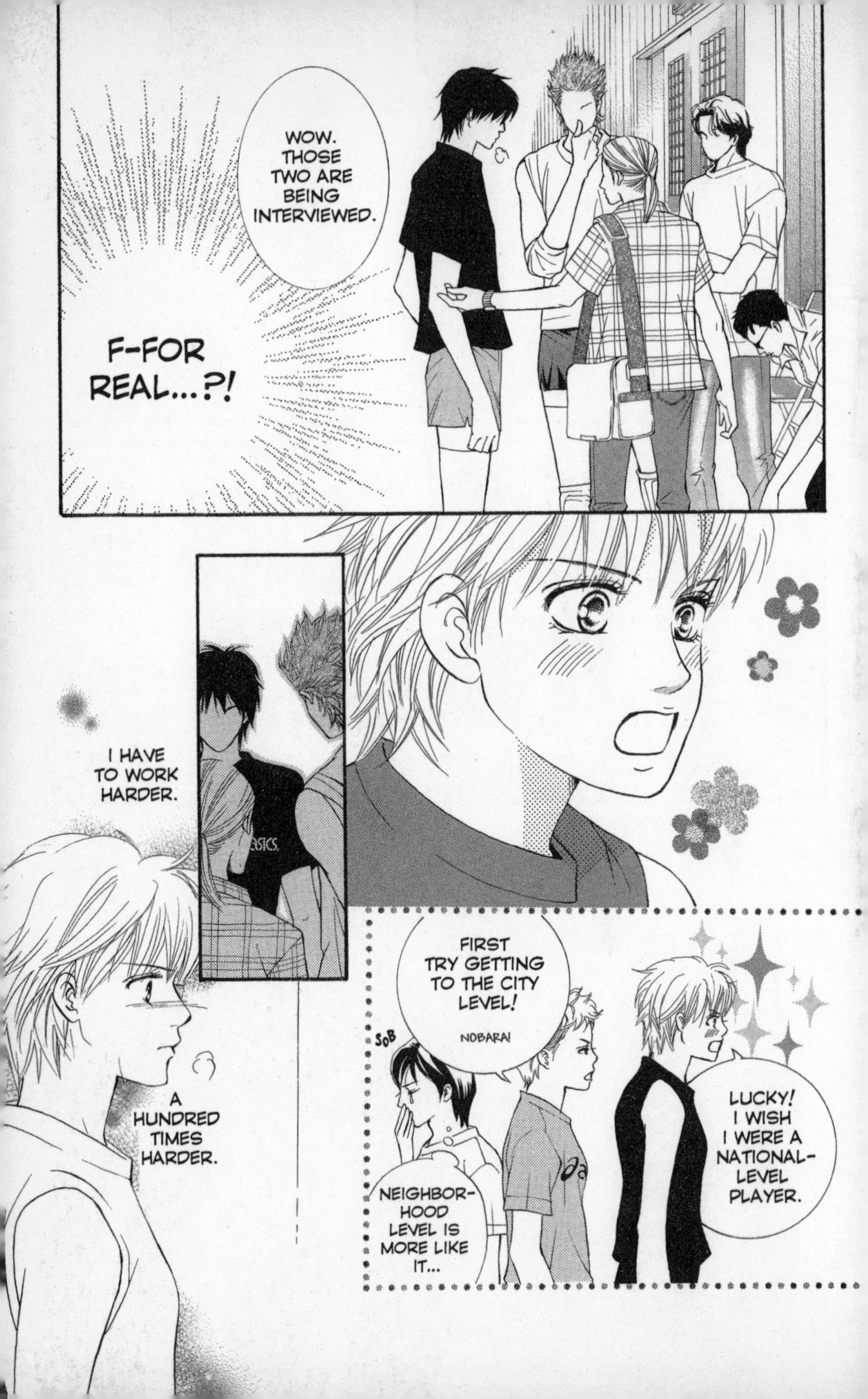
WOW. THOSE TWO ARE BEING INTERVIEWED.
F-FOR REAL...?!
LUCKY! I WISH I WERE A NATIONAL-LEVEL PLAYER.
FIRST TRY GETTING TO THE CITY LEVEL!
NOBARA!
SOB
NEIGHBORHOOD LEVEL IS MORE LIKE IT...
I HAVE TO WORK HARDER.
A HUNDRED TIMES HARDER.

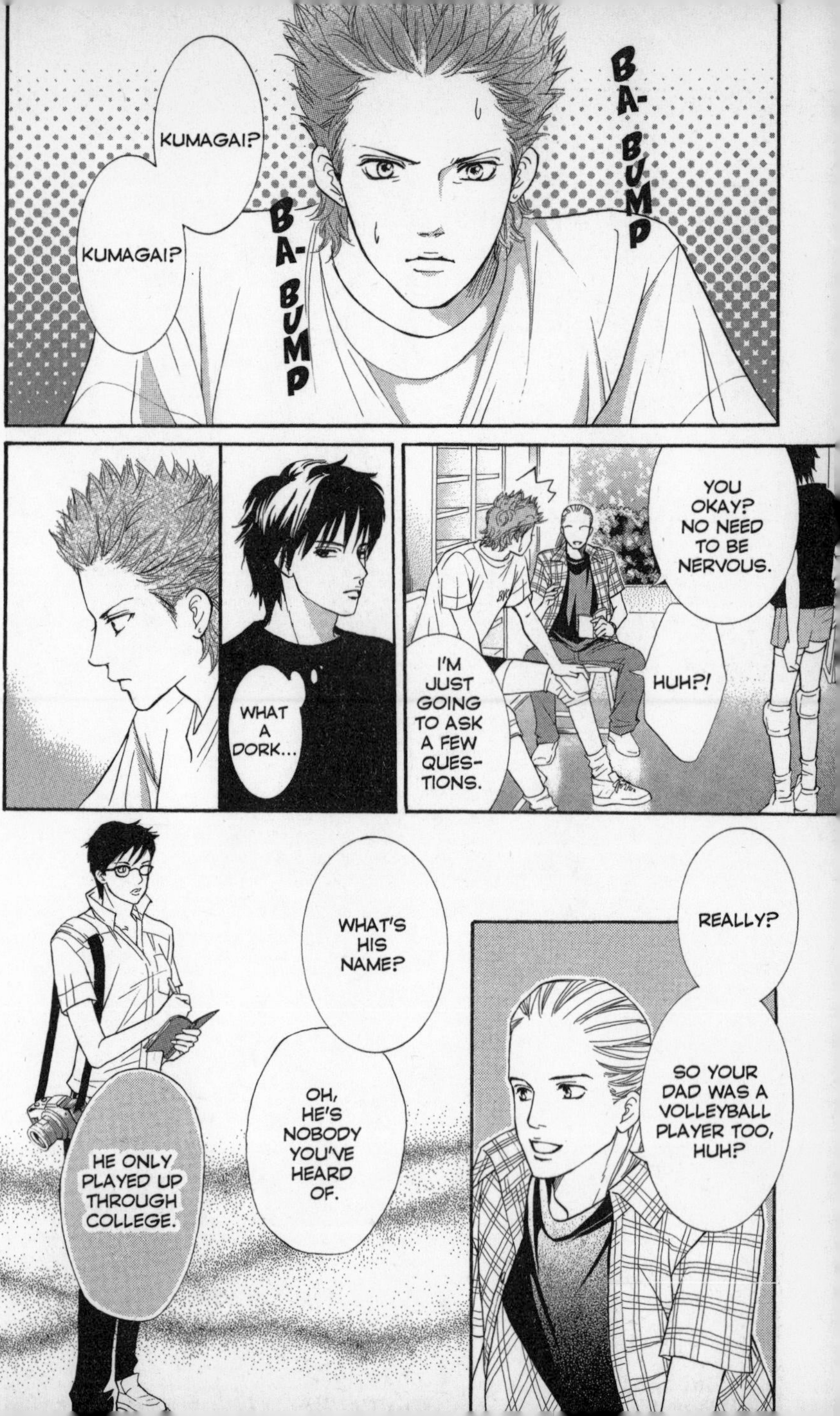
BA-BUMP
KUMAGAI?
KUMAGAI?
BA-BUMP
YOU OKAY? NO NEED TO BE NERVOUS.
HUH?!
I'M JUST GOING TO ASK A FEW QUES-TIONS.
WHAT A DORK...
REALLY?
SO YOUR DAD WAS A VOLLEYBALL PLAYER TOO, HUH?
WHAT'S HIS NAME?
OH, HE'S NOBODY YOU'VE HEARD OF.
HE ONLY PLAYED UP THROUGH COLLEGE.

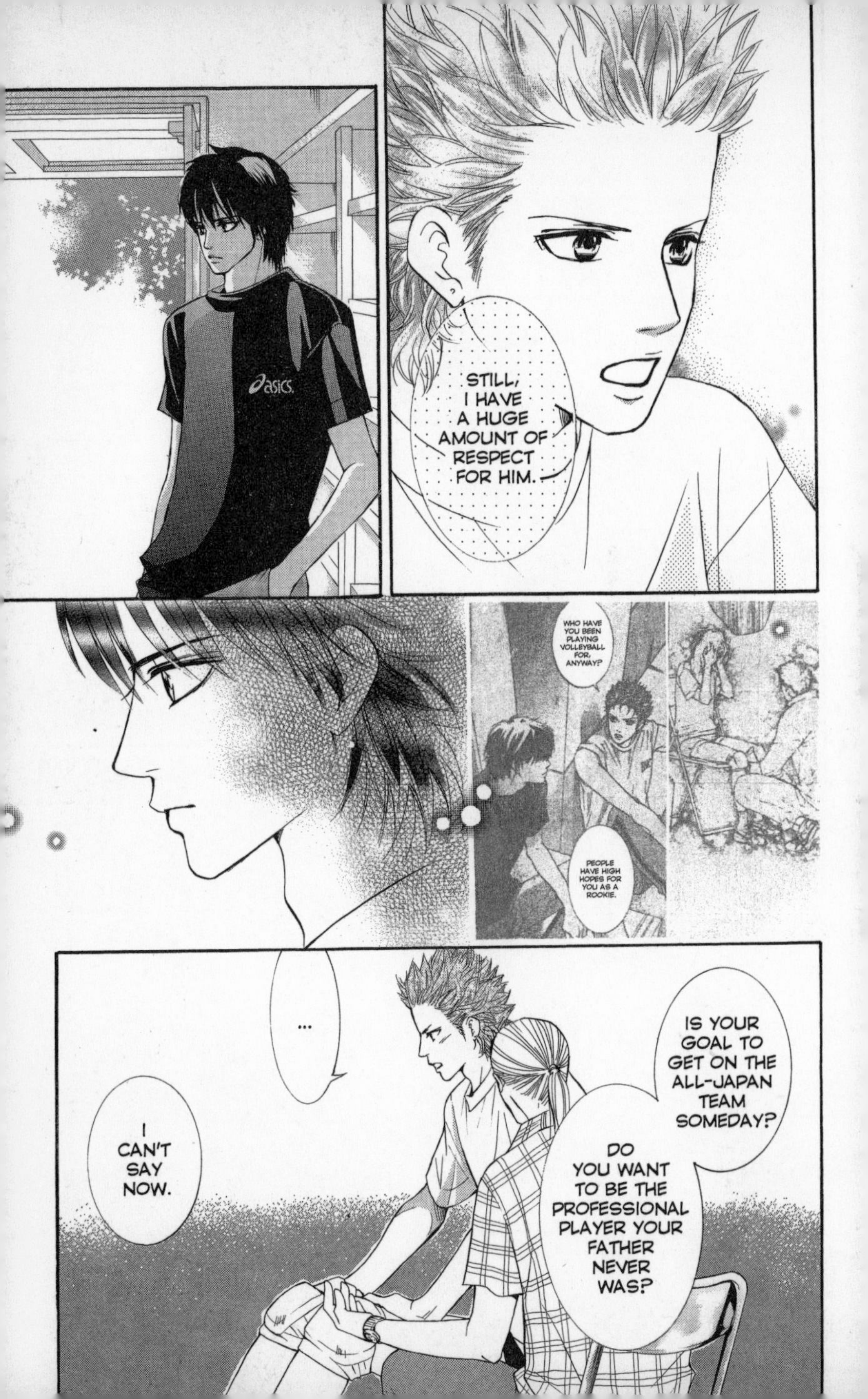
STILL, I HAVE A HUGE AMOUNT OF RESPECT FOR HIM.
WHO HAVE YOU BEEN PLAYING VOLLEYBALL FOR, ANYWAY?
PEOPLE HAVE HIGH HOPES FOR YOU AS A ROOKIE.
IS YOUR GOAL TO GET ON THE ALL-JAPAN TEAM SOMEDAY?
DO YOU WANT TO BE THE PROFESSIONAL PLAYER YOUR FATHER NEVER WAS?
...
I CAN'T SAY NOW.

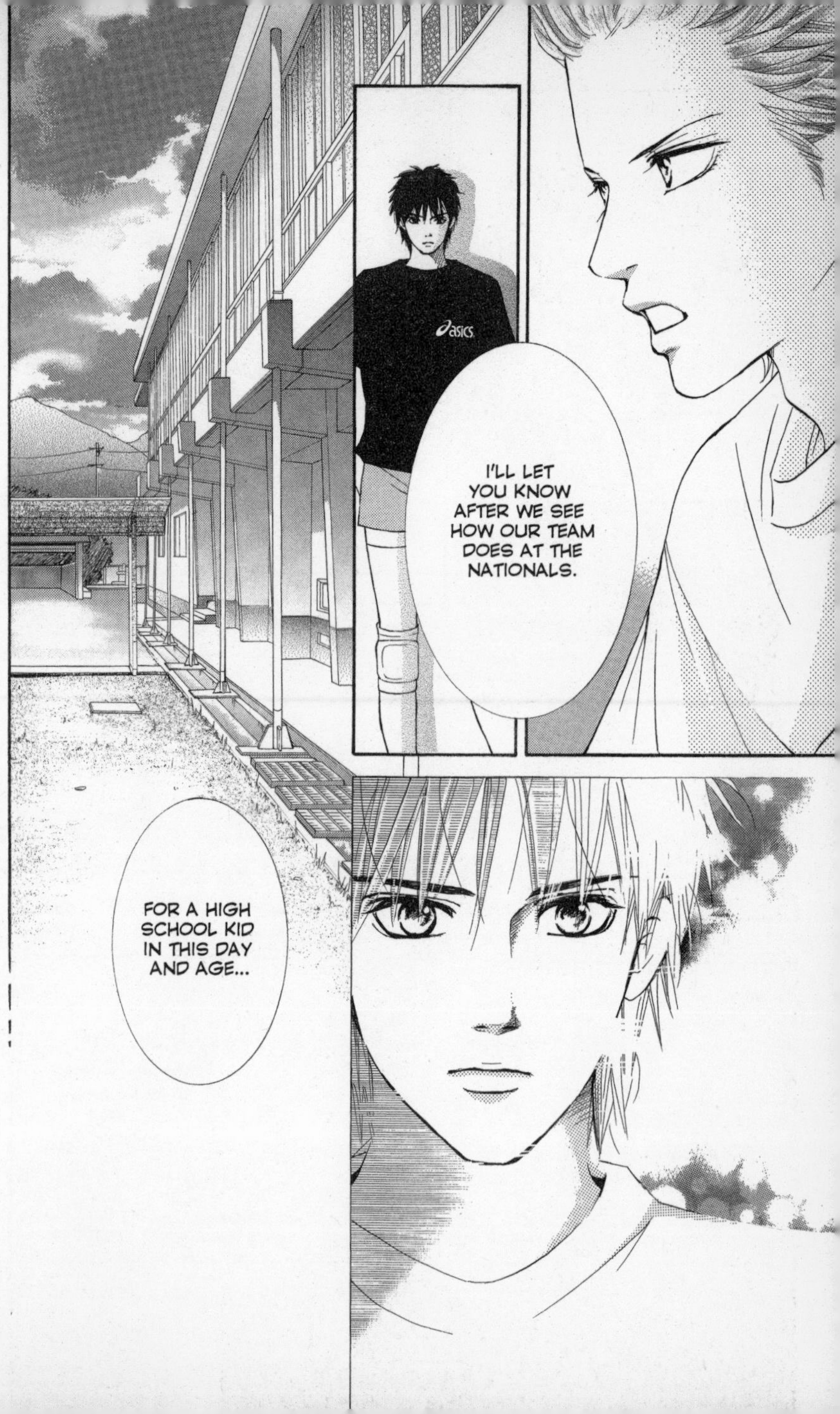
I'LL LET YOU KNOW AFTER WE SEE HOW OUR TEAM DOES AT THE NATIONALS.
FOR A HIGH SCHOOL KID IN THIS DAY AND AGE...

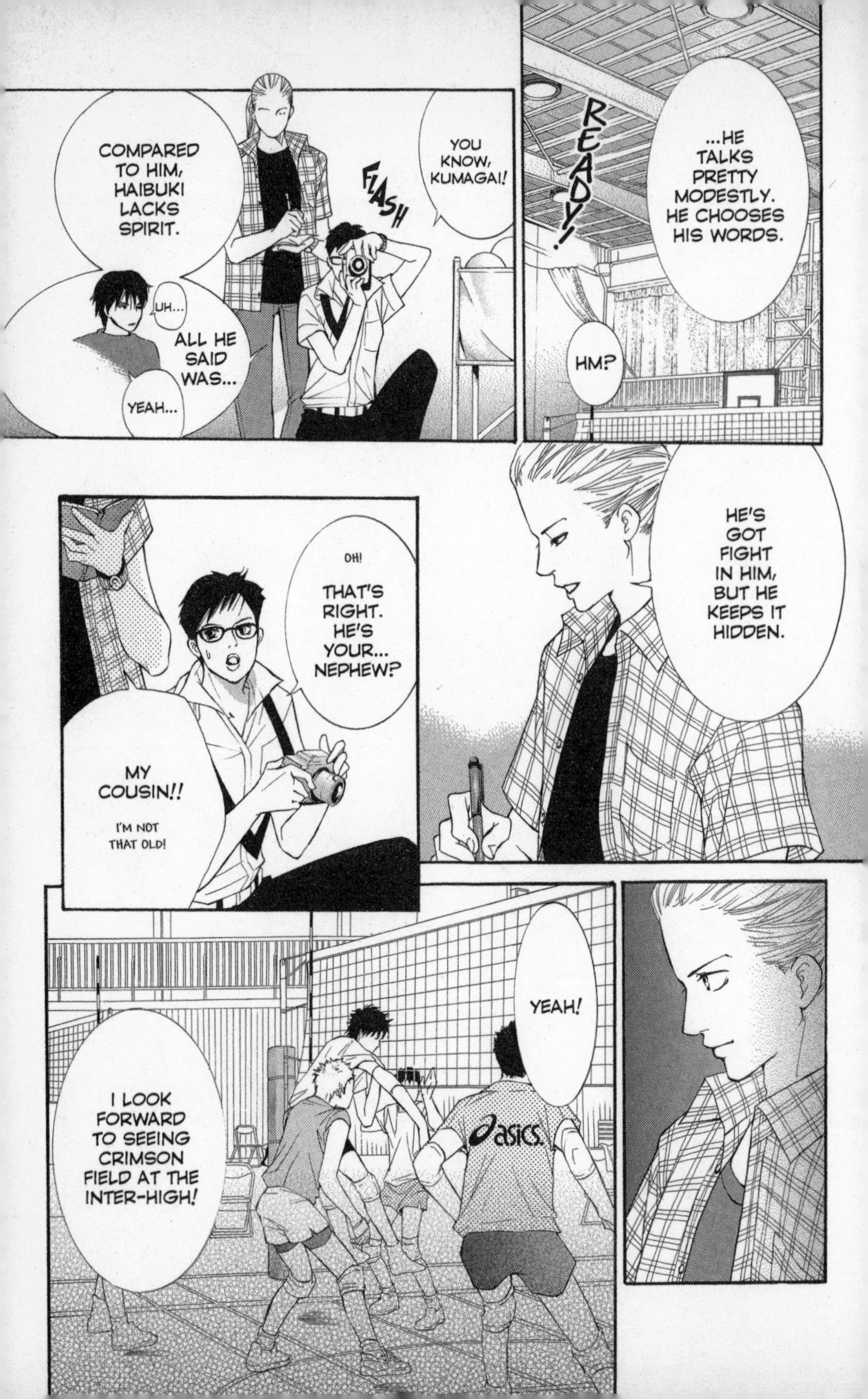
...HE TALKS PRETTY MODESTLY. HE CHOOSES HIS WORDS.
READY!
HM?
YOU KNOW, KUMAGAI!
FLASH
COMPARED TO HIM, HAIBUKI LACKS SPIRIT.
UH...
ALL HE SAID WAS...
YEAH...
HE'S GOT FIGHT IN HIM, BUT HE KEEPS IT HIDDEN.
OH!
THAT'S RIGHT. HE'S YOUR... NEPHEW?
MY COUSIN!!
I'M NOT THAT OLD!
YEAH!
I LOOK FORWARD TO SEEING CRIMSON FIELD AT THE INTER-HIGH!
asics

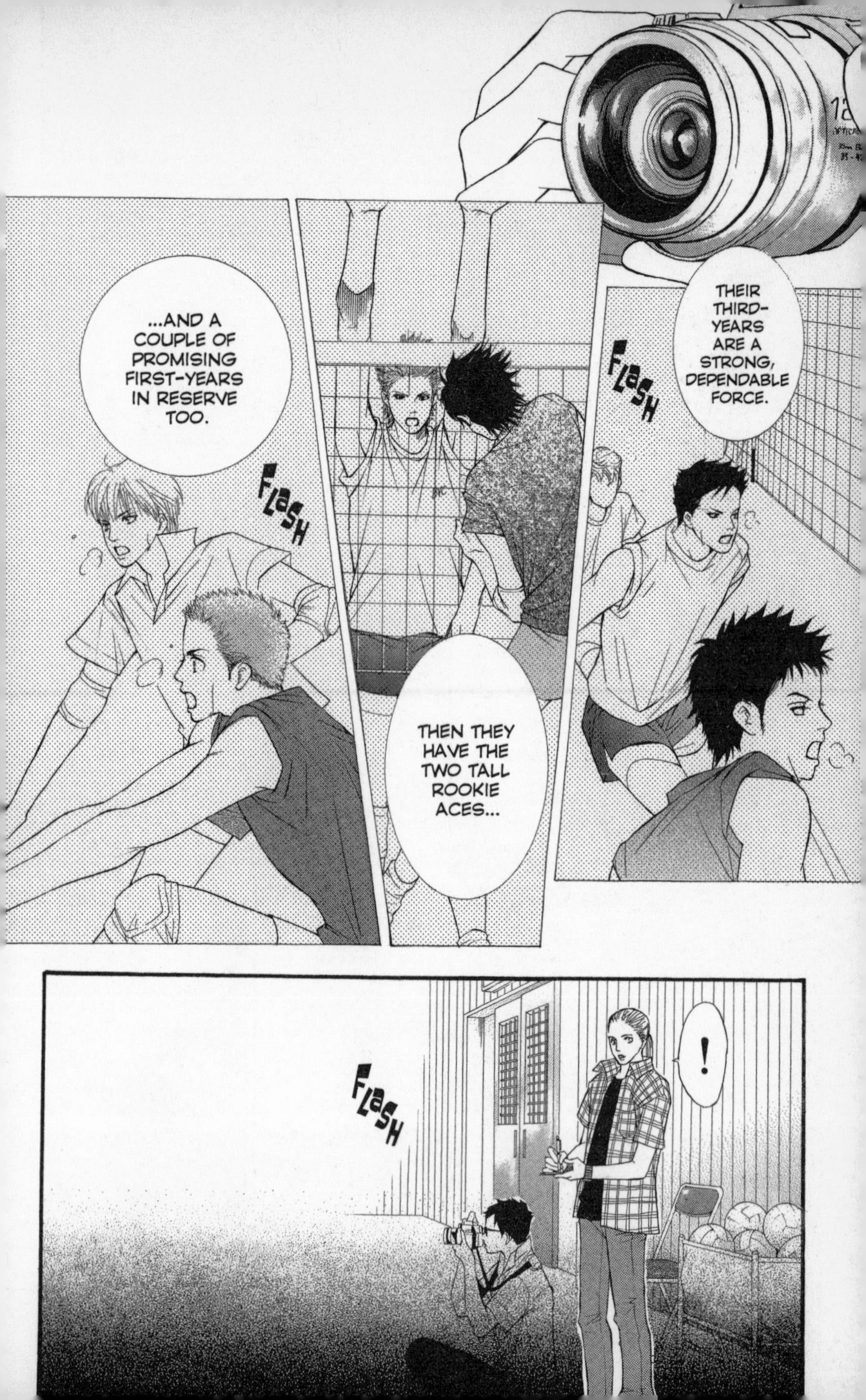
THEIR THIRD-YEARS ARE A STRONG, DEPENDABLE FORCE.
FLASH
THEN THEY HAVE THE TWO TALL ROOKIE ACES...
...AND A COUPLE OF PROMISING FIRST-YEARS IN RESERVE TOO.
FLASH
!
FLASH

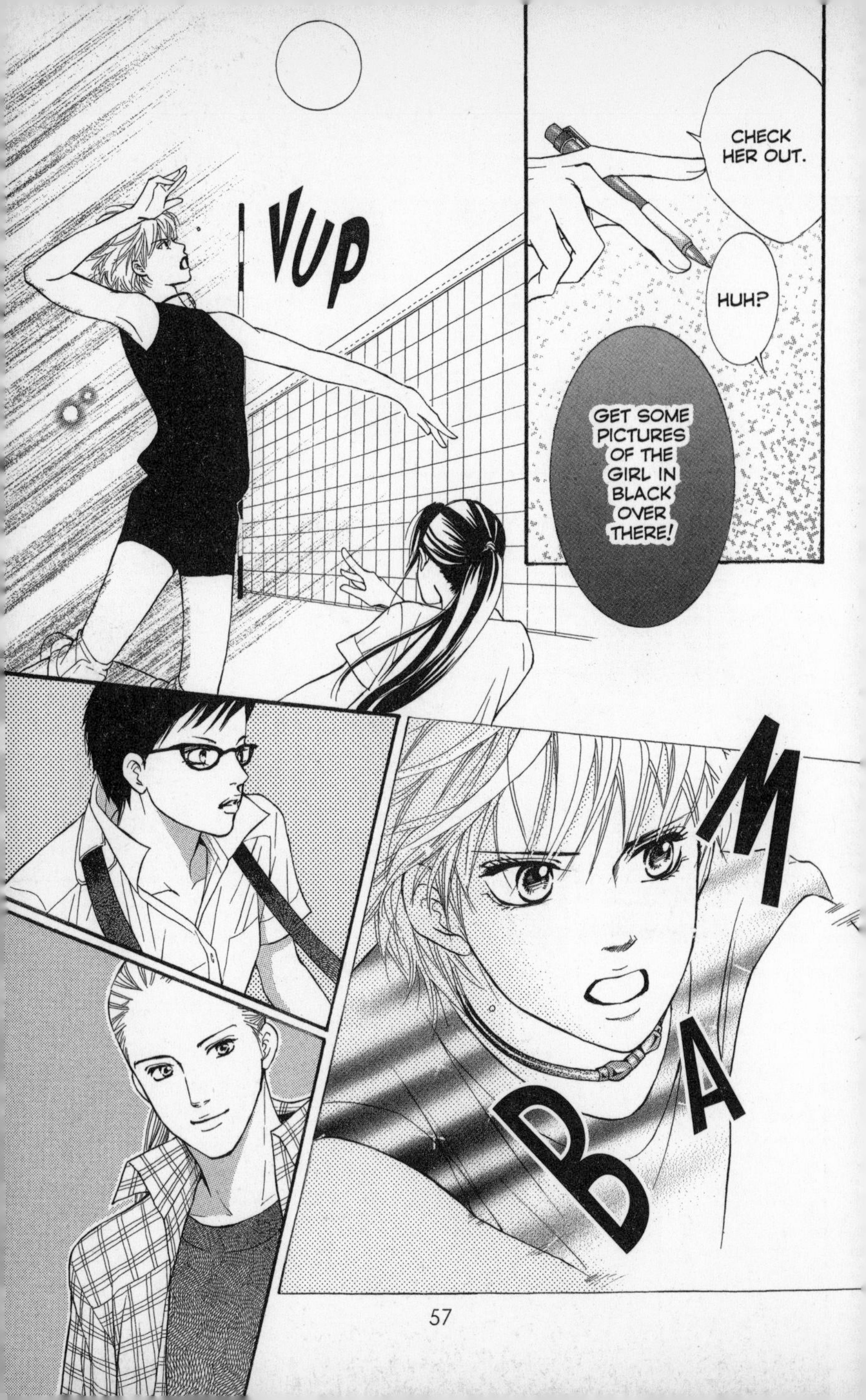
CHECK HER OUT.
HUH?
GET SOME PICTURES OF THE GIRL IN BLACK OVER THERE!
VUP
BAM

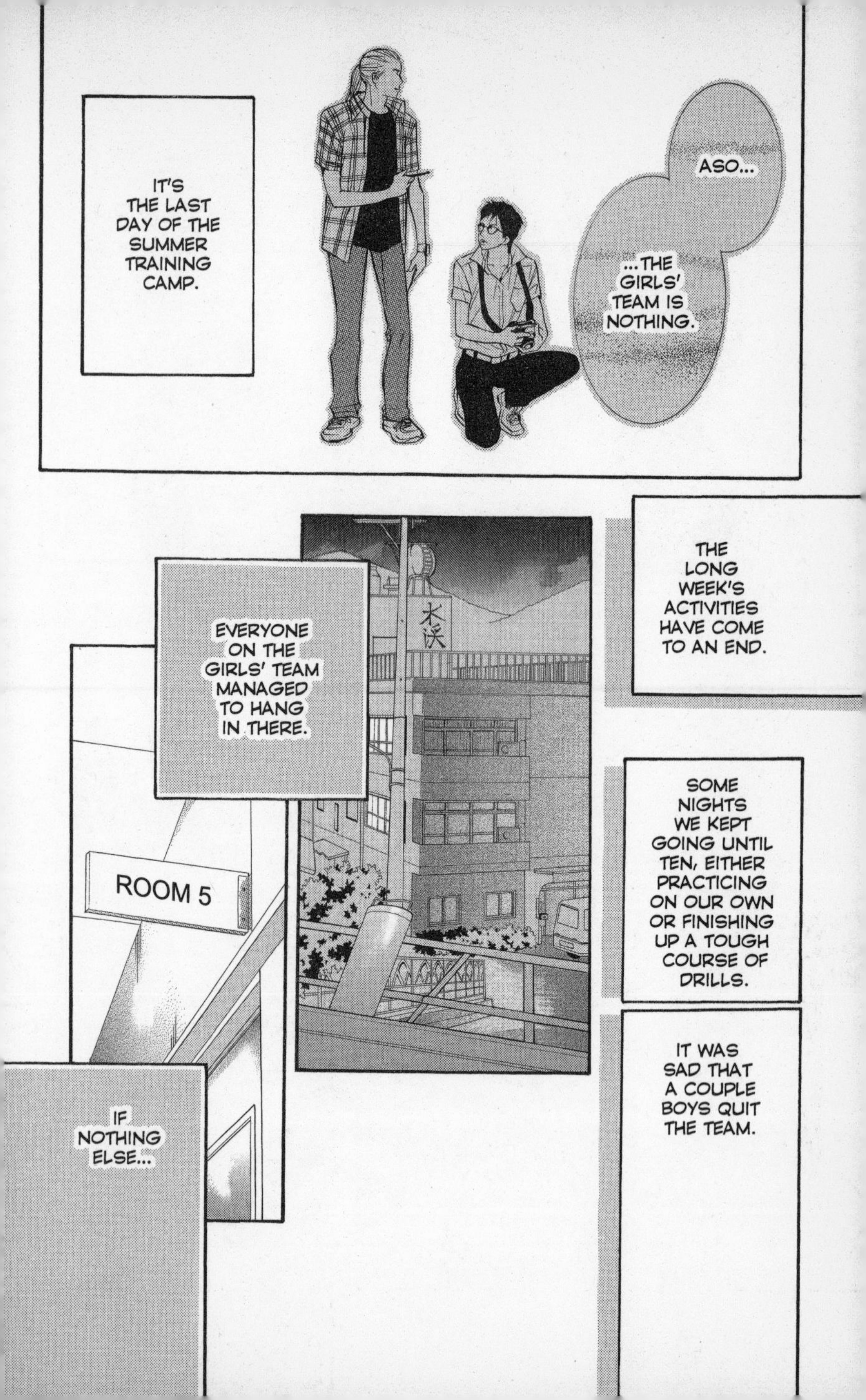
ASO...
...THE GIRLS' TEAM IS NOTHING.
IT'S THE LAST DAY OF THE SUMMER TRAINING CAMP.
THE LONG WEEK'S ACTIVITIES HAVE COME TO AN END.
SOME NIGHTS WE KEPT GOING UNTIL TEN, EITHER PRACTICING ON OUR OWN OR FINISHING UP A TOUGH COURSE OF DRILLS.
IT WAS SAD THAT A COUPLE BOYS QUIT THE TEAM.
EVERYONE ON THE GIRLS' TEAM MANAGED TO HANG IN THERE.
ROOM 5
IF NOTHING ELSE...

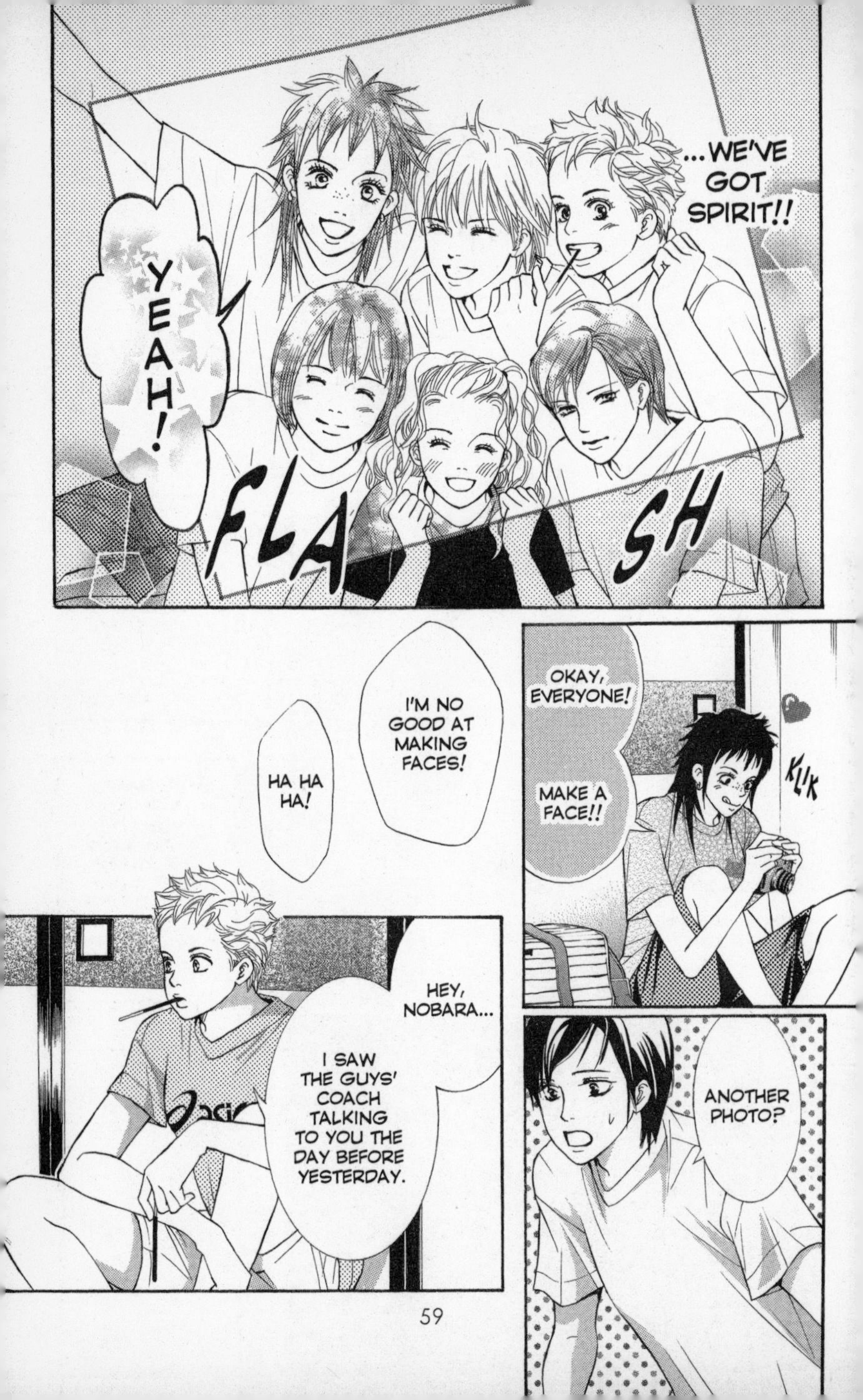
...WE'VE GOT SPIRIT!!
YEAH!
FLASH
OKAY, EVERYONE!
MAKE A FACE!!
KLIK
ANOTHER PHOTO?
I'M NO GOOD AT MAKING FACES!
HA HA HA!
HEY, NOBARA...
I SAW THE GUYS' COACH TALKING TO YOU THE DAY BEFORE YESTERDAY.

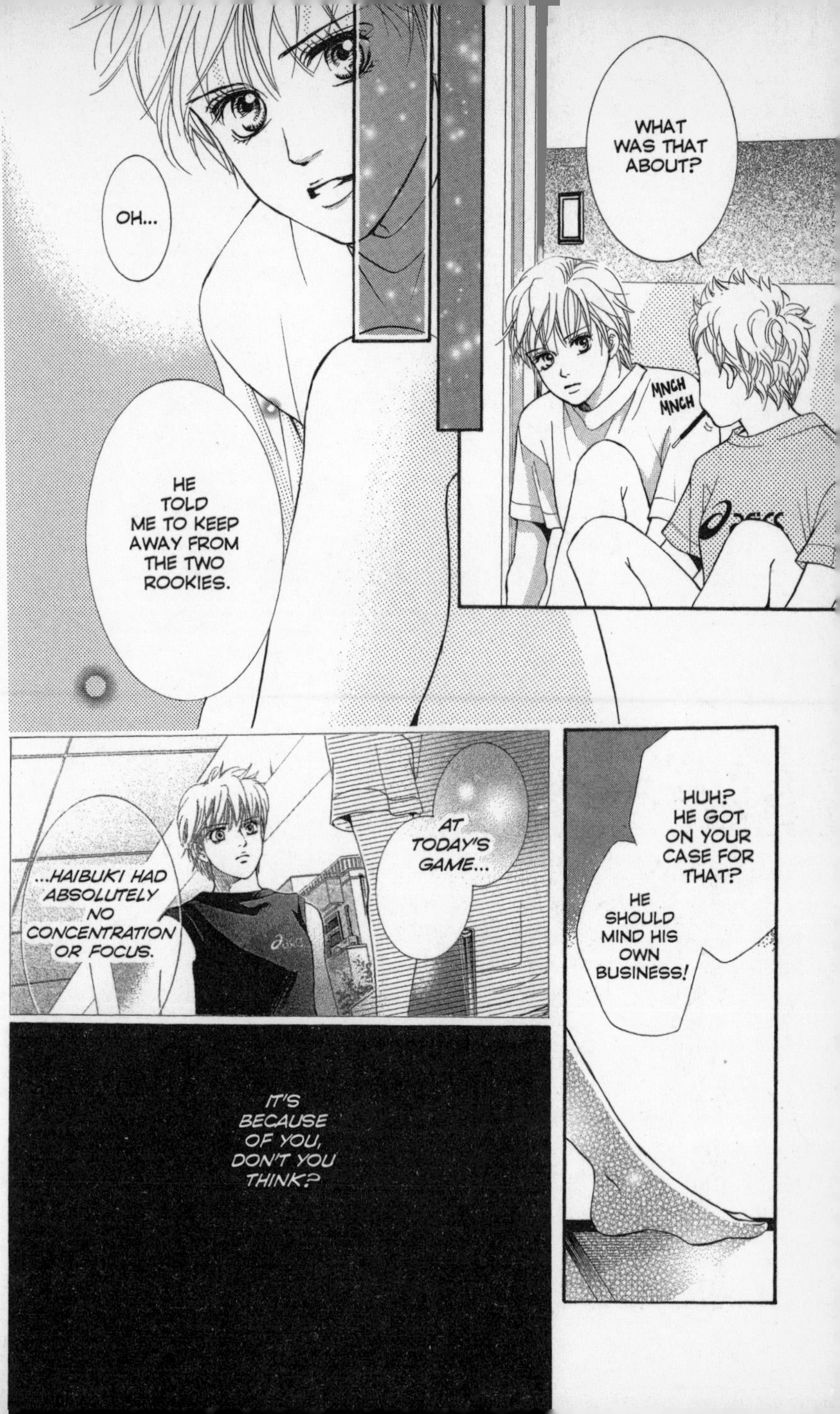
WHAT WAS THAT ABOUT?
MNCH MNCH
OH...
HE TOLD ME TO KEEP AWAY FROM THE TWO ROOKIES.
HUH? HE GOT ON YOUR CASE FOR THAT?
HE SHOULD MIND HIS OWN BUSINESS!
AT TODAY'S GAME...
...HAIBUKI HAD ABSOLUTELY NO CONCENTRATION OR FOCUS.
IT'S BECAUSE OF YOU, DON'T YOU THINK?

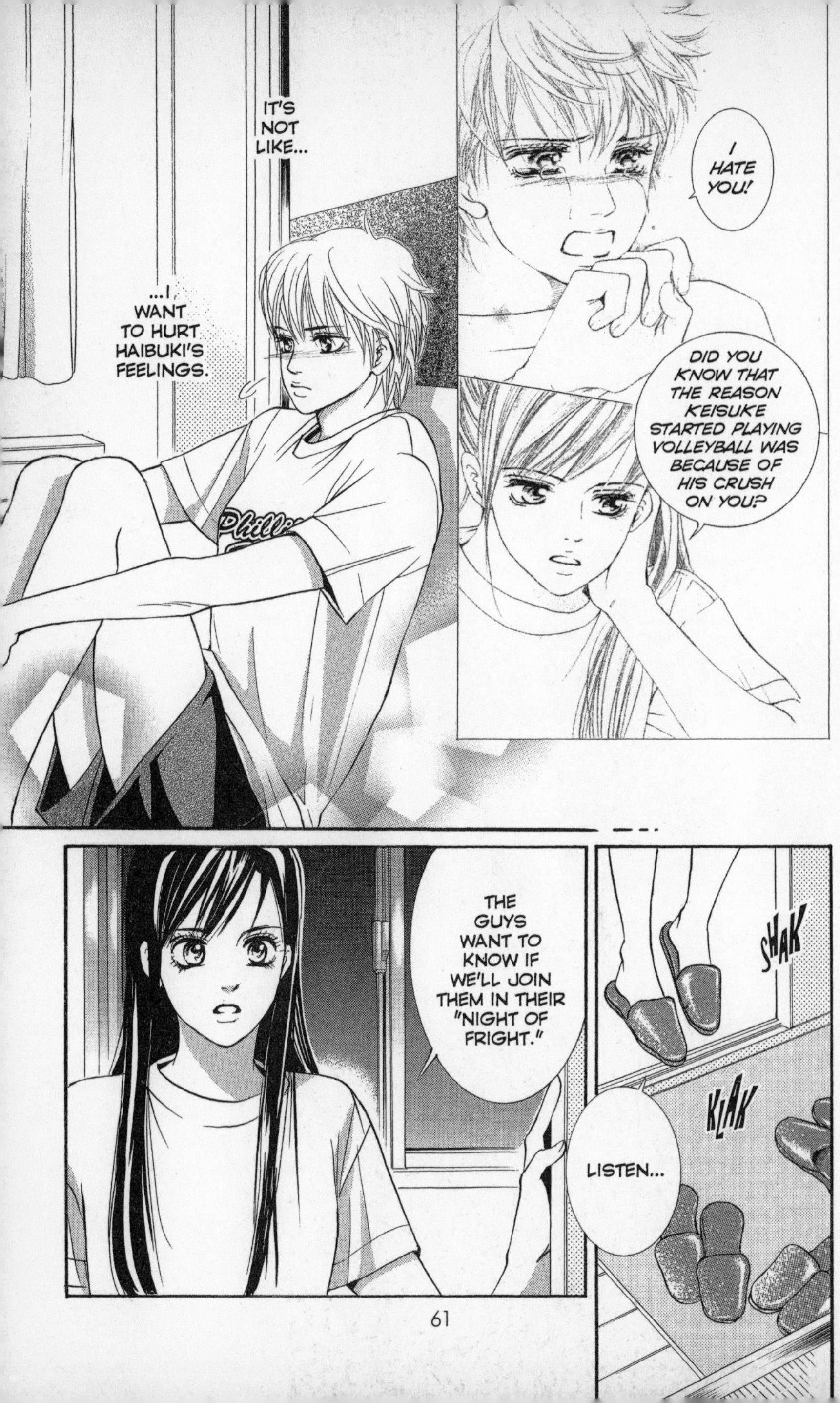
I HATE YOU!
DID YOU KNOW THAT THE REASON KEISUKE STARTED PLAYING VOLLEYBALL WAS BECAUSE OF HIS CRUSH ON YOU?
IT'S NOT LIKE...
...I WANT TO HURT HAIBUKI'S FEELINGS.
SHAK
KLAK
LISTEN...
THE GUYS WANT TO KNOW IF WE'LL JOIN THEM IN THEIR "NIGHT OF FRIGHT."

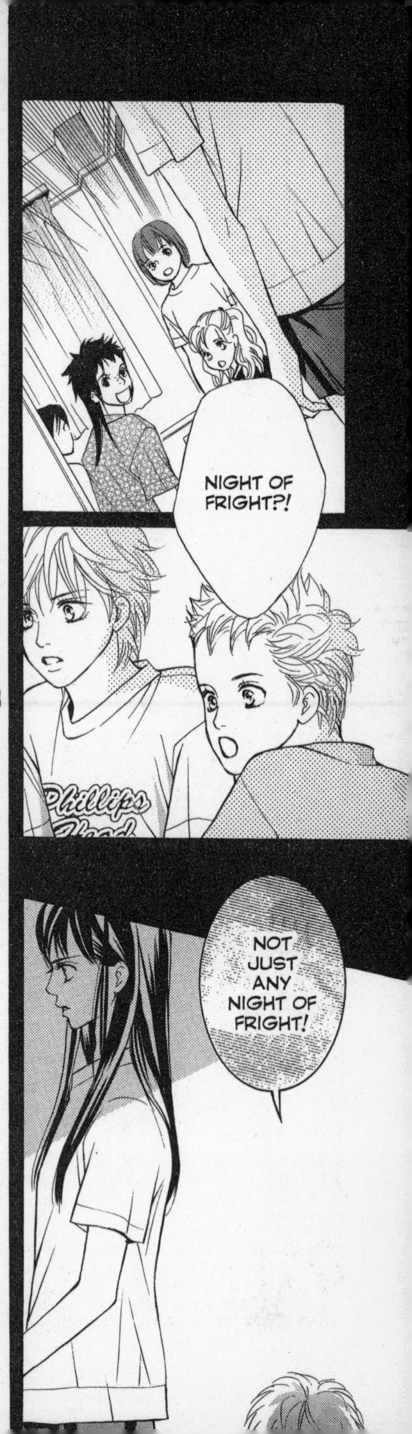
NIGHT OF FRIGHT?!
NOT JUST ANY NIGHT OF FRIGHT!

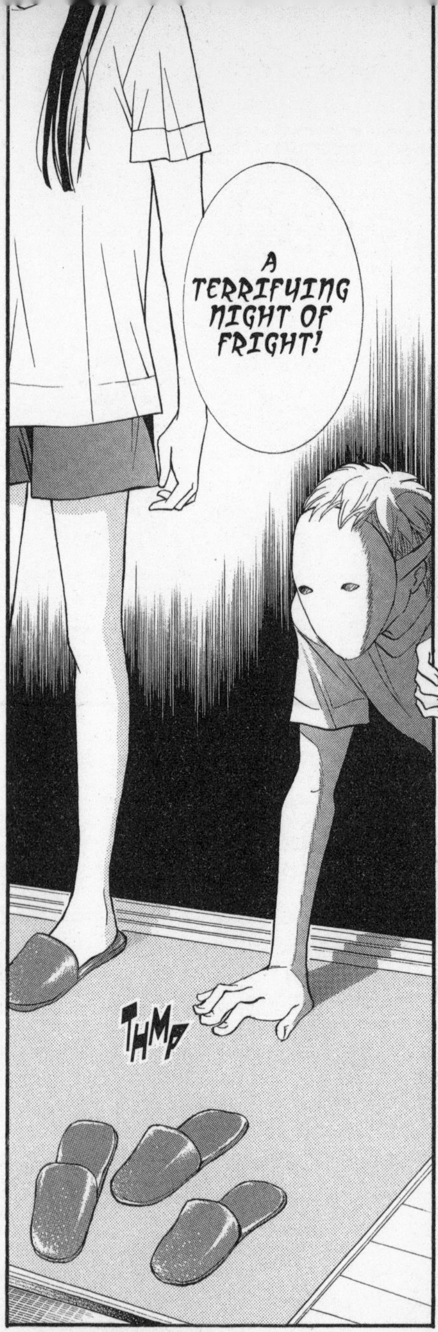
A TERRIFYING NIGHT OF FRIGHT!
THMP

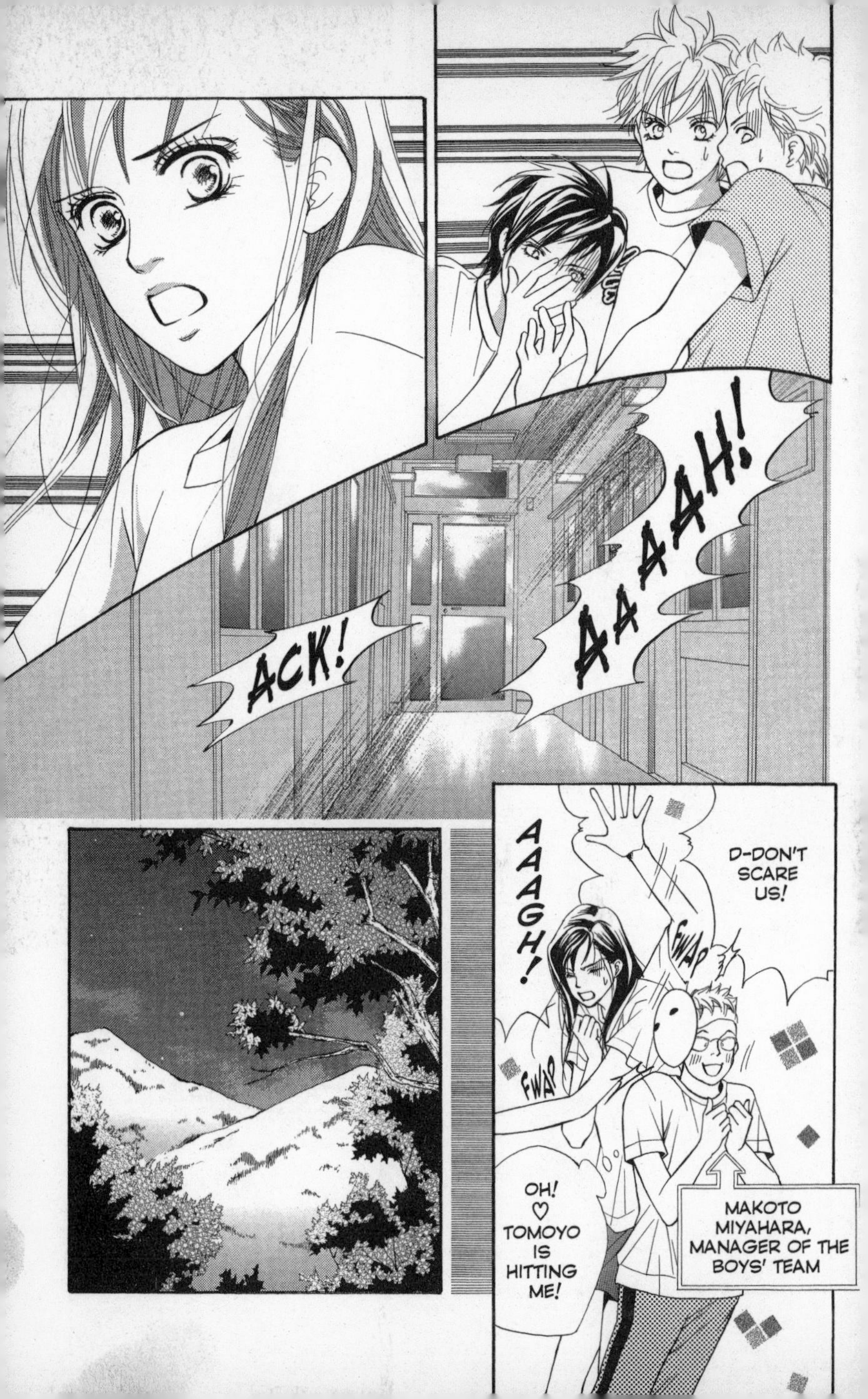
AAAAH!
ACK!
D-DON'T SCARE US!
AAAAGH!
FWAP
FWAP
MAKOTO MIYAHARA, MANAGER OF THE BOYS' TEAM
OH! ♡ TOMOYO IS HITTING ME!

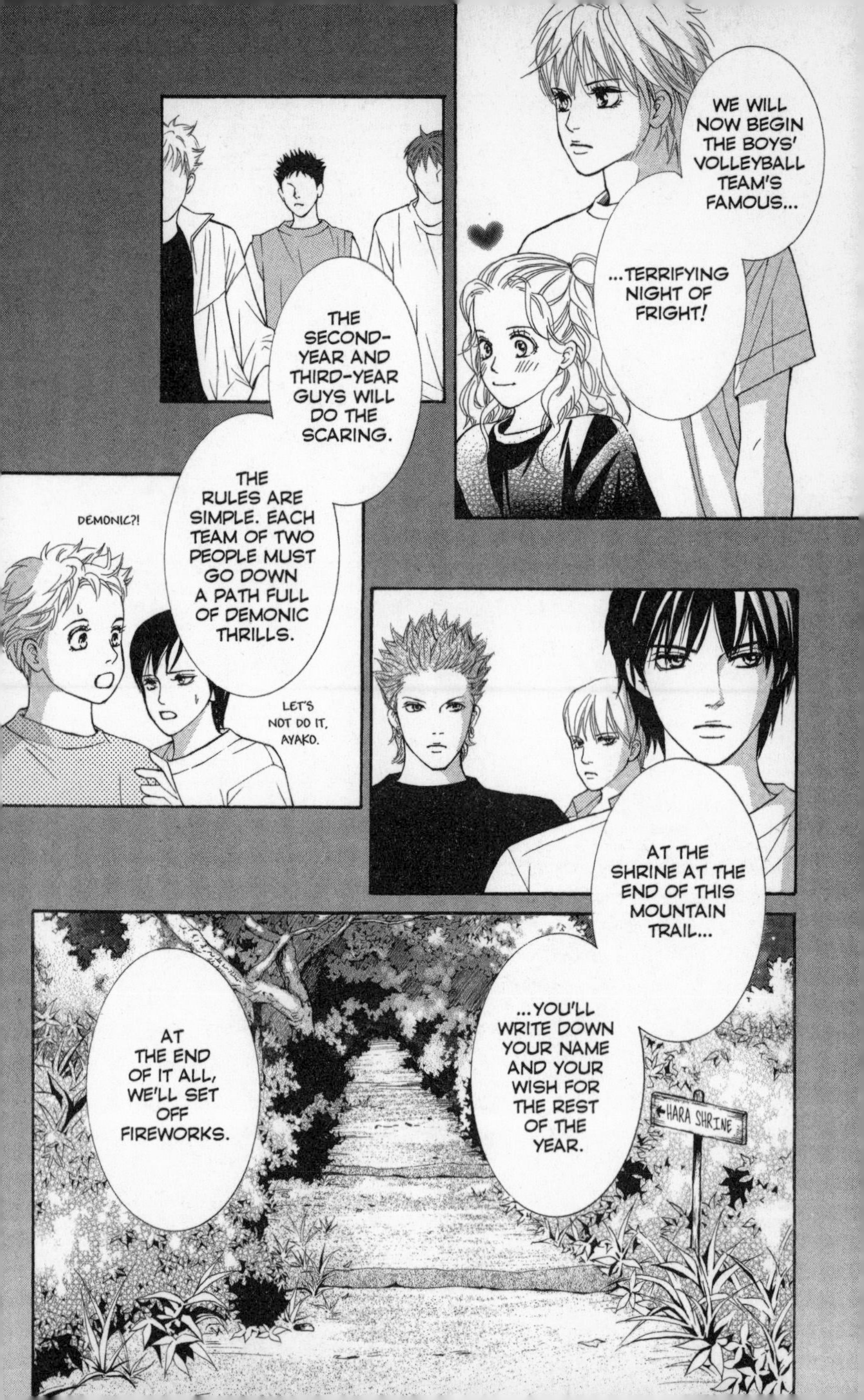
WE WILL NOW BEGIN THE BOYS' VOLLEYBALL TEAM'S FAMOUS...
...TERRIFYING NIGHT OF FRIGHT!
THE SECOND-YEAR AND THIRD-YEAR GUYS WILL DO THE SCARING.
THE RULES ARE SIMPLE. EACH TEAM OF TWO PEOPLE MUST GO DOWN A PATH FULL OF DEMONIC THRILLS.
DEMONIC?!
LET'S NOT DO IT, AYAKO.
AT THE SHRINE AT THE END OF THIS MOUNTAIN TRAIL...
...YOU'LL WRITE DOWN YOUR NAME AND YOUR WISH FOR THE REST OF THE YEAR.
HARA SHRINE
AT THE END OF IT ALL, WE'LL SET OFF FIREWORKS.

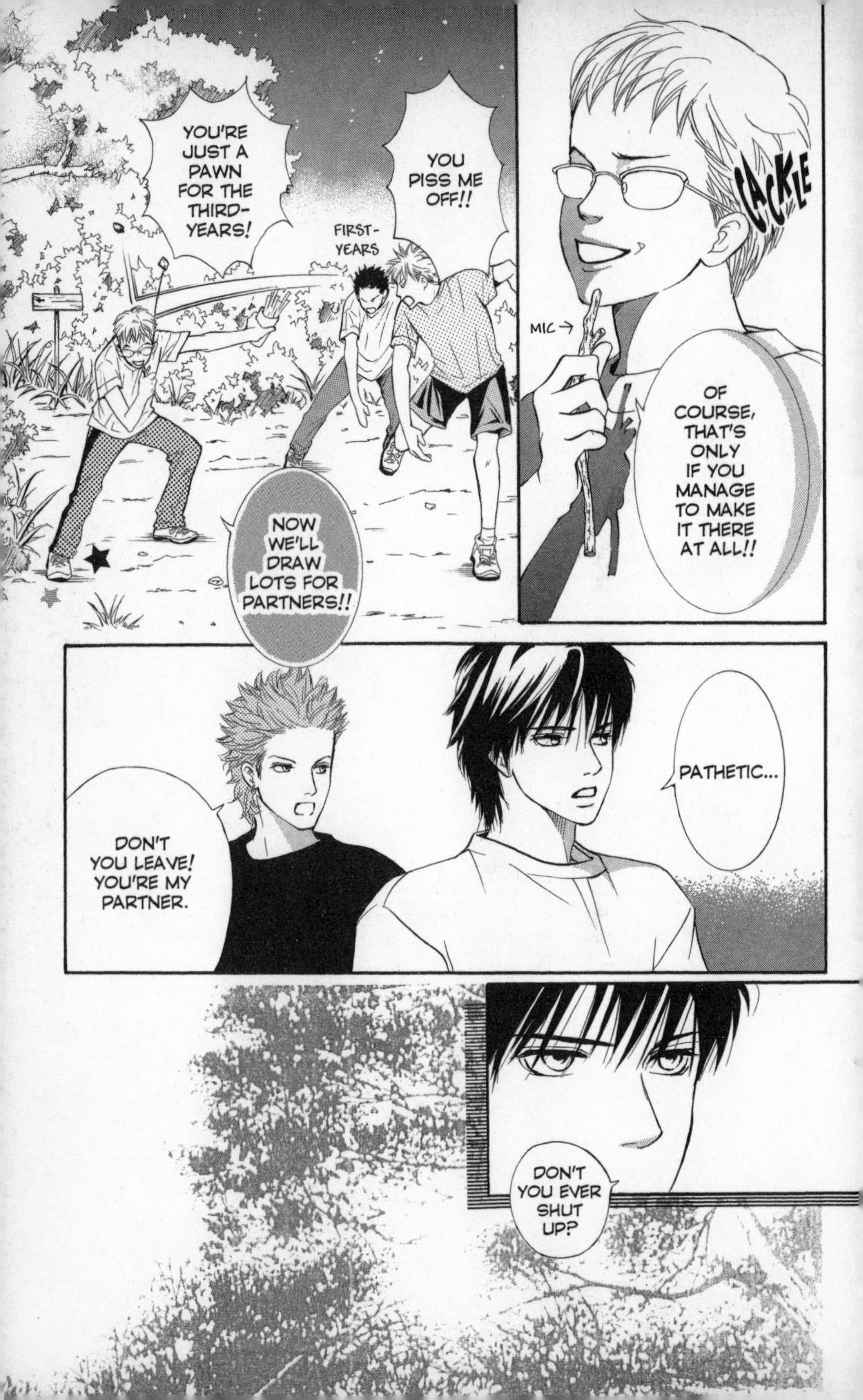
CACKLE
MIC →
OF COURSE, THAT'S ONLY IF YOU MANAGE TO MAKE IT THERE AT ALL!!
YOU PISS ME OFF!!
YOU'RE JUST A PAWN FOR THE THIRD-YEARS!
FIRST-YEARS
NOW WE'LL DRAW LOTS FOR PARTNERS!!
PATHETIC...
DON'T YOU LEAVE! YOU'RE MY PARTNER.
DON'T YOU EVER SHUT UP?

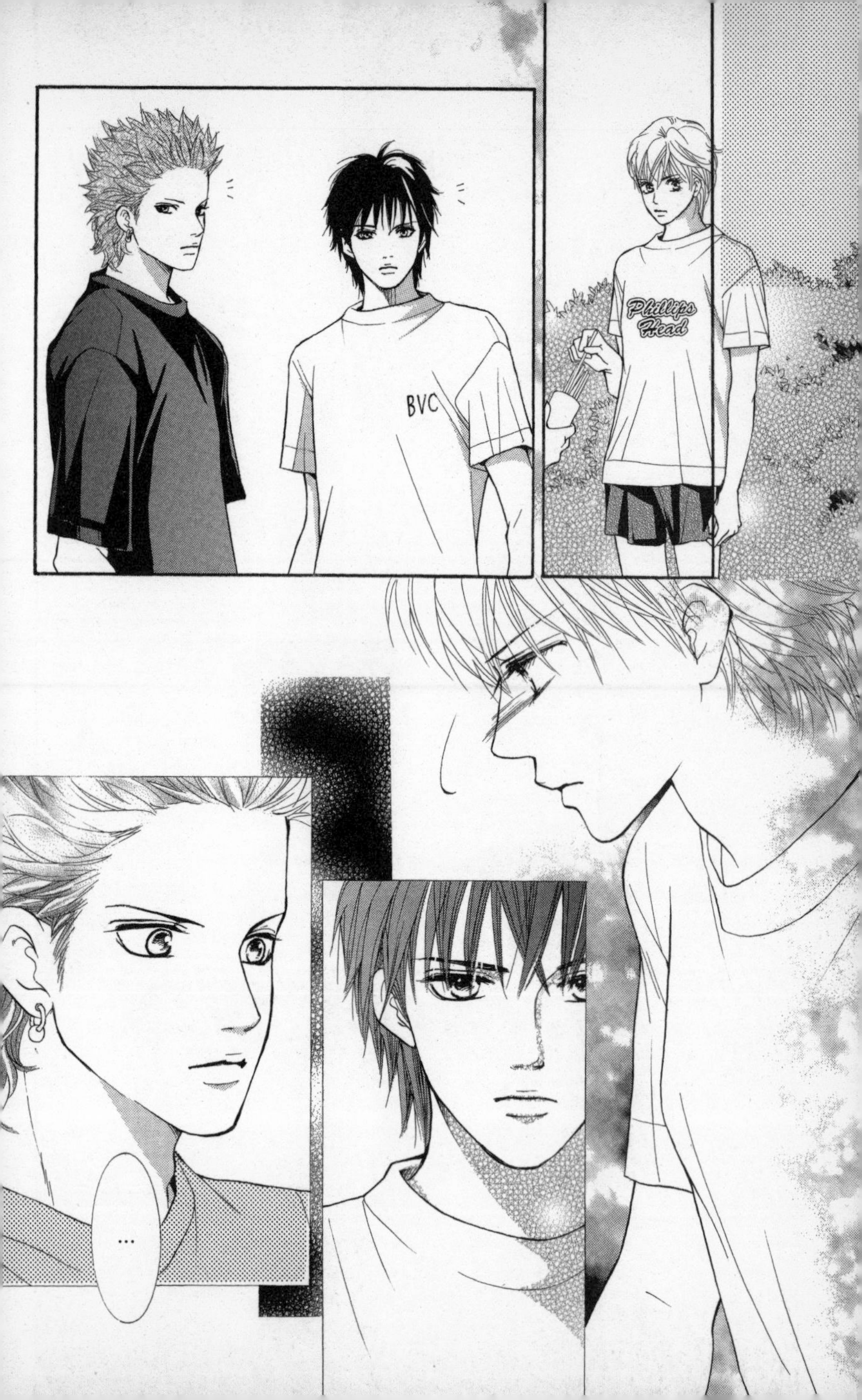
Phillips Head
BVC
...

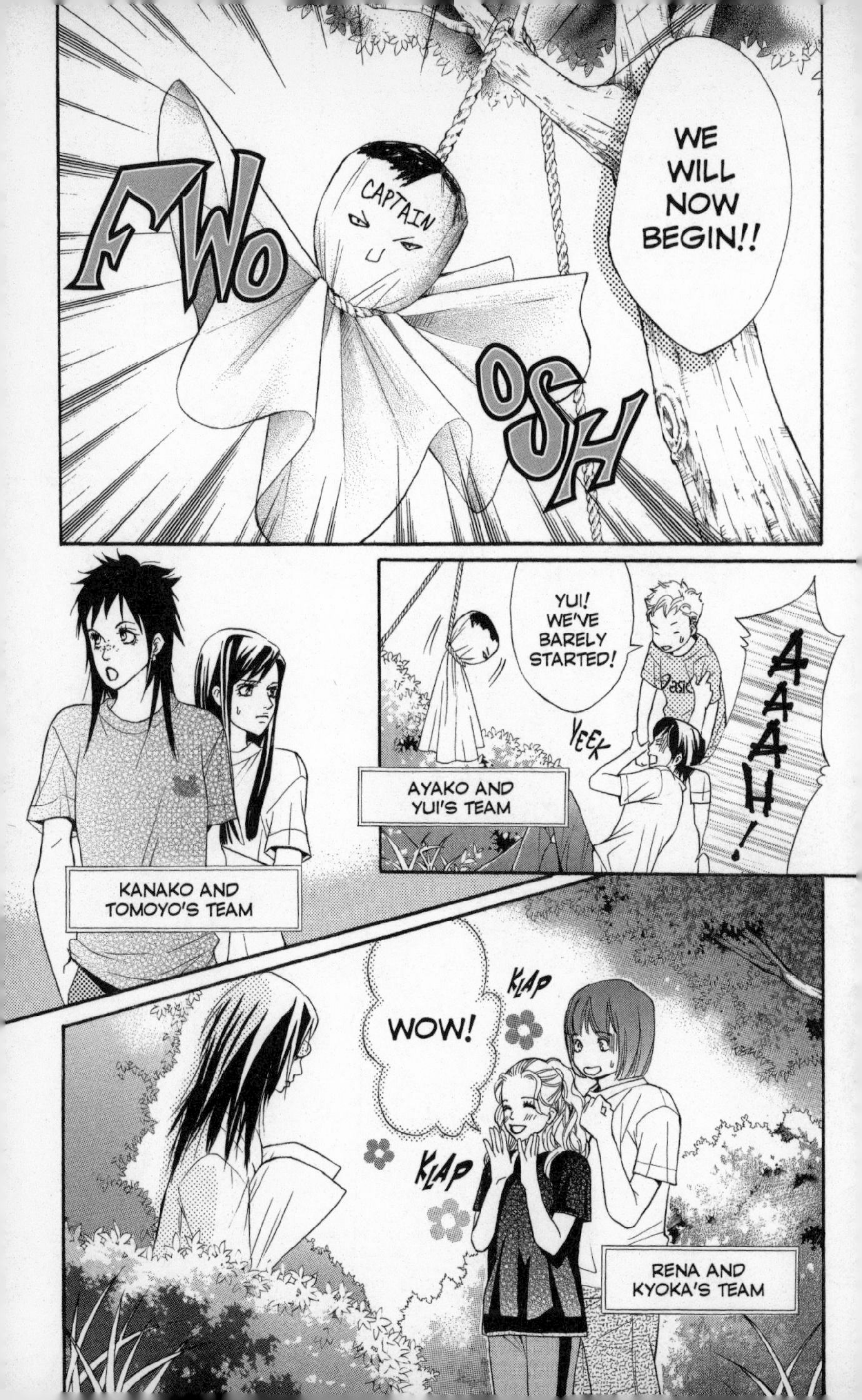
WE WILL NOW BEGIN!!
FWOOSH
CAPTAIN
AAAAH!
YUI! WE'VE BARELY STARTED!
YEEK
AYAKO AND YUI'S TEAM
KANAKO AND TOMOYO'S TEAM
RENA AND KYOKA'S TEAM
KLAP
WOW!
KLAP

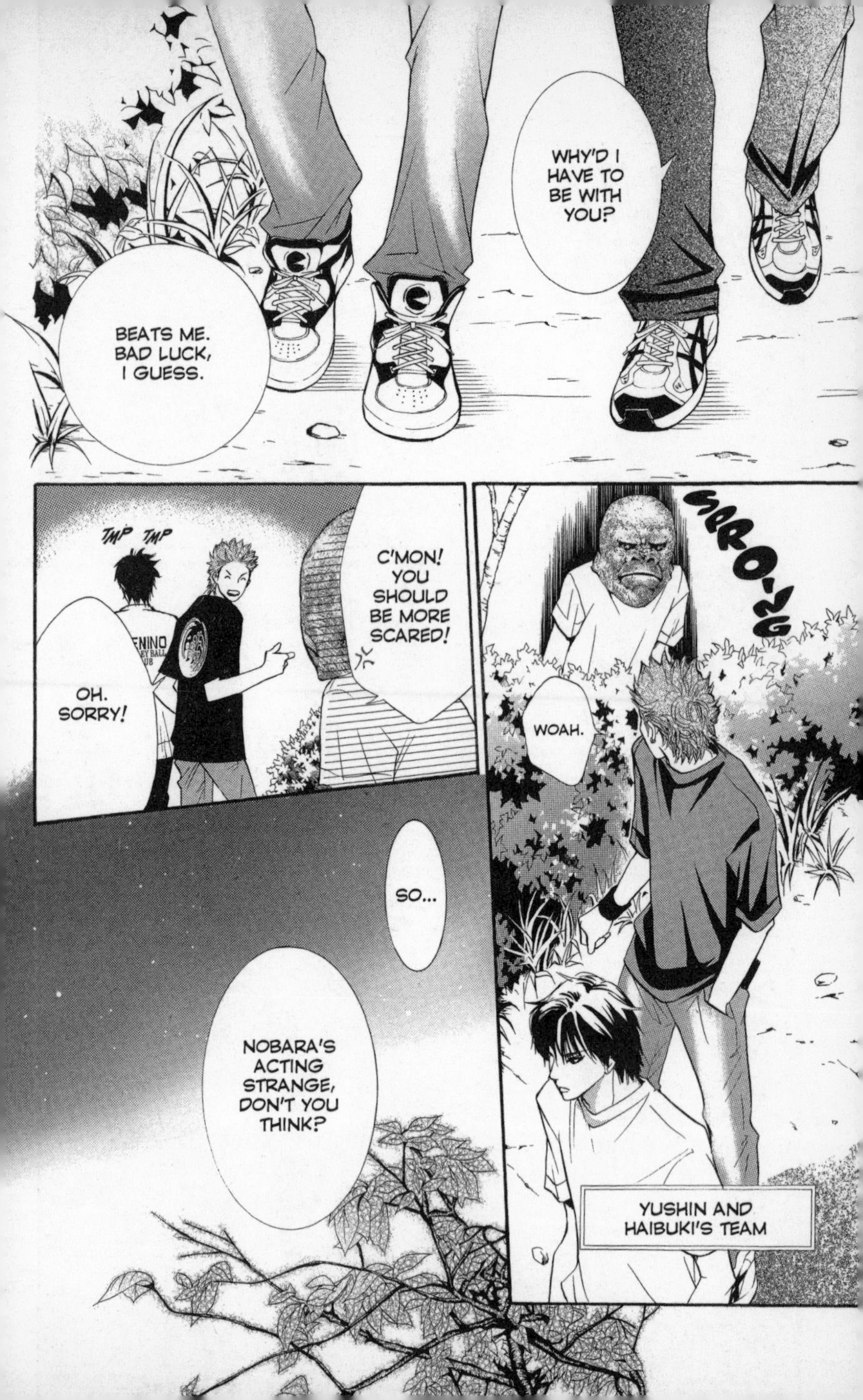
WHY'D I HAVE TO BE WITH YOU?
BEATS ME. BAD LUCK, I GUESS.
SPROING
WOAH.
YUSHIN AND HAIBUKI'S TEAM
TMP TMP
C'MON! YOU SHOULD BE MORE SCARED!
OH. SORRY!
SO...
NOBARA'S ACTING STRANGE, DON'T YOU THINK?

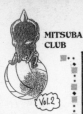

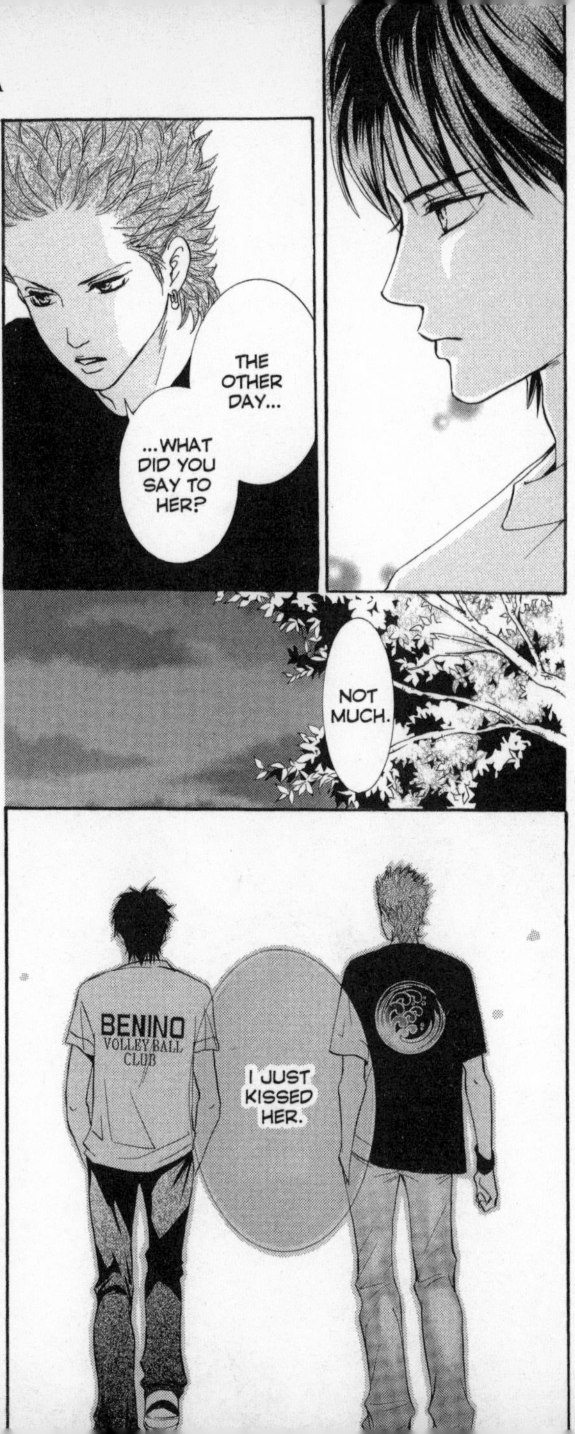
THE OTHER DAY...
...WHAT DID YOU SAY TO HER?
NOT MUCH.
I JUST KISSED HER.

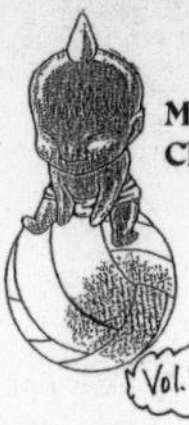
Vol.2

MITSUBA CLUB

CRIMSON HERO IS ONLY JUST BEGINNING. IT STILL HASN'T GOTTEN TO WHAT I HAVE IN MIND FOR IT--DUE TO MY LACK OF ABILITY AS WELL AS OTHER REASONS. RIGHT NOW I FEEL LIKE I'M PUSHING AND PUSHING TO GET MORE INTO IT.

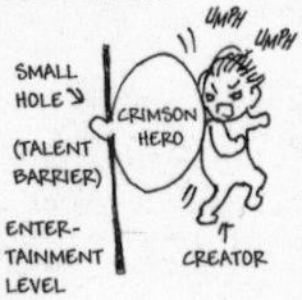
UMPH
UMPH
SMALL HOLE
CRIMSON HERO
(TALENT BARRIER)
ENTER-TAINMENT LEVEL
CREATOR

SOMETIMES I GET DEPRESSED OVER MY LACK OF TALENT, BUT MY PASSION FOR MANGA NEVER WANES, AND I SIT AT MY DESK EVERY DAY. THE OTHER DAY I WAS ON THE PHONE WITH KARUHO SHIINA AND I TOLD HER ABOUT A JOURNAL EX-CHANGE I DID IN JUNIOR HIGH WITH A FRIEND (THAT WAS THE "IN" THING TO DO). RECENTLY I DISCOVERED IT AT MY PARENTS' HOUSE. AND IN IT ALMOST EVERY DAY I HAD WRITTEN "I WANT TO BECOME A MANGA-KA." KARUHO SAID, "AND NOW YOU ARE A MANGA-KA." THAT'S RIGHT. I AM. I DID IT. BACK IN THOSE DAYS, I WAS OBSESSED WITH THE DESIRE TO BECOME A MANGA-KA. AND NOW I'VE BECOME ONE.

ME IN JUNIOR HIGH

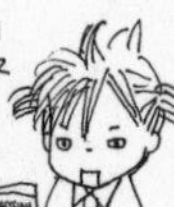

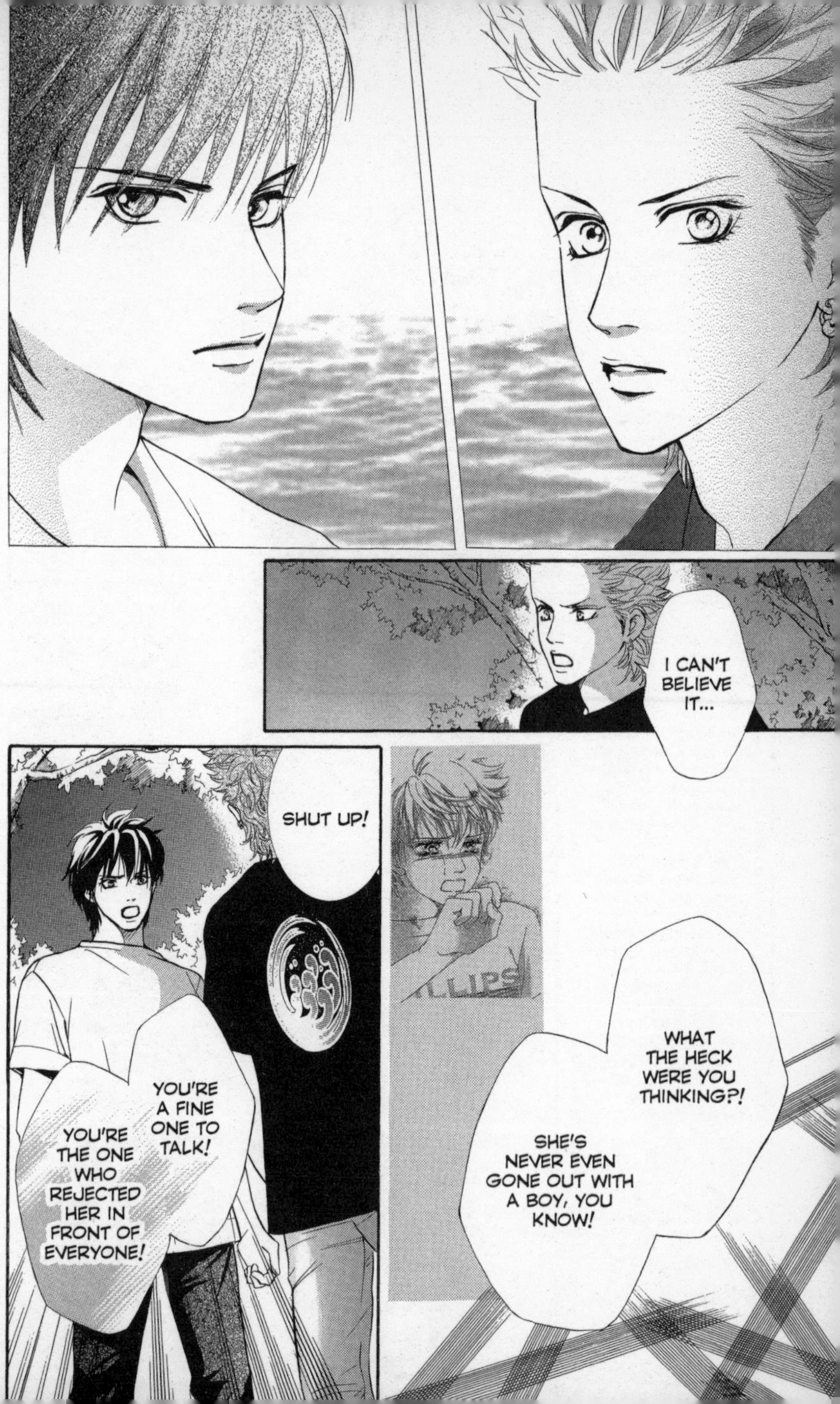
I CAN'T BELIEVE IT...
WHAT THE HECK WERE YOU THINKING?!
SHE'S NEVER EVEN GONE OUT WITH A BOY, YOU KNOW!
SHUT UP!
YOU'RE A FINE ONE TO TALK!
YOU'RE THE ONE WHO REJECTED HER IN FRONT OF EVERYONE!

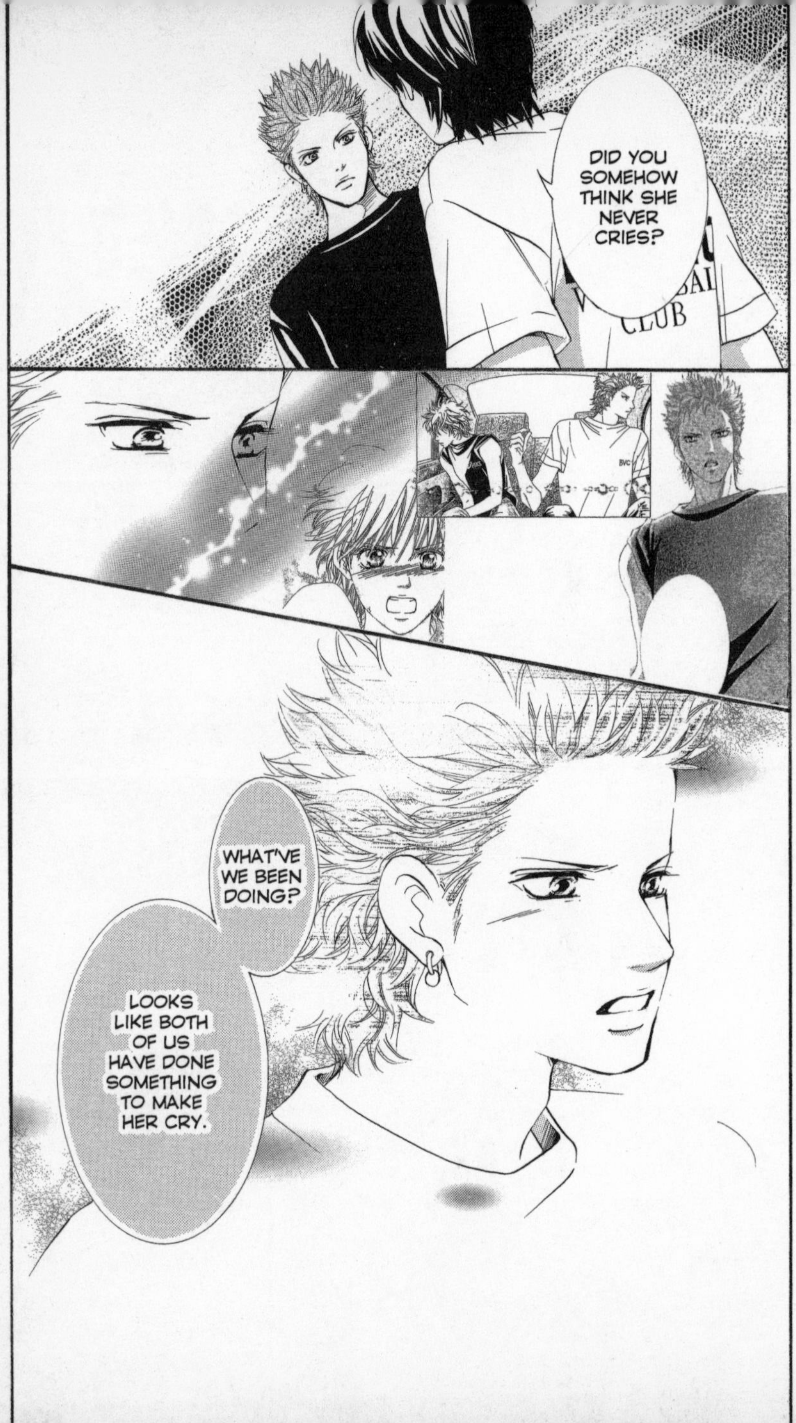
DID YOU SOMEHOW THINK SHE NEVER CRIES?
CLUB
BVC
WHAT'VE WE BEEN DOING?
LOOKS LIKE BOTH OF US HAVE DONE SOMETHING TO MAKE HER CRY.

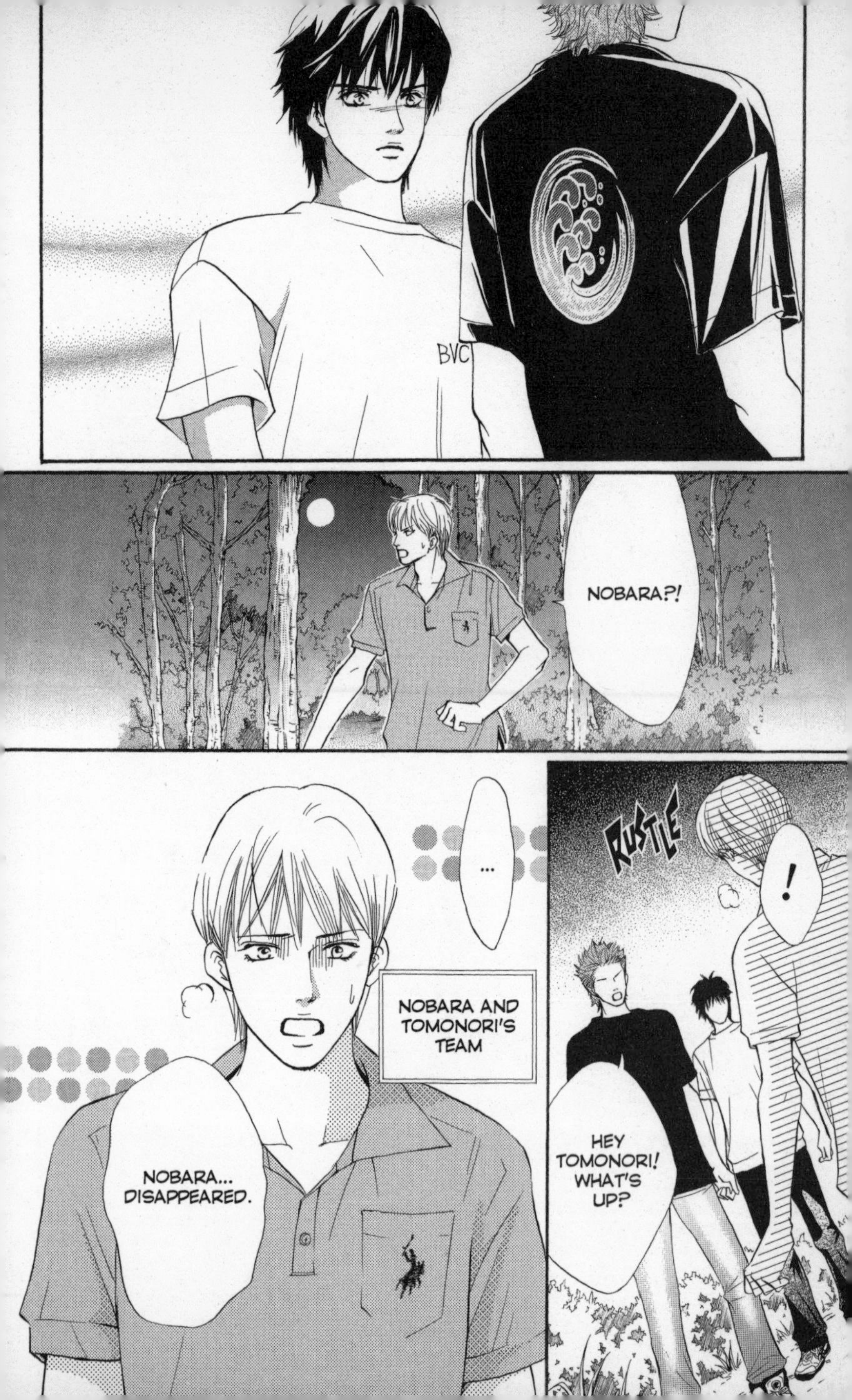
NOBARA?!
RUSTLE
!
HEY TOMONORI! WHAT'S UP?
...
NOBARA AND TOMONORI'S TEAM
NOBARA... DISAPPEARED.

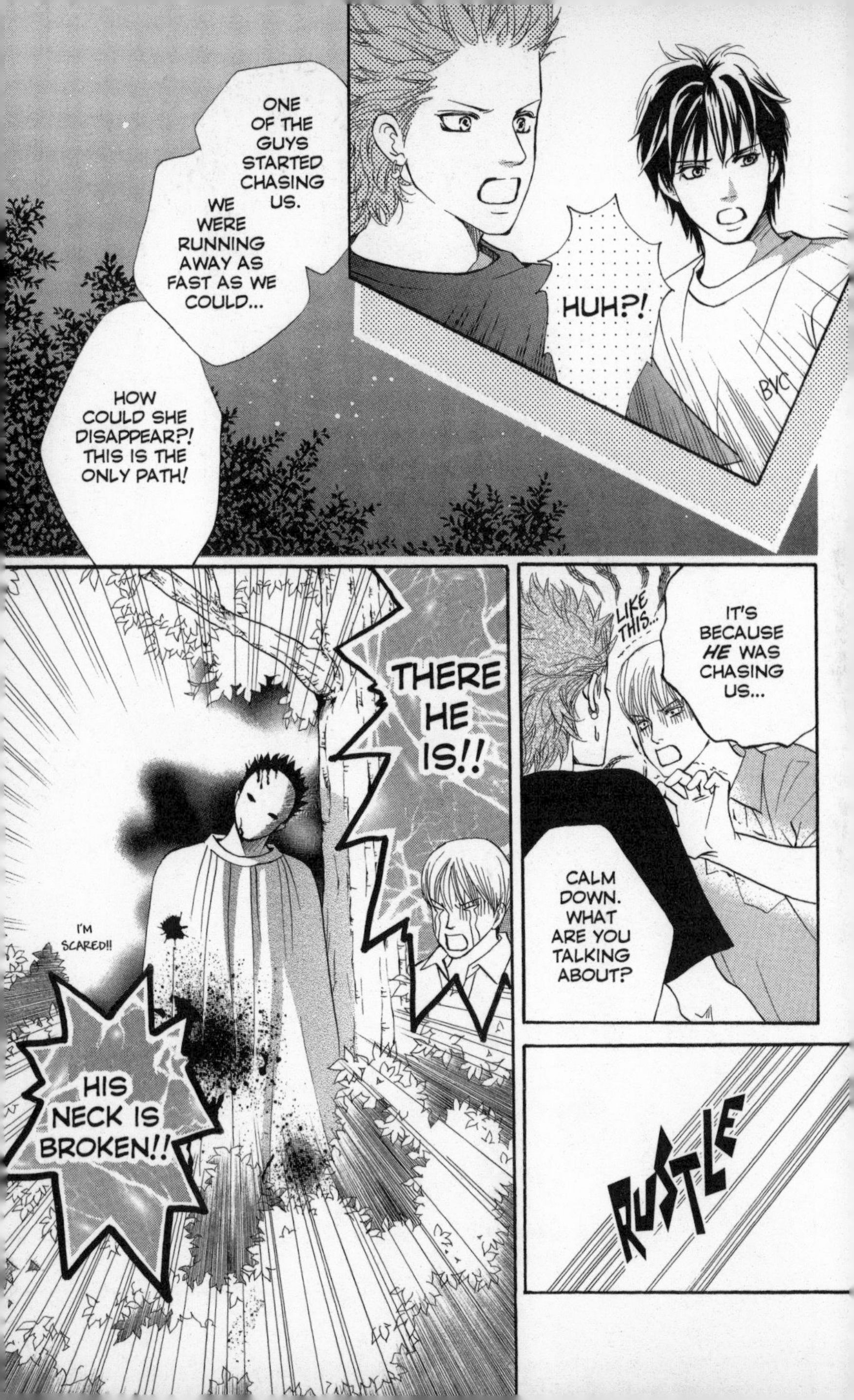
HUH?!
ONE OF THE GUYS STARTED CHASING US.
WE WERE RUNNING AWAY AS FAST AS WE COULD...
HOW COULD SHE DISAPPEAR?! THIS IS THE ONLY PATH!
IT'S BECAUSE *HE* WAS CHASING US...
LIKE THIS...
CALM DOWN. WHAT ARE YOU TALKING ABOUT?
RUSTLE
THERE HE IS!!
I'M SCARED!!
HIS NECK IS BROKEN!!

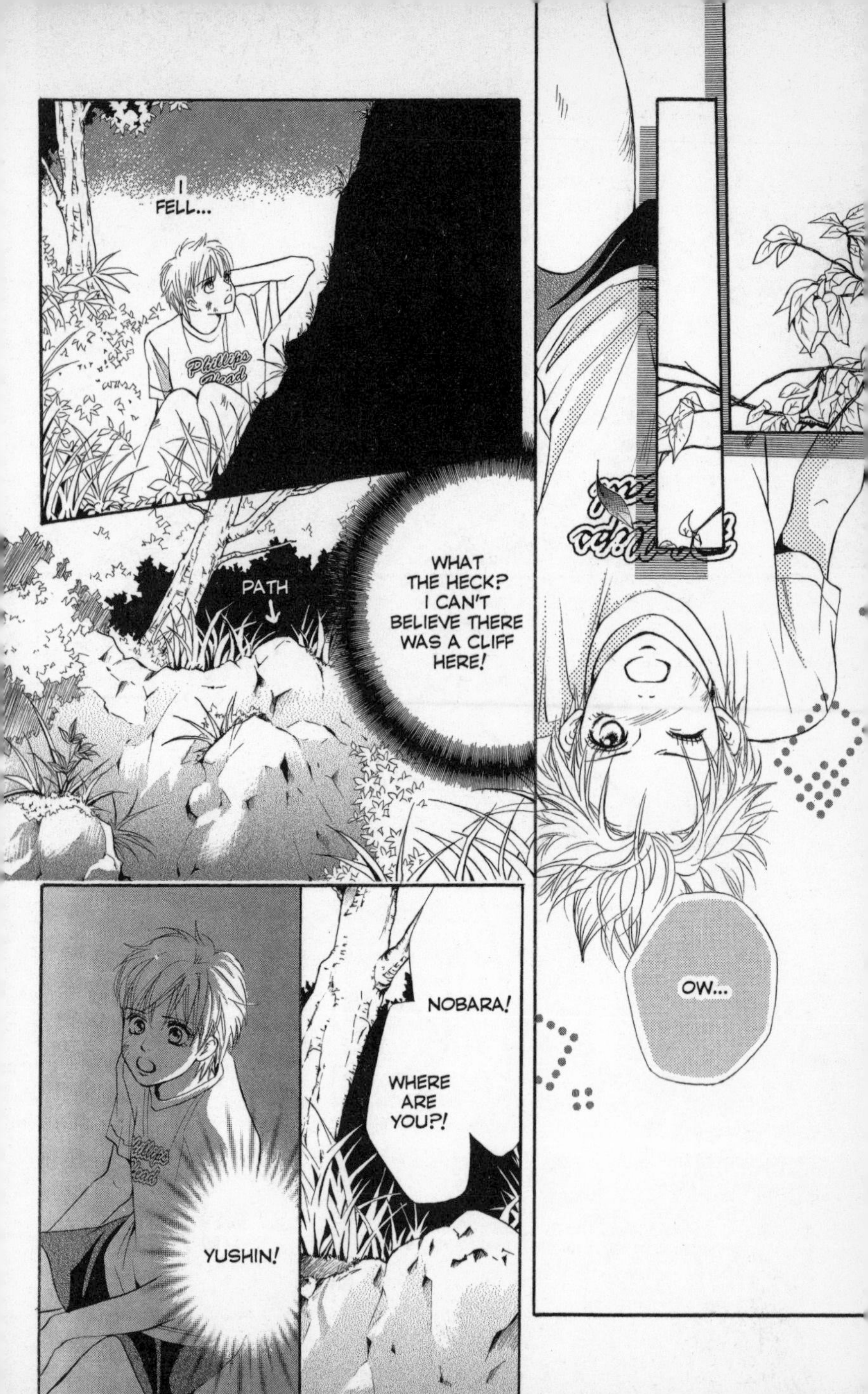
OW...
I FELL...
WHAT THE HECK? I CAN'T BELIEVE THERE WAS A CLIFF HERE!
PATH
NOBARA!
WHERE ARE YOU?!
YUSHIN!

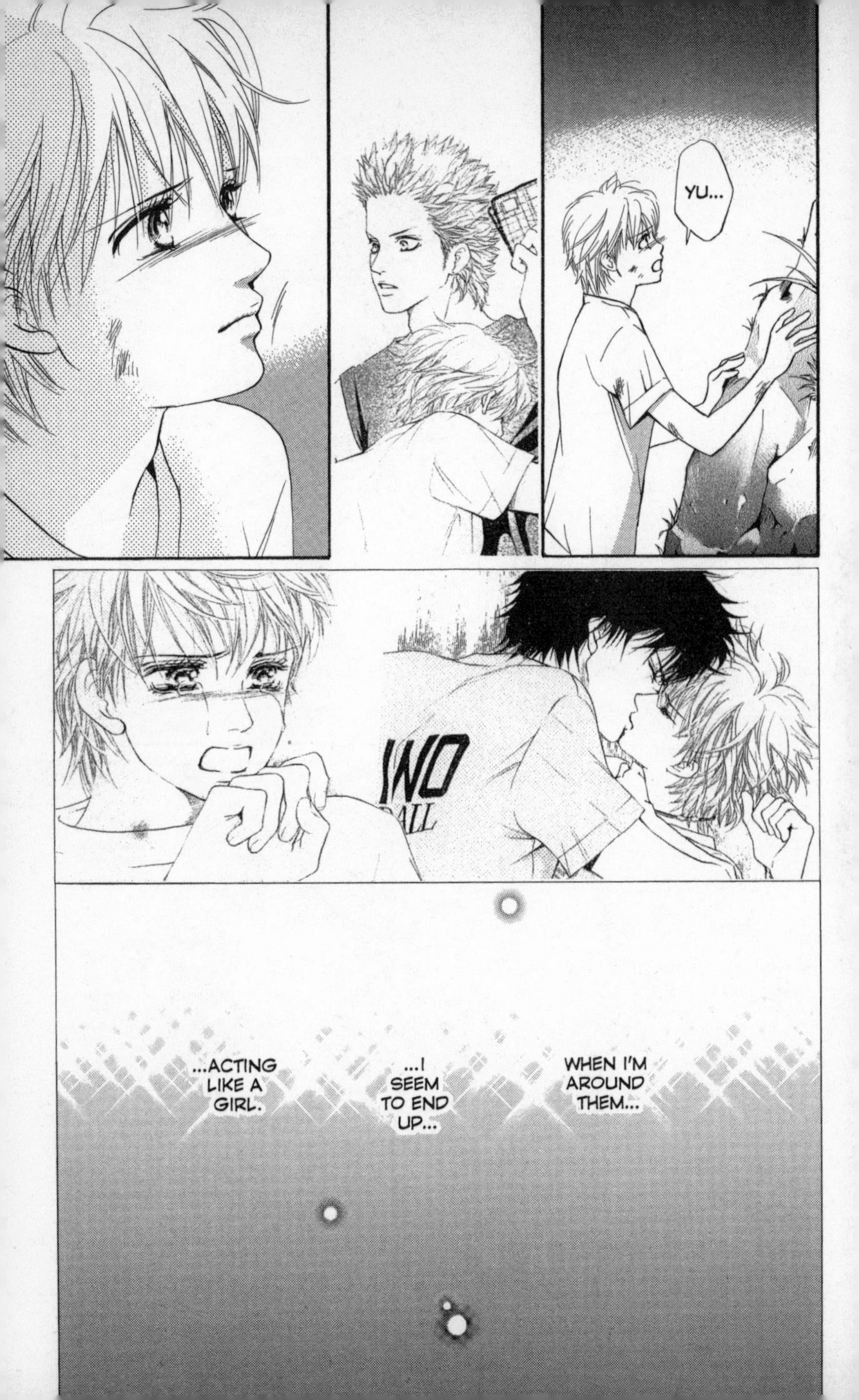
YU...
WHEN I'M AROUND THEM...
...I SEEM TO END UP...
...ACTING LIKE A GIRL.

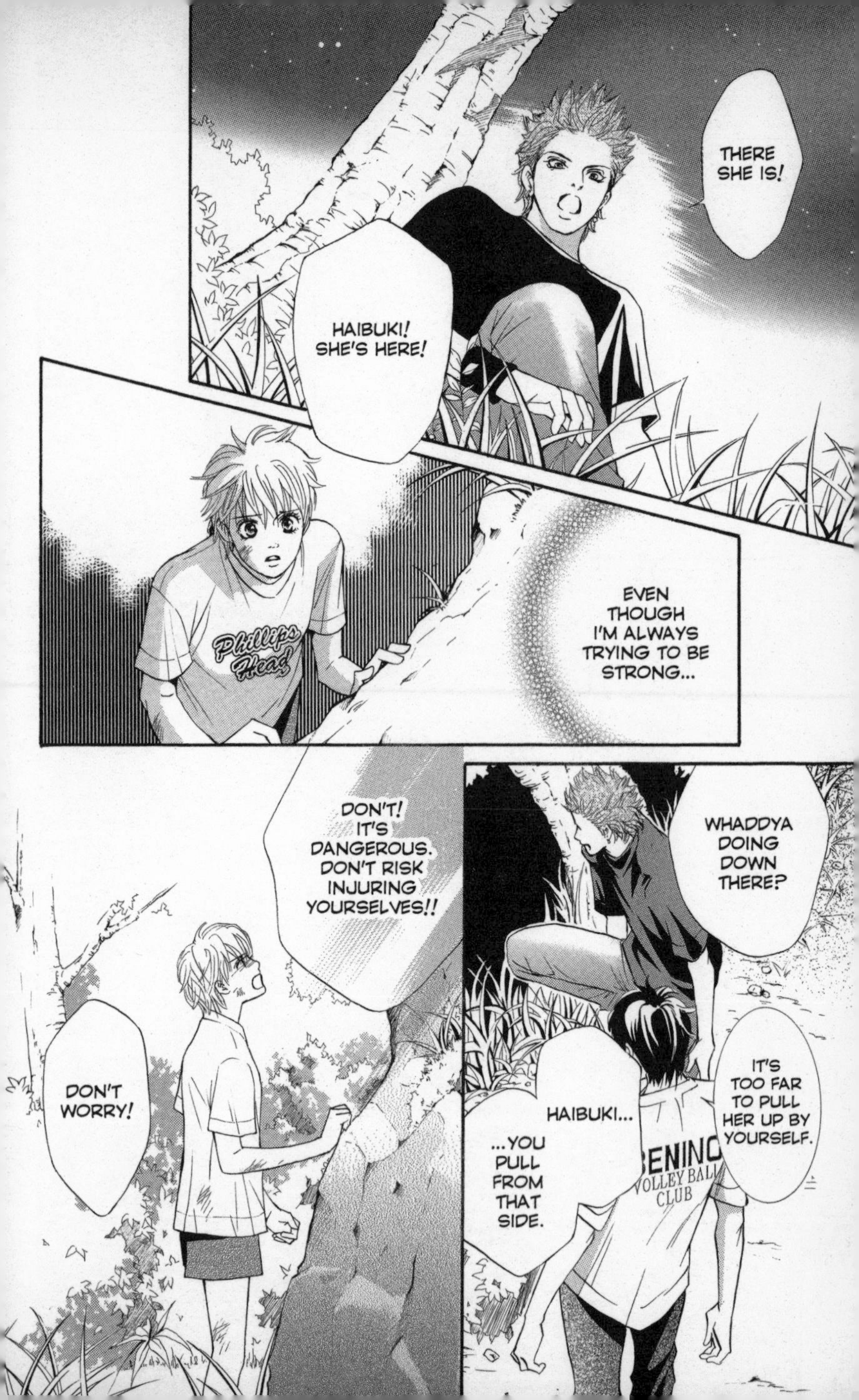
THERE SHE IS!
HAIBUKI! SHE'S HERE!
EVEN THOUGH I'M ALWAYS TRYING TO BE STRONG...
Phillips Head
WHADDYA DOING DOWN THERE?
IT'S TOO FAR TO PULL HER UP BY YOURSELF.
HAIBUKI...
...YOU PULL FROM THAT SIDE.
VOLLEY BALL CLUB
DON'T! IT'S DANGEROUS. DON'T RISK INJURING YOURSELVES!!
DON'T WORRY!

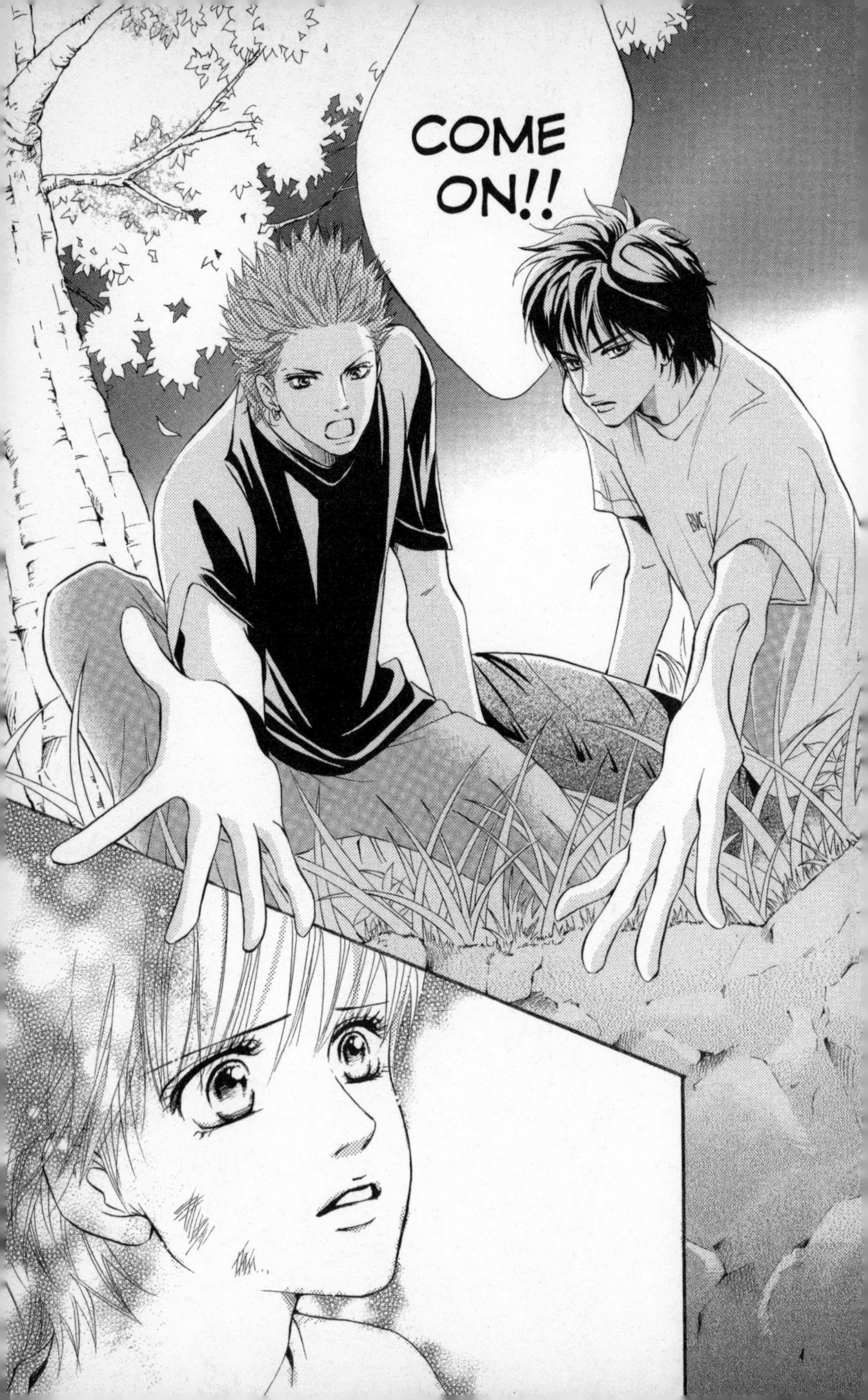
COME ON!!

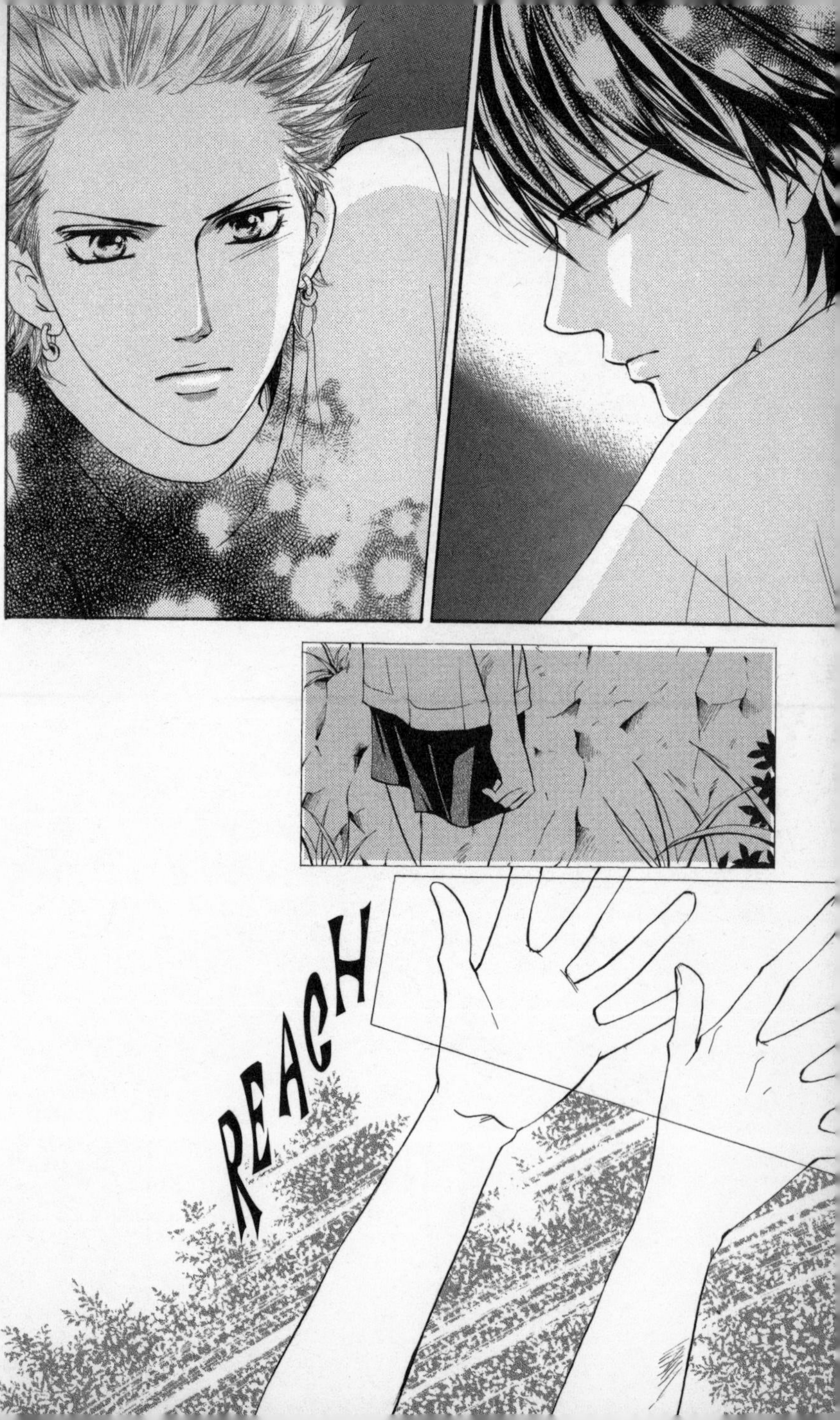
REACH

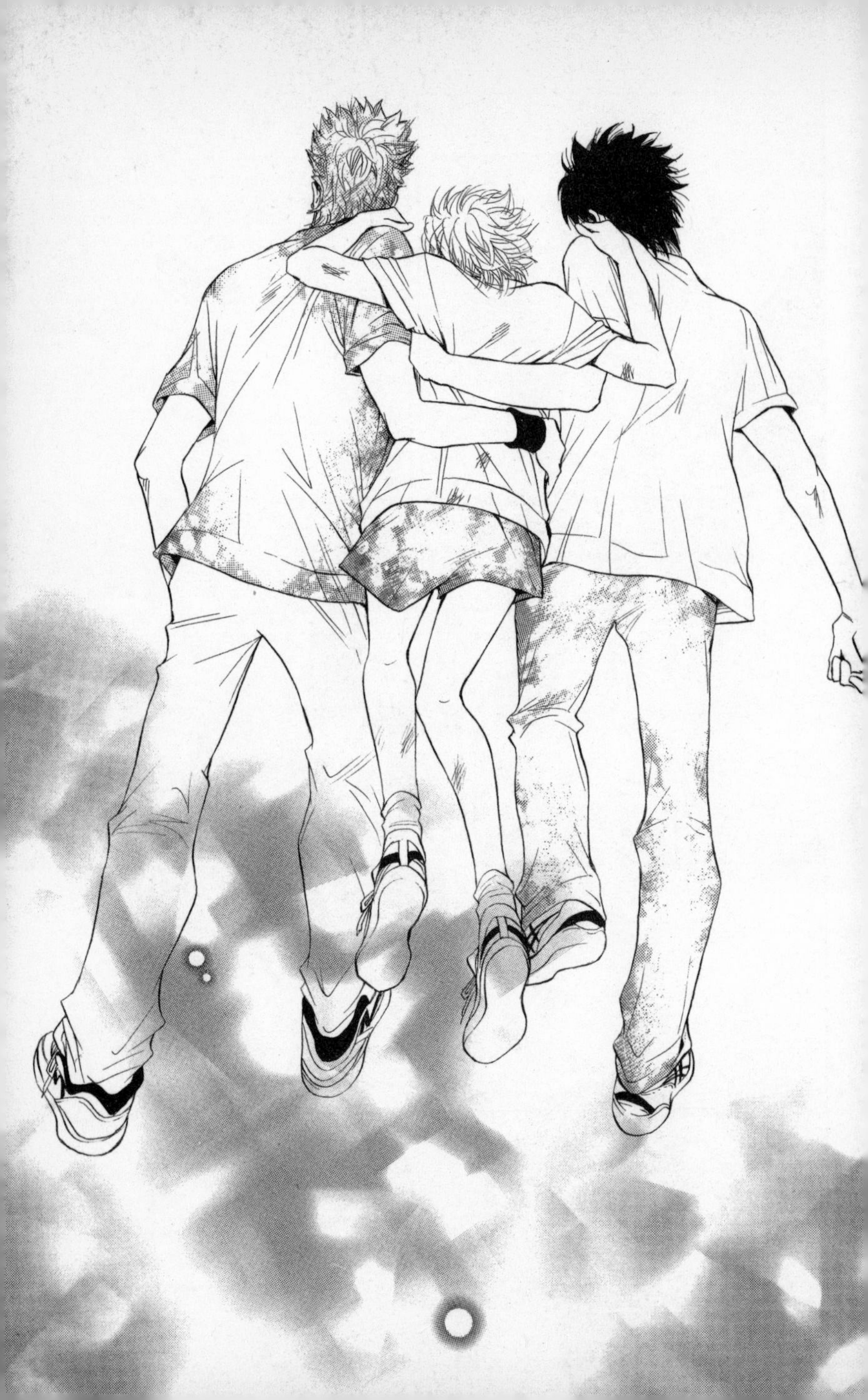

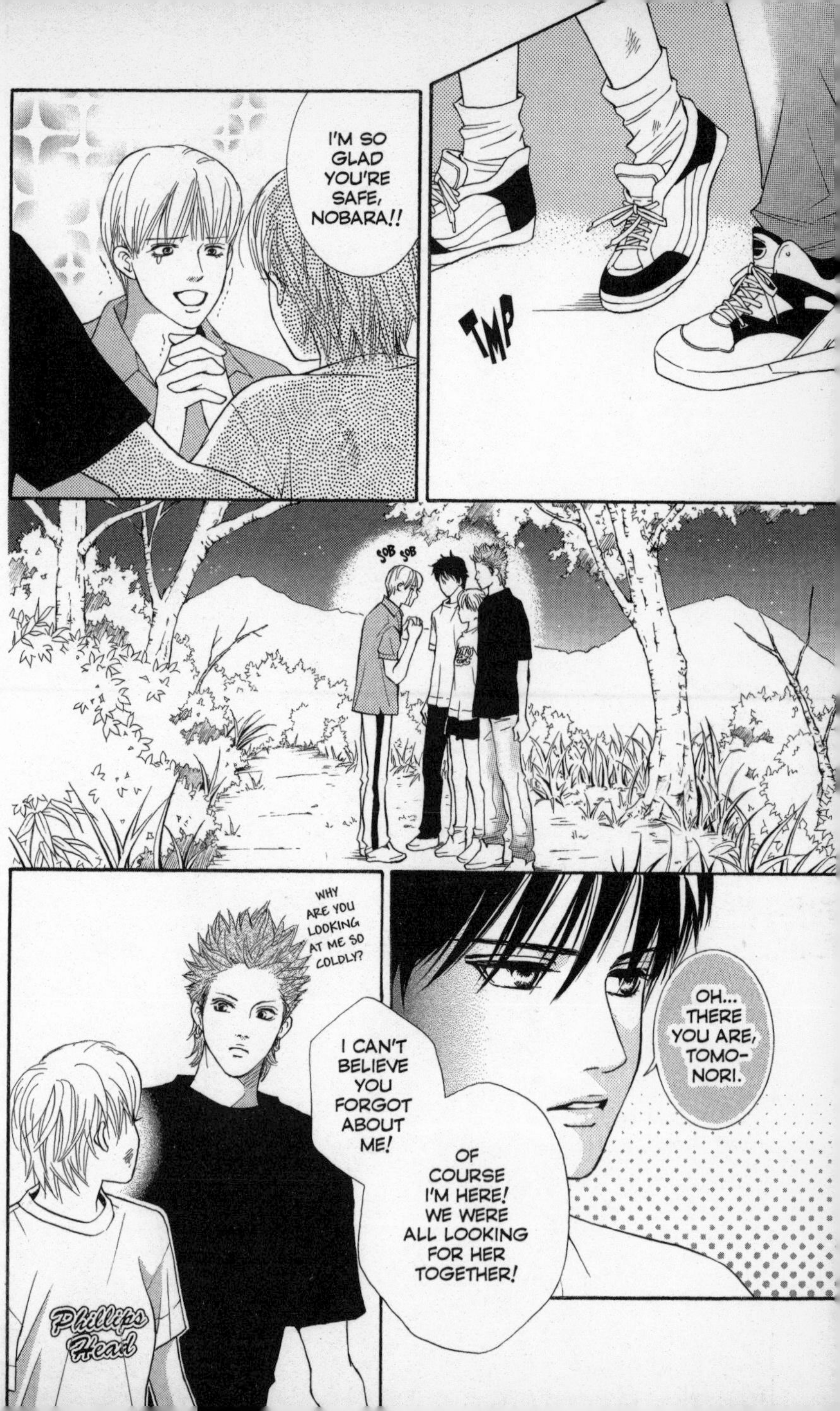
TMP
I'M SO GLAD YOU'RE SAFE, NOBARA!!
SOB SOB
OH... THERE YOU ARE, TOMO-NORI.
WHY ARE YOU LOOKING AT ME SO COLDLY?
I CAN'T BELIEVE YOU FORGOT ABOUT ME!
OF COURSE I'M HERE! WE WERE ALL LOOKING FOR HER TOGETHER!
Phillips Head

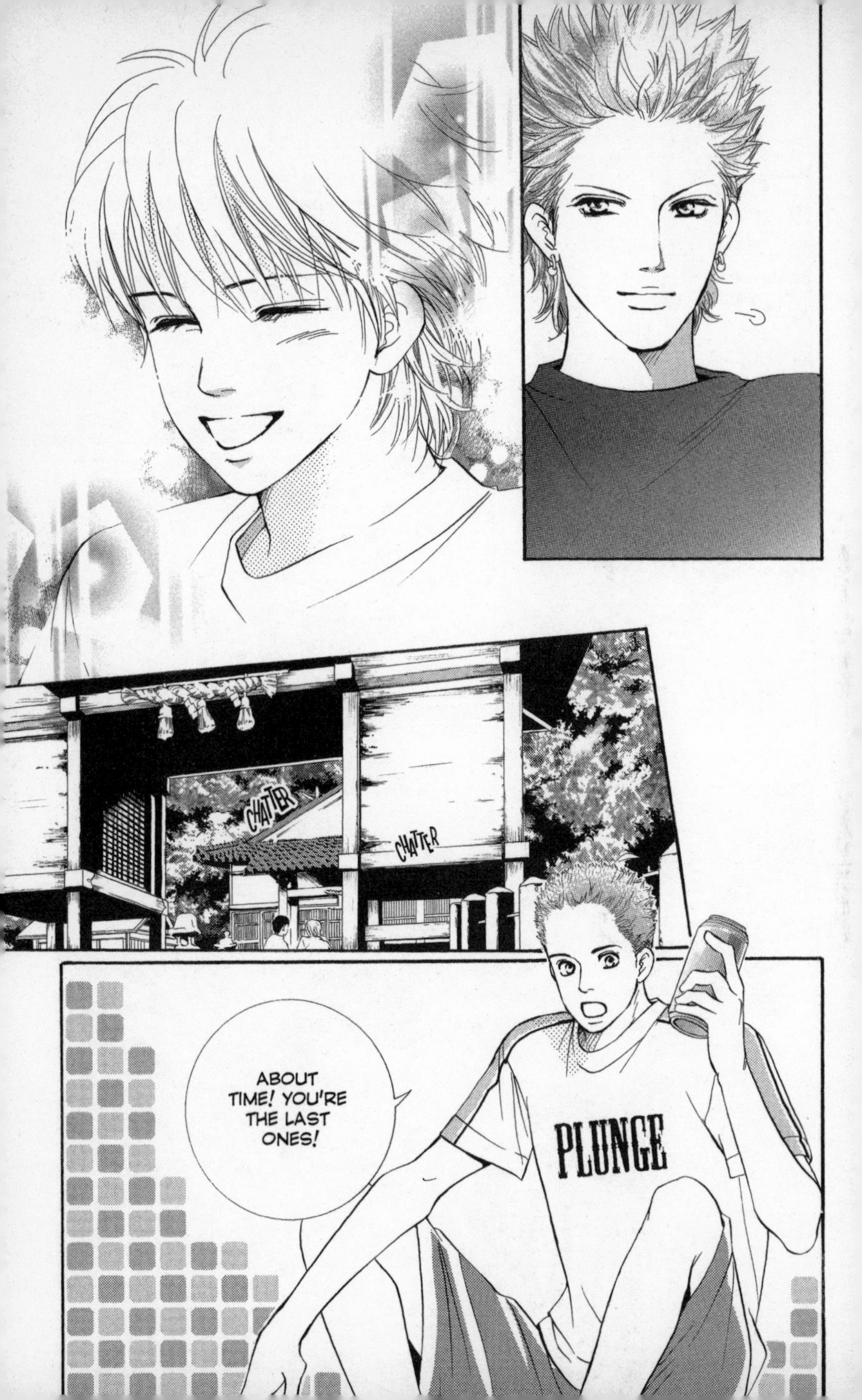
CHATTER
CHATTER
ABOUT TIME! YOU'RE THE LAST ONES!
PLUNGE

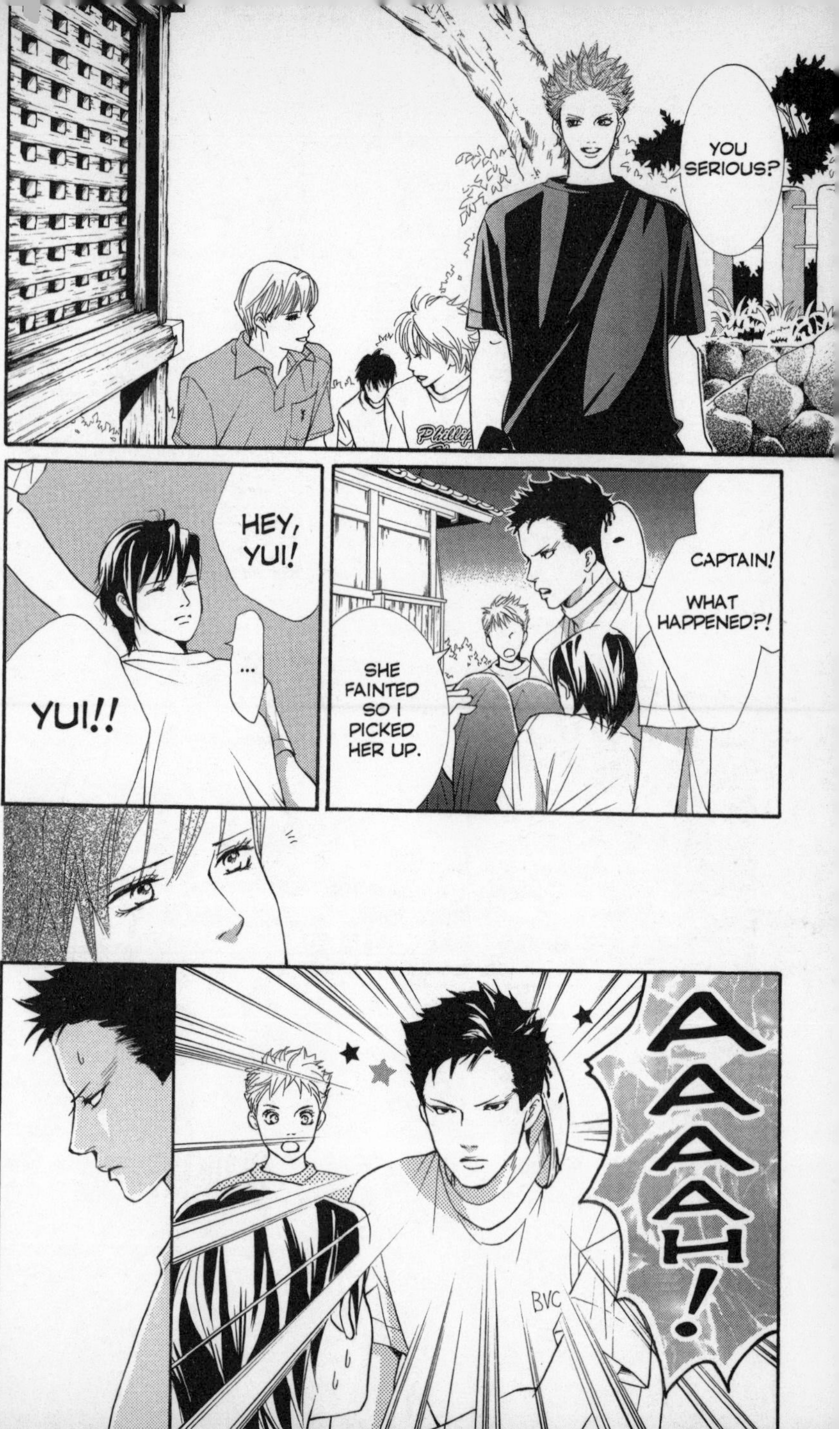
YOU SERIOUS?
CAPTAIN!
WHAT HAPPENED?!
SHE FAINTED SO I PICKED HER UP.
HEY, YUI!
...
YUI!!
AAAAH!

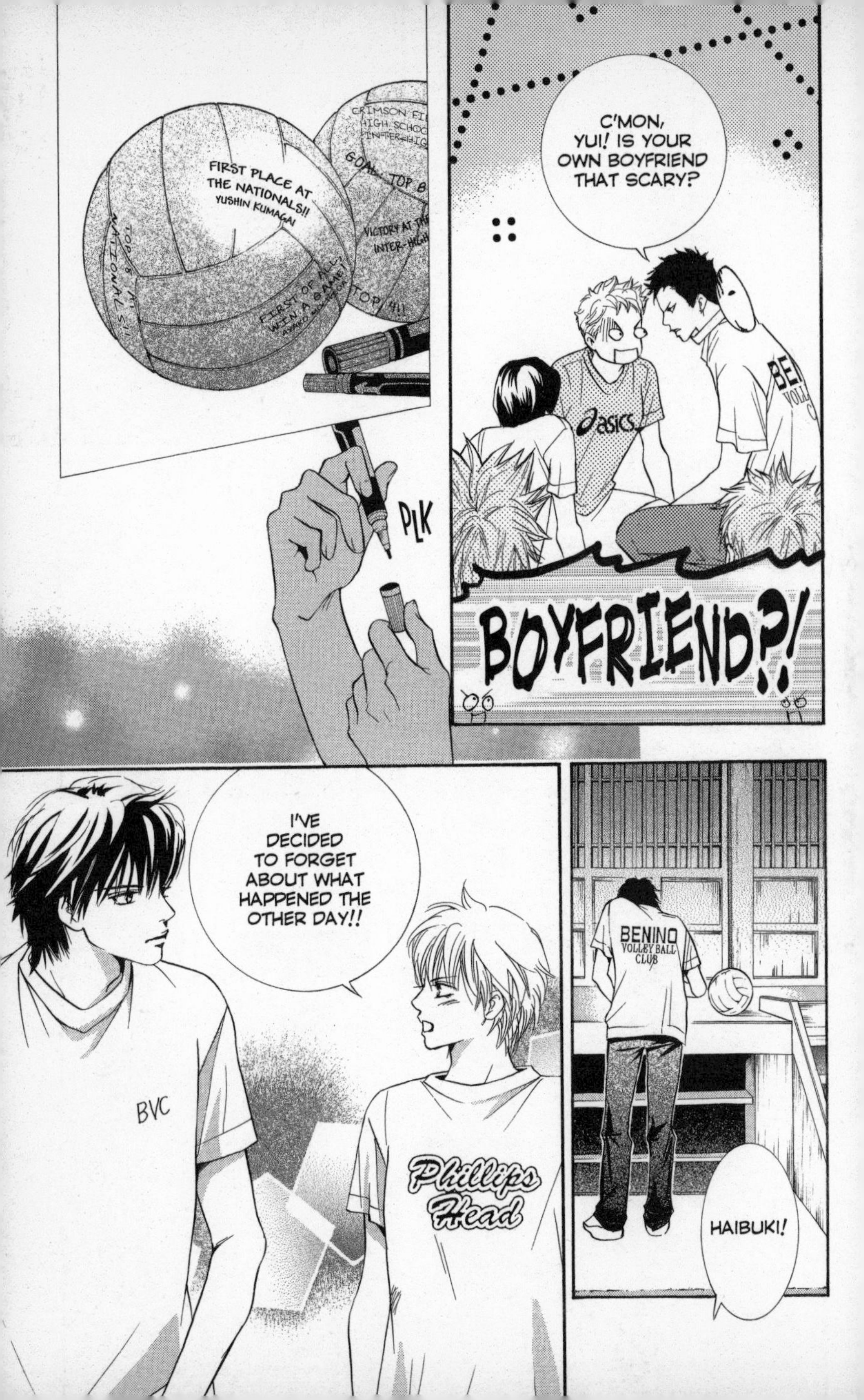
C'MON, YUI! IS YOUR OWN BOYFRIEND THAT SCARY?
asics
BOYFRIEND?!
FIRST PLACE AT THE NATIONALS!! YUSHIN KUMAGAI
FIRST OF ALL, WIN A GAME!
VICTORY AT THE INTER-HIGH
TOP 4!!
PLK
BENINO VOLLEY BALL CLUB
HAIBUKI!
I'VE DECIDED TO FORGET ABOUT WHAT HAPPENED THE OTHER DAY!!
BVC
Phillips Head

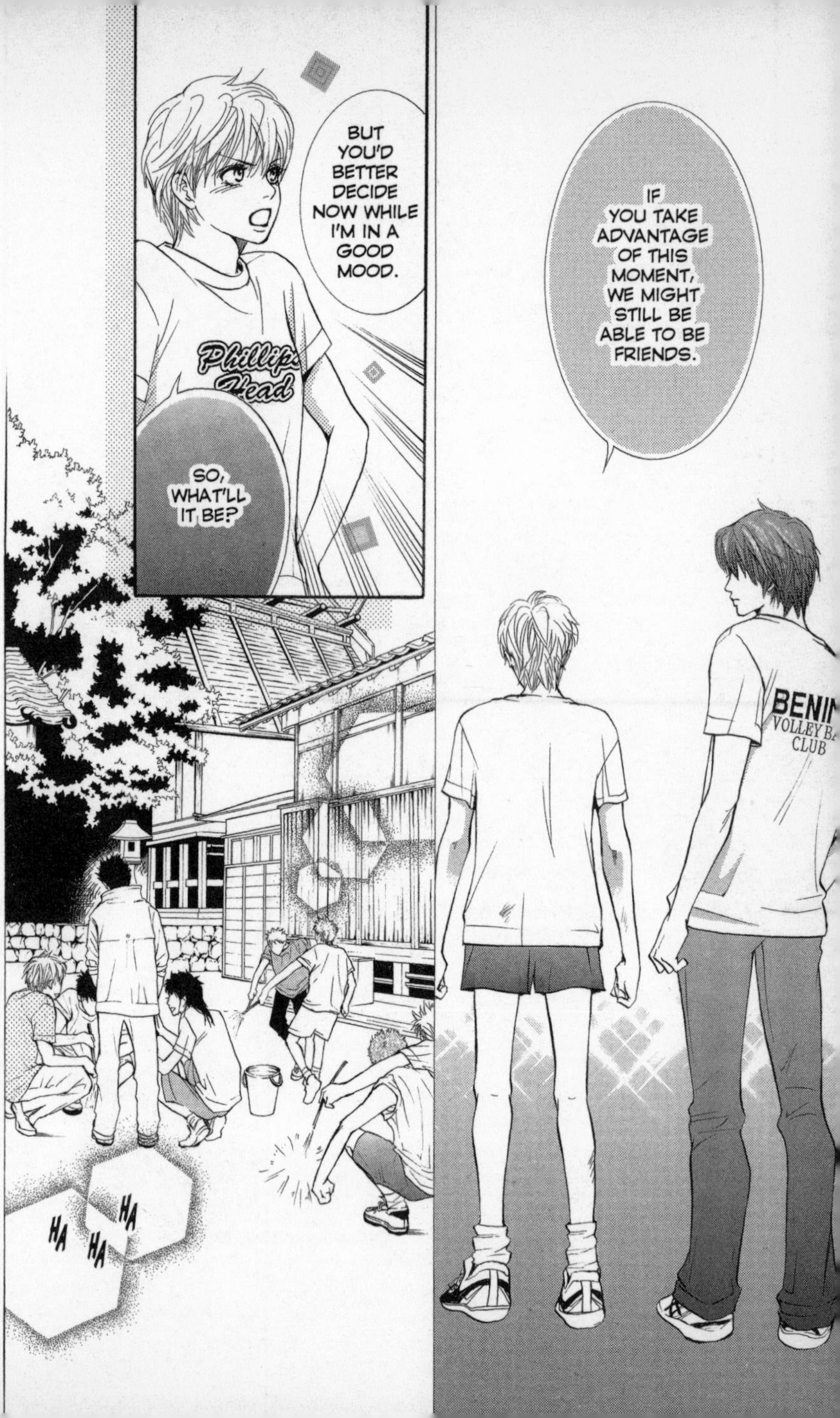
IF YOU TAKE ADVANTAGE OF THIS MOMENT, WE MIGHT STILL BE ABLE TO BE FRIENDS.
BUT YOU'D BETTER DECIDE NOW WHILE I'M IN A GOOD MOOD.
SO, WHAT'LL IT BE?
HA HA HA

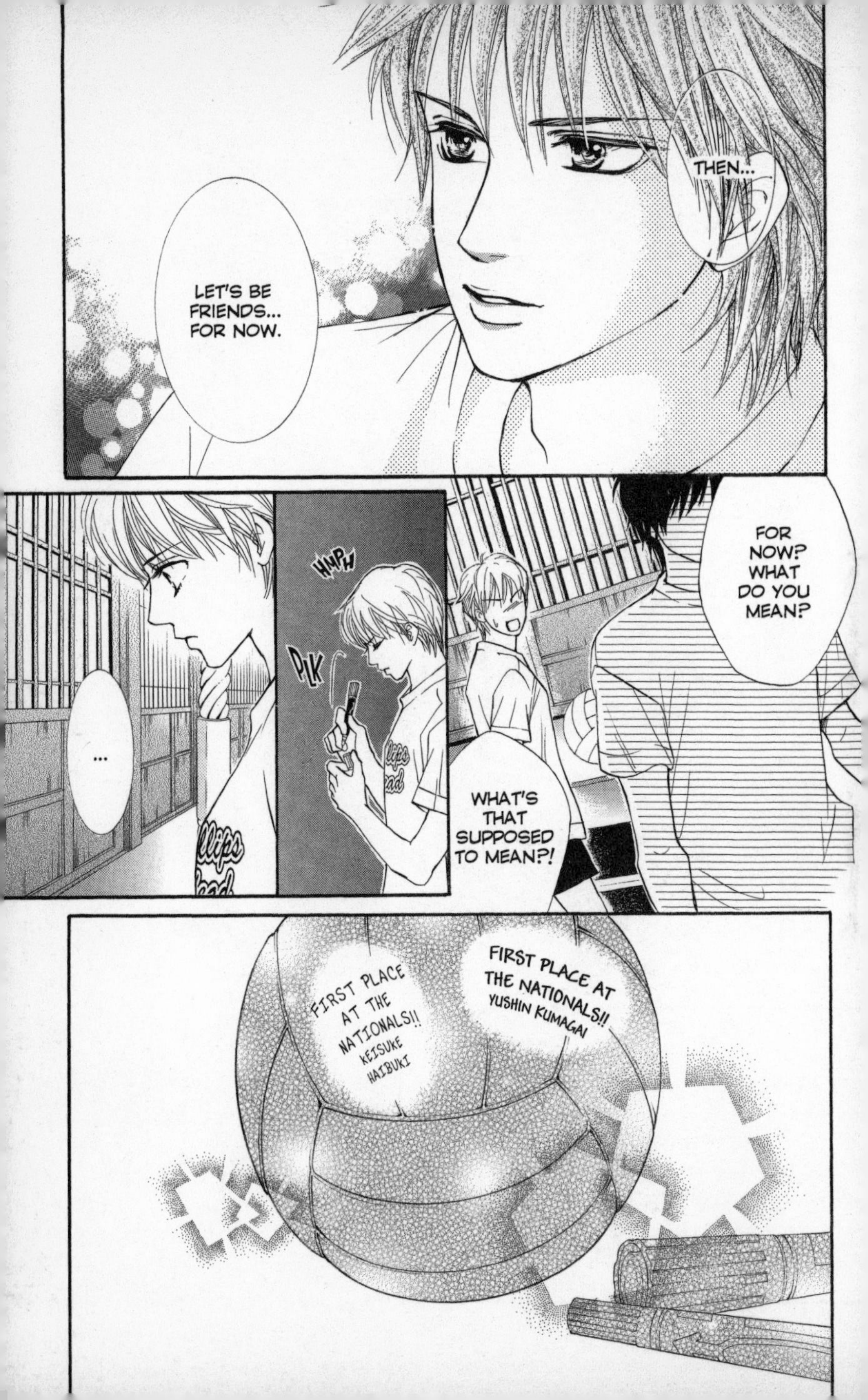
THEN...
LET'S BE FRIENDS... FOR NOW.
FOR NOW? WHAT DO YOU MEAN?
WHAT'S THAT SUPPOSED TO MEAN?!
HMPH
PLK
...
FIRST PLACE AT THE NATIONALS!! YUSHIN KUMAGAI
FIRST PLACE AT THE NATIONALS!! KEISUKE HAIBUKI

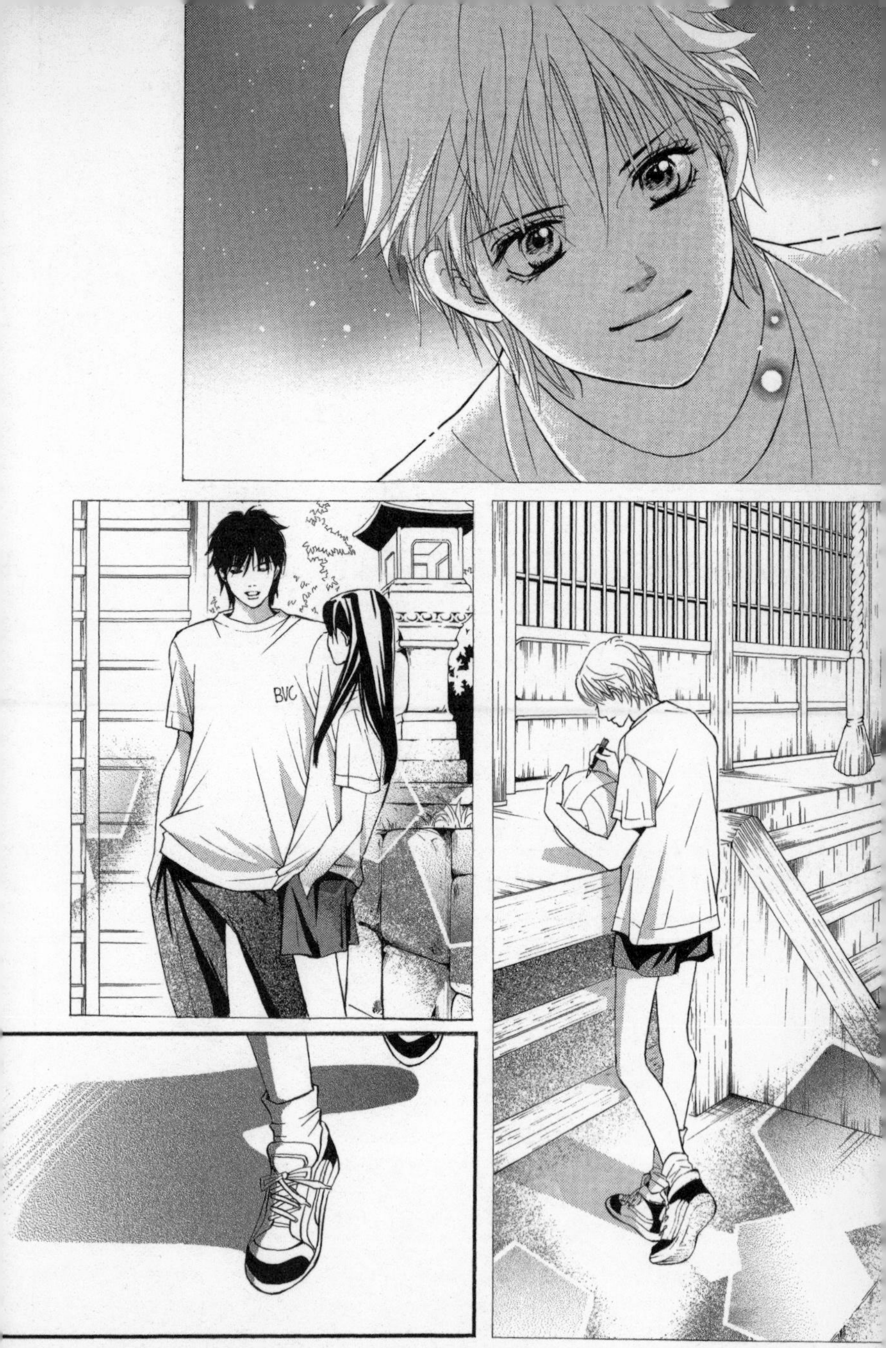
BVC

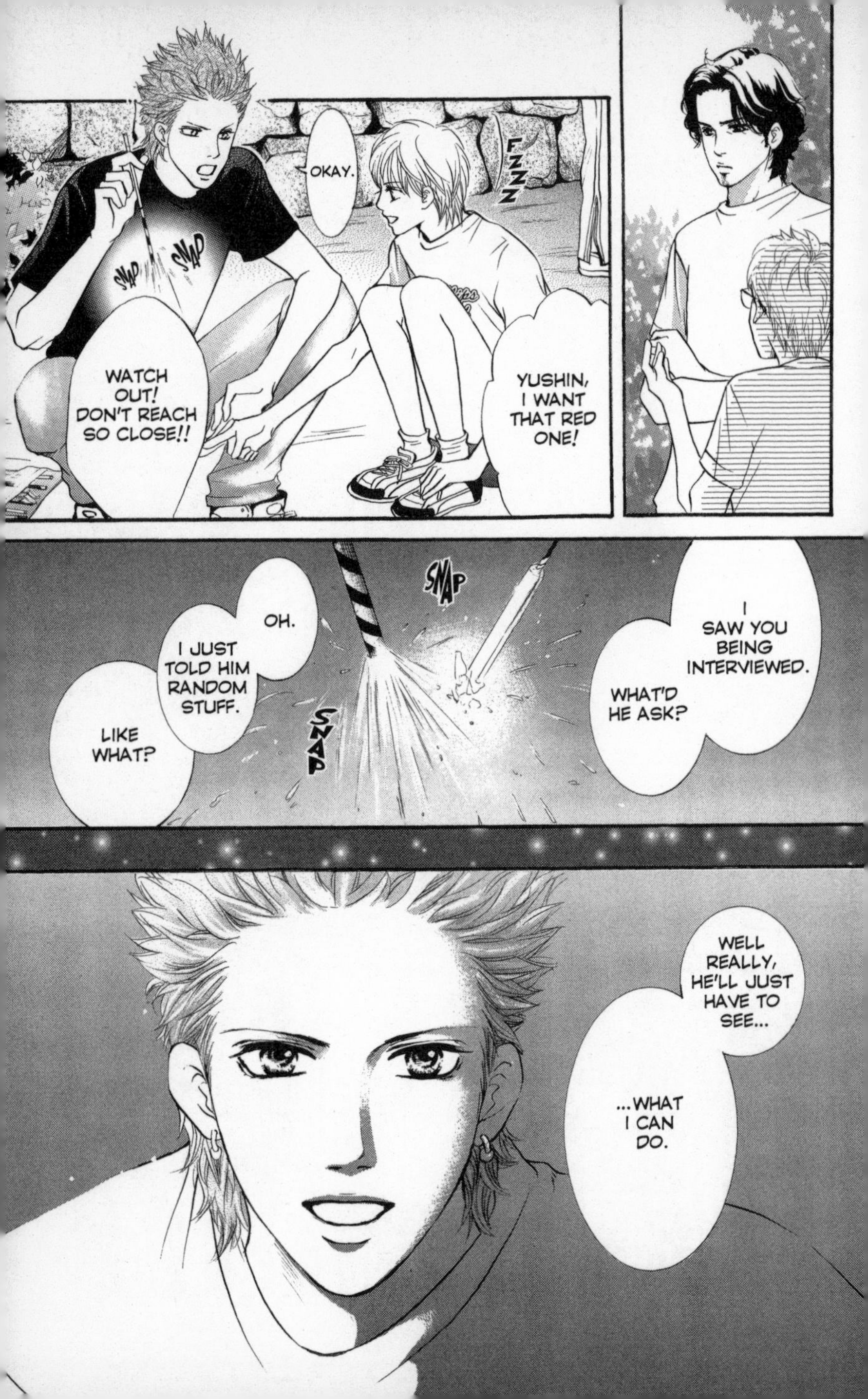
FZZZ
YUSHIN, I WANT THAT RED ONE!
OKAY.
SNAP SNAP
WATCH OUT! DON'T REACH SO CLOSE!!
SNAP
I SAW YOU BEING INTERVIEWED.
WHAT'D HE ASK?
OH.
I JUST TOLD HIM RANDOM STUFF.
SNAP
LIKE WHAT?
WELL REALLY, HE'LL JUST HAVE TO SEE...
...WHAT I CAN DO.

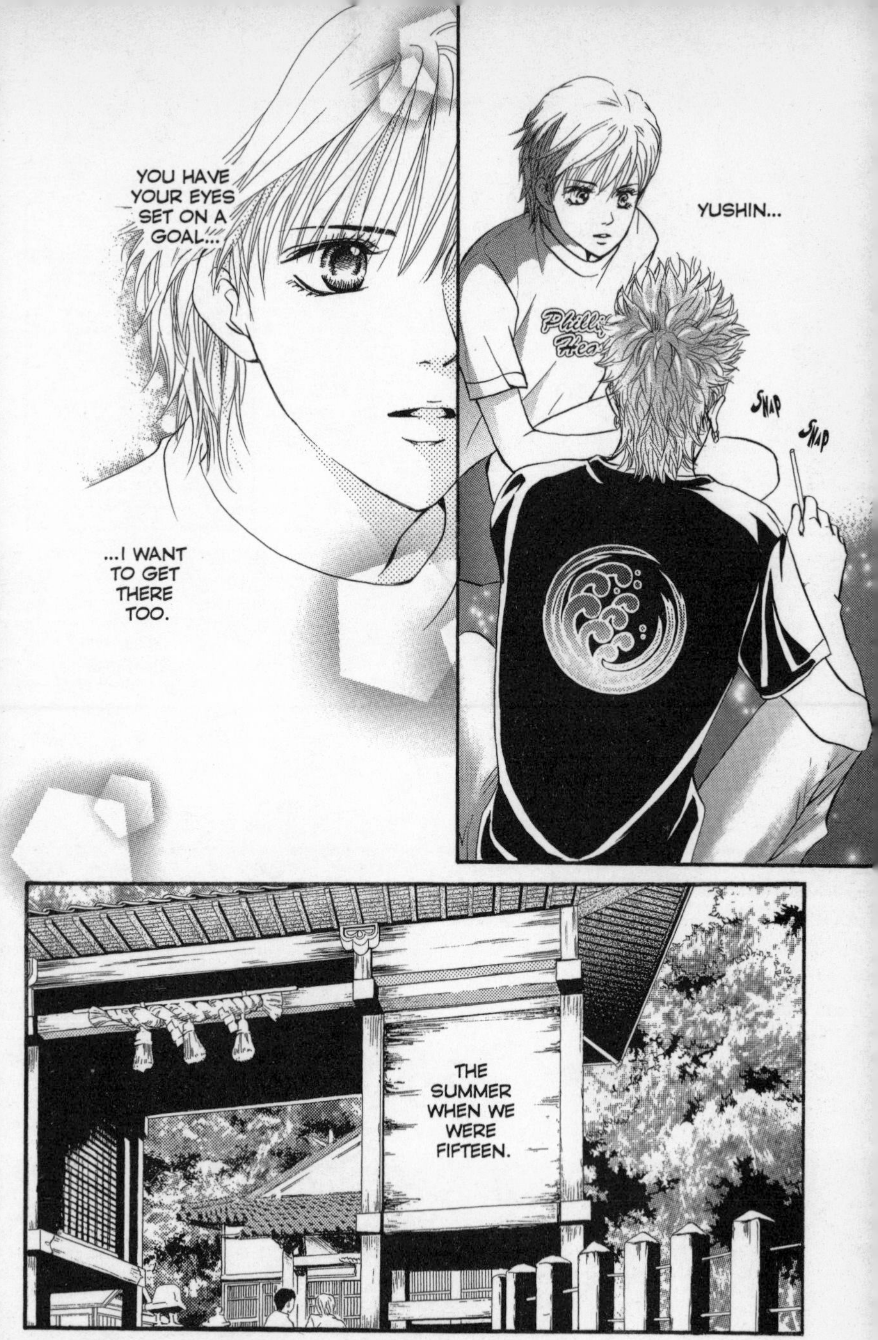
YUSHIN...
SNAP
SNAP
YOU HAVE YOUR EYES SET ON A GOAL...
...I WANT TO GET THERE TOO.
THE SUMMER WHEN WE WERE FIFTEEN.

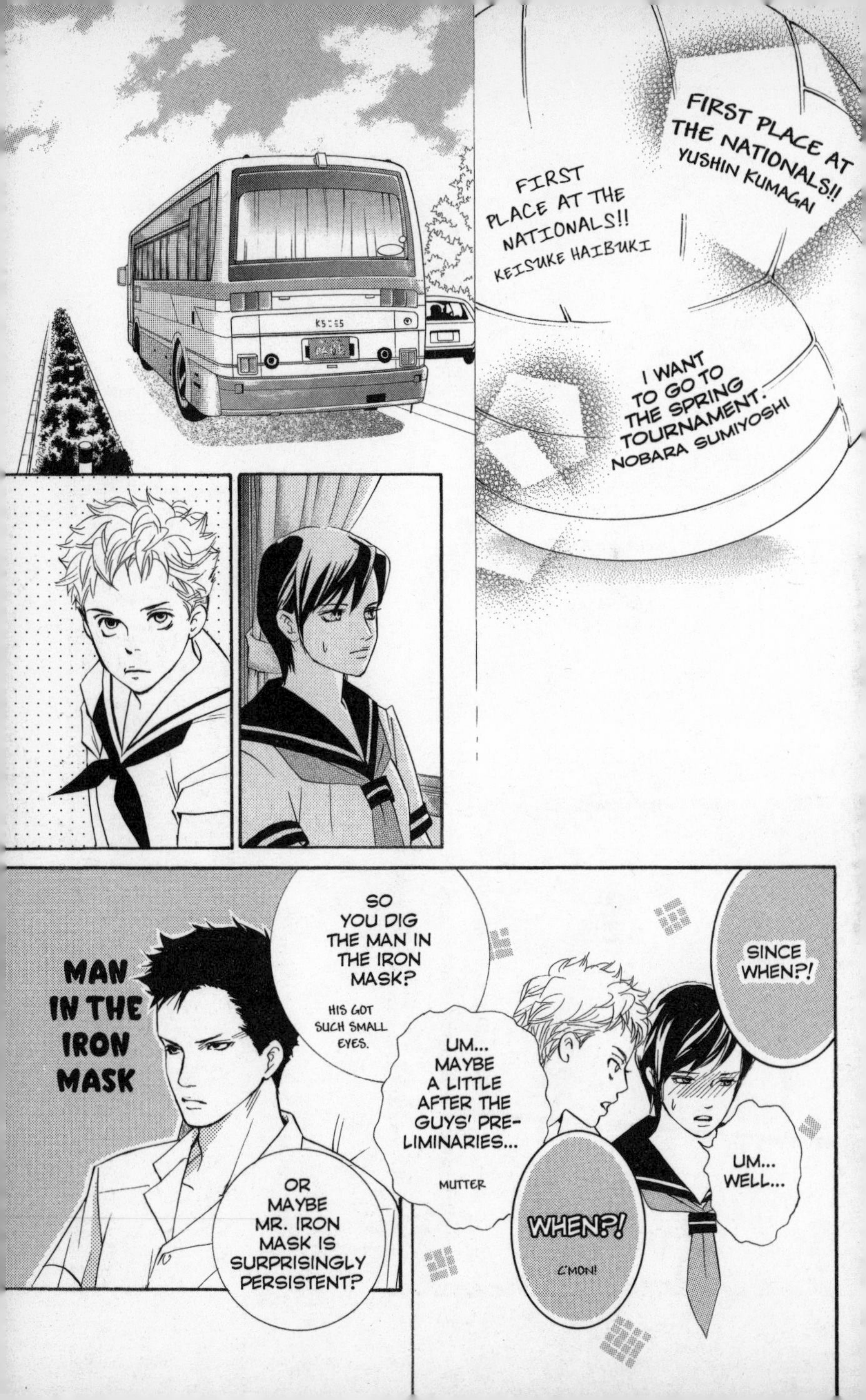
FIRST PLACE AT THE NATIONALS!! YUSHIN KUMAGAI
FIRST PLACE AT THE NATIONALS!! KEISUKE HAIBUKI
I WANT TO GO TO THE SPRING TOURNAMENT. NOBARA SUMIYOSHI
SINCE WHEN?!
SO YOU DIG THE MAN IN THE IRON MASK?
HIS GOT SUCH SMALL EYES.
UM... WELL...
WHEN?!
C'MON!
UM... MAYBE A LITTLE AFTER THE GUYS' PRE-LIMINARIES...
MUTTER
OR MAYBE MR. IRON MASK IS SURPRISINGLY PERSISTENT?
MAN IN THE IRON MASK

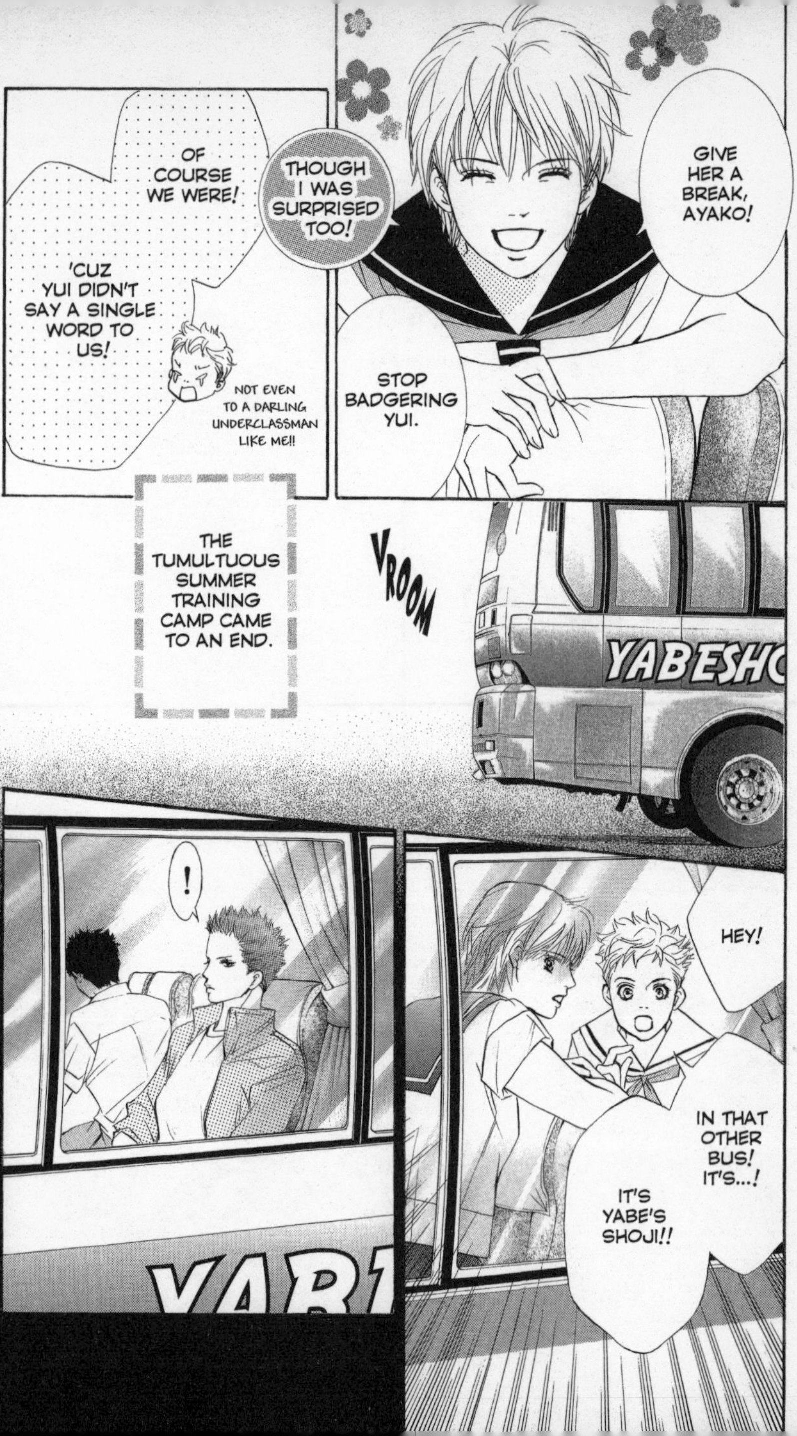
GIVE HER A BREAK, AYAKO!
STOP BADGERING YUI.
THOUGH I WAS SURPRISED TOO!
OF COURSE WE WERE!
'CUZ YUI DIDN'T SAY A SINGLE WORD TO US!
NOT EVEN TO A DARLING UNDERCLASSMAN LIKE ME!!
VROOM
YABESHO
THE TUMULTUOUS SUMMER TRAINING CAMP CAME TO AN END.
HEY!
IN THAT OTHER BUS! IT'S...!
IT'S YABE'S SHOJI!!
!

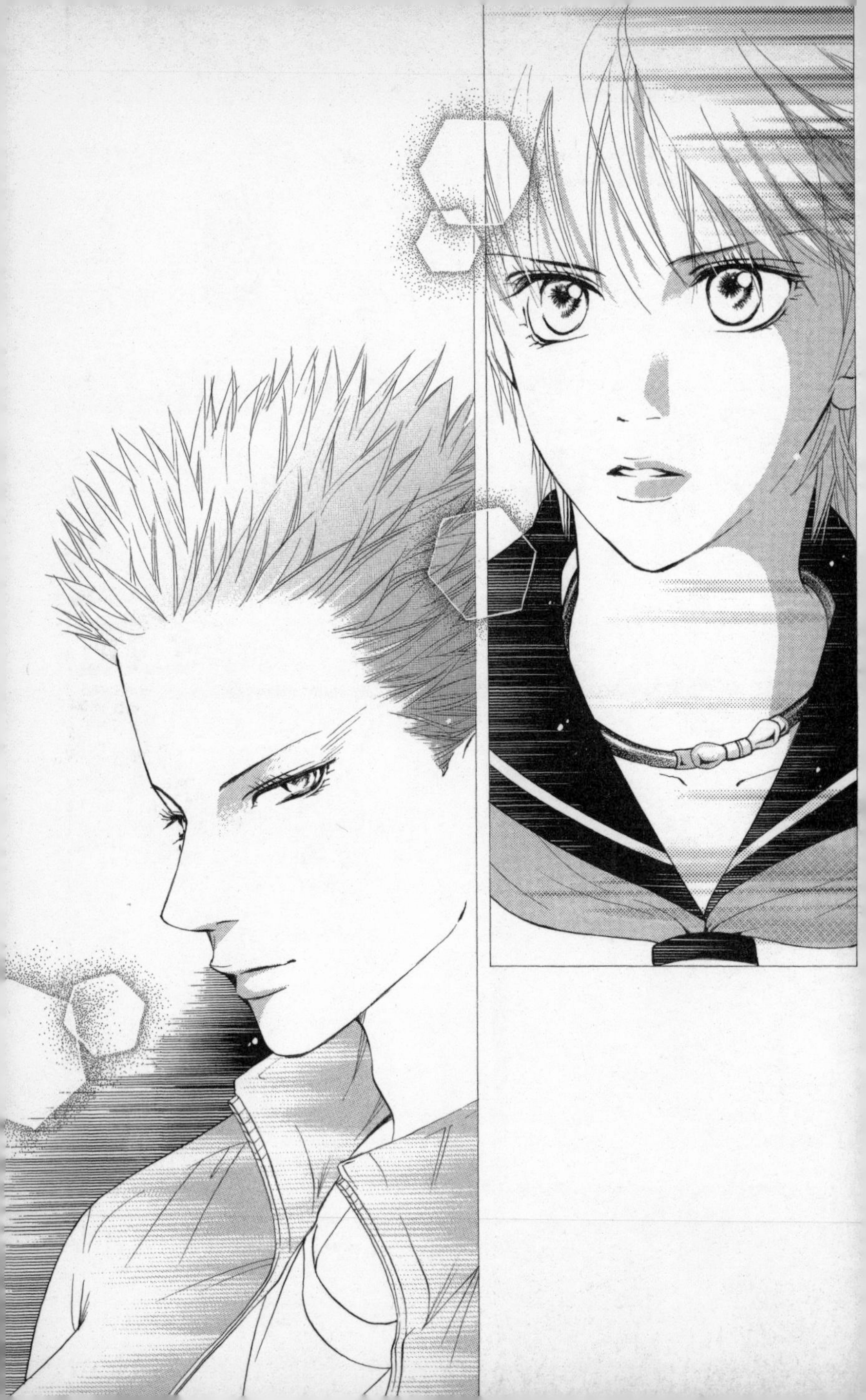

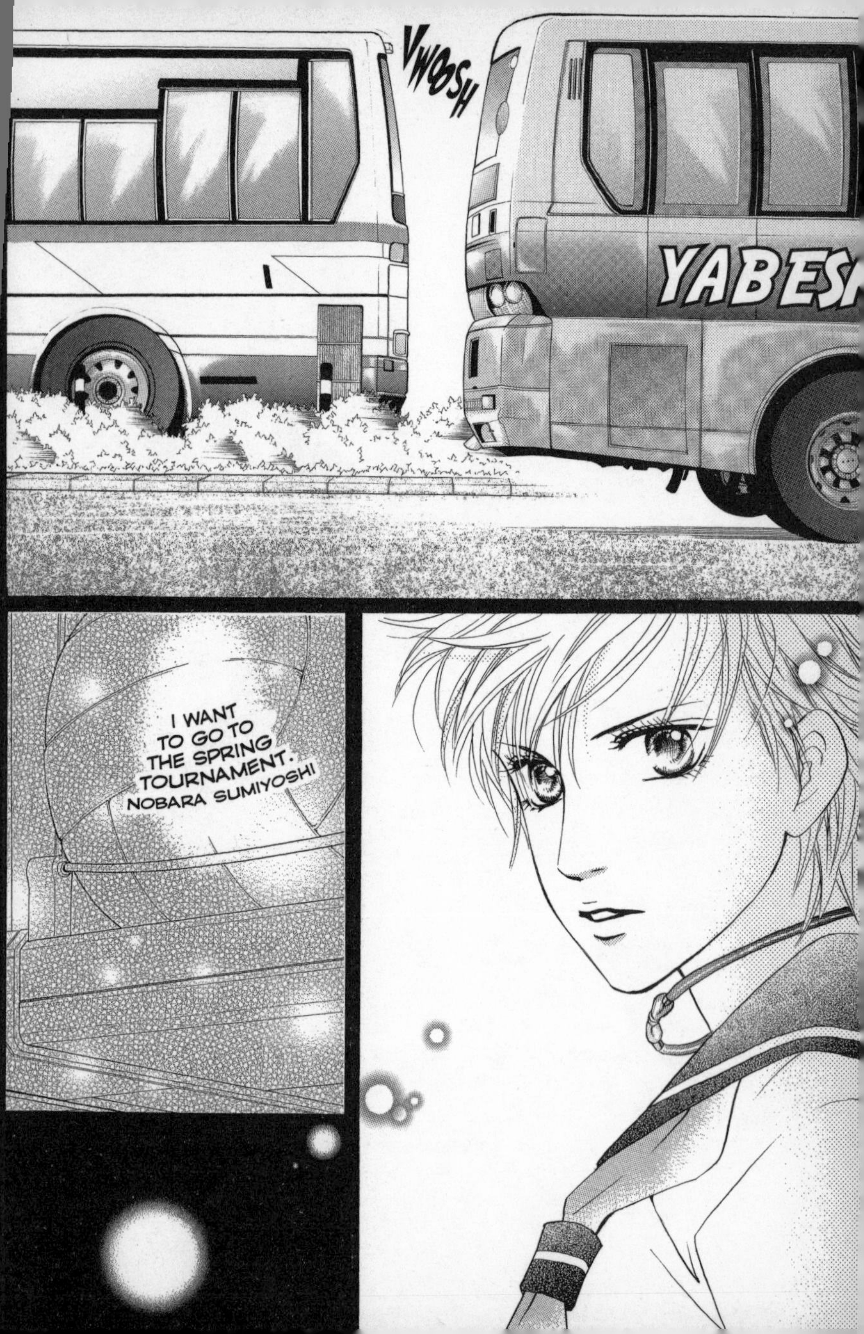
VWOOSH
YABESH
I WANT TO GO TO THE SPRING TOURNAMENT. NOBARA SUMIYOSHI

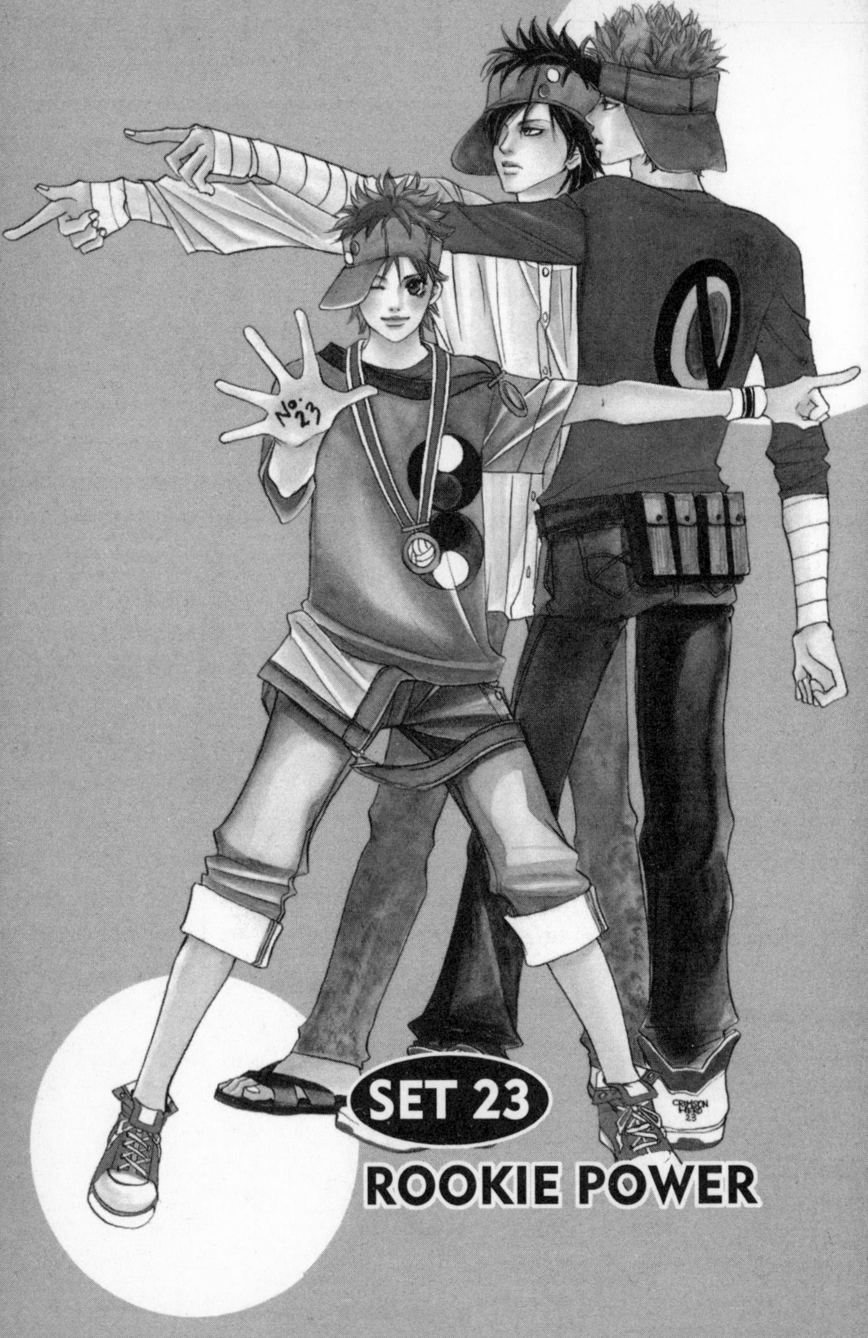
No. 23
CRIMSON HERO 23

SET 23
ROOKIE POWER

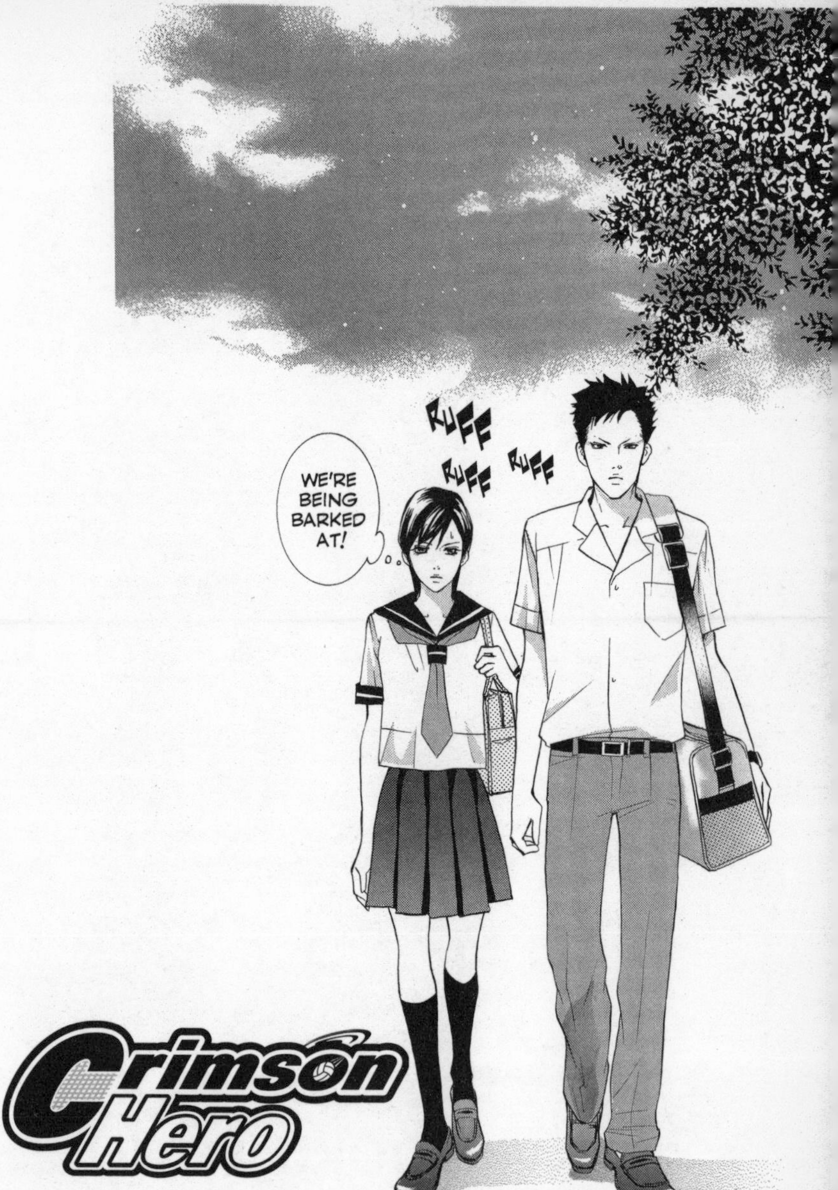
RUFF
RUFF RUFF
WE'RE BEING BARKED AT!
Crimson Hero

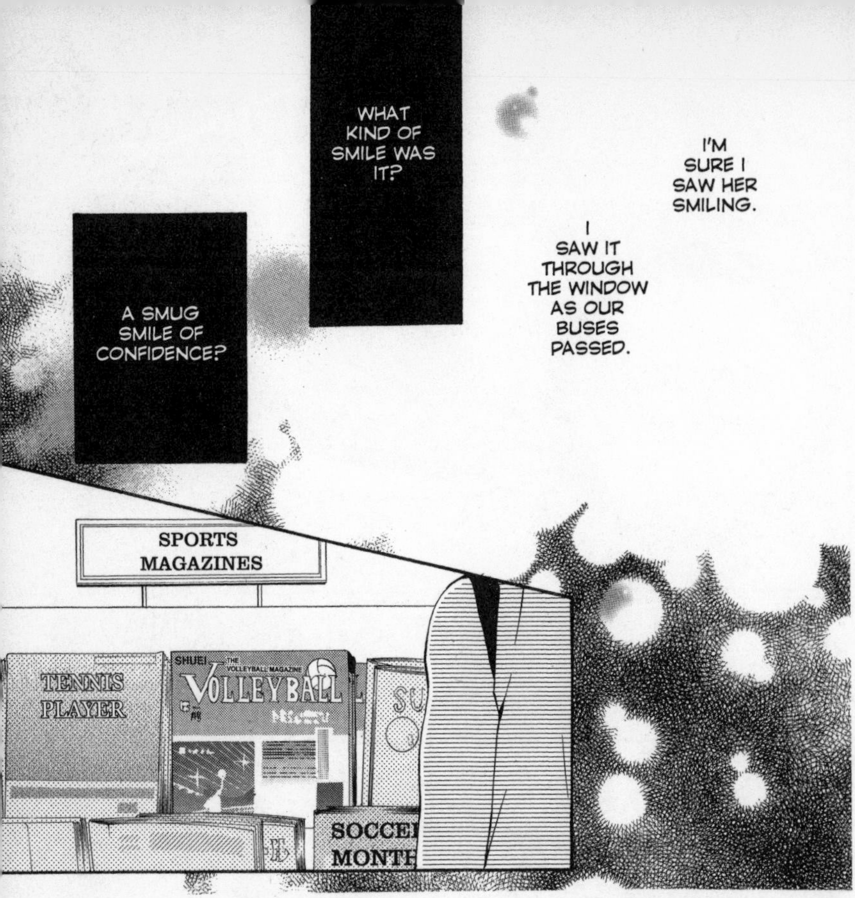
I'M SURE I SAW HER SMILING.
I SAW IT THROUGH THE WINDOW AS OUR BUSES PASSED.
WHAT KIND OF SMILE WAS IT?
A SMUG SMILE OF CONFIDENCE?
SPORTS MAGAZINES
SHUEI THE VOLLEYBALL MAGAZINE VOLLEYBALL
TENNIS PLAYER
SOCCER MONTH

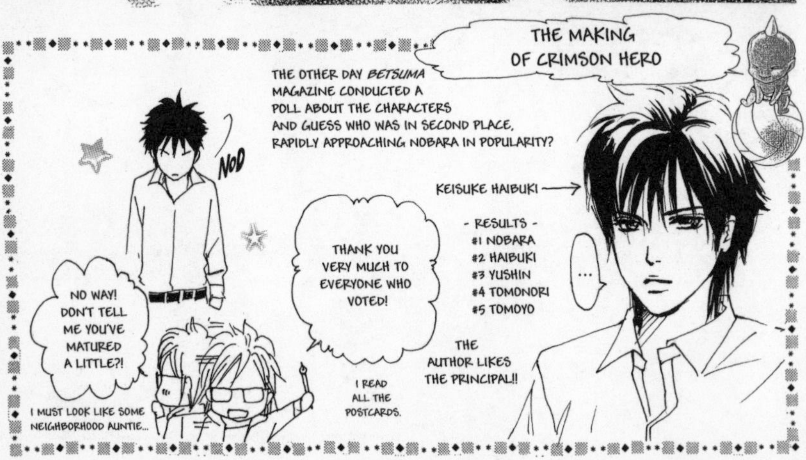
THE MAKING OF CRIMSON HERO
THE OTHER DAY *BETSUMA* MAGAZINE CONDUCTED A POLL ABOUT THE CHARACTERS AND GUESS WHO WAS IN SECOND PLACE, RAPIDLY APPROACHING NOBARA IN POPULARITY?
KEISUKE HAIBUKI
...
- RESULTS -
#1 NOBARA
#2 HAIBUKI
#3 YUSHIN
#4 TOMONORI
#5 TOMOYO
THE AUTHOR LIKES THE PRINCIPAL!!
NOD
THANK YOU VERY MUCH TO EVERYONE WHO VOTED!
I READ ALL THE POSTCARDS.
NO WAY! DON'T TELL ME YOU'VE MATURED A LITTLE?!
I MUST LOOK LIKE SOME NEIGHBORHOOD AUNTIE...

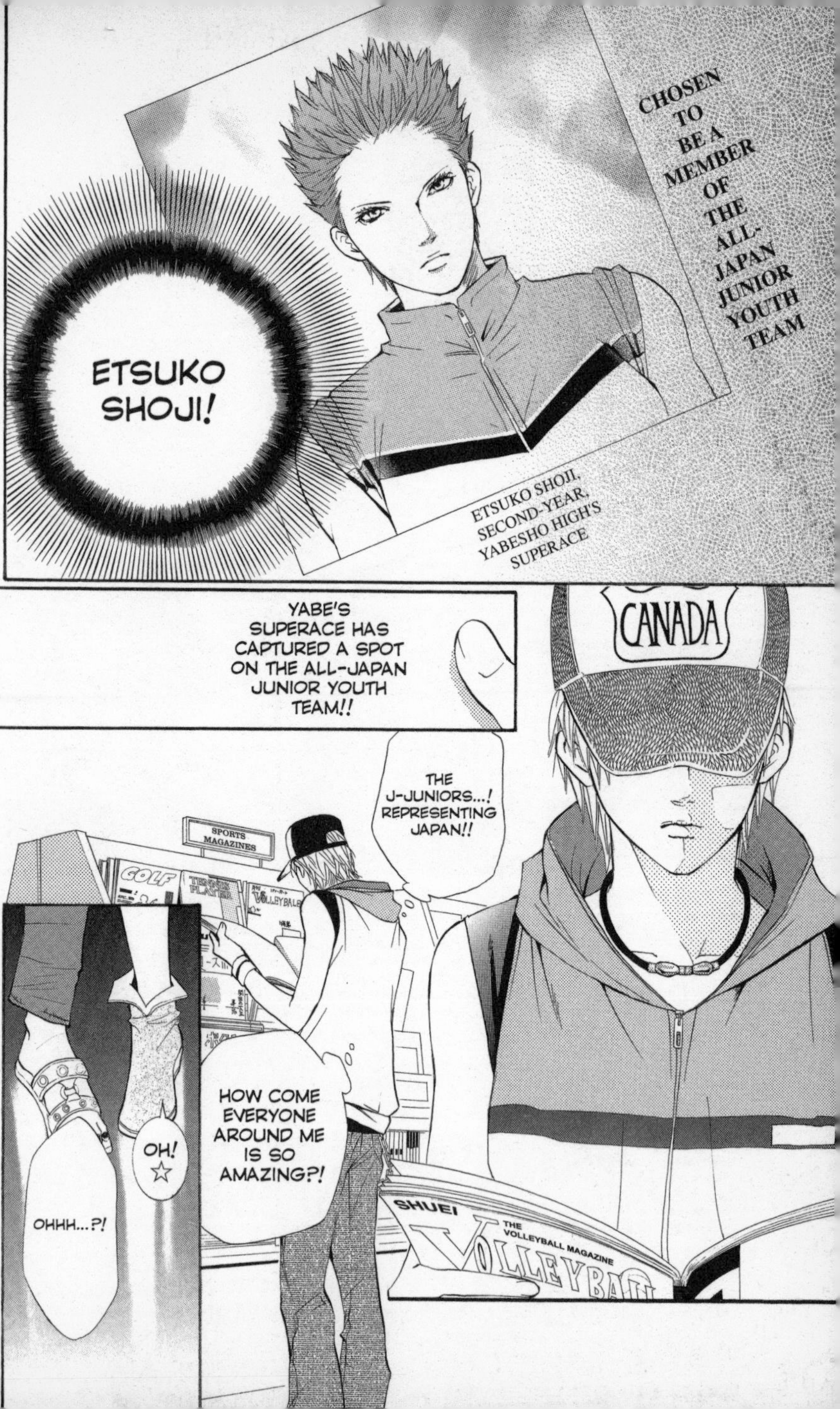
CHOSEN TO BE A MEMBER OF THE ALL-JAPAN JUNIOR YOUTH TEAM
ETSUKO SHOJI, SECOND-YEAR, YABESHO HIGH'S SUPERACE
ETSUKO SHOJI!
CANADA
YABE'S SUPERACE HAS CAPTURED A SPOT ON THE ALL-JAPAN JUNIOR YOUTH TEAM!!
THE J-JUNIORS...! REPRESENTING JAPAN!!
SHUEI
THE VOLLEYBALL MAGAZINE
VOLLEYBALL
SPORTS MAGAZINES
GOLF
TENNIS PLAYER
VOLLEYBALL
HOW COME EVERYONE AROUND ME IS SO AMAZING?!
OH! ☆
OHHH...?!

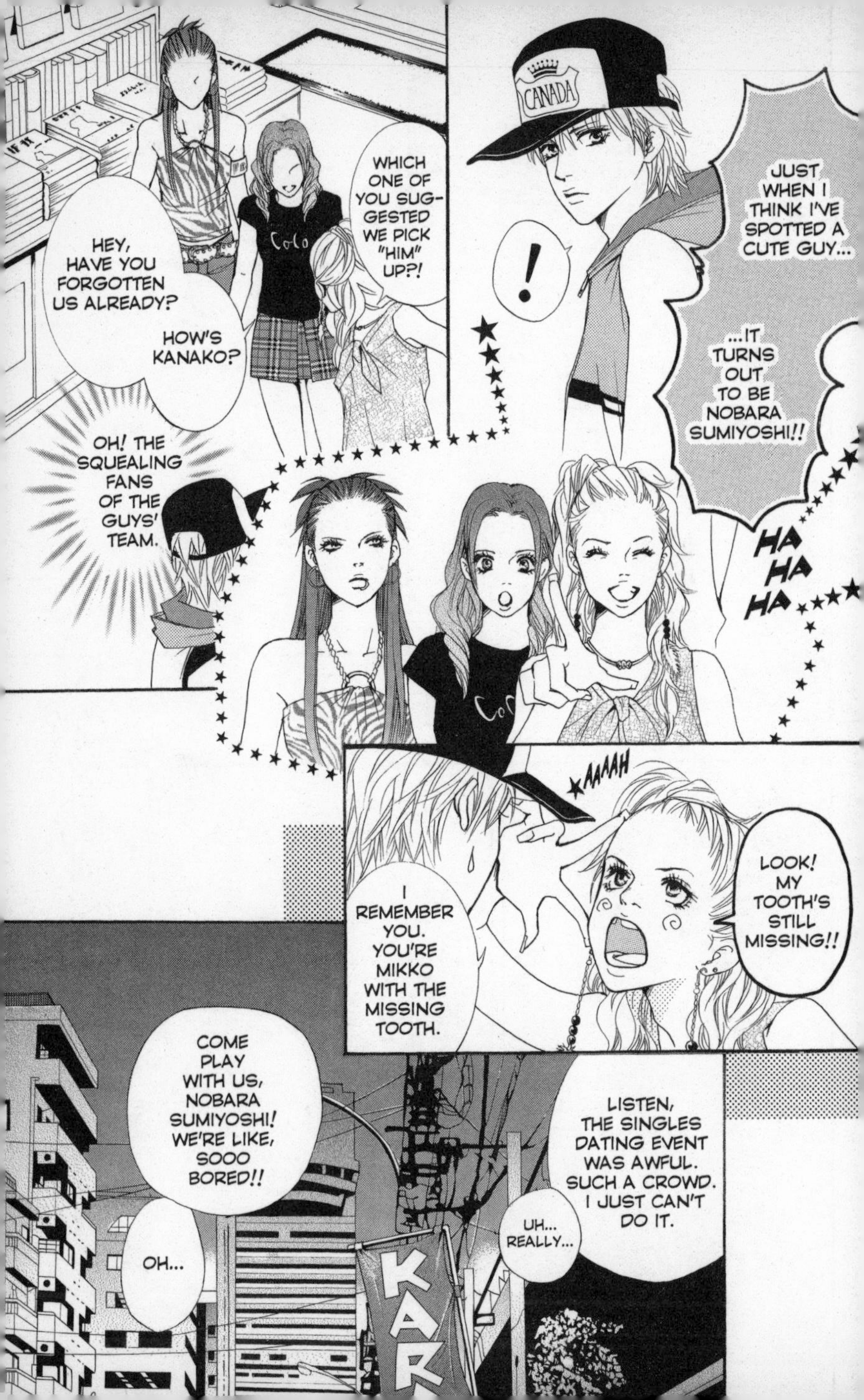
!
JUST WHEN I THINK I'VE SPOTTED A CUTE GUY...
...IT TURNS OUT TO BE NOBARA SUMIYOSHI!!
WHICH ONE OF YOU SUG-GESTED WE PICK "HIM" UP?!
HEY, HAVE YOU FORGOTTEN US ALREADY?
HOW'S KANAKO?
Colo
HA HA HA
OH! THE SQUEALING FANS OF THE GUYS' TEAM.
AAAAH
LOOK! MY TOOTH'S STILL MISSING!!
I REMEMBER YOU. YOU'RE MIKKO WITH THE MISSING TOOTH.
LISTEN, THE SINGLES DATING EVENT WAS AWFUL. SUCH A CROWD. I JUST CAN'T DO IT.
UH... REALLY...
COME PLAY WITH US, NOBARA SUMIYOSHI! WE'RE LIKE, SOOO BORED!!
OH...
KAR

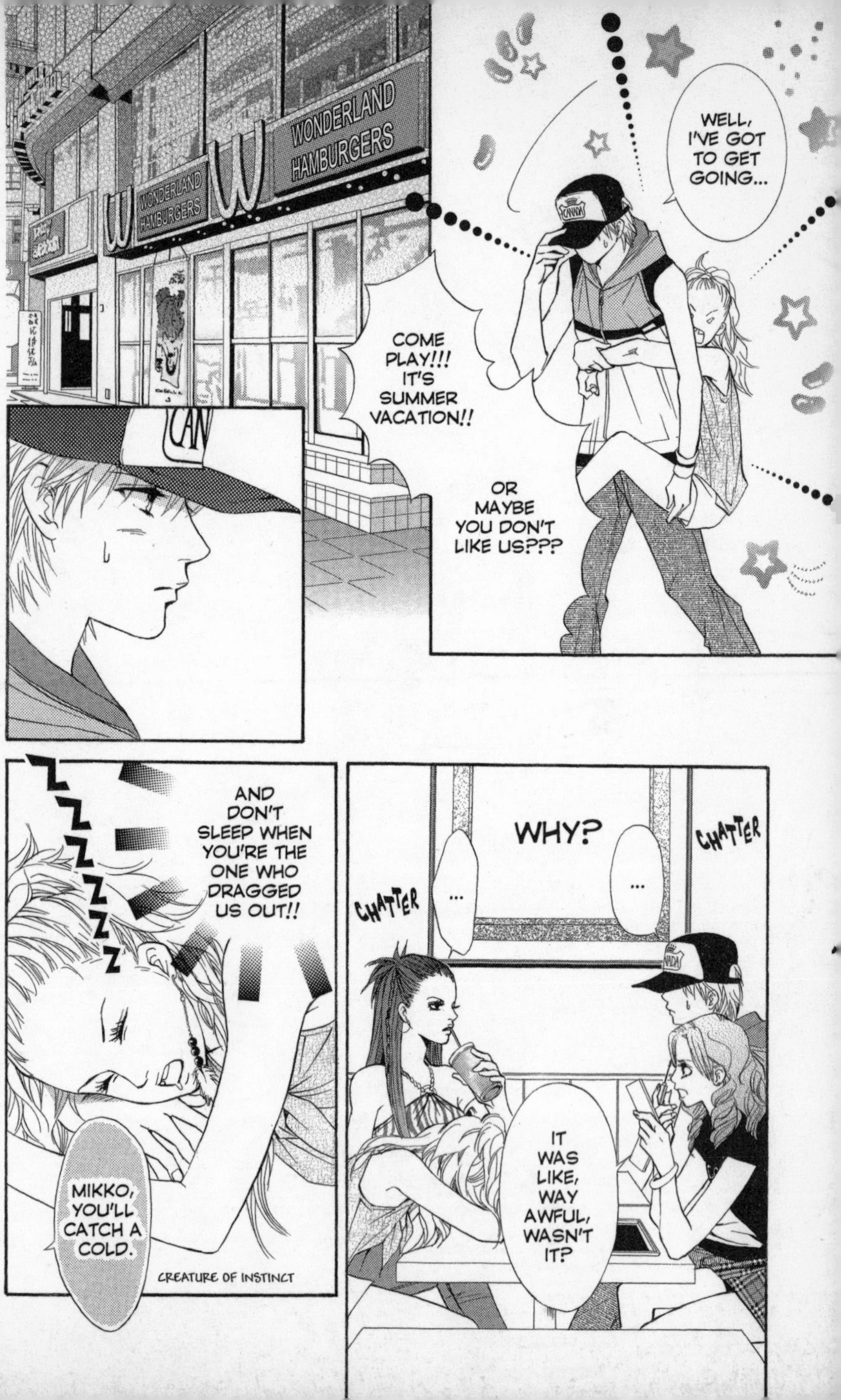
WONDERLAND HAMBURGERS
WONDERLAND HAMBURGERS
WELL, I'VE GOT TO GET GOING...
COME PLAY!!! IT'S SUMMER VACATION!!
OR MAYBE YOU DON'T LIKE US???
CHATTER
WHY?
...
...
CHATTER
IT WAS LIKE, WAY AWFUL, WASN'T IT?
AND DON'T SLEEP WHEN YOU'RE THE ONE WHO DRAGGED US OUT!!
ZZZZZZZ
MIKKO, YOU'LL CATCH A COLD.
CREATURE OF INSTINCT

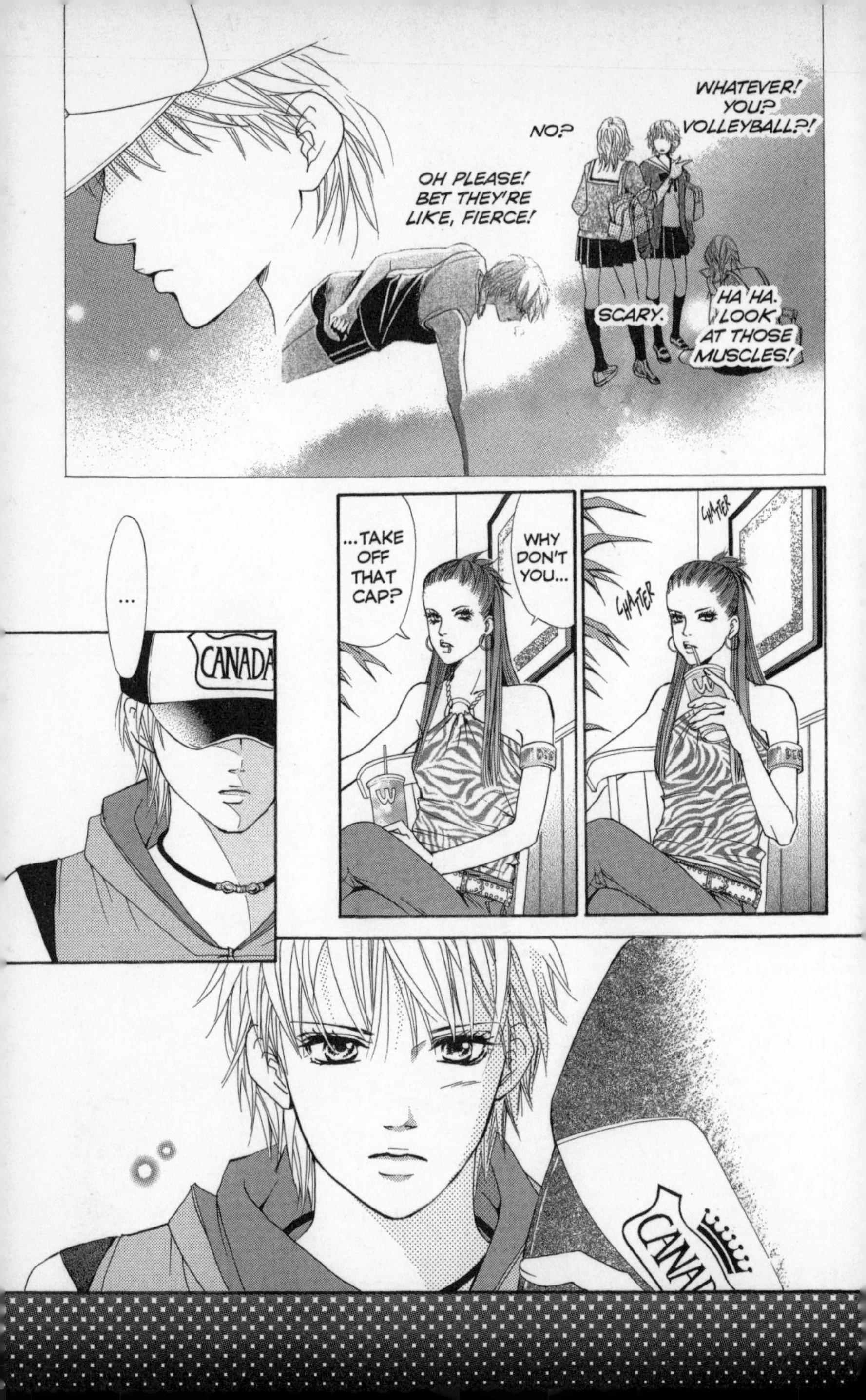
WHATEVER! YOU? VOLLEYBALL?!
NO?
OH PLEASE! BET THEY'RE LIKE, FIERCE!
HA HA. LOOK AT THOSE MUSCLES!
SCARY.
CHATTER
CHATTER
WHY DON'T YOU...
...TAKE OFF THAT CAP?
...
CANADA

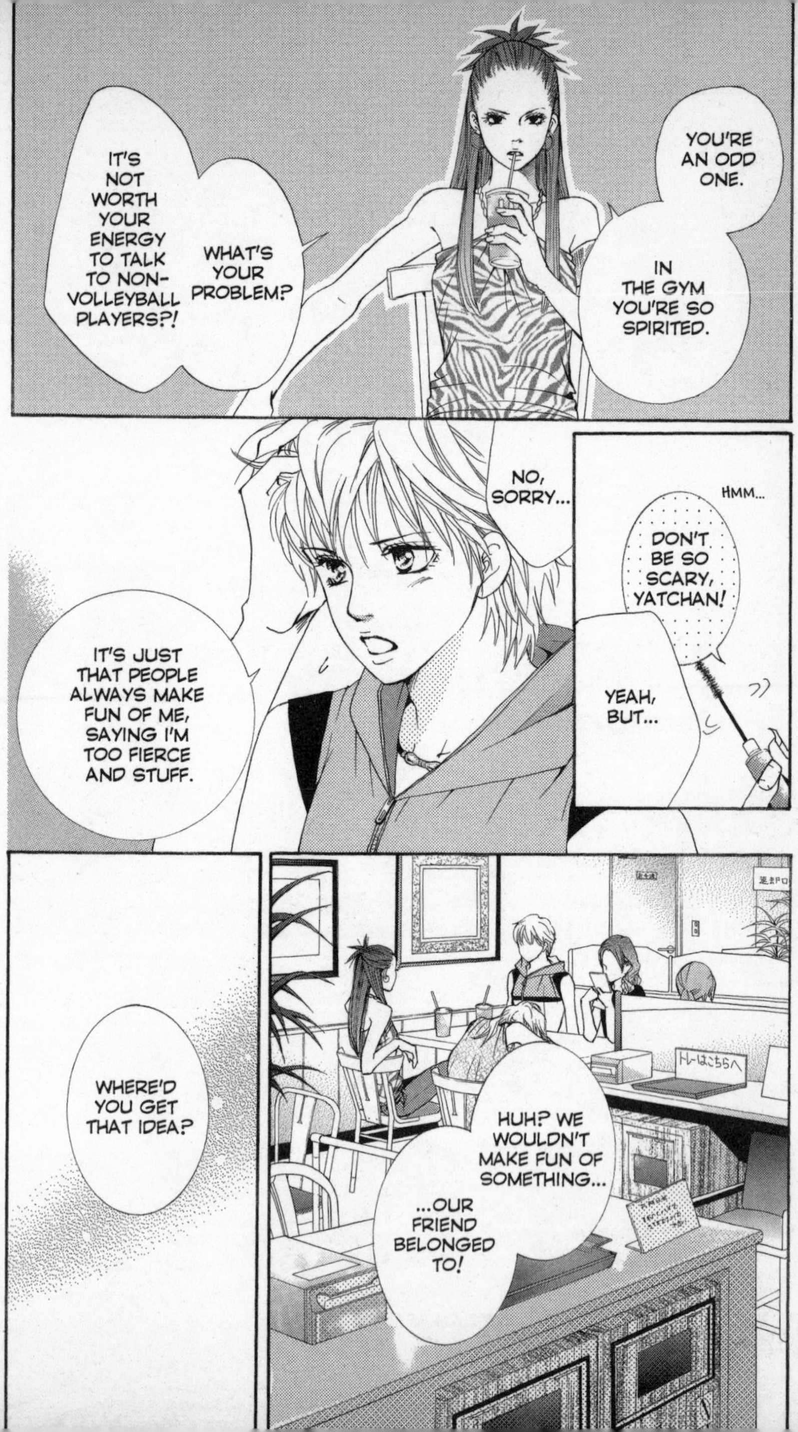
YOU'RE AN ODD ONE.
IN THE GYM YOU'RE SO SPIRITED.
WHAT'S YOUR PROBLEM?
IT'S NOT WORTH YOUR ENERGY TO TALK TO NON-VOLLEYBALL PLAYERS?!
HMM...
DON'T BE SO SCARY, YATCHAN!
YEAH, BUT...
NO, SORRY...
IT'S JUST THAT PEOPLE ALWAYS MAKE FUN OF ME, SAYING I'M TOO FIERCE AND STUFF.
トレーはこちらへ
HUH? WE WOULDN'T MAKE FUN OF SOMETHING...
...OUR FRIEND BELONGED TO!
WHERE'D YOU GET THAT IDEA?

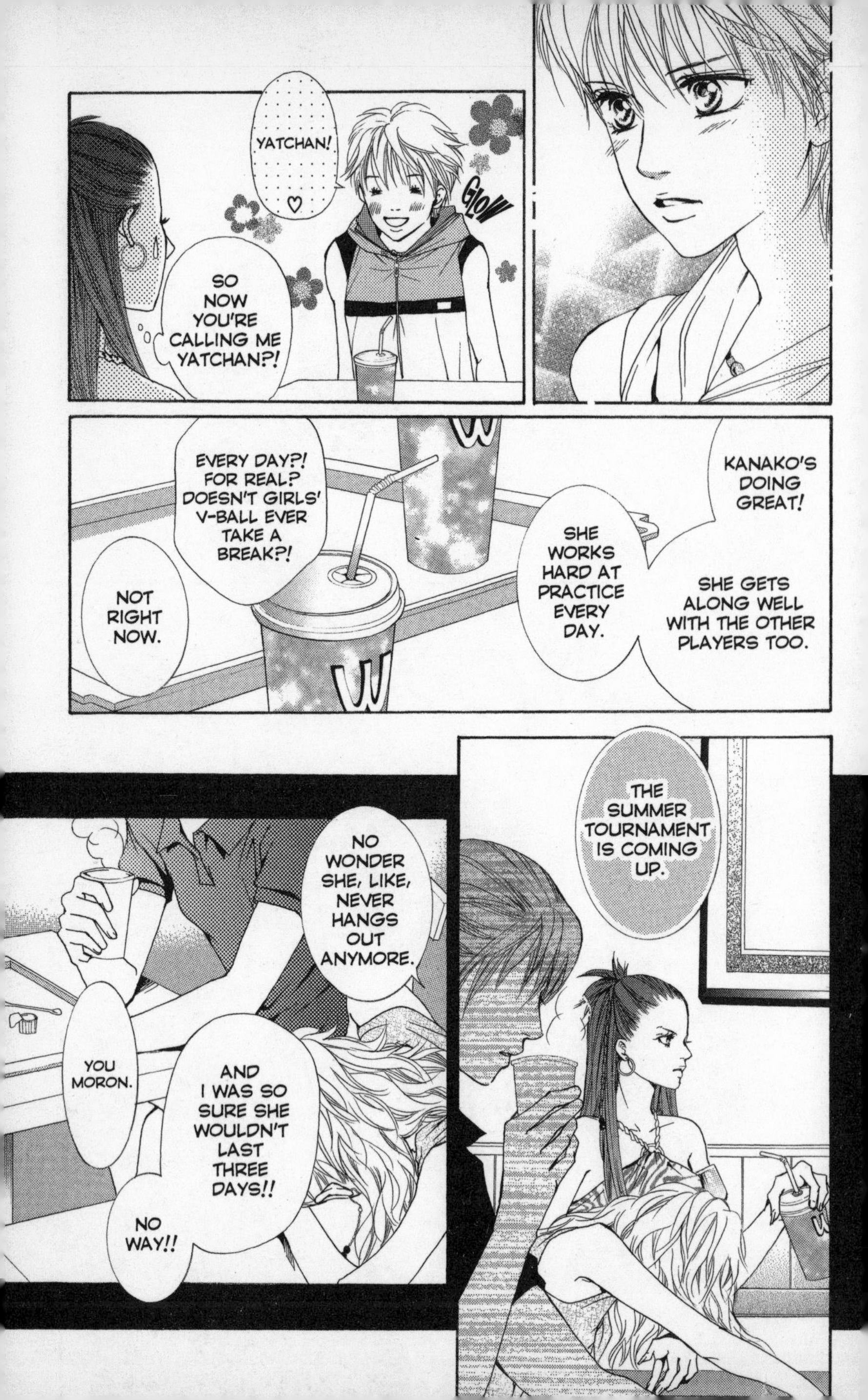
YATCHAN! ♡
GLOW
SO NOW YOU'RE CALLING ME YATCHAN?!
KANAKO'S DOING GREAT!
SHE GETS ALONG WELL WITH THE OTHER PLAYERS TOO.
SHE WORKS HARD AT PRACTICE EVERY DAY.
EVERY DAY?! FOR REAL? DOESN'T GIRLS' V-BALL EVER TAKE A BREAK?!
NOT RIGHT NOW.
THE SUMMER TOURNAMENT IS COMING UP.
NO WONDER SHE, LIKE, NEVER HANGS OUT ANYMORE.
AND I WAS SO SURE SHE WOULDN'T LAST THREE DAYS!!
YOU MORON.
NO WAY!!

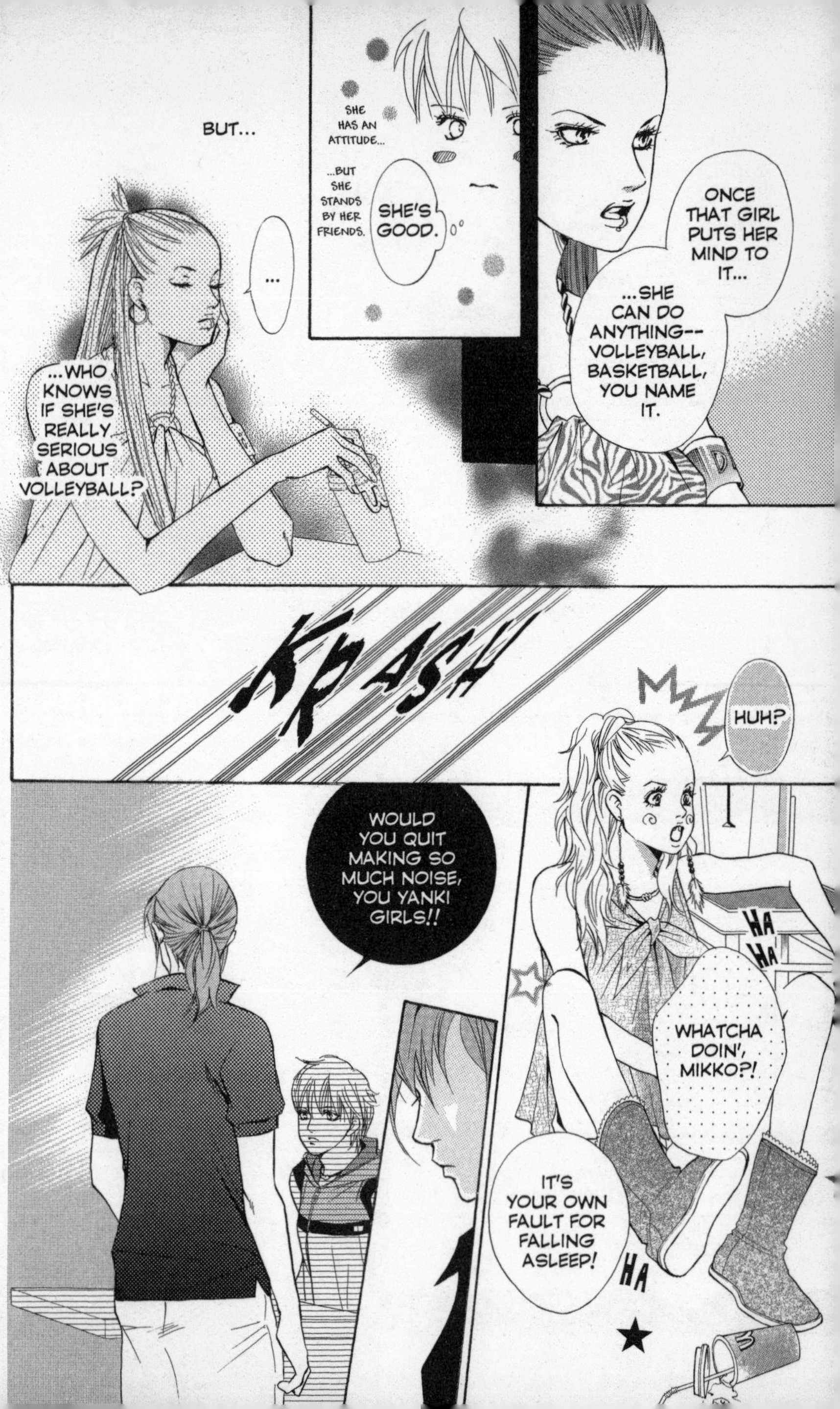
ONCE THAT GIRL PUTS HER MIND TO IT...
...SHE CAN DO ANYTHING--VOLLEYBALL, BASKETBALL, YOU NAME IT.
SHE HAS AN ATTITUDE...
...BUT SHE STANDS BY HER FRIENDS.
SHE'S GOOD.
BUT...
...
...WHO KNOWS IF SHE'S REALLY SERIOUS ABOUT VOLLEYBALL?
KRASH
HUH?
HA HA
WHATCHA DOIN', MIKKO?!
IT'S YOUR OWN FAULT FOR FALLING ASLEEP!
HA
WOULD YOU QUIT MAKING SO MUCH NOISE, YOU YANKI GIRLS!!

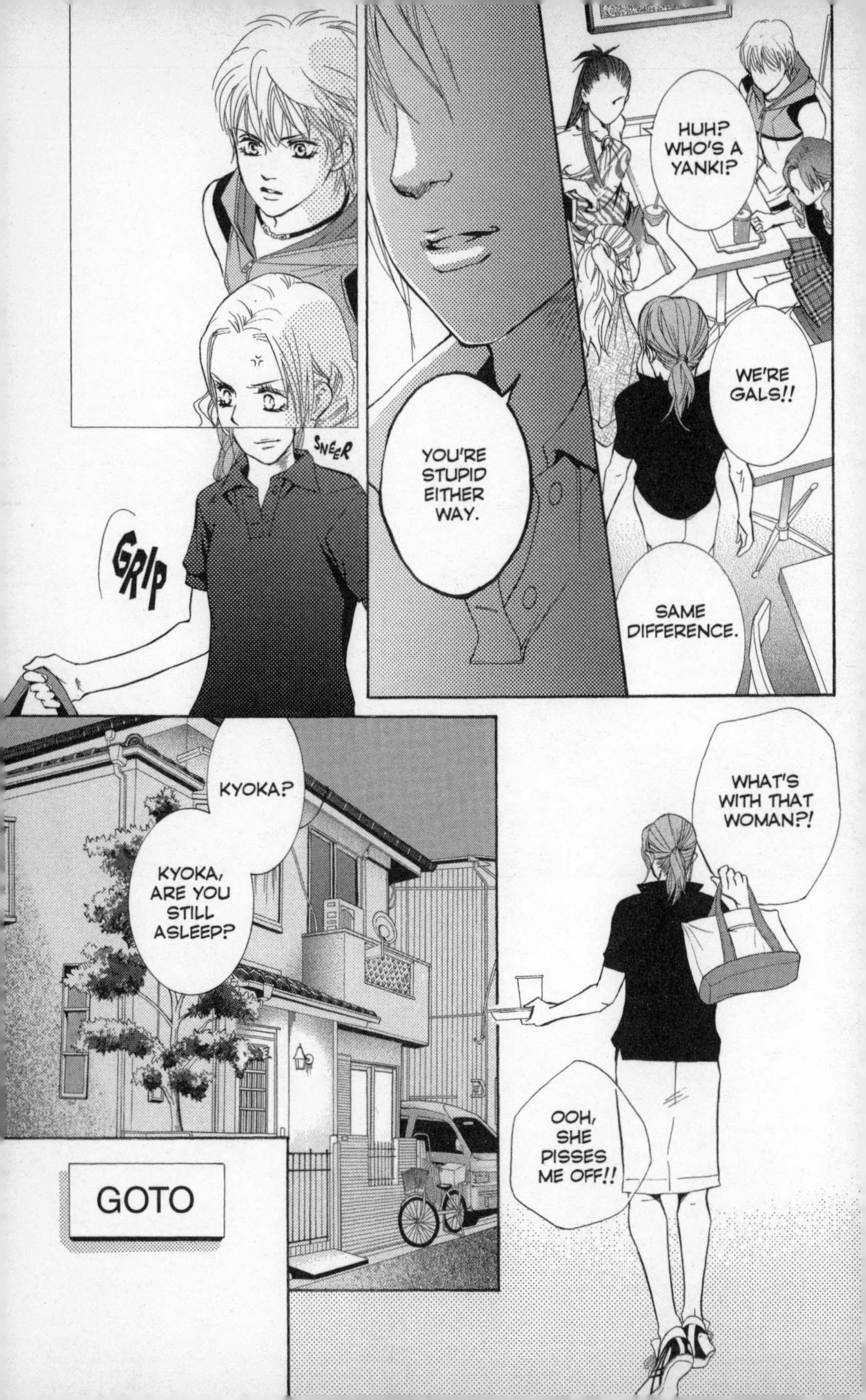
HUH? WHO'S A YANKI?
WE'RE GALS!!
SAME DIFFERENCE.
YOU'RE STUPID EITHER WAY.
SNEER
GRIP
WHAT'S WITH THAT WOMAN?!
OOH, SHE PISSES ME OFF!!
KYOKA?
KYOKA, ARE YOU STILL ASLEEP?
GOTO

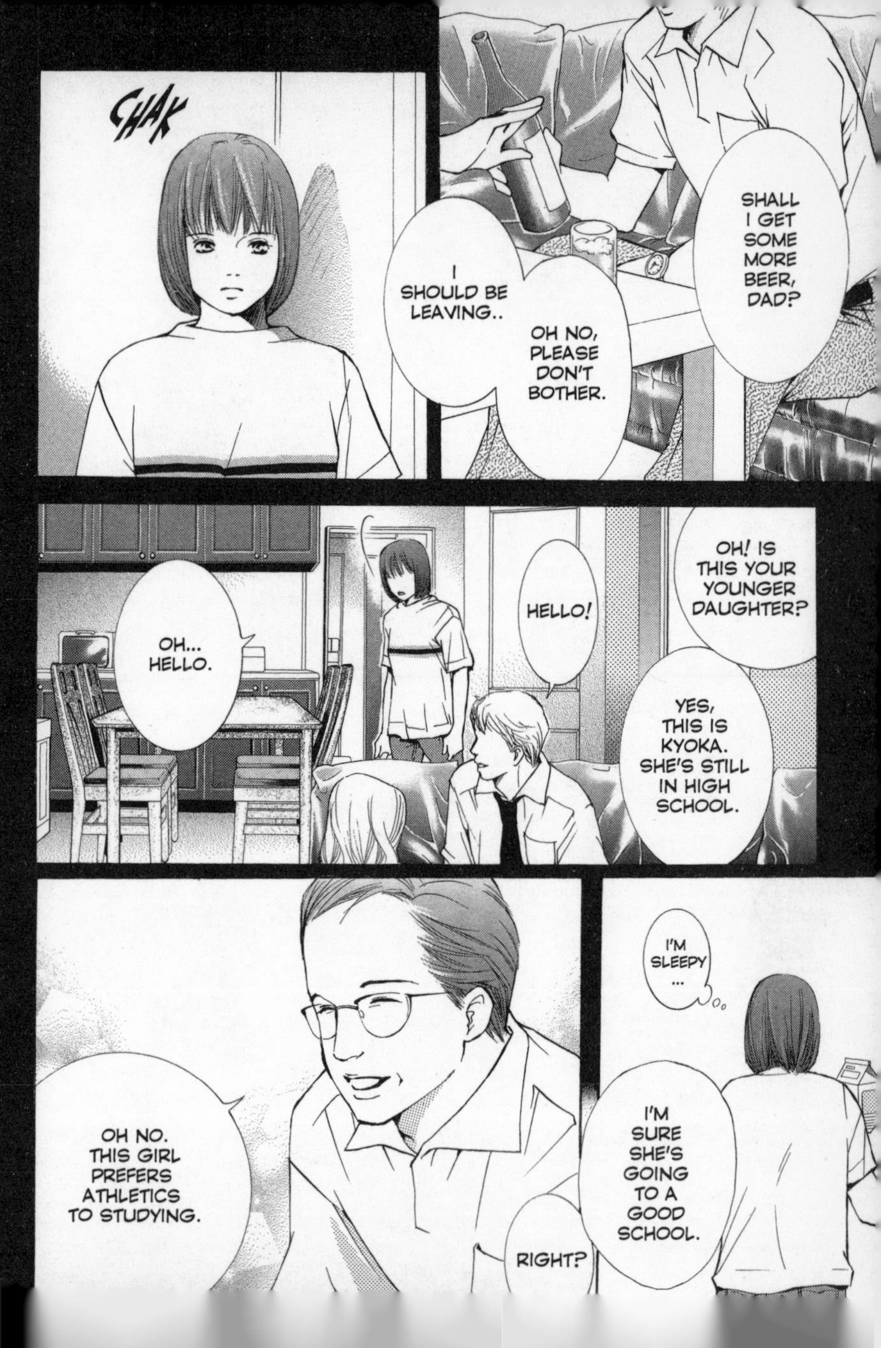
SHALL I GET SOME MORE BEER, DAD?
I SHOULD BE LEAVING..
OH NO, PLEASE DON'T BOTHER.
CHAK
OH! IS THIS YOUR YOUNGER DAUGHTER?
YES, THIS IS KYOKA. SHE'S STILL IN HIGH SCHOOL.
HELLO!
OH... HELLO.
I'M SLEEPY ...
I'M SURE SHE'S GOING TO A GOOD SCHOOL.
RIGHT?
OH NO. THIS GIRL PREFERS ATHLETICS TO STUDYING.

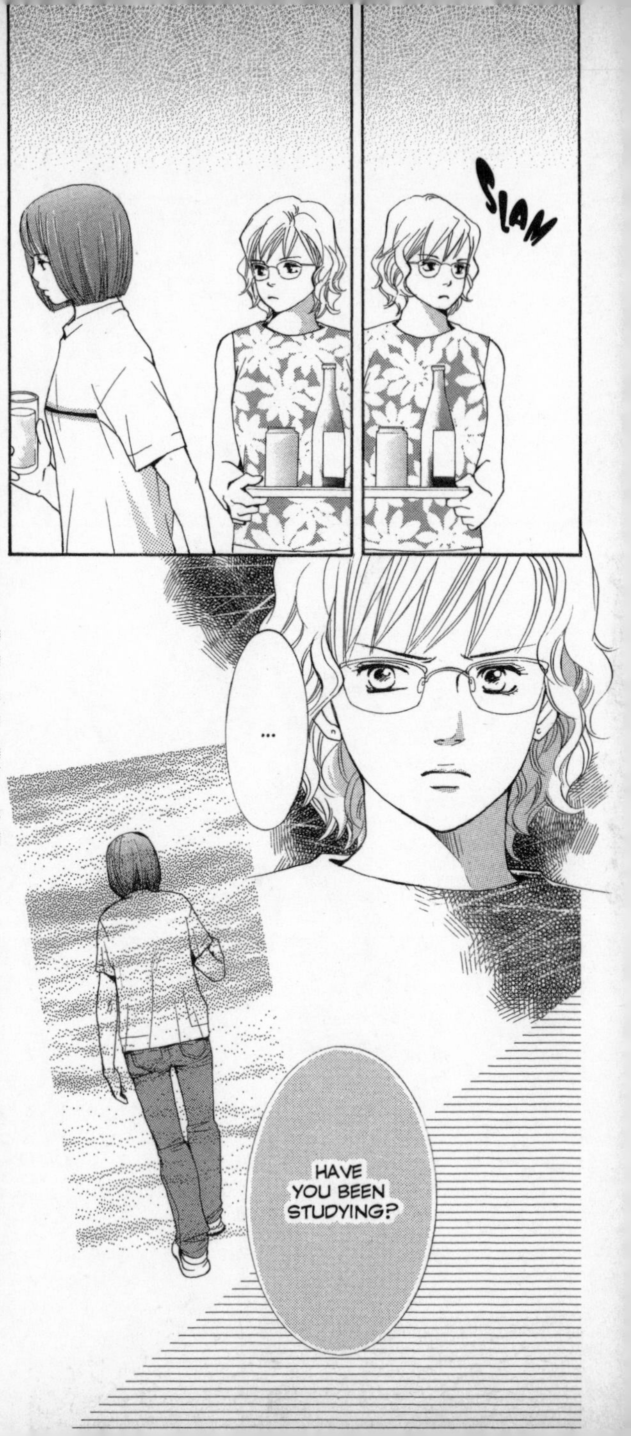
SLAM
...
HAVE YOU BEEN STUDYING?

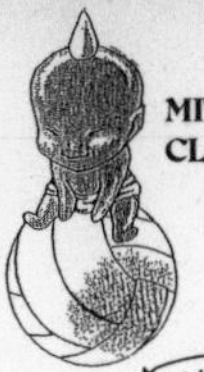

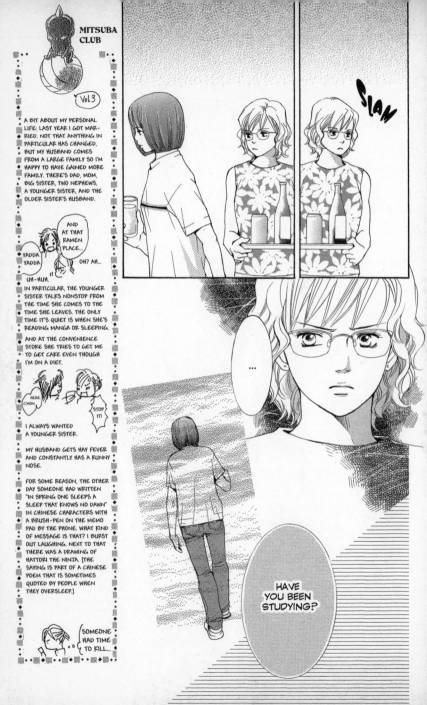

MITSUBA CLUB

Vol.3

A BIT ABOUT MY PERSONAL LIFE: LAST YEAR I GOT MARRIED. NOT THAT ANYTHING IN PARTICULAR HAS CHANGED, BUT MY HUSBAND COMES FROM A LARGE FAMILY SO I'M HAPPY TO HAVE GAINED MORE FAMILY. THERE'S DAD, MOM, BIG SISTER, TWO NEPHEWS, A YOUNGER SISTER, AND THE OLDER SISTER'S HUSBAND.

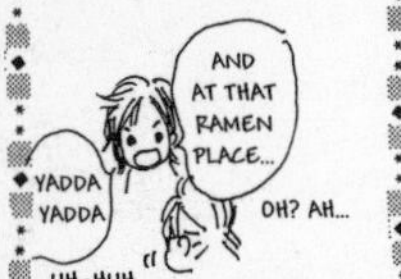
AND AT THAT RAMEN PLACE...
YADDA YADDA
OH? AH...
UH-HUH.

IN PARTICULAR, THE YOUNGER SISTER TALKS NONSTOP FROM THE TIME SHE COMES TO THE TIME SHE LEAVES. THE ONLY TIME IT'S QUIET IS WHEN SHE'S READING MANGA OR SLEEPING.

AND AT THE CONVENIENCE STORE SHE TRIES TO GET ME TO GET CAKE EVEN THOUGH I'M ON A DIET.

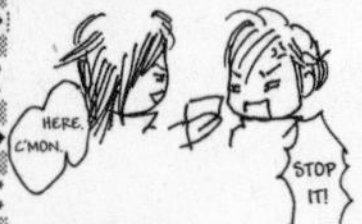
HERE, C'MON.
STOP IT!

I ALWAYS WANTED A YOUNGER SISTER.

MY HUSBAND GETS HAY FEVER AND CONSTANTLY HAS A RUNNY NOSE.

FOR SOME REASON, THE OTHER DAY SOMEONE HAD WRITTEN "IN SPRING ONE SLEEPS A SLEEP THAT KNOWS NO DAWN" IN CHINESE CHARACTERS WITH A BRUSH-PEN ON THE MEMO PAD BY THE PHONE. WHAT KIND OF MESSAGE IS THAT? I BURST OUT LAUGHING. NEXT TO THAT THERE WAS A DRAWING OF HATTORI THE NINJA. [THE SAYING IS PART OF A CHINESE POEM THAT IS SOMETIMES QUOTED BY PEOPLE WHEN THEY OVERSLEEP.]

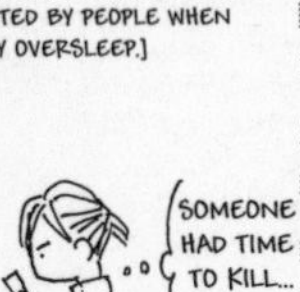
SOMEONE HAD TIME TO KILL...

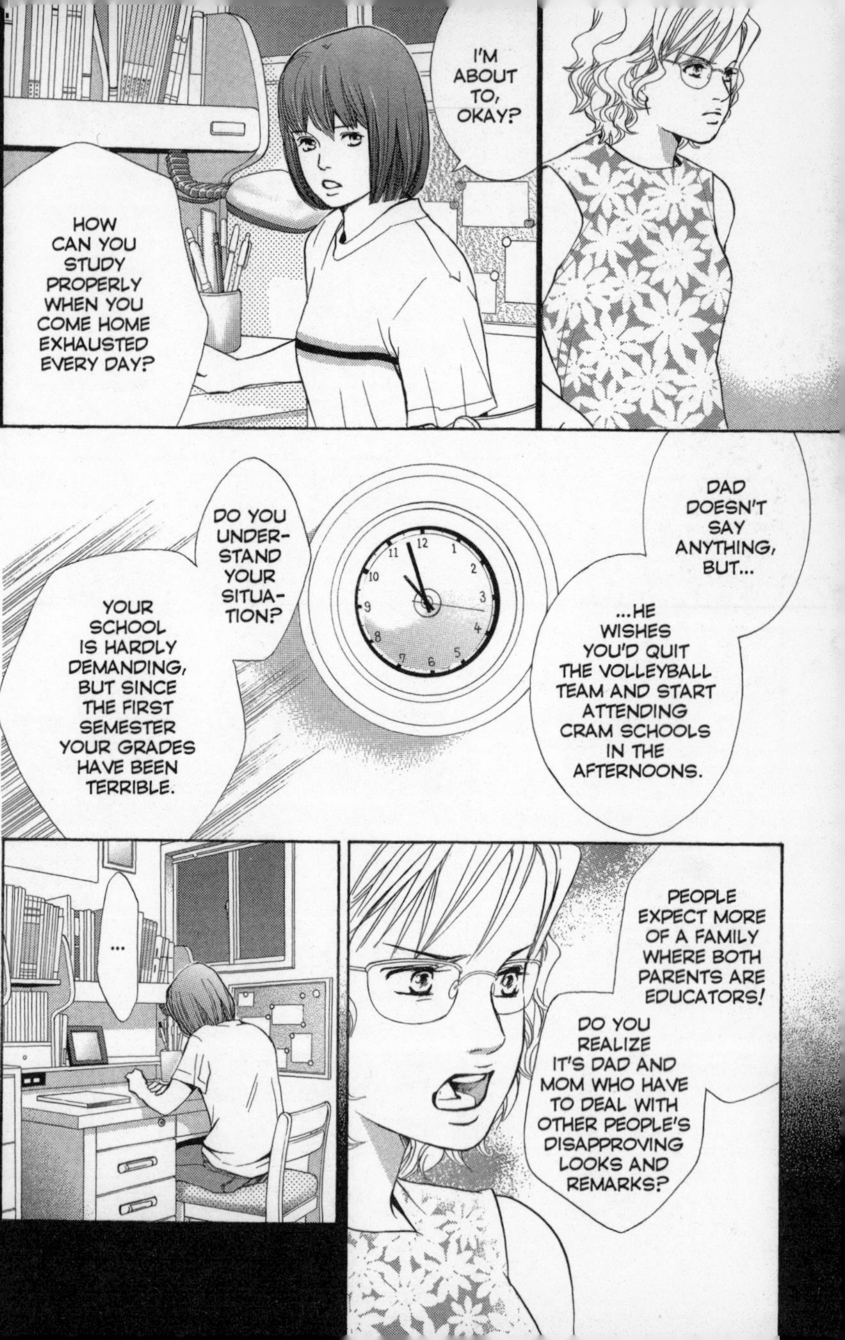
I'M ABOUT TO, OKAY?
HOW CAN YOU STUDY PROPERLY WHEN YOU COME HOME EXHAUSTED EVERY DAY?
DAD DOESN'T SAY ANYTHING, BUT...
...HE WISHES YOU'D QUIT THE VOLLEYBALL TEAM AND START ATTENDING CRAM SCHOOLS IN THE AFTERNOONS.
DO YOU UNDER-STAND YOUR SITUA-TION?
YOUR SCHOOL IS HARDLY DEMANDING, BUT SINCE THE FIRST SEMESTER YOUR GRADES HAVE BEEN TERRIBLE.
PEOPLE EXPECT MORE OF A FAMILY WHERE BOTH PARENTS ARE EDUCATORS!
DO YOU REALIZE IT'S DAD AND MOM WHO HAVE TO DEAL WITH OTHER PEOPLE'S DISAPPROVING LOOKS AND REMARKS?
...

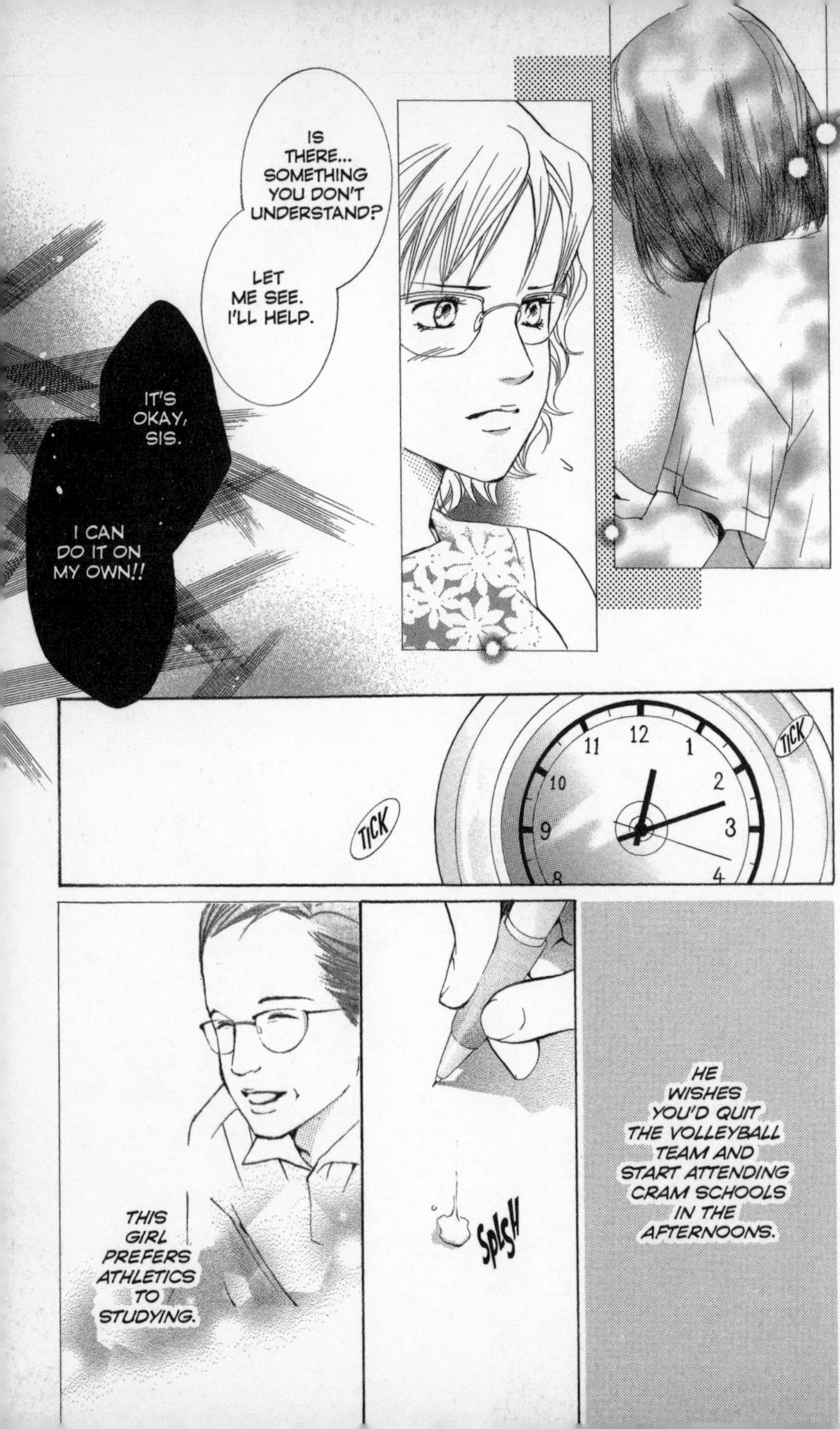
IS THERE... SOMETHING YOU DON'T UNDERSTAND?
LET ME SEE. I'LL HELP.
IT'S OKAY, SIS.
I CAN DO IT ON MY OWN!!
TICK
TICK
12
1
2
3
4
8
9
10
11
HE WISHES YOU'D QUIT THE VOLLEYBALL TEAM AND START ATTENDING CRAM SCHOOLS IN THE AFTERNOONS.
SPLSH
THIS GIRL PREFERS ATHLETICS TO STUDYING.

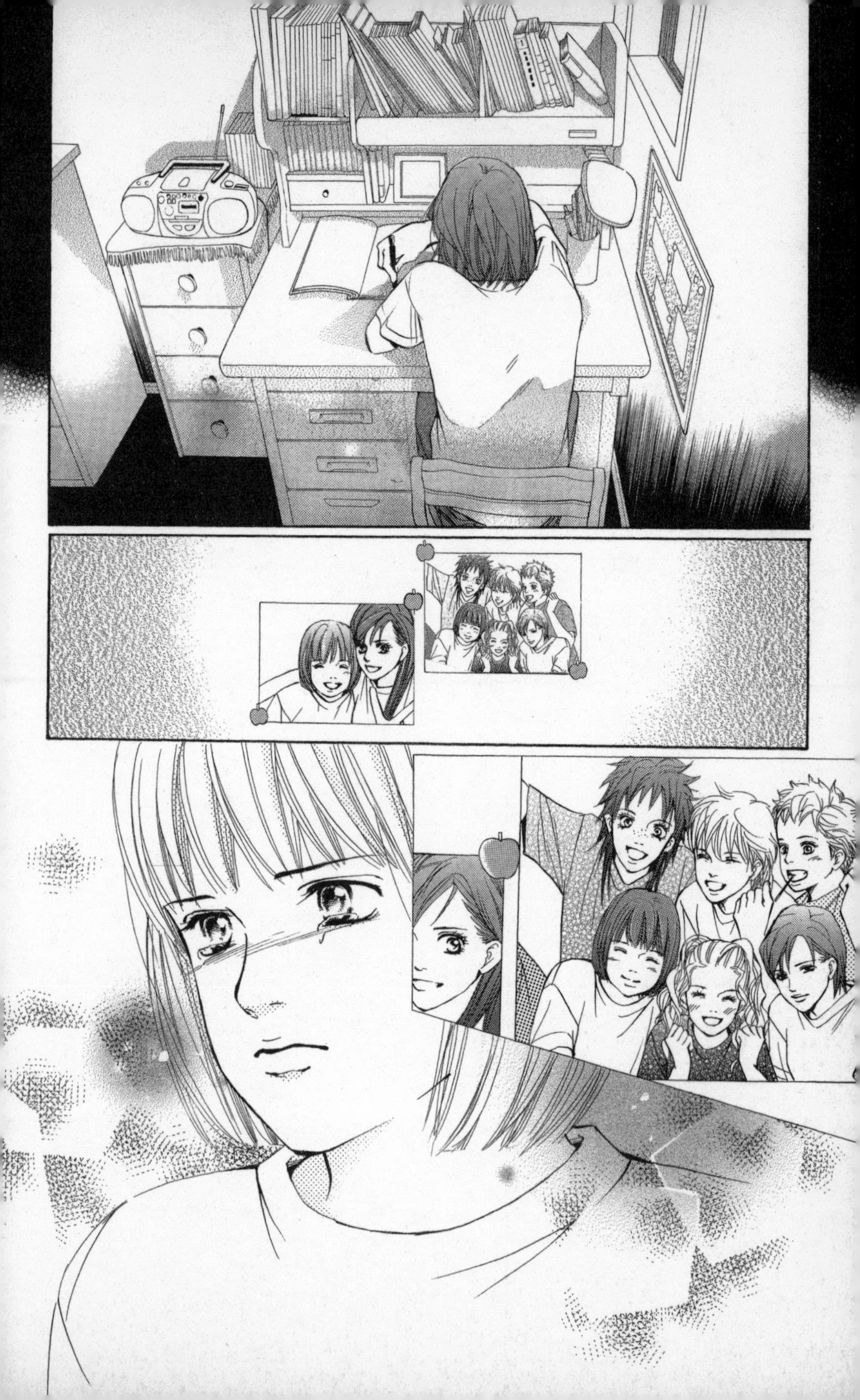

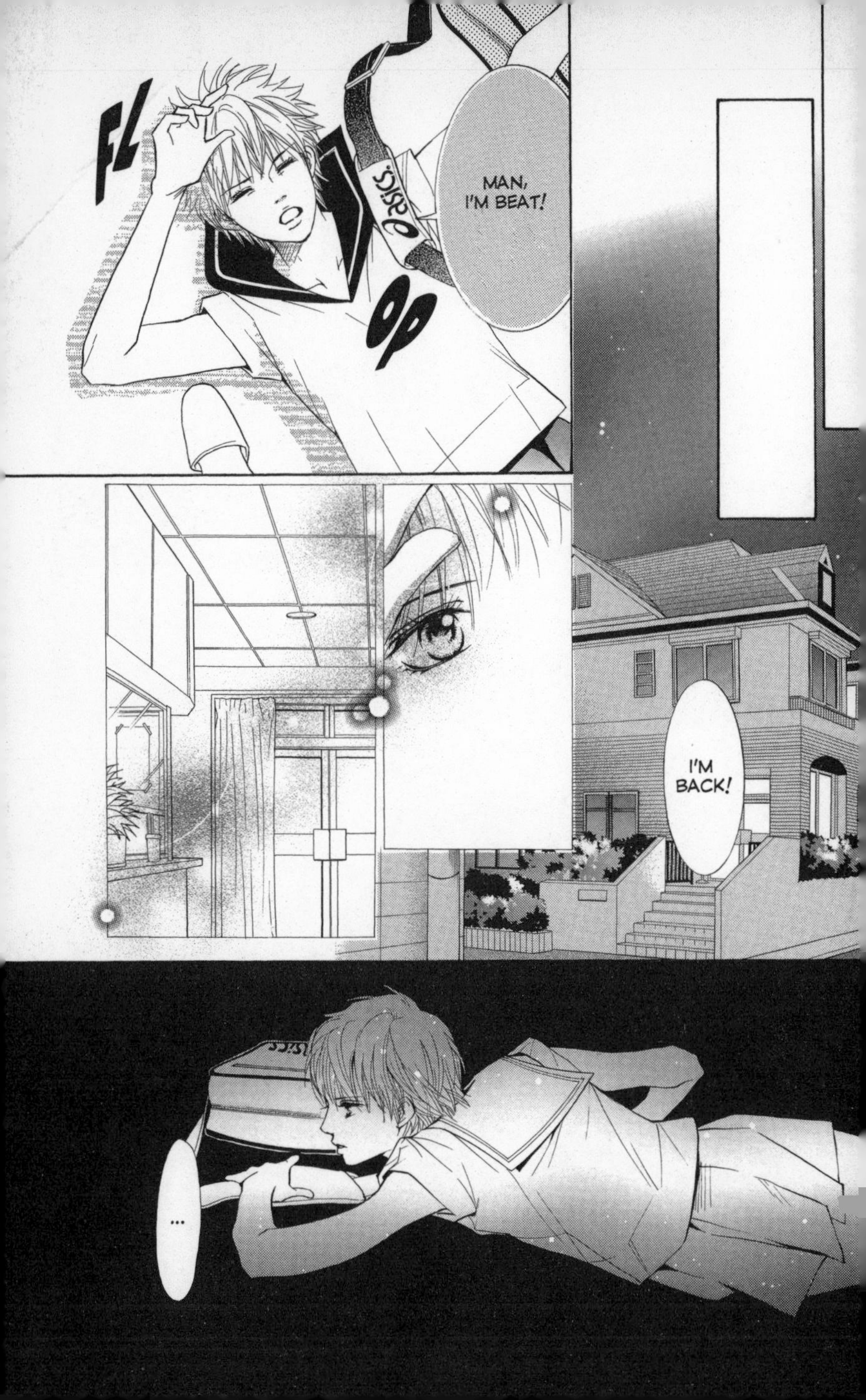
MAN, I'M BEAT!
I'M BACK!
...

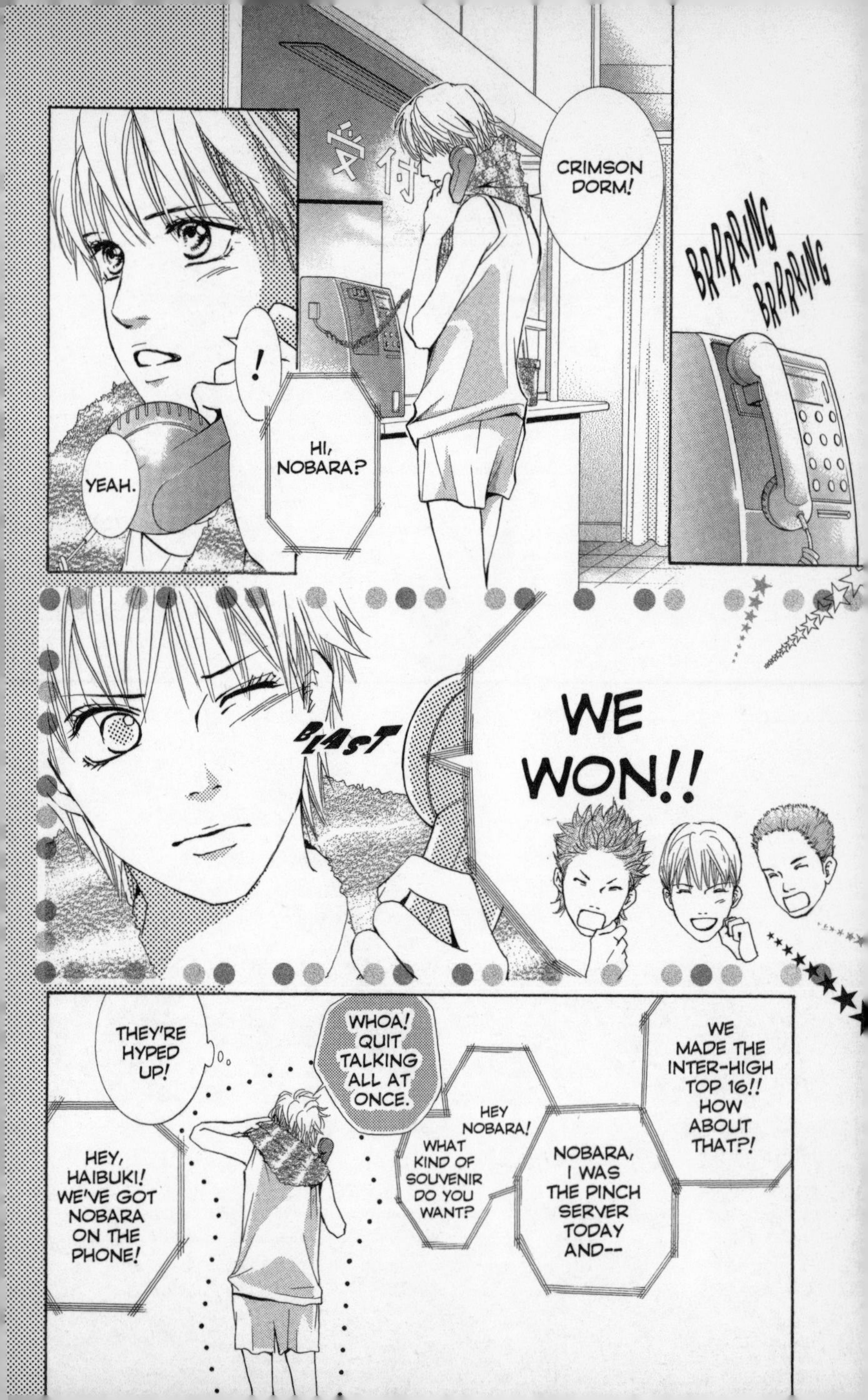
BRRRING BRRRING
受付
CRIMSON DORM!
HI, NOBARA?
!
YEAH.
WE WON!!
BLAST
WE MADE THE INTER-HIGH TOP 16!! HOW ABOUT THAT?!
NOBARA, I WAS THE PINCH SERVER TODAY AND--
HEY NOBARA! WHAT KIND OF SOUVENIR DO YOU WANT?
WHOA! QUIT TALKING ALL AT ONCE.
THEY'RE HYPED UP!
HEY, HAIBUKI! WE'VE GOT NOBARA ON THE PHONE!

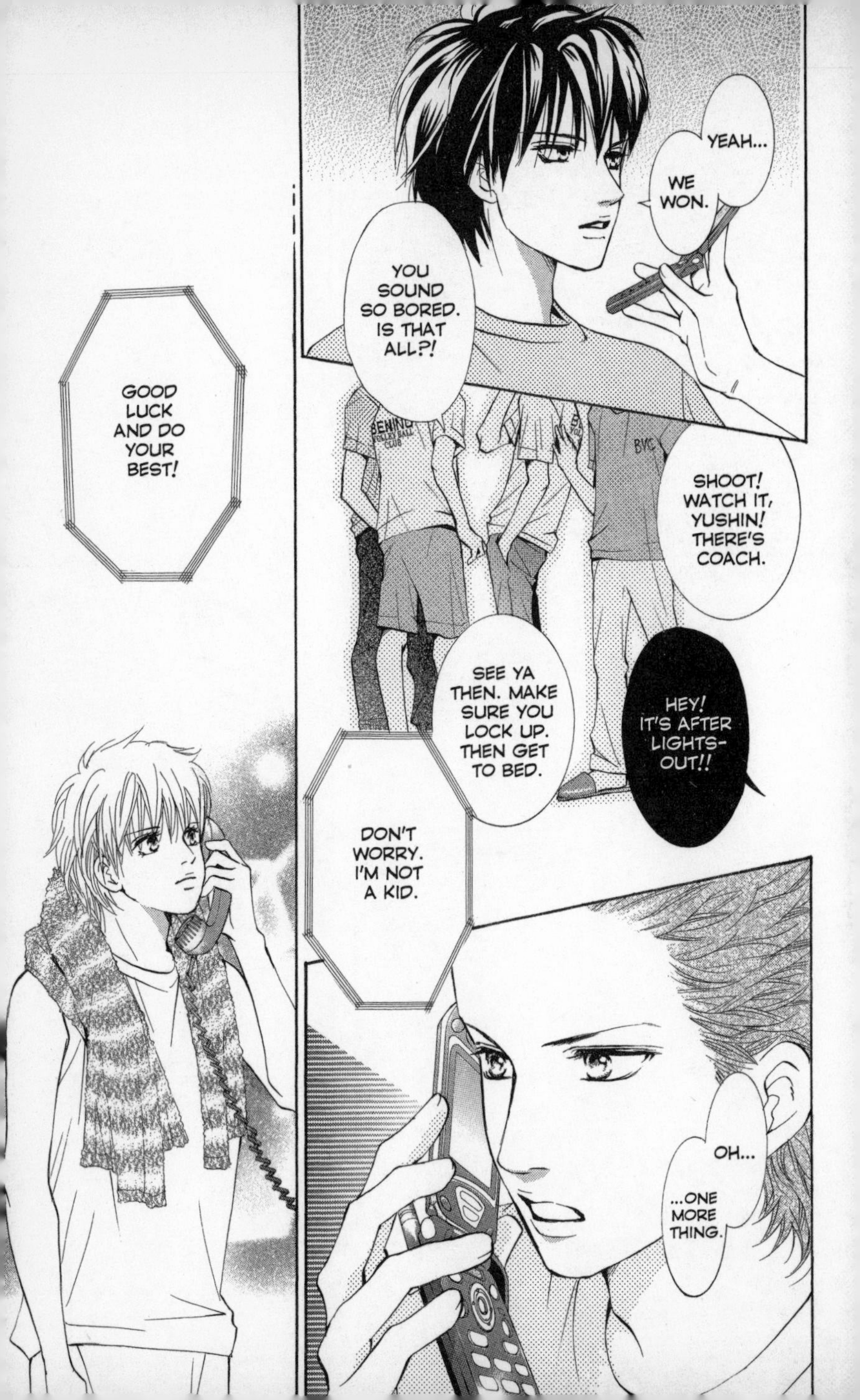
YEAH...
WE WON.
YOU SOUND SO BORED. IS THAT ALL?!
SHOOT! WATCH IT, YUSHIN! THERE'S COACH.
HEY! IT'S AFTER LIGHTS-OUT!!
SEE YA THEN. MAKE SURE YOU LOCK UP. THEN GET TO BED.
DON'T WORRY. I'M NOT A KID.
OH...
...ONE MORE THING.
GOOD LUCK AND DO YOUR BEST!

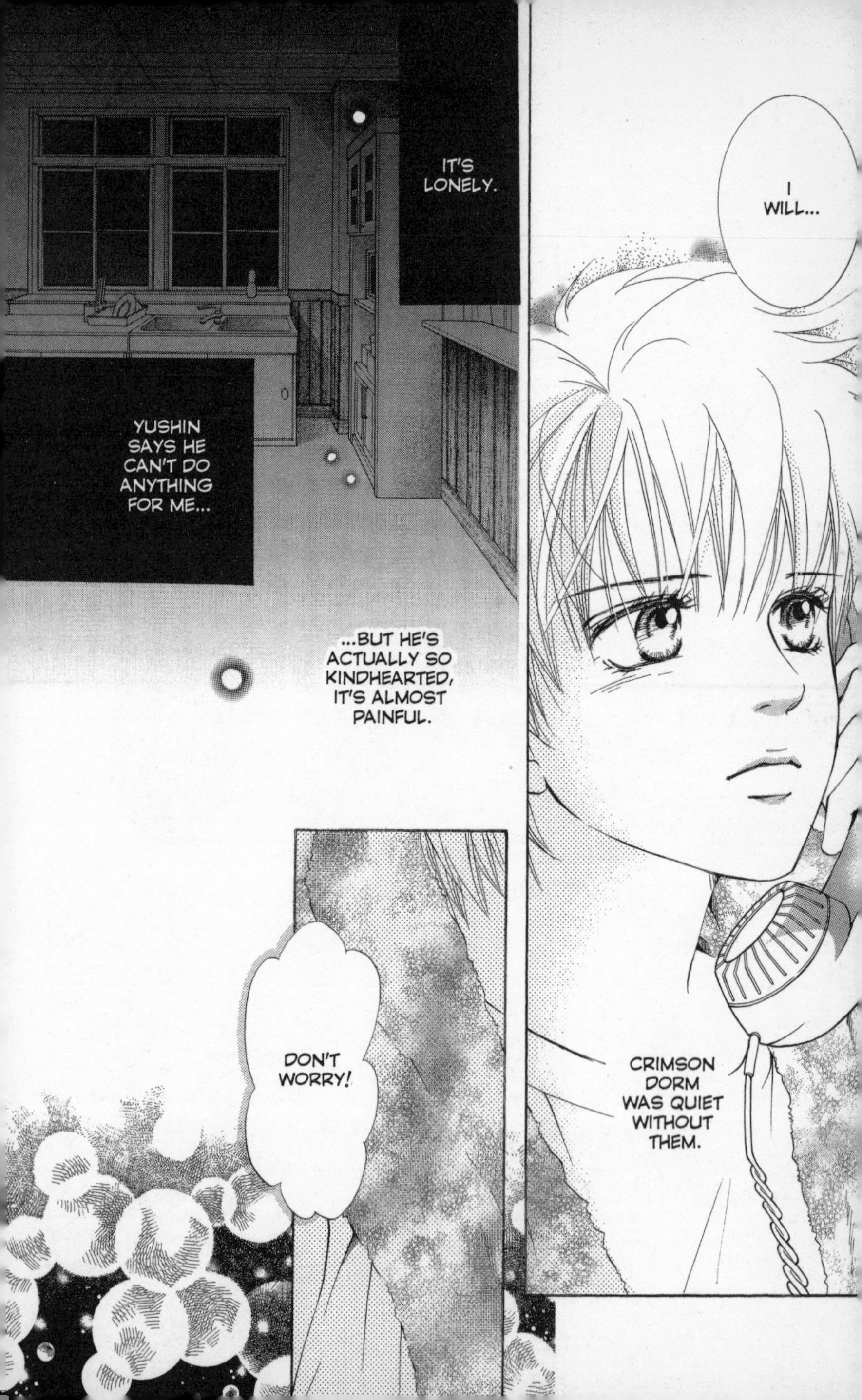
I WILL...
CRIMSON DORM WAS QUIET WITHOUT THEM.
IT'S LONELY.
YUSHIN SAYS HE CAN'T DO ANYTHING FOR ME...
...BUT HE'S ACTUALLY SO KINDHEARTED, IT'S ALMOST PAINFUL.
DON'T WORRY!

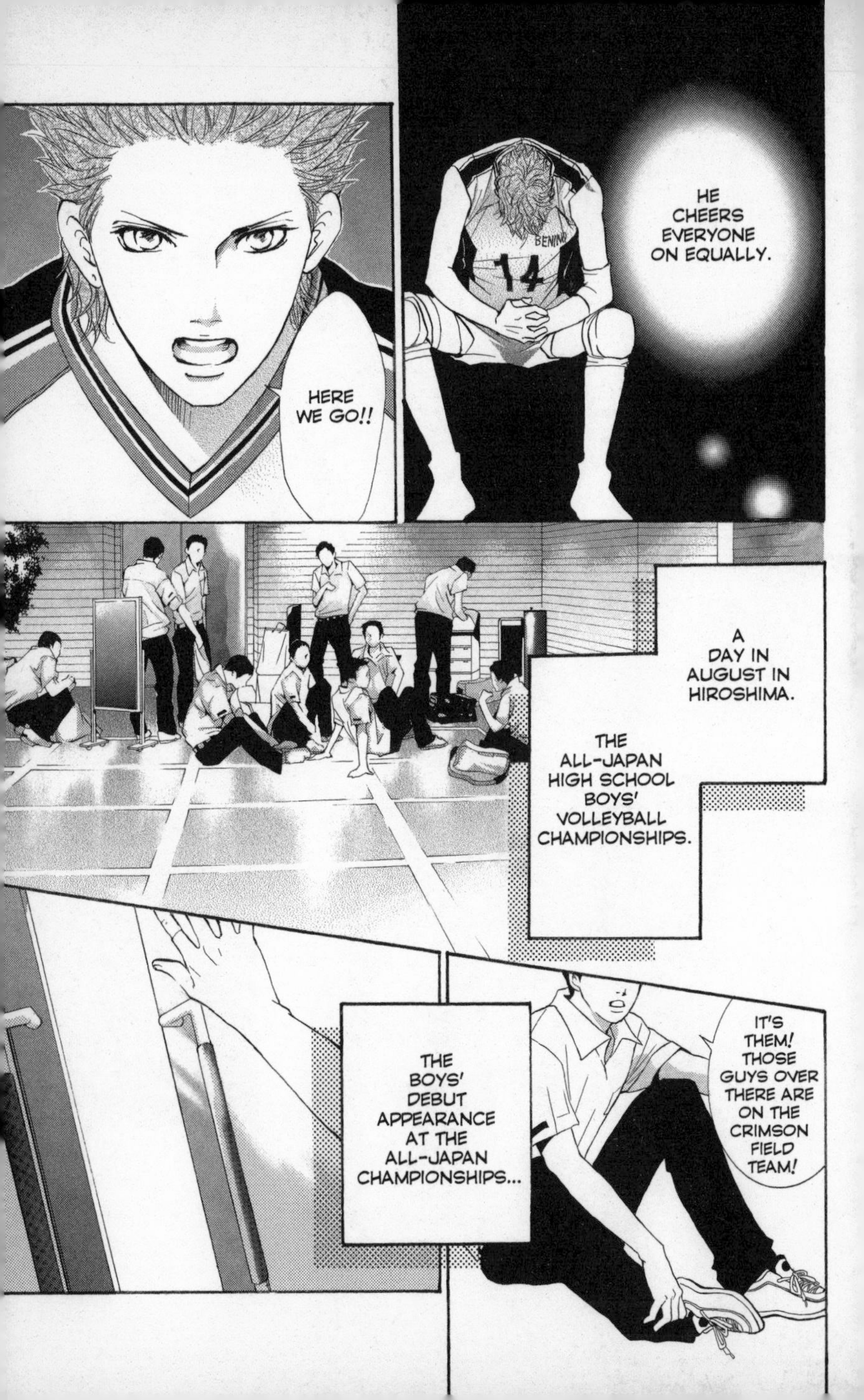
HE CHEERS EVERYONE ON EQUALLY.
HERE WE GO!!
A DAY IN AUGUST IN HIROSHIMA.
THE ALL-JAPAN HIGH SCHOOL BOYS' VOLLEYBALL CHAMPIONSHIPS.
IT'S THEM! THOSE GUYS OVER THERE ARE ON THE CRIMSON FIELD TEAM!
THE BOYS' DEBUT APPEARANCE AT THE ALL-JAPAN CHAMPIONSHIPS...

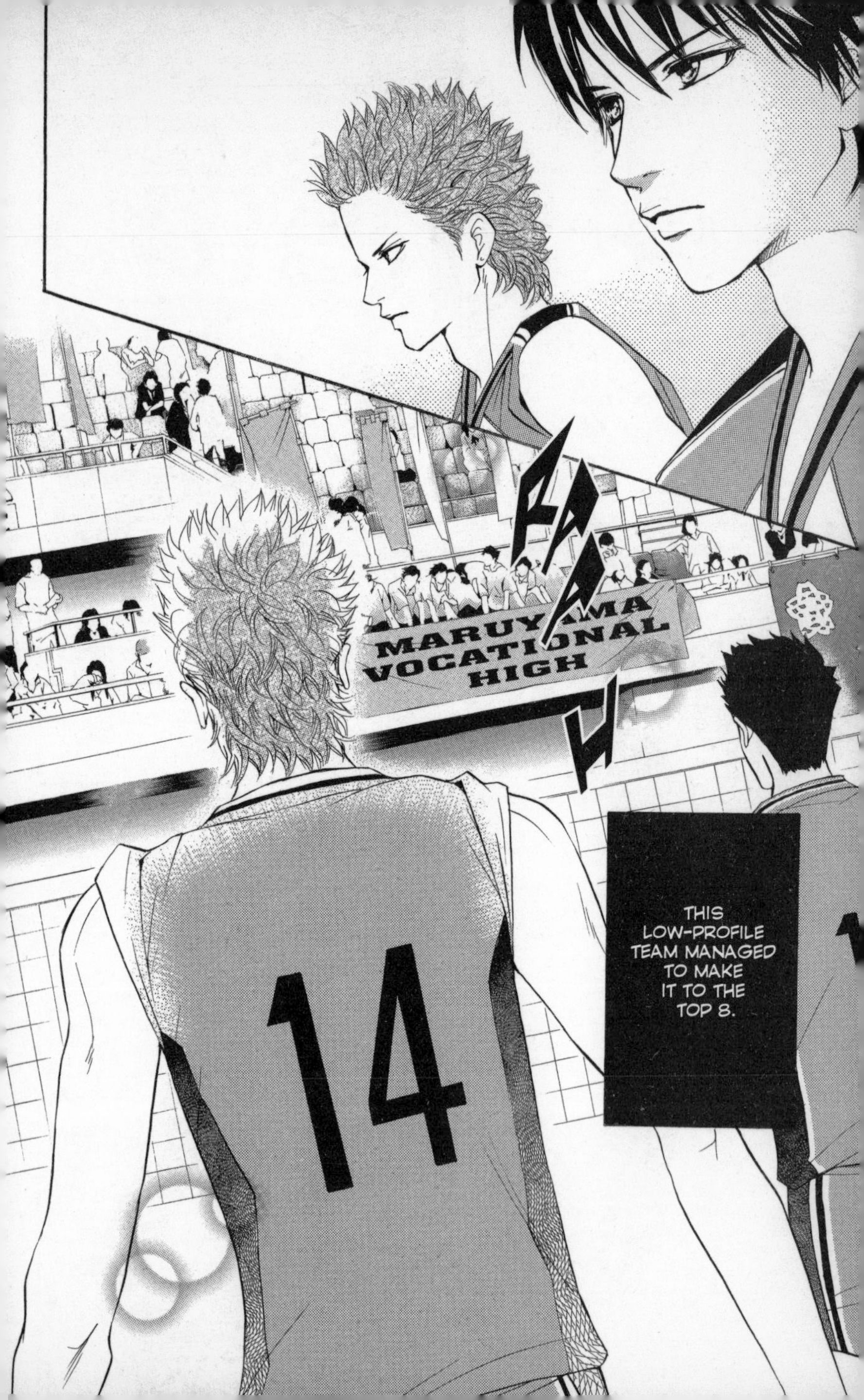
MARUYAMA VOCATIONAL HIGH
THIS LOW-PROFILE TEAM MANAGED TO MAKE IT TO THE TOP 8.

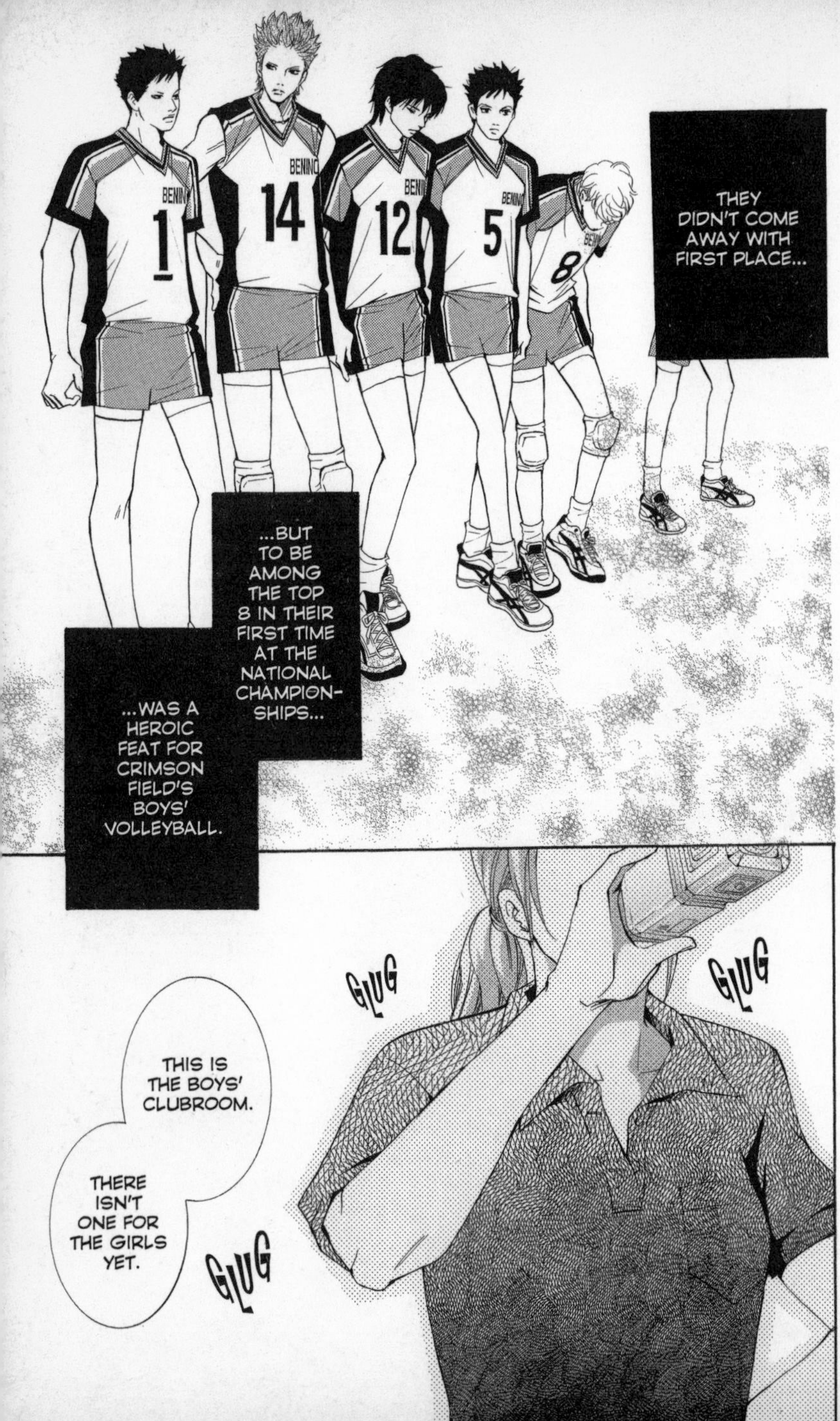

THEY DIDN'T COME AWAY WITH FIRST PLACE...
...BUT TO BE AMONG THE TOP 8 IN THEIR FIRST TIME AT THE NATIONAL CHAMPION-SHIPS...
...WAS A HEROIC FEAT FOR CRIMSON FIELD'S BOYS' VOLLEYBALL.
GLUG
GLUG
THIS IS THE BOYS' CLUBROOM.
THERE ISN'T ONE FOR THE GIRLS YET.
GLUG

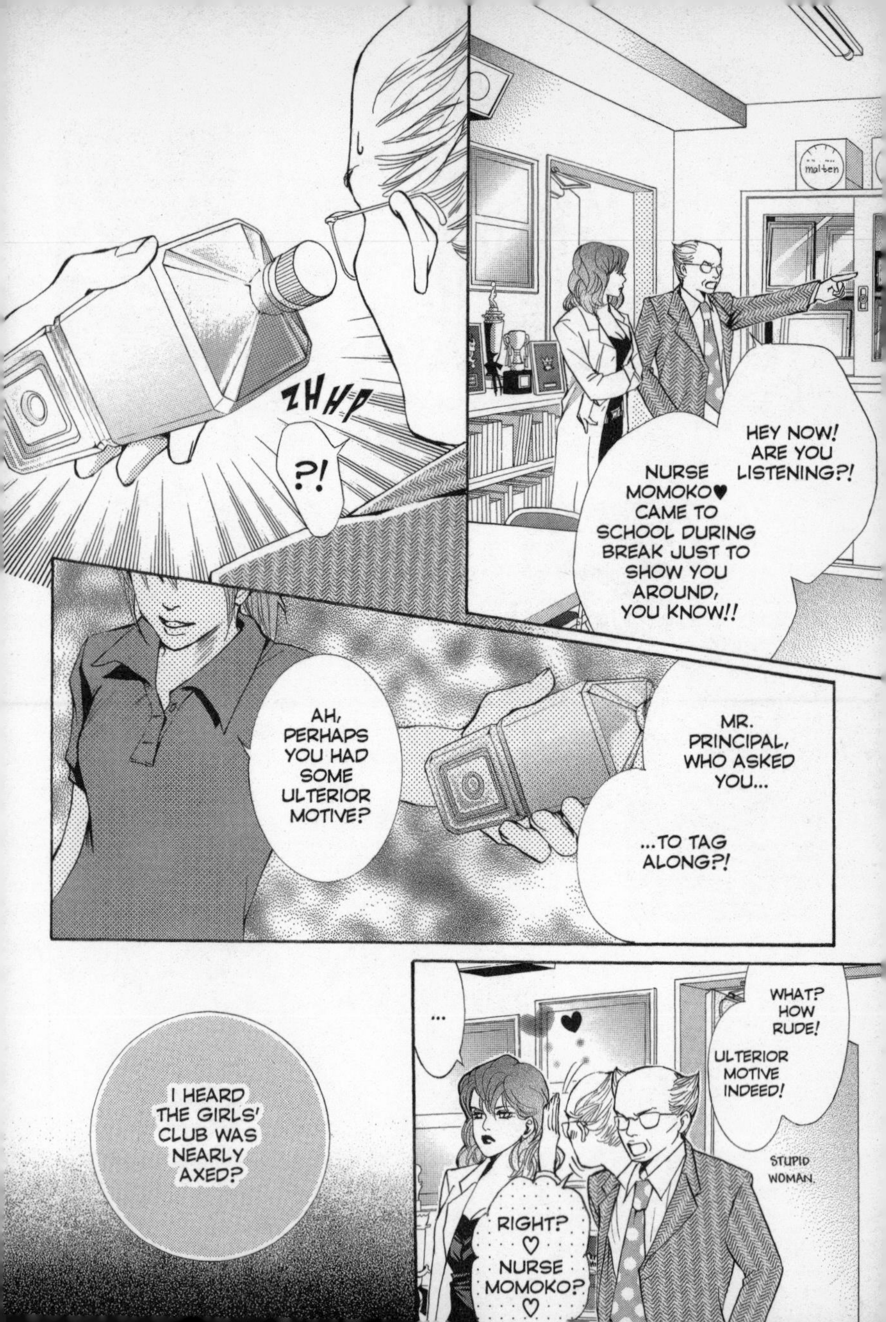
HEY NOW! ARE YOU LISTENING?!
NURSE MOMOKO♥ CAME TO SCHOOL DURING BREAK JUST TO SHOW YOU AROUND, YOU KNOW!!
ZHHP
?!
MR. PRINCIPAL, WHO ASKED YOU...
...TO TAG ALONG?!
AH, PERHAPS YOU HAD SOME ULTERIOR MOTIVE?
WHAT? HOW RUDE!
...
ULTERIOR MOTIVE INDEED!
STUPID WOMAN.
RIGHT? ♡ NURSE MOMOKO? ♡
I HEARD THE GIRLS' CLUB WAS NEARLY AXED?

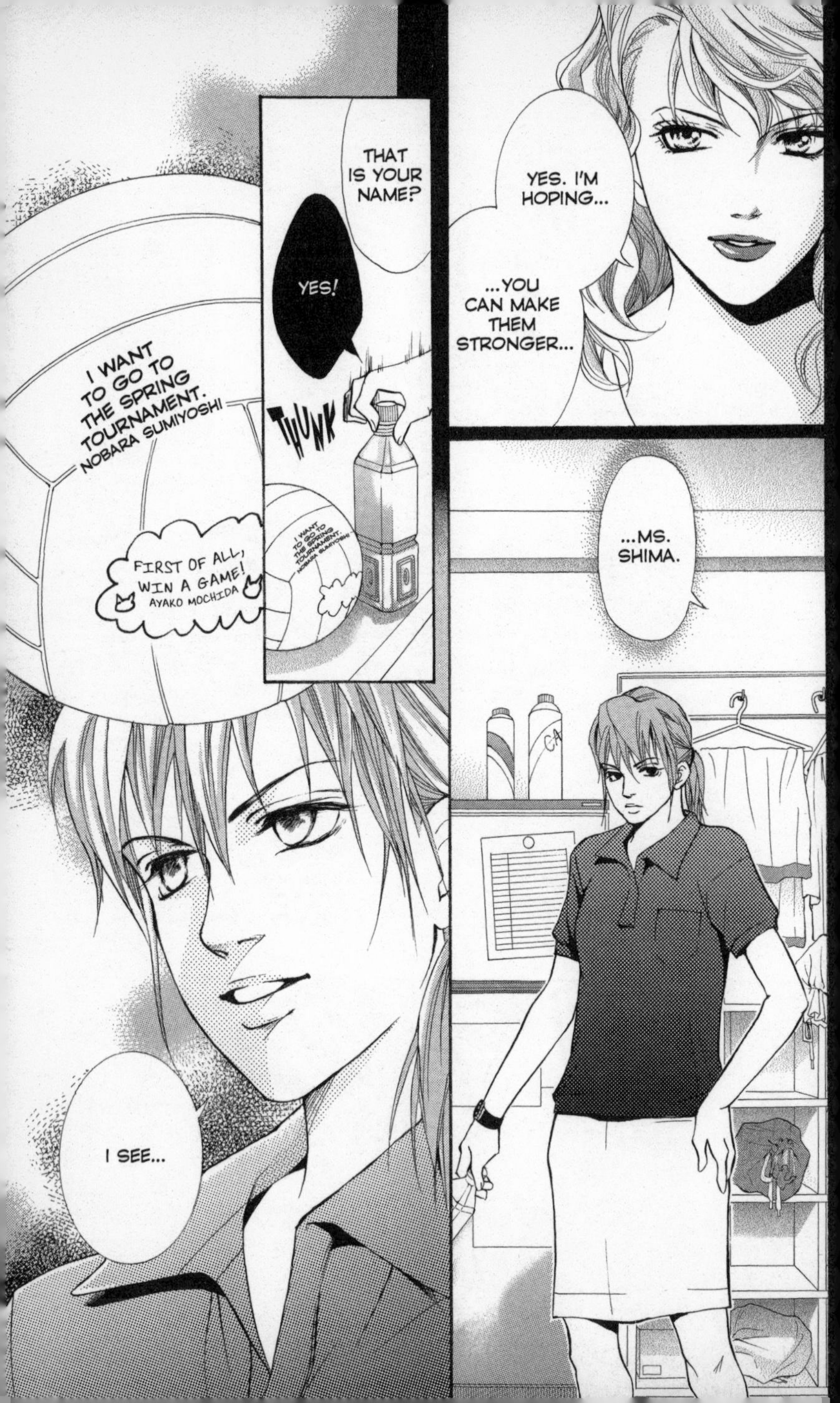
YES. I'M HOPING...
...YOU CAN MAKE THEM STRONGER...
...MS. SHIMA.
THAT IS YOUR NAME?
YES!
THUNK
I WANT TO GO TO THE SPRING TOURNAMENT. NOBARA SUMIYOSHI
FIRST OF ALL, WIN A GAME! AYAKO MOCHIDA
I SEE...

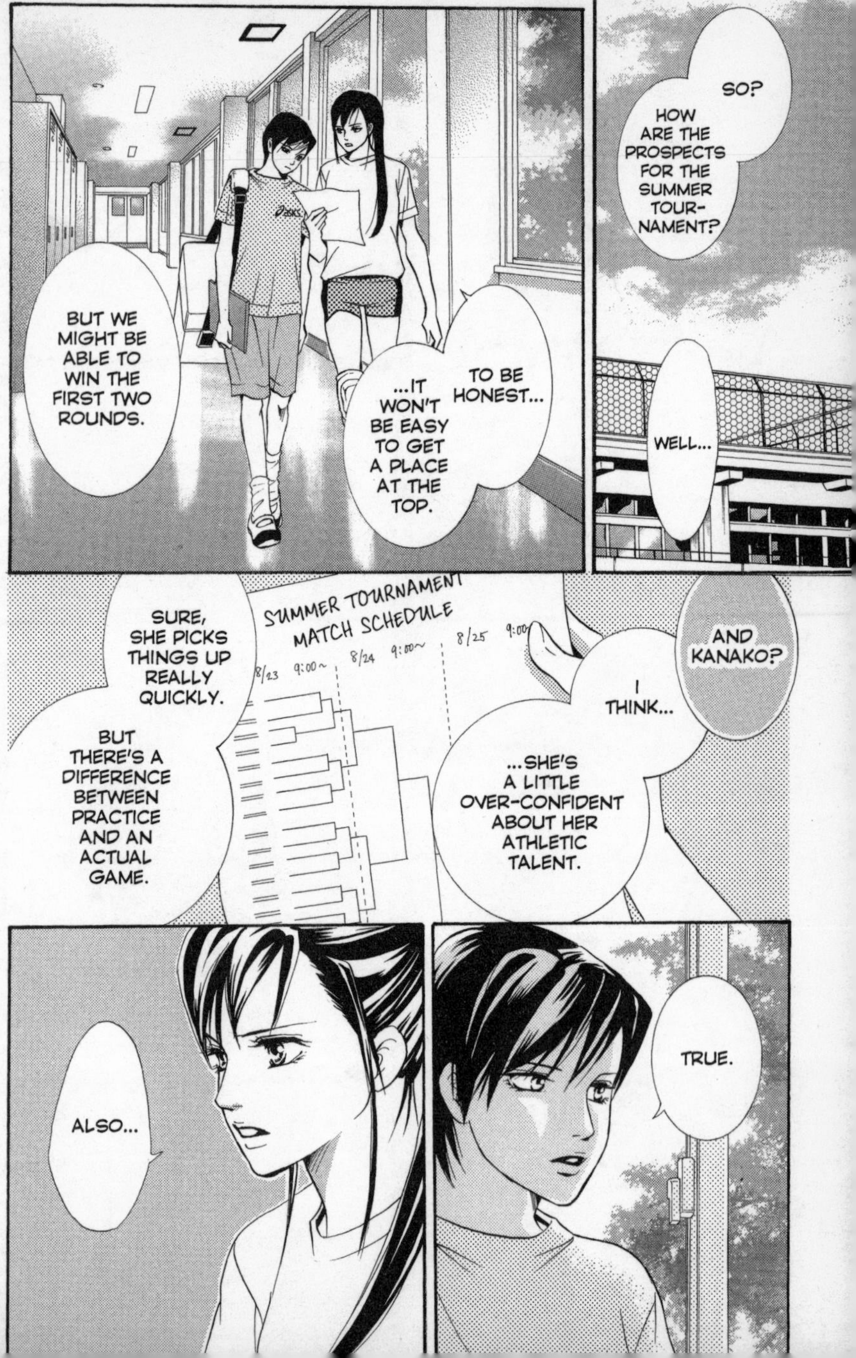
SO?
HOW ARE THE PROSPECTS FOR THE SUMMER TOUR-NAMENT?
WELL...
TO BE HONEST...
...IT WON'T BE EASY TO GET A PLACE AT THE TOP.
BUT WE MIGHT BE ABLE TO WIN THE FIRST TWO ROUNDS.
AND KANAKO?
I THINK...
...SHE'S A LITTLE OVER-CONFIDENT ABOUT HER ATHLETIC TALENT.
SUMMER TOURNAMENT MATCH SCHEDULE
8/23 9:00~
8/24 9:00~
8/25 9:00
SURE, SHE PICKS THINGS UP REALLY QUICKLY.
BUT THERE'S A DIFFERENCE BETWEEN PRACTICE AND AN ACTUAL GAME.
TRUE.
ALSO...

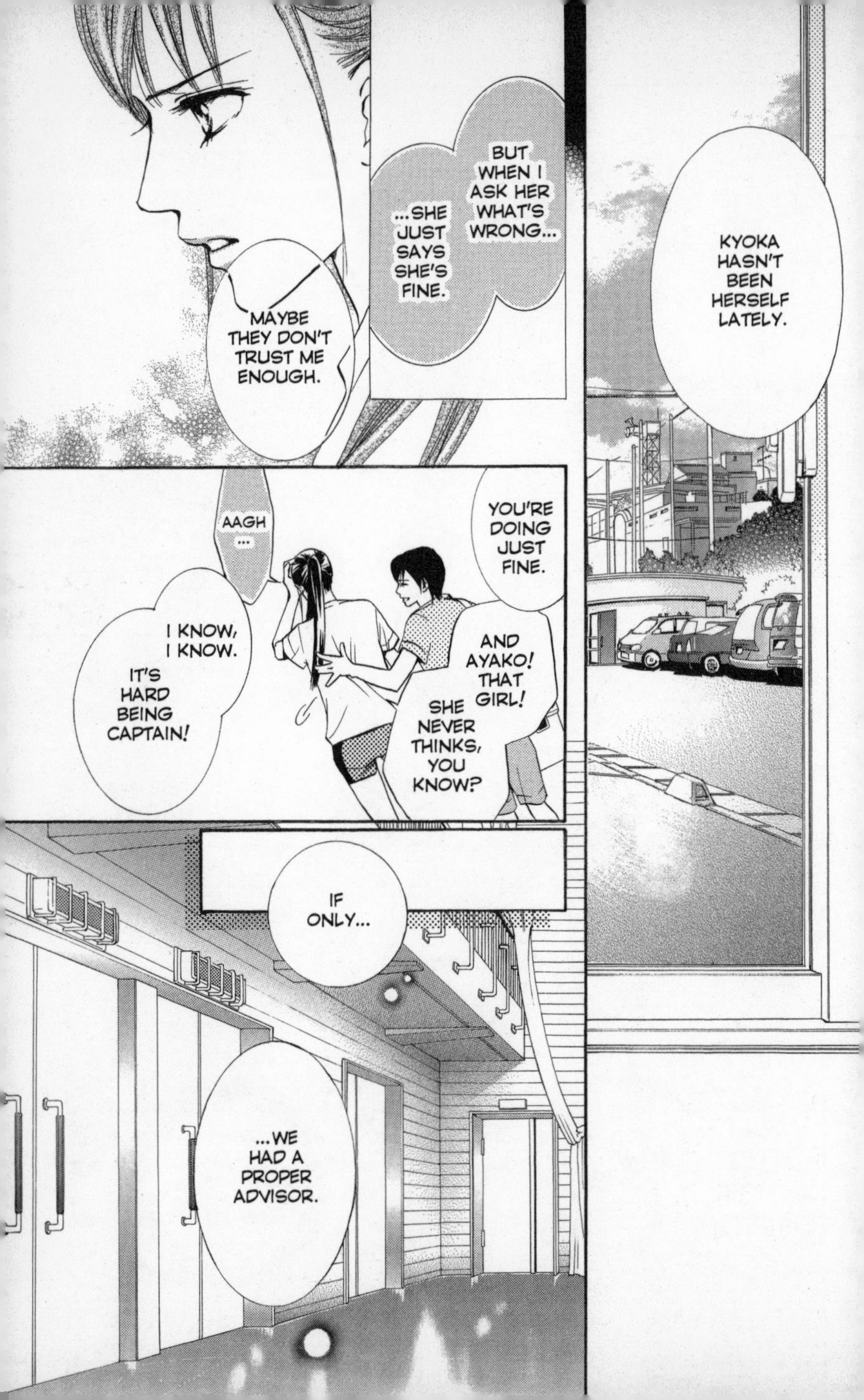
KYOKA HASN'T BEEN HERSELF LATELY.
BUT WHEN I ASK HER WHAT'S WRONG...
...SHE JUST SAYS SHE'S FINE.
MAYBE THEY DON'T TRUST ME ENOUGH.
YOU'RE DOING JUST FINE.
AND AYAKO! THAT GIRL!
SHE NEVER THINKS, YOU KNOW?
AAGH ...
I KNOW, I KNOW.
IT'S HARD BEING CAPTAIN!
IF ONLY...
...WE HAD A PROPER ADVISOR.

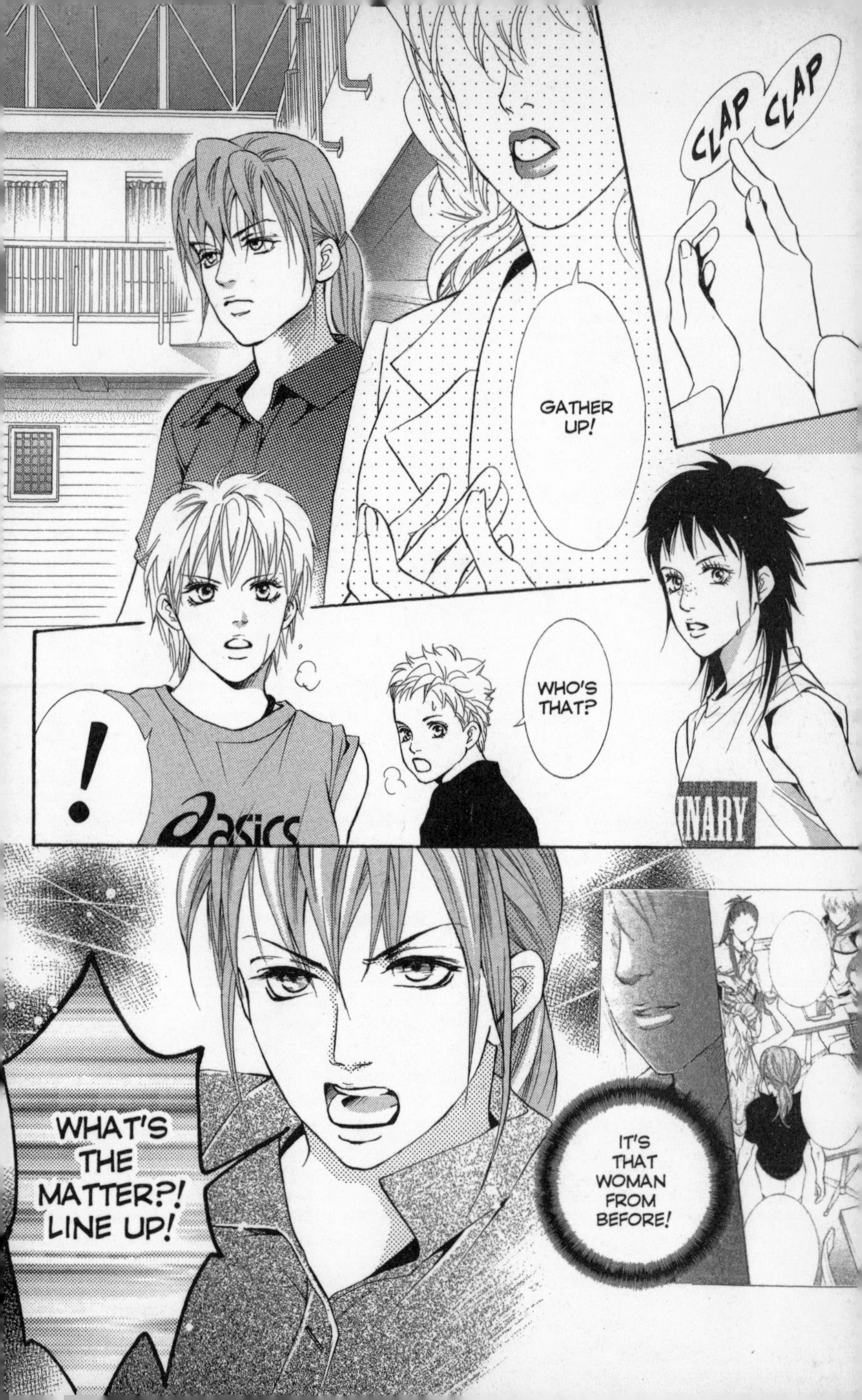
CLAP CLAP
GATHER UP!
WHO'S THAT?
!
asics
INARY
IT'S THAT WOMAN FROM BEFORE!
WHAT'S THE MATTER?! LINE UP!

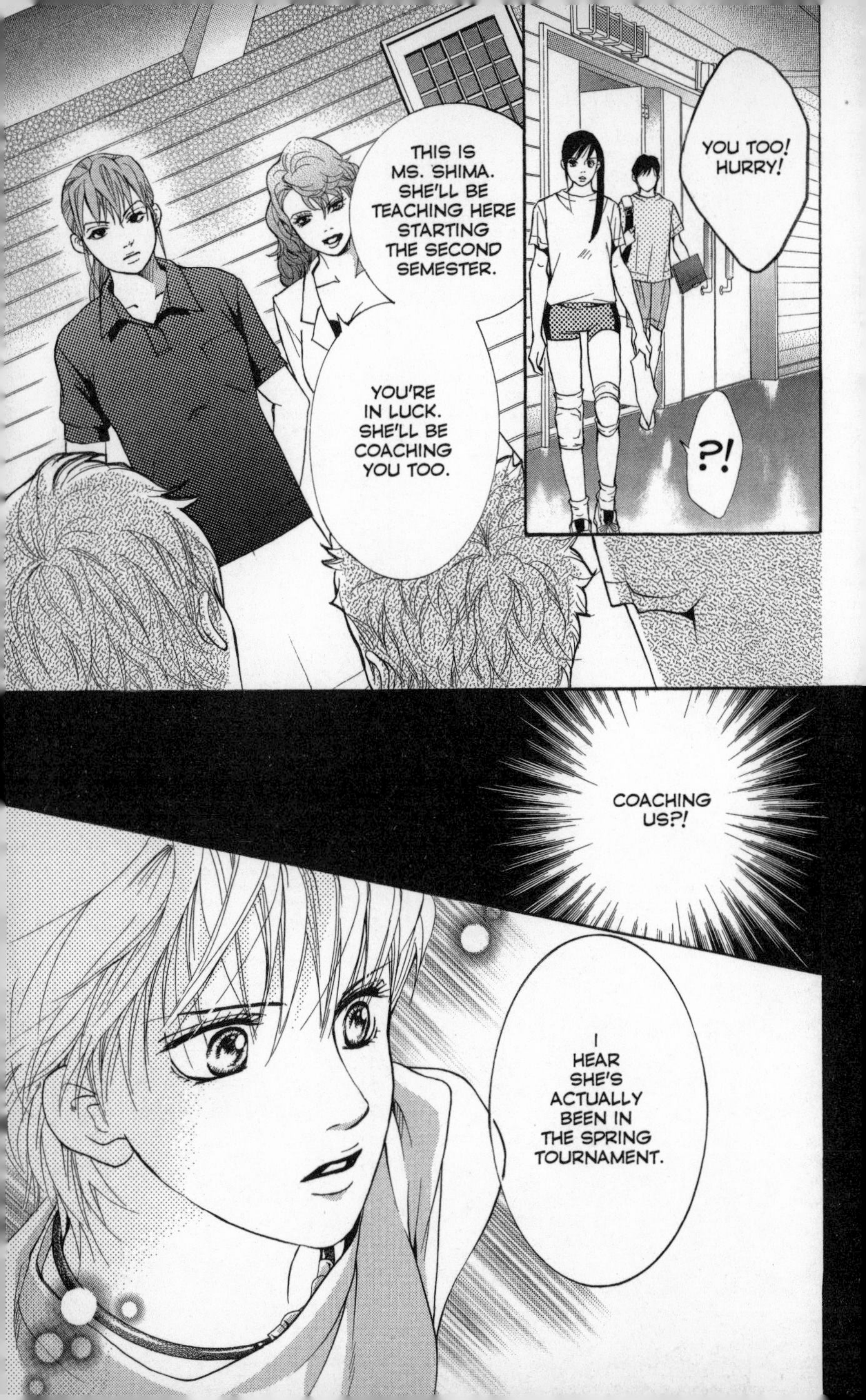
YOU TOO! HURRY!
?!
THIS IS MS. SHIMA. SHE'LL BE TEACHING HERE STARTING THE SECOND SEMESTER.
YOU'RE IN LUCK. SHE'LL BE COACHING YOU TOO.
COACHING US?!
I HEAR SHE'S ACTUALLY BEEN IN THE SPRING TOURNAMENT.

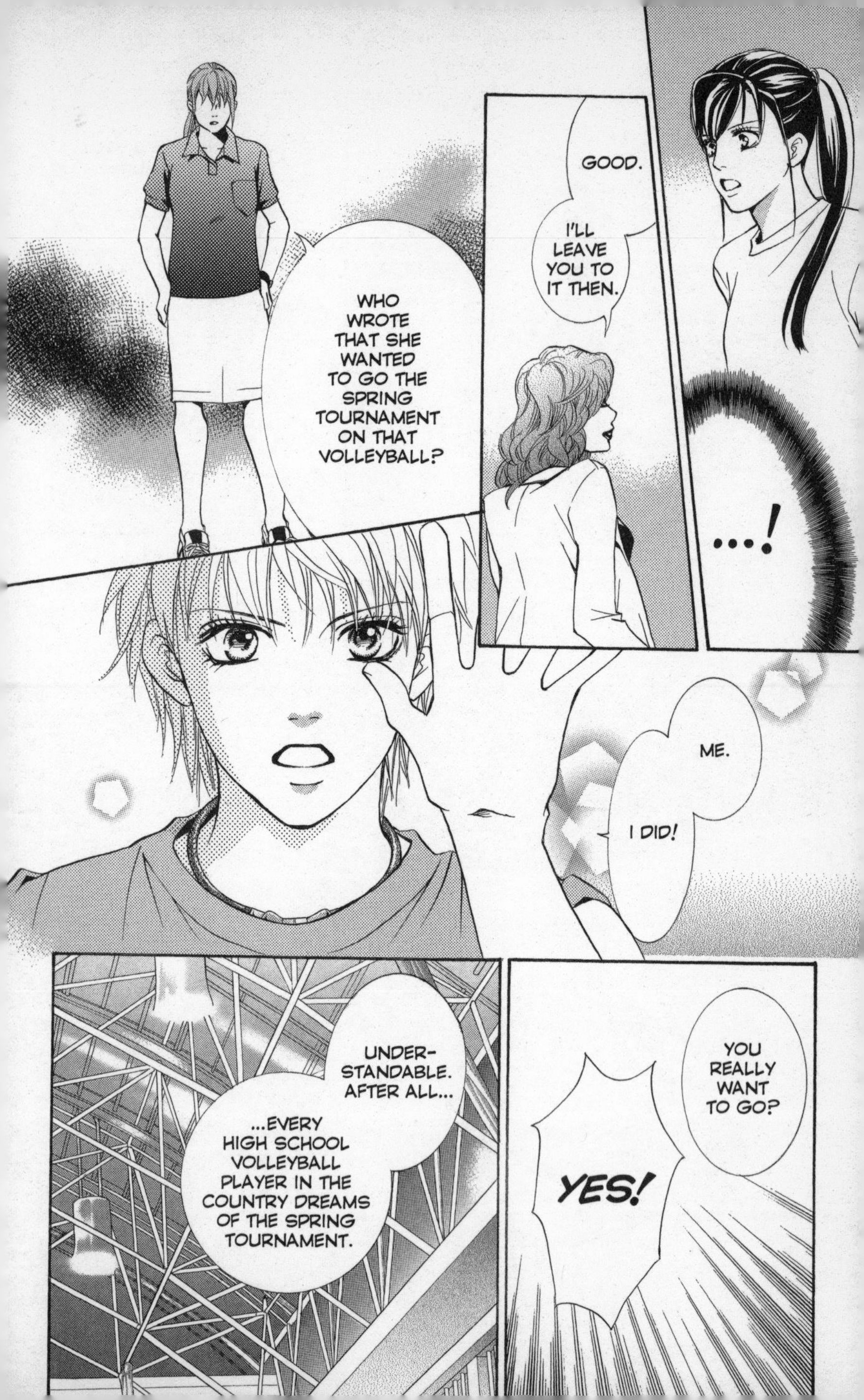

...!
GOOD.
I'LL LEAVE YOU TO IT THEN.
WHO WROTE THAT SHE WANTED TO GO THE SPRING TOURNAMENT ON THAT VOLLEYBALL?
ME.
I DID!
YOU REALLY WANT TO GO?
YES!
UNDER-STANDABLE. AFTER ALL...
...EVERY HIGH SCHOOL VOLLEYBALL PLAYER IN THE COUNTRY DREAMS OF THE SPRING TOURNAMENT.

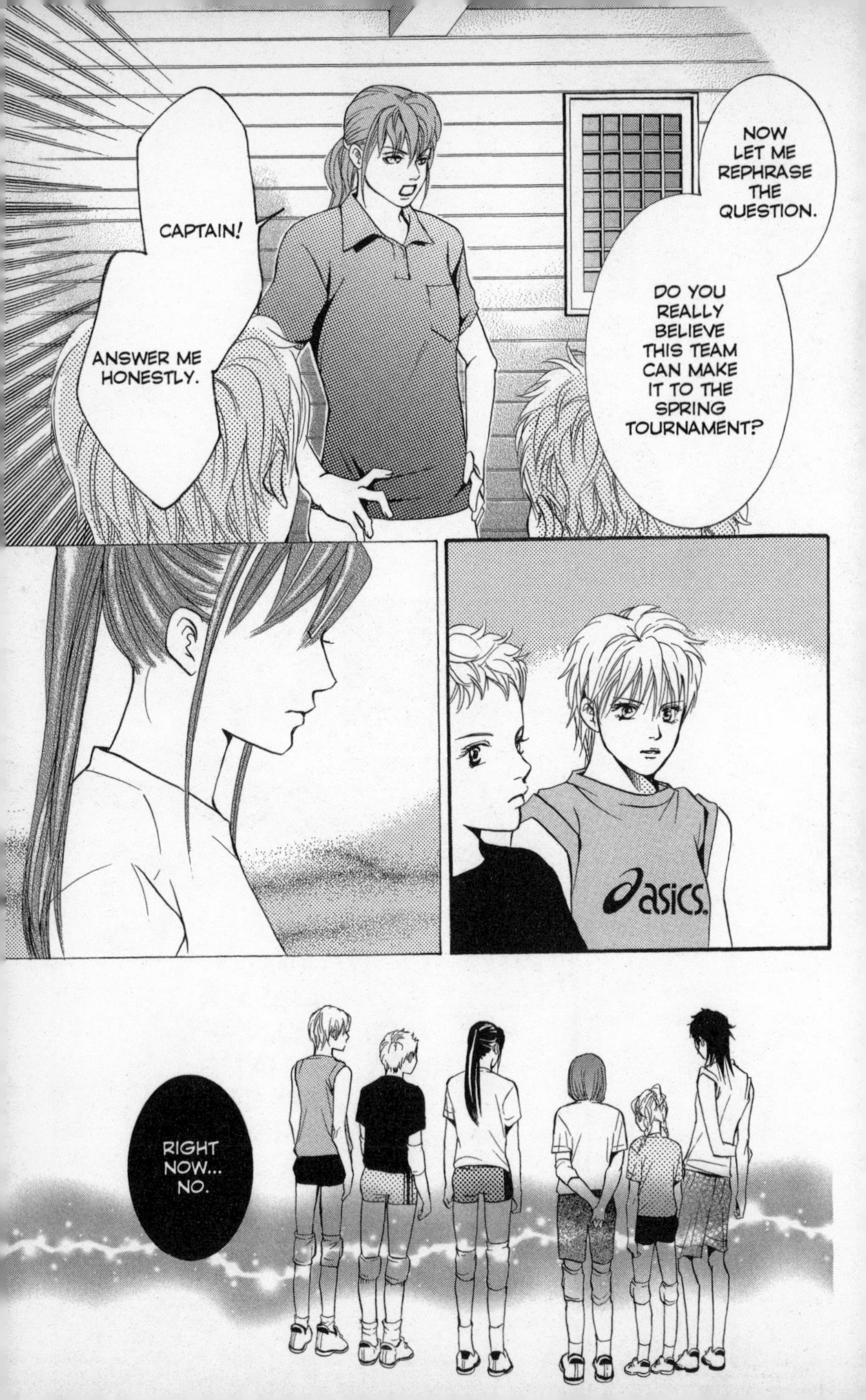
NOW LET ME REPHRASE THE QUESTION.
DO YOU REALLY BELIEVE THIS TEAM CAN MAKE IT TO THE SPRING TOURNAMENT?
CAPTAIN!
ANSWER ME HONESTLY.
asics
RIGHT NOW... NO.

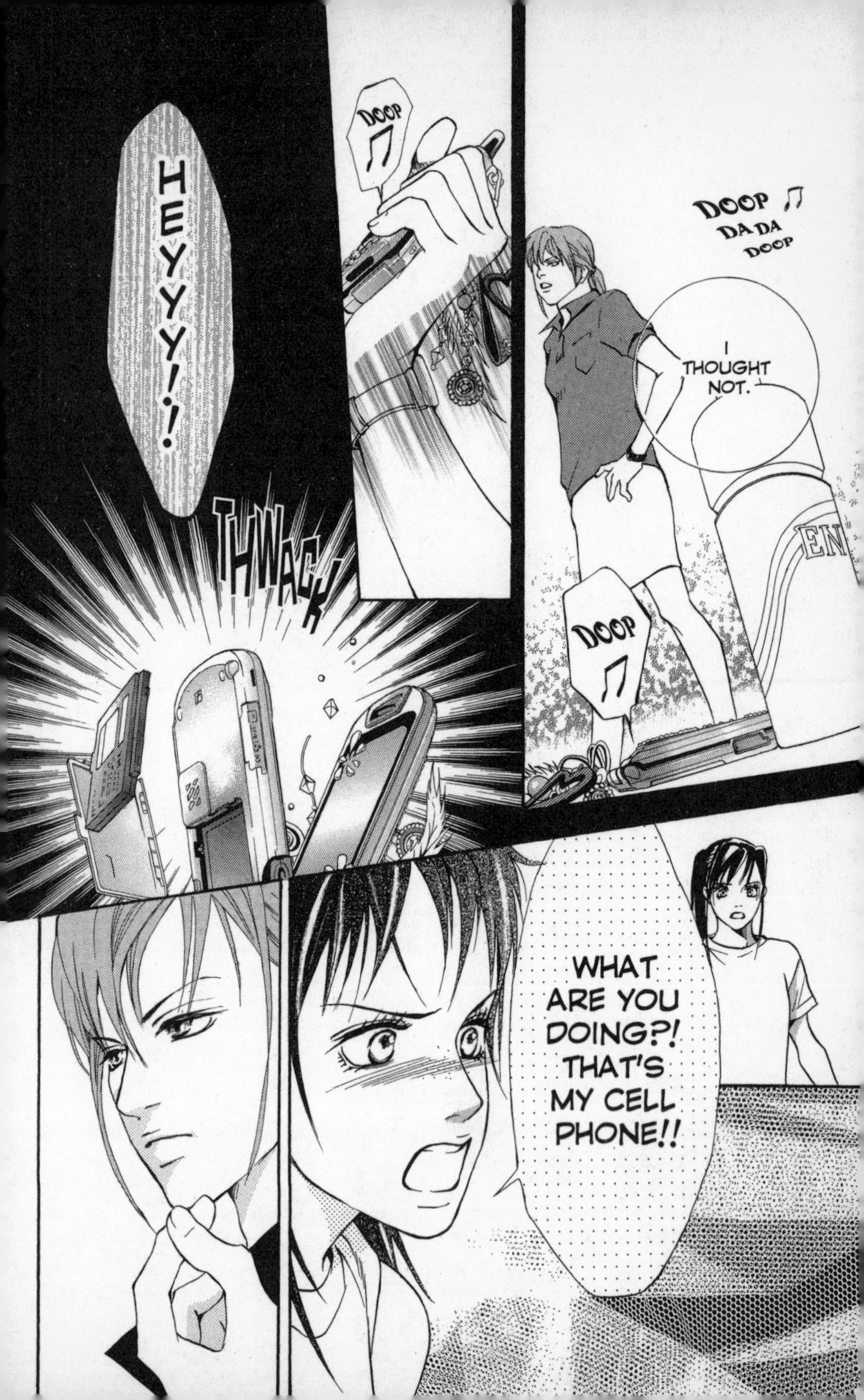
DOOP ♫ DA DA DOOP
I THOUGHT NOT.
DOOP ♫
DOOP ♫
HEYYY!!
THWACK!
WHAT ARE YOU DOING?! THAT'S MY CELL PHONE!!

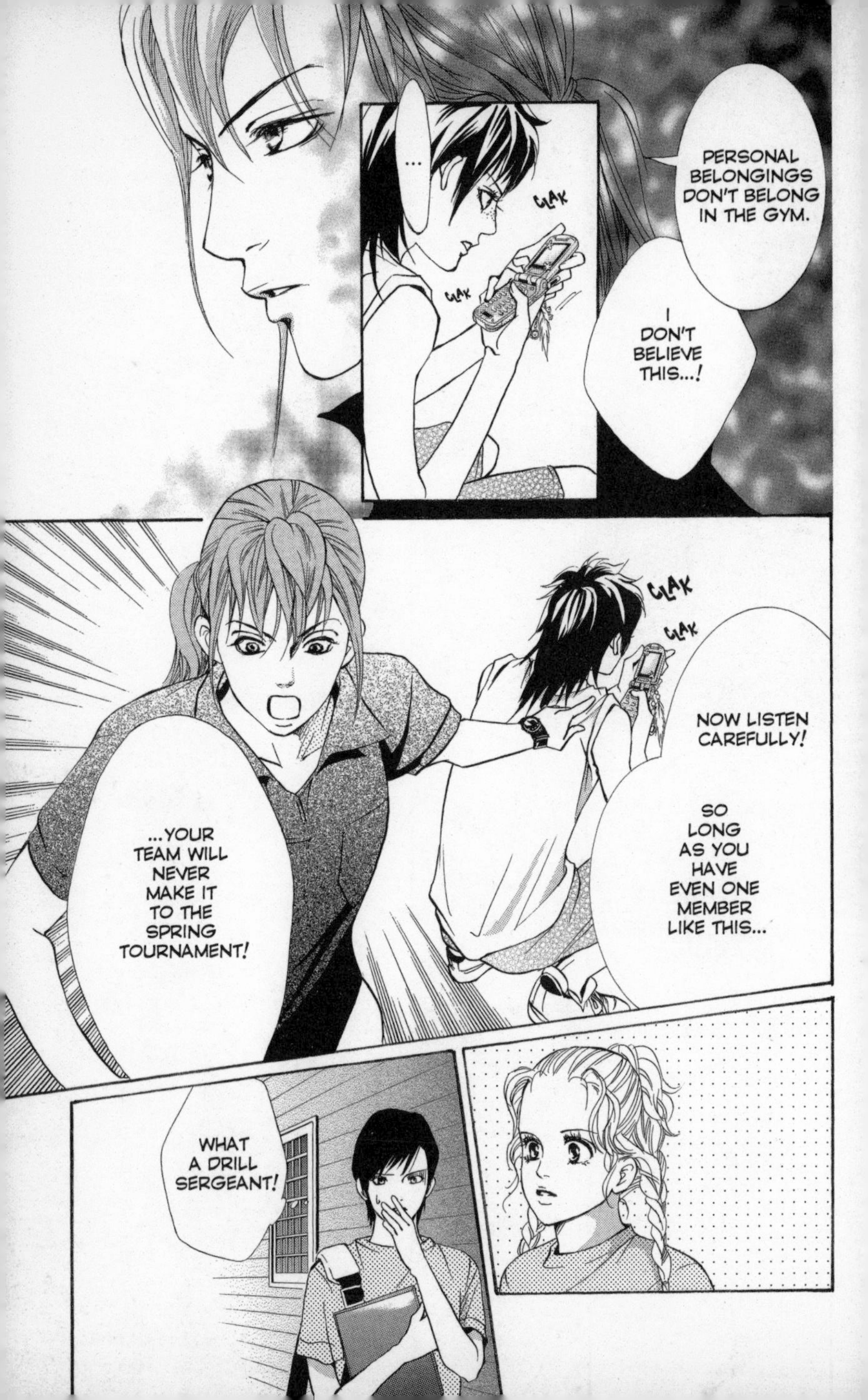
PERSONAL BELONGINGS DON'T BELONG IN THE GYM.
I DON'T BELIEVE THIS...!
CLAK
CLAK
...
CLAK
CLAK
NOW LISTEN CAREFULLY!
SO LONG AS YOU HAVE EVEN ONE MEMBER LIKE THIS...
...YOUR TEAM WILL NEVER MAKE IT TO THE SPRING TOURNAMENT!
WHAT A DRILL SERGEANT!

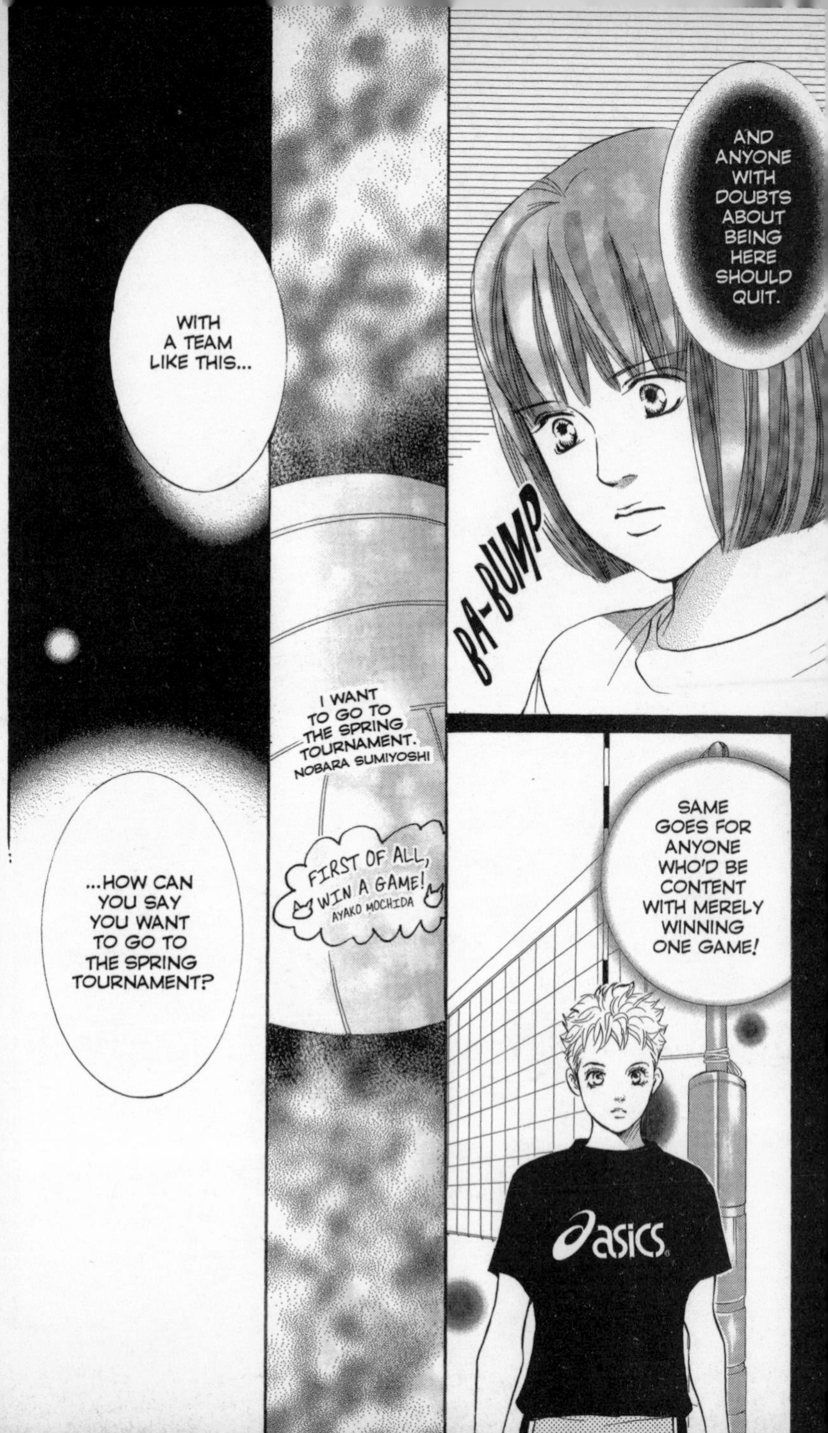
AND ANYONE WITH DOUBTS ABOUT BEING HERE SHOULD QUIT.
BA-BUMP
SAME GOES FOR ANYONE WHO'D BE CONTENT WITH MERELY WINNING ONE GAME!
asics
I WANT TO GO TO THE SPRING TOURNAMENT.
NOBARA SUMIYOSHI
FIRST OF ALL, WIN A GAME!
AYAKO MOCHIDA
WITH A TEAM LIKE THIS...
...HOW CAN YOU SAY YOU WANT TO GO TO THE SPRING TOURNAMENT?

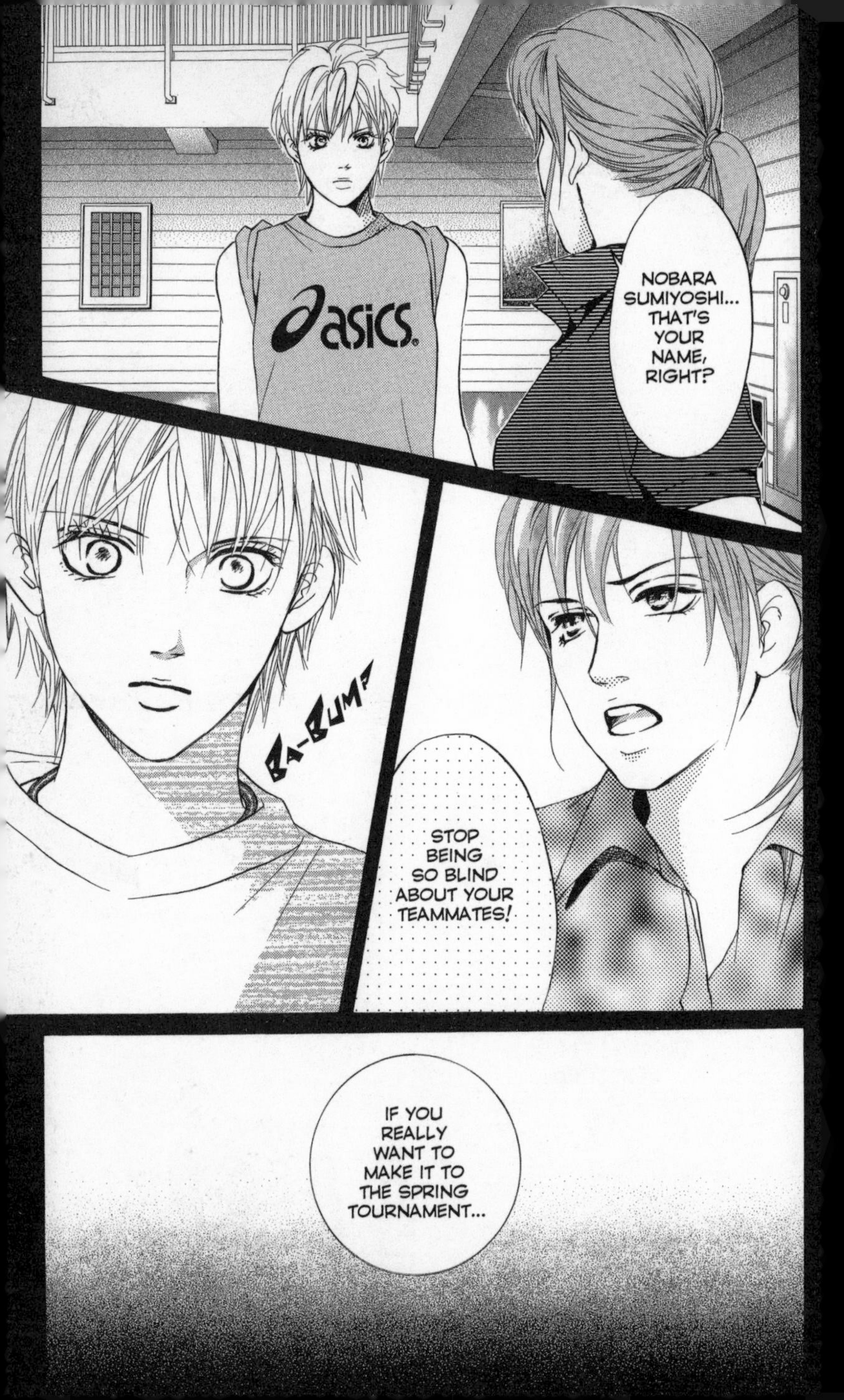
NOBARA SUMIYOSHI... THAT'S YOUR NAME, RIGHT?
STOP BEING SO BLIND ABOUT YOUR TEAMMATES!
BA-BUMP
IF YOU REALLY WANT TO MAKE IT TO THE SPRING TOURNAMENT...

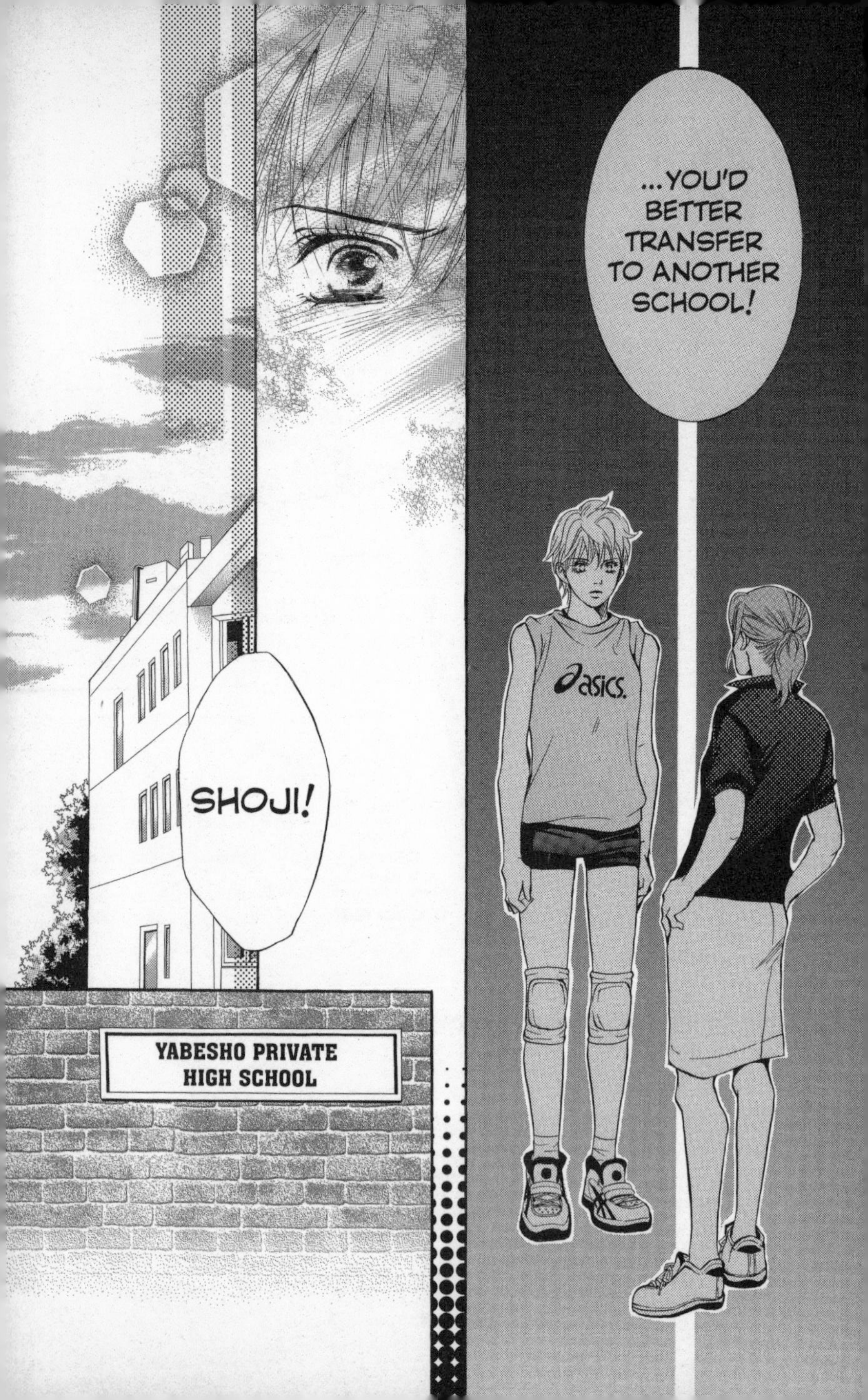
...YOU'D BETTER TRANSFER TO ANOTHER SCHOOL!
SHOJI!
YABESHO PRIVATE HIGH SCHOOL

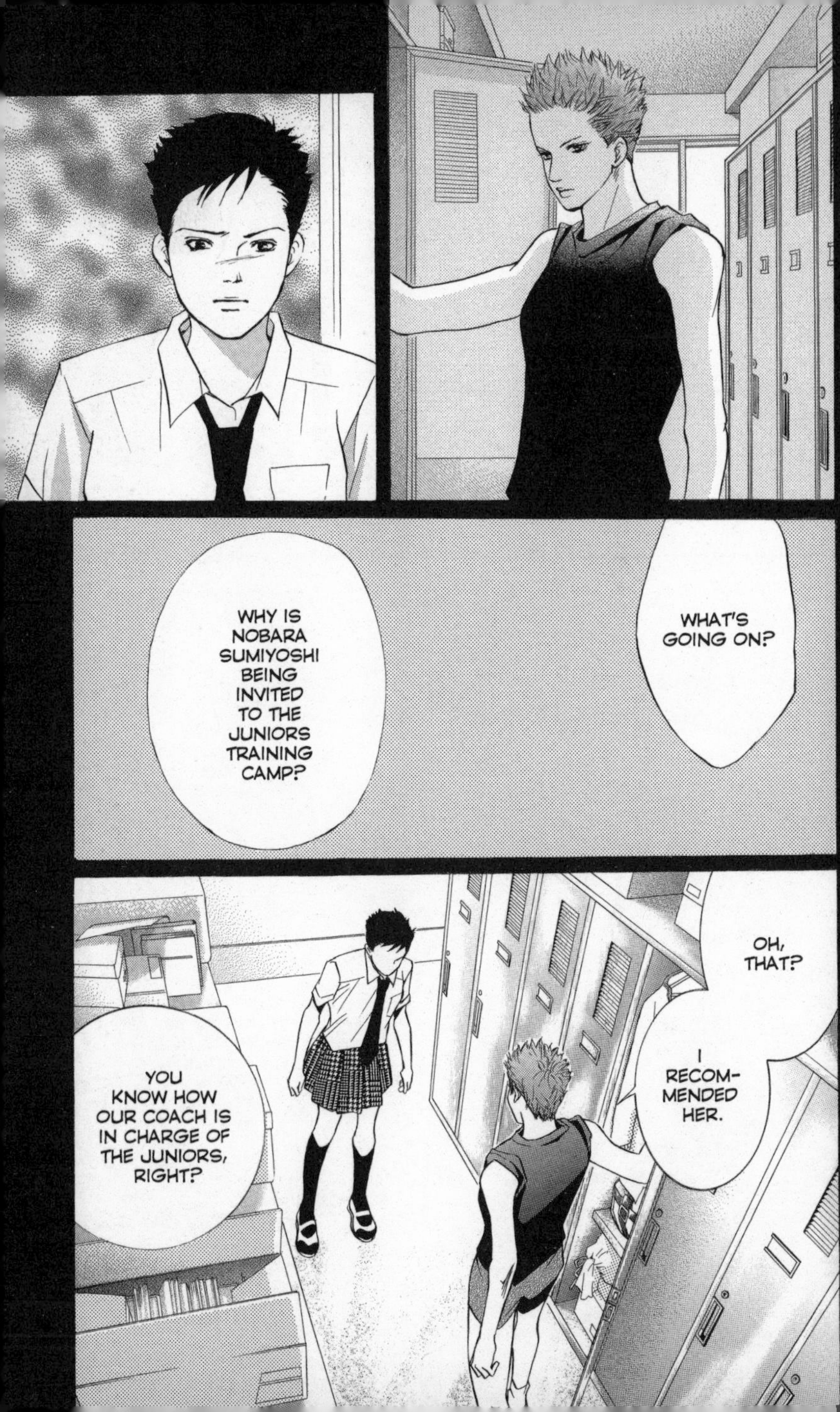
WHAT'S GOING ON?
WHY IS NOBARA SUMIYOSHI BEING INVITED TO THE JUNIORS TRAINING CAMP?
OH, THAT?
I RECOM-MENDED HER.
YOU KNOW HOW OUR COACH IS IN CHARGE OF THE JUNIORS, RIGHT?

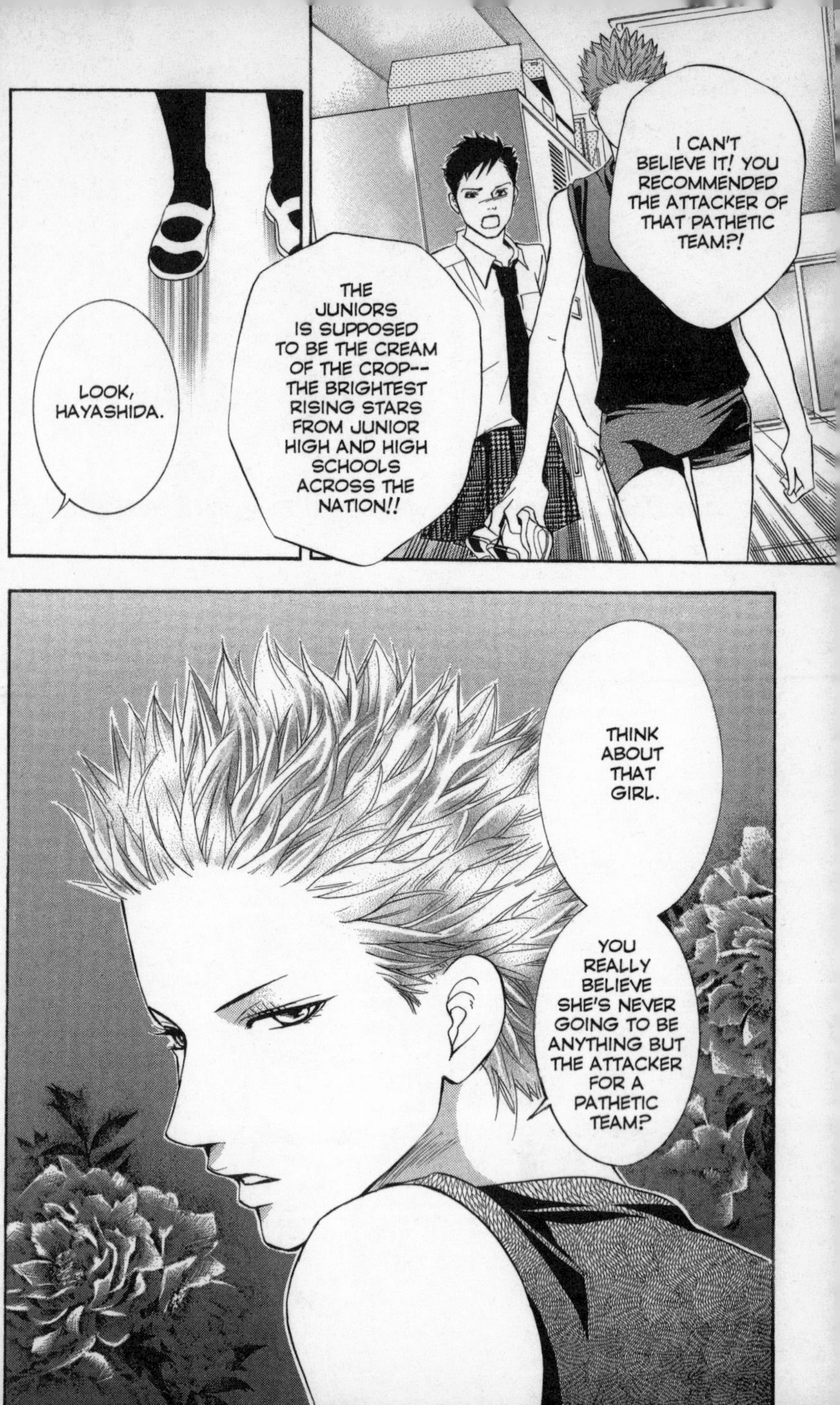
I CAN'T BELIEVE IT! YOU RECOMMENDED THE ATTACKER OF THAT PATHETIC TEAM?!
THE JUNIORS IS SUPPOSED TO BE THE CREAM OF THE CROP-- THE BRIGHTEST RISING STARS FROM JUNIOR HIGH AND HIGH SCHOOLS ACROSS THE NATION!!
LOOK, HAYASHIDA.
THINK ABOUT THAT GIRL.
YOU REALLY BELIEVE SHE'S NEVER GOING TO BE ANYTHING BUT THE ATTACKER FOR A PATHETIC TEAM?

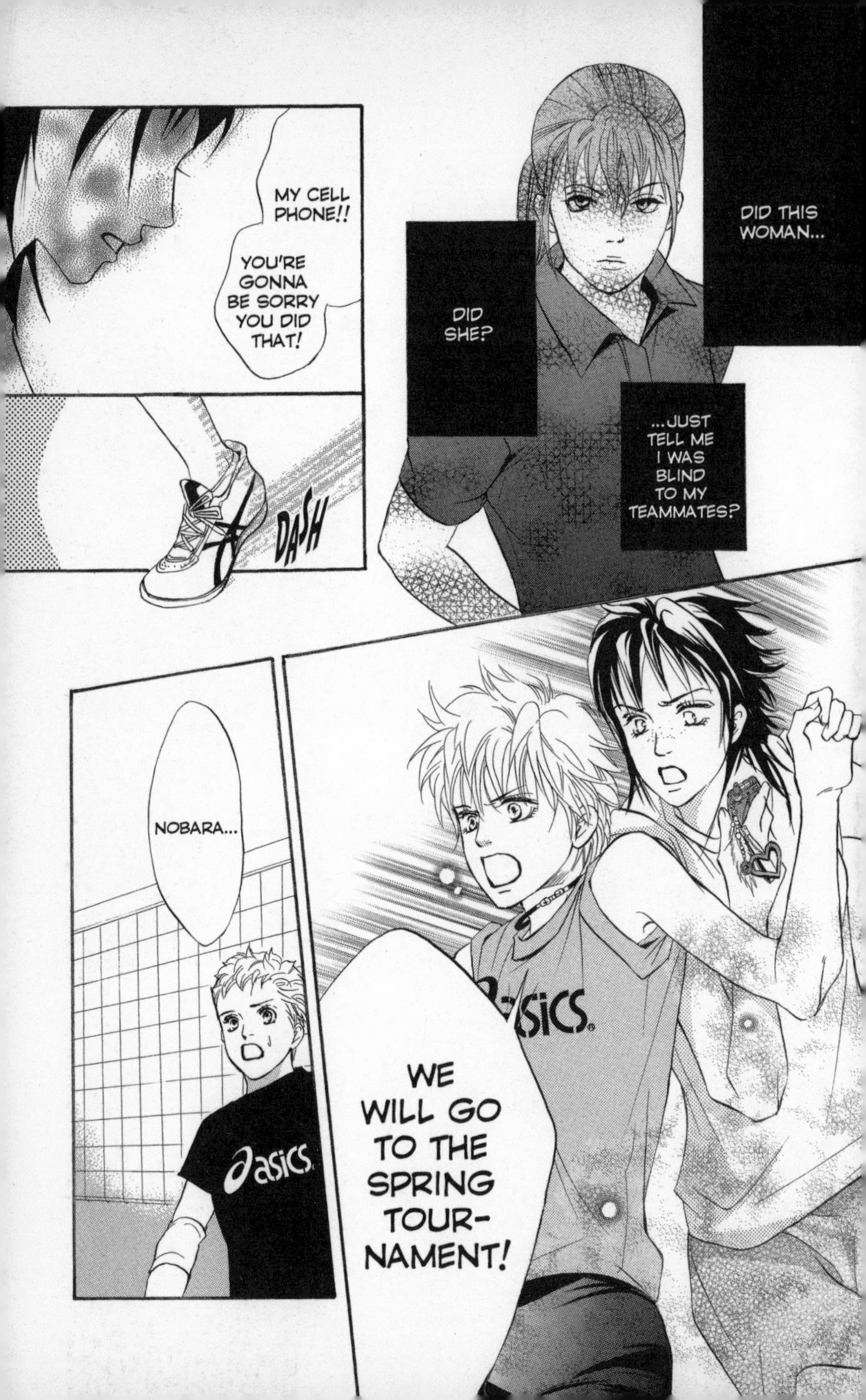
DID THIS WOMAN...
...JUST TELL ME I WAS BLIND TO MY TEAMMATES?
DID SHE?
MY CELL PHONE!!
YOU'RE GONNA BE SORRY YOU DID THAT!
DASH
WE WILL GO TO THE SPRING TOUR-NAMENT!
NOBARA...

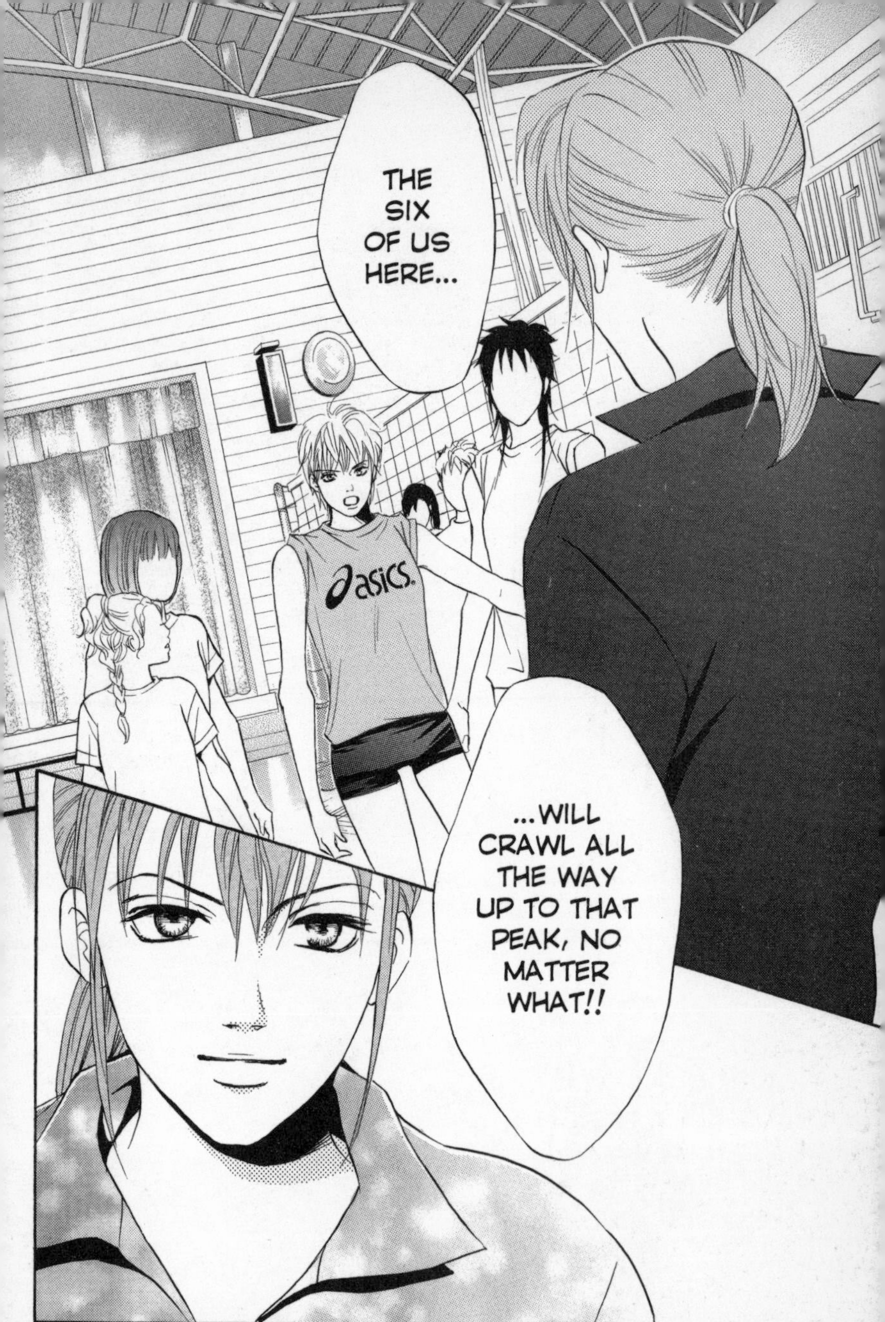
THE SIX OF US HERE...
...WILL CRAWL ALL THE WAY UP TO THAT PEAK, NO MATTER WHAT!!

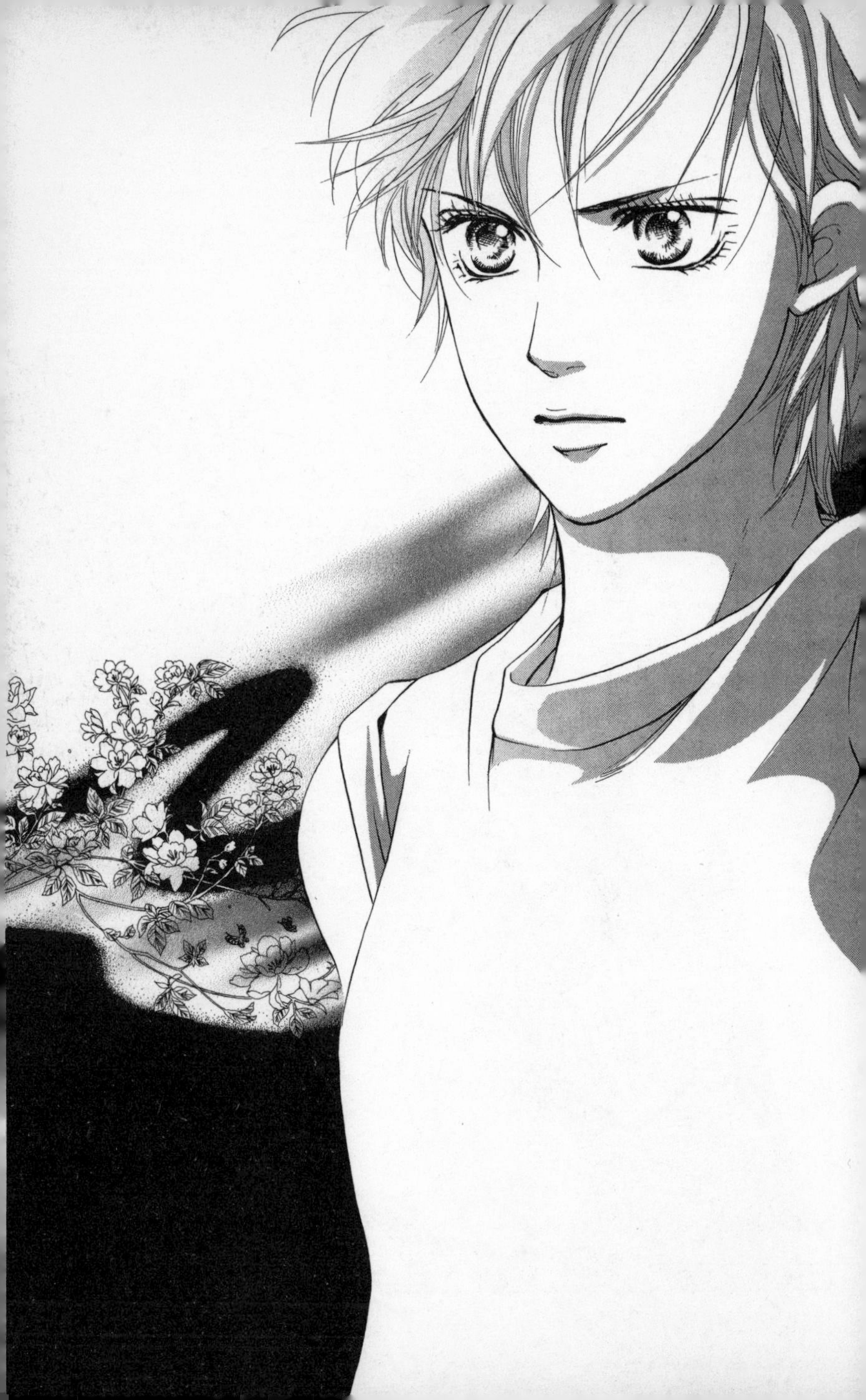

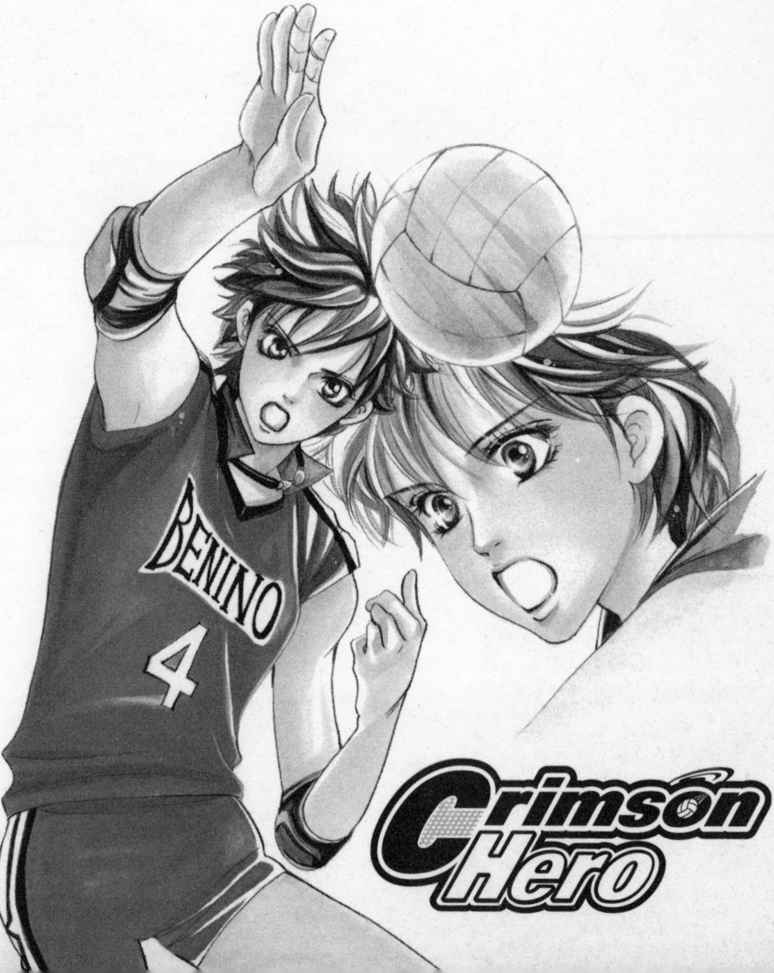
BENINO
4
Crimson Hero

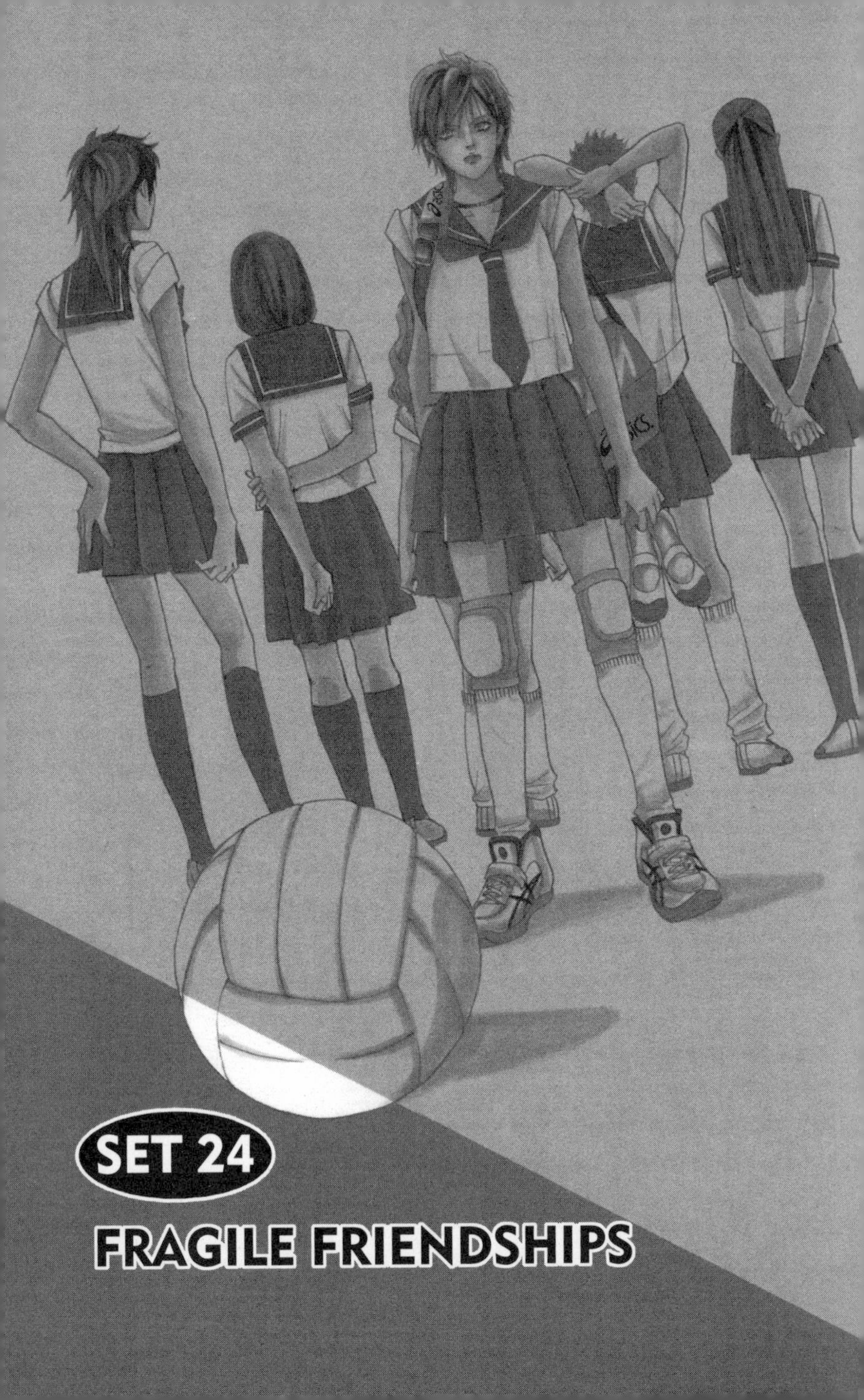

SET 24

FRAGILE FRIENDSHIPS

Crimson Hero

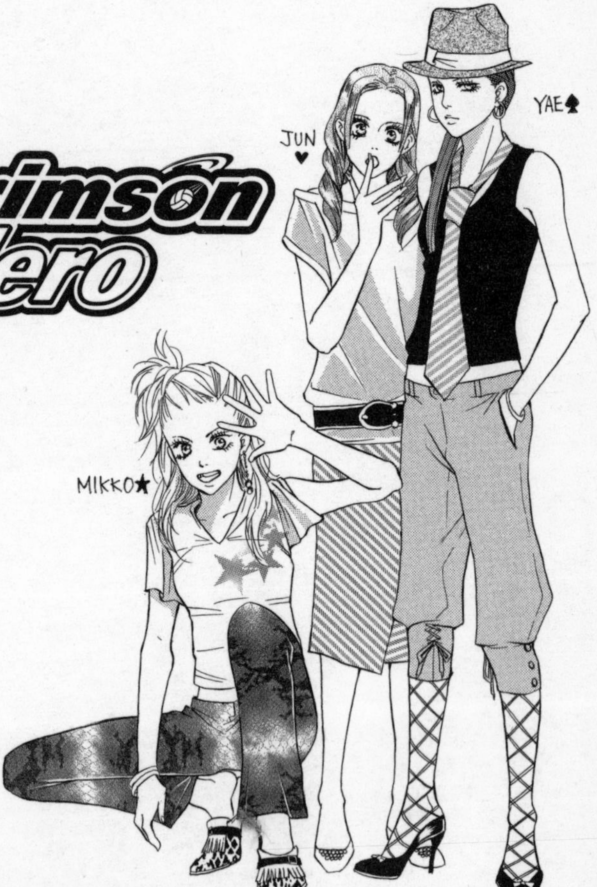
YAE
JUN
MIKKO

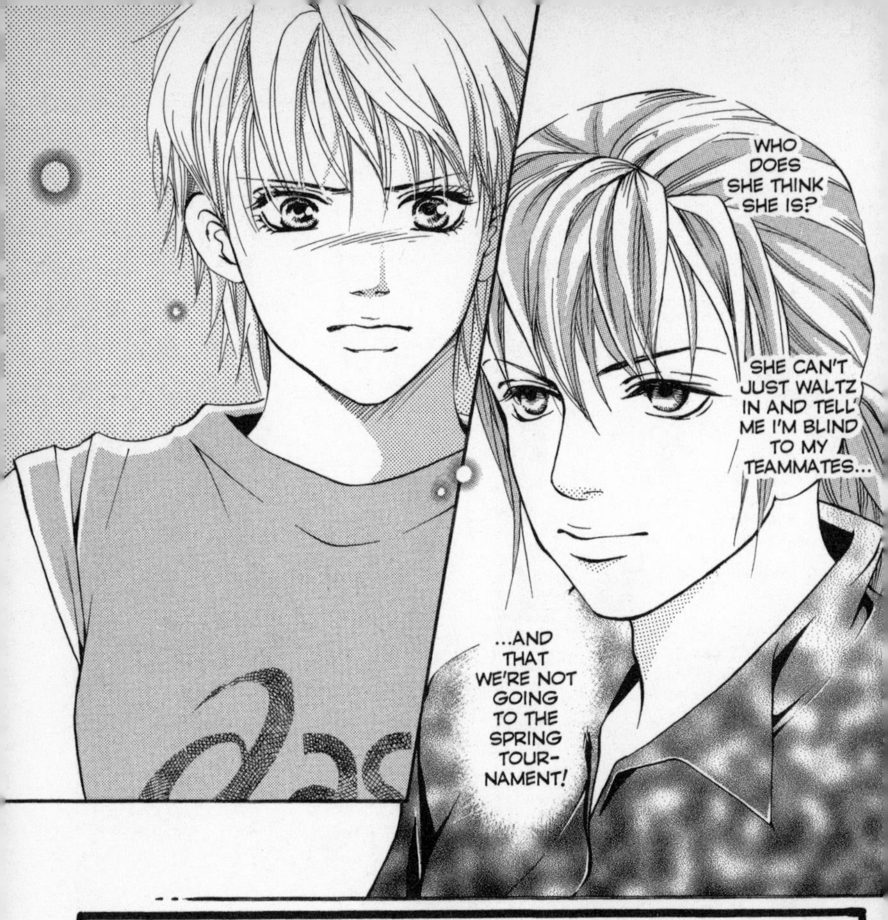
WHO DOES SHE THINK SHE IS?
SHE CAN'T JUST WALTZ IN AND TELL ME I'M BLIND TO MY TEAMMATES...
...AND THAT WE'RE NOT GOING TO THE SPRING TOURNAMENT!

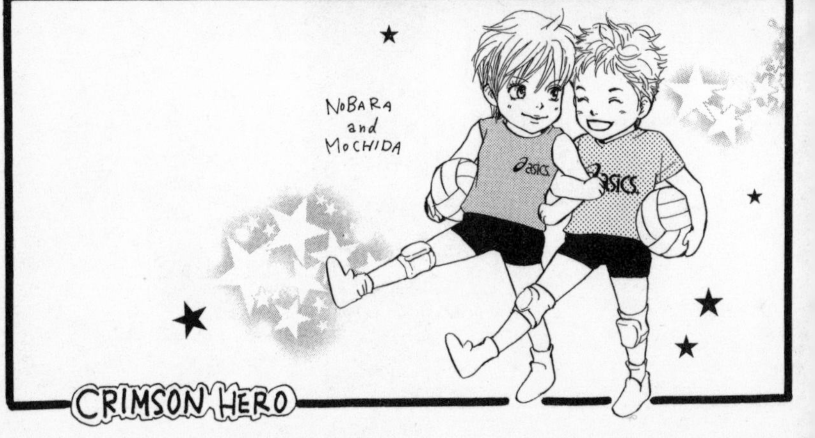
NOBARA and MOCHIDA
CRIMSON HERO

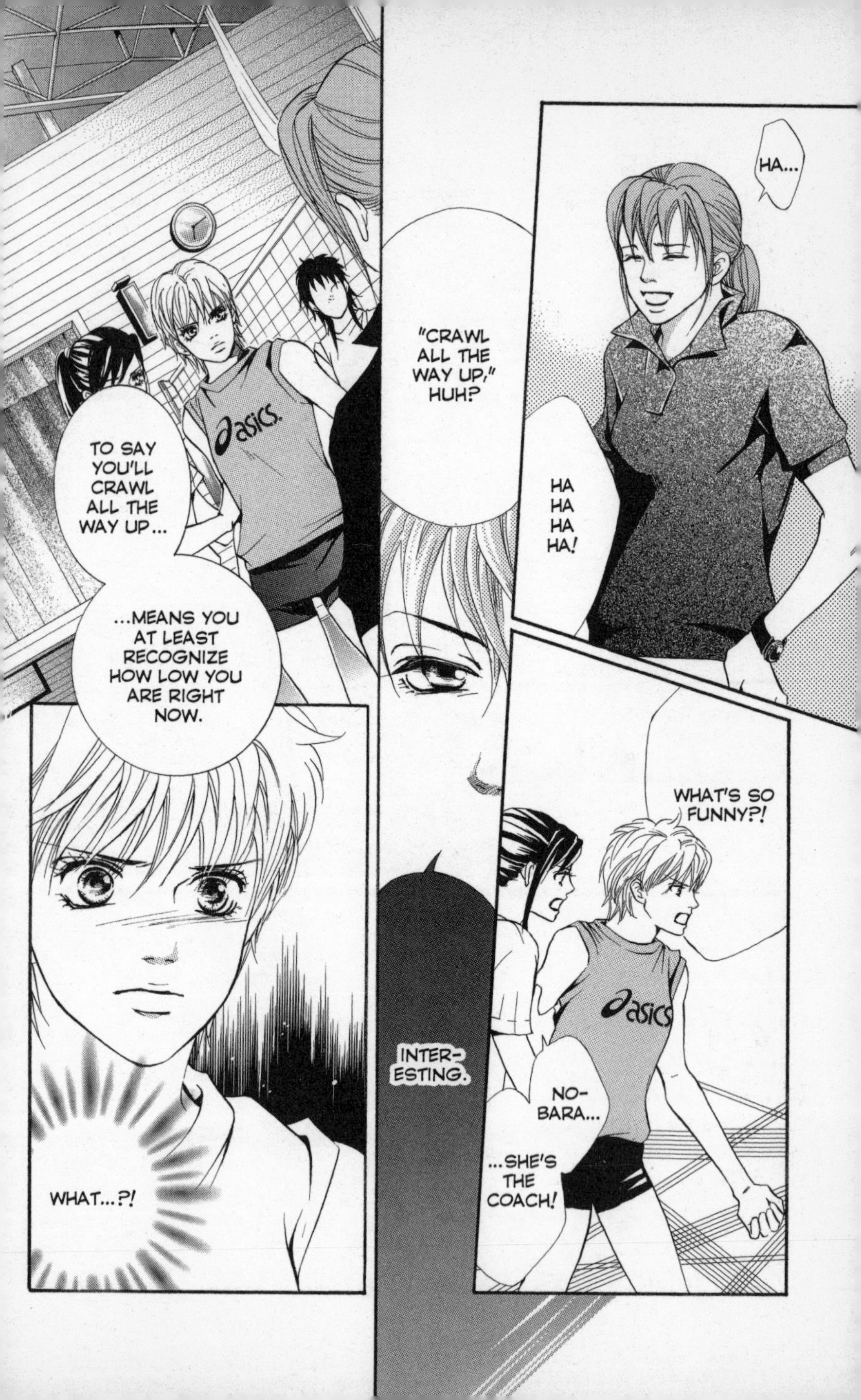
HA...
HA HA HA HA!
WHAT'S SO FUNNY?!
NO-BARA...
...SHE'S THE COACH!
"CRAWL ALL THE WAY UP," HUH?
INTER-ESTING.
TO SAY YOU'LL CRAWL ALL THE WAY UP...
...MEANS YOU AT LEAST RECOGNIZE HOW LOW YOU ARE RIGHT NOW.
WHAT...?!

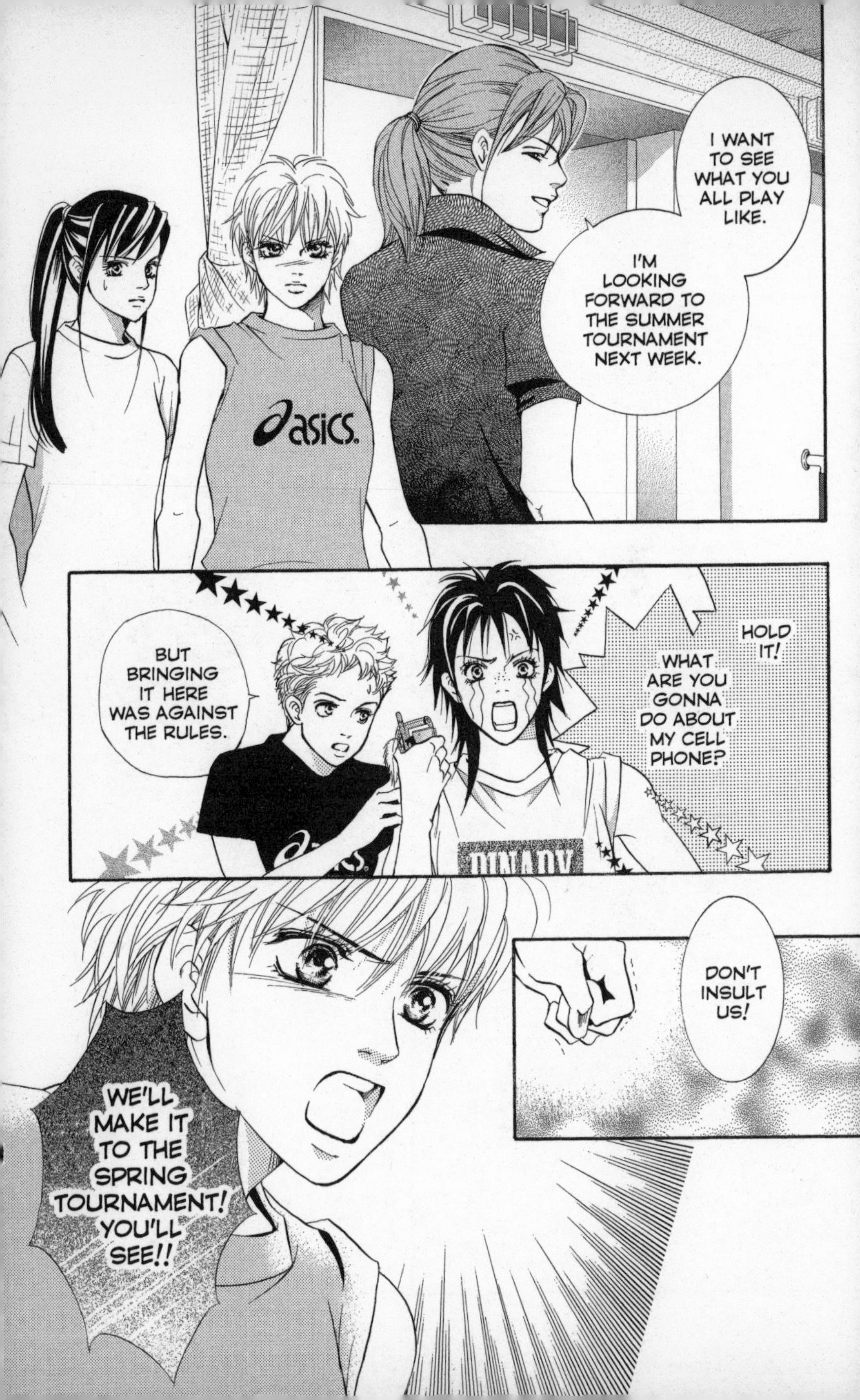
I WANT TO SEE WHAT YOU ALL PLAY LIKE.
I'M LOOKING FORWARD TO THE SUMMER TOURNAMENT NEXT WEEK.
HOLD IT!
WHAT ARE YOU GONNA DO ABOUT MY CELL PHONE?
BUT BRINGING IT HERE WAS AGAINST THE RULES.
DON'T INSULT US!
WE'LL MAKE IT TO THE SPRING TOURNAMENT! YOU'LL SEE!!

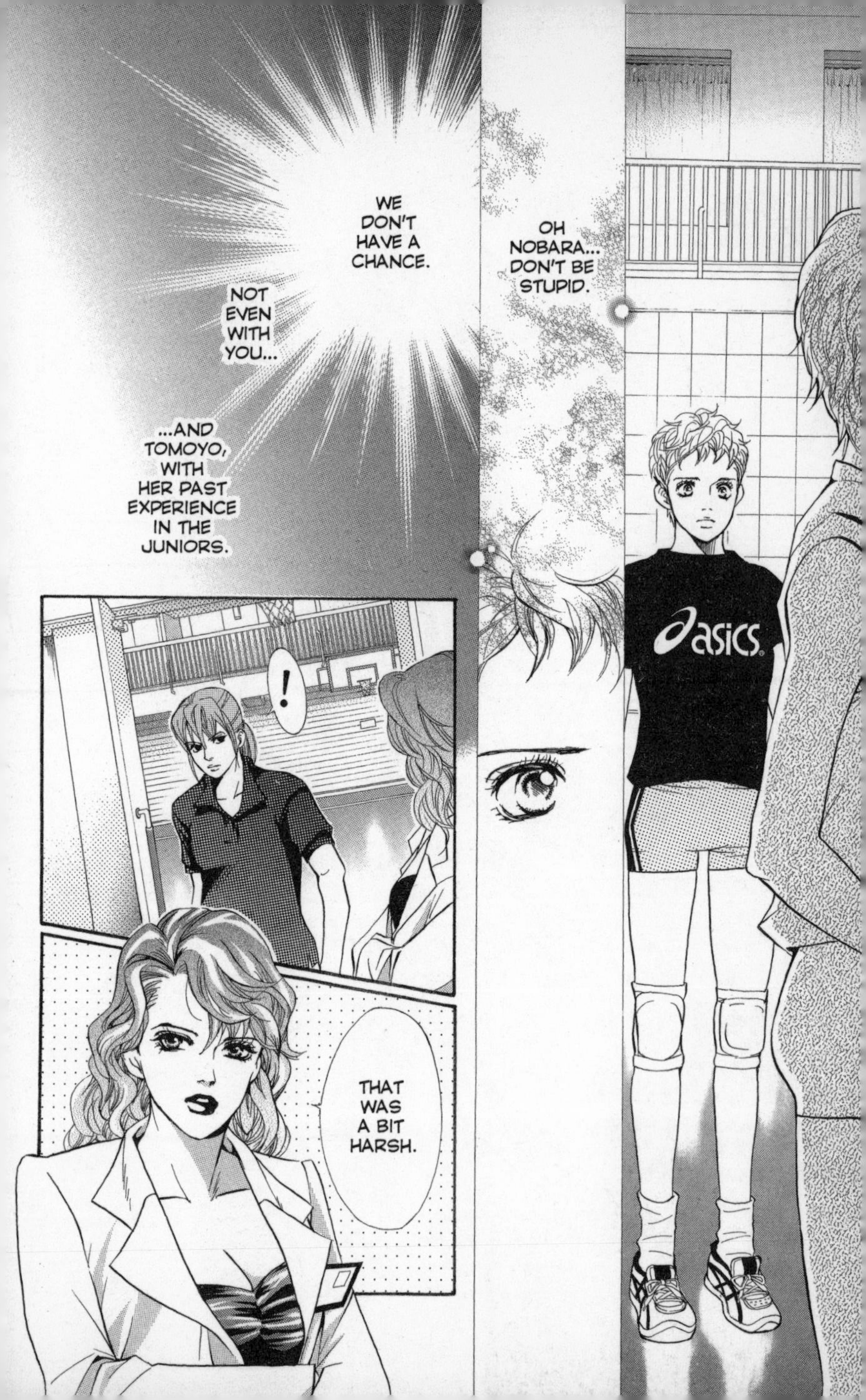
OH NOBARA... DON'T BE STUPID.
WE DON'T HAVE A CHANCE.
NOT EVEN WITH YOU...
...AND TOMOYO, WITH HER PAST EXPERIENCE IN THE JUNIORS.
!
THAT WAS A BIT HARSH.

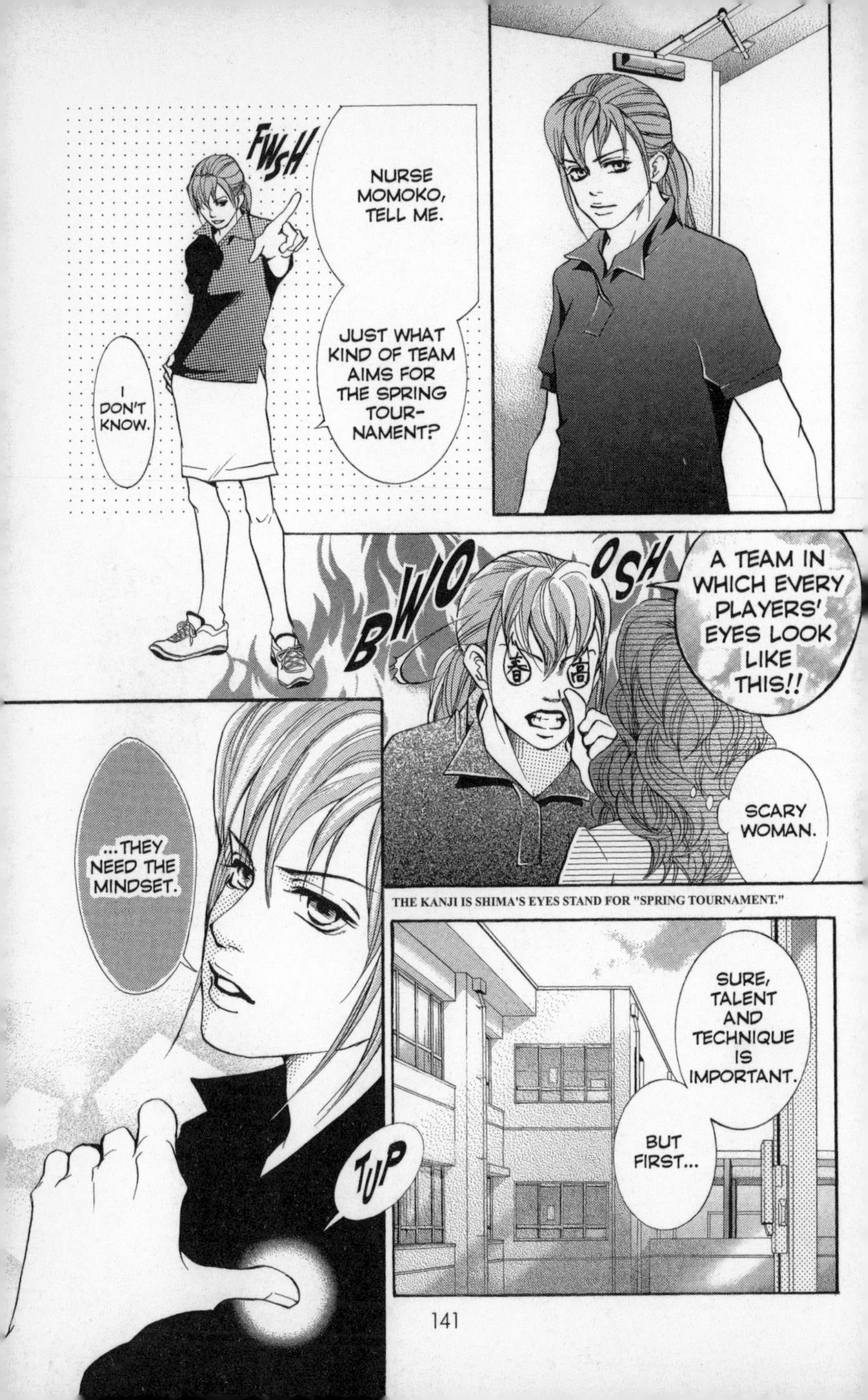
FWSH
NURSE MOMOKO, TELL ME.
JUST WHAT KIND OF TEAM AIMS FOR THE SPRING TOURNAMENT?
I DON'T KNOW.
BWOOSH
A TEAM IN WHICH EVERY PLAYERS' EYES LOOK LIKE THIS!!
SCARY WOMAN.
SURE, TALENT AND TECHNIQUE IS IMPORTANT.
BUT FIRST...
...THEY NEED THE MINDSET.
TUP

THE KANJI IS SHIMA'S EYES STAND FOR "SPRING TOURNAMENT."

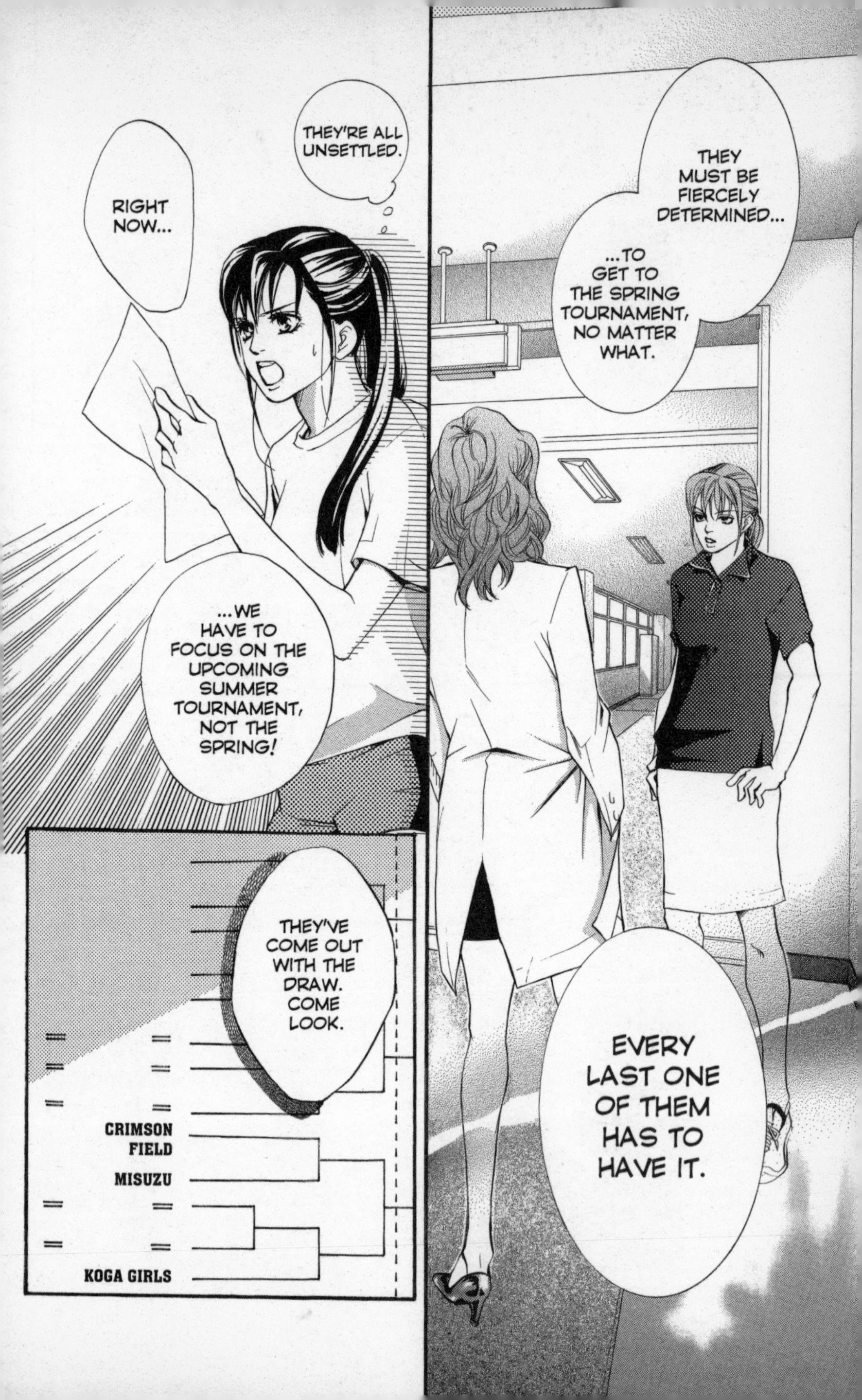
THEY MUST BE FIERCELY DETERMINED...
...TO GET TO THE SPRING TOURNAMENT, NO MATTER WHAT.
EVERY LAST ONE OF THEM HAS TO HAVE IT.
THEY'RE ALL UNSETTLED.
RIGHT NOW...
...WE HAVE TO FOCUS ON THE UPCOMING SUMMER TOURNAMENT, NOT THE SPRING!
THEY'VE COME OUT WITH THE DRAW. COME LOOK.
CRIMSON FIELD
MISUZU
KOGA GIRLS

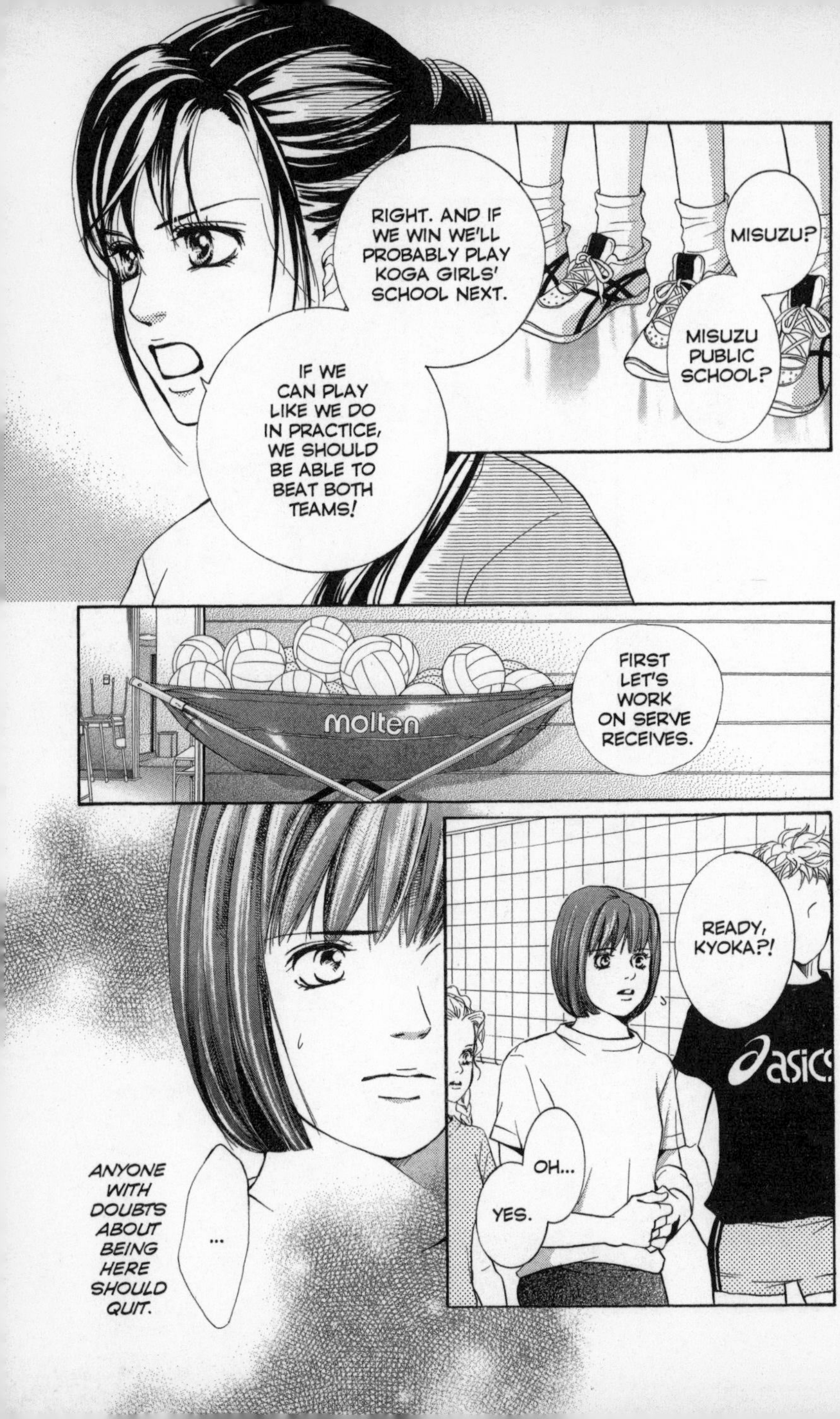
MISUZU?
MISUZU PUBLIC SCHOOL?
RIGHT. AND IF WE WIN WE'LL PROBABLY PLAY KOGA GIRLS' SCHOOL NEXT.
IF WE CAN PLAY LIKE WE DO IN PRACTICE, WE SHOULD BE ABLE TO BEAT BOTH TEAMS!
molten
FIRST LET'S WORK ON SERVE RECEIVES.
READY, KYOKA?!
asics
OH... YES.
...
ANYONE WITH DOUBTS ABOUT BEING HERE SHOULD QUIT.

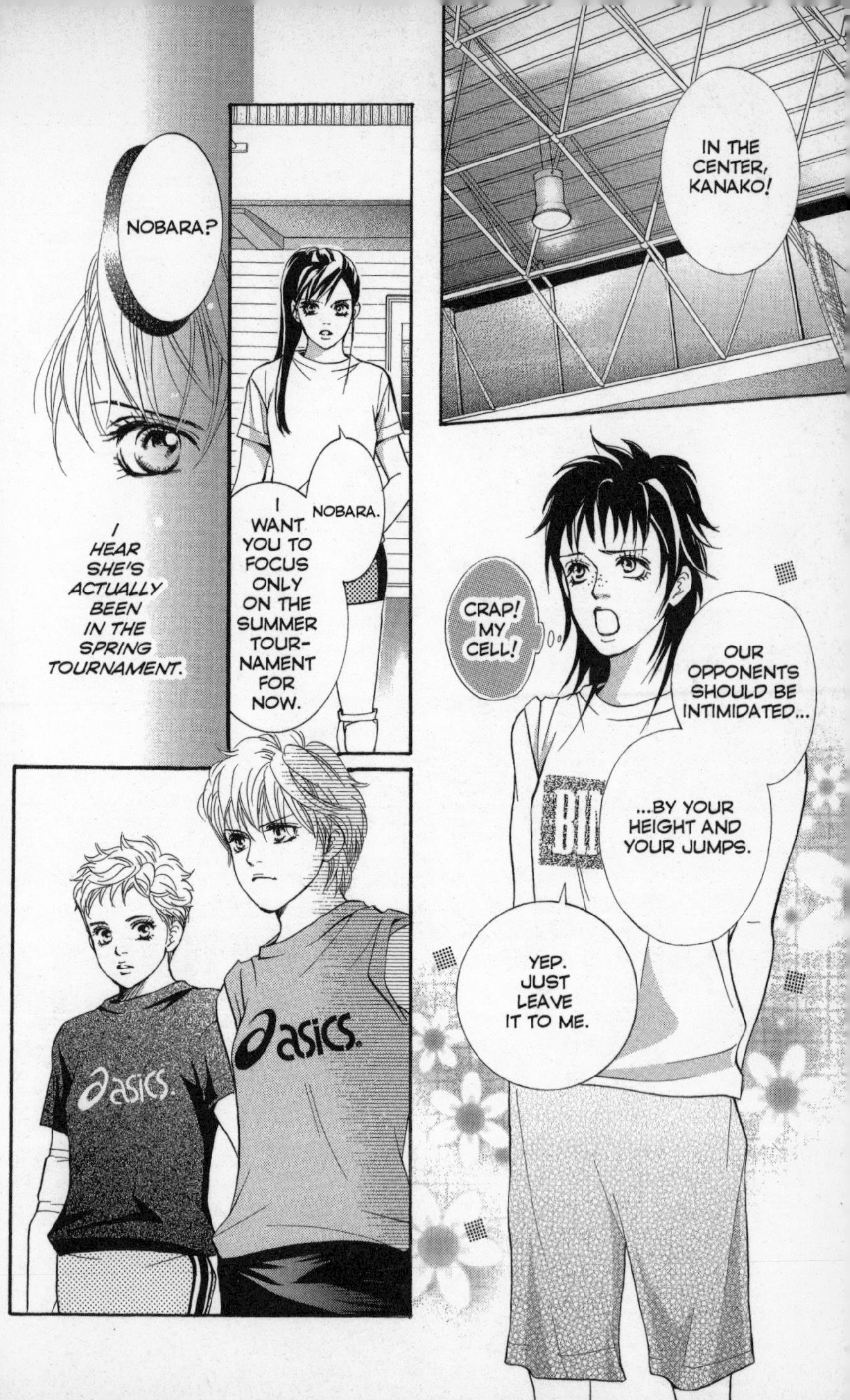
IN THE CENTER, KANAKO!
NOBARA.
I WANT YOU TO FOCUS ONLY ON THE SUMMER TOURNAMENT FOR NOW.
NOBARA?
I HEAR SHE'S ACTUALLY BEEN IN THE SPRING TOURNAMENT.
OUR OPPONENTS SHOULD BE INTIMIDATED...
...BY YOUR HEIGHT AND YOUR JUMPS.
YEP. JUST LEAVE IT TO ME.
CRAP! MY CELL!

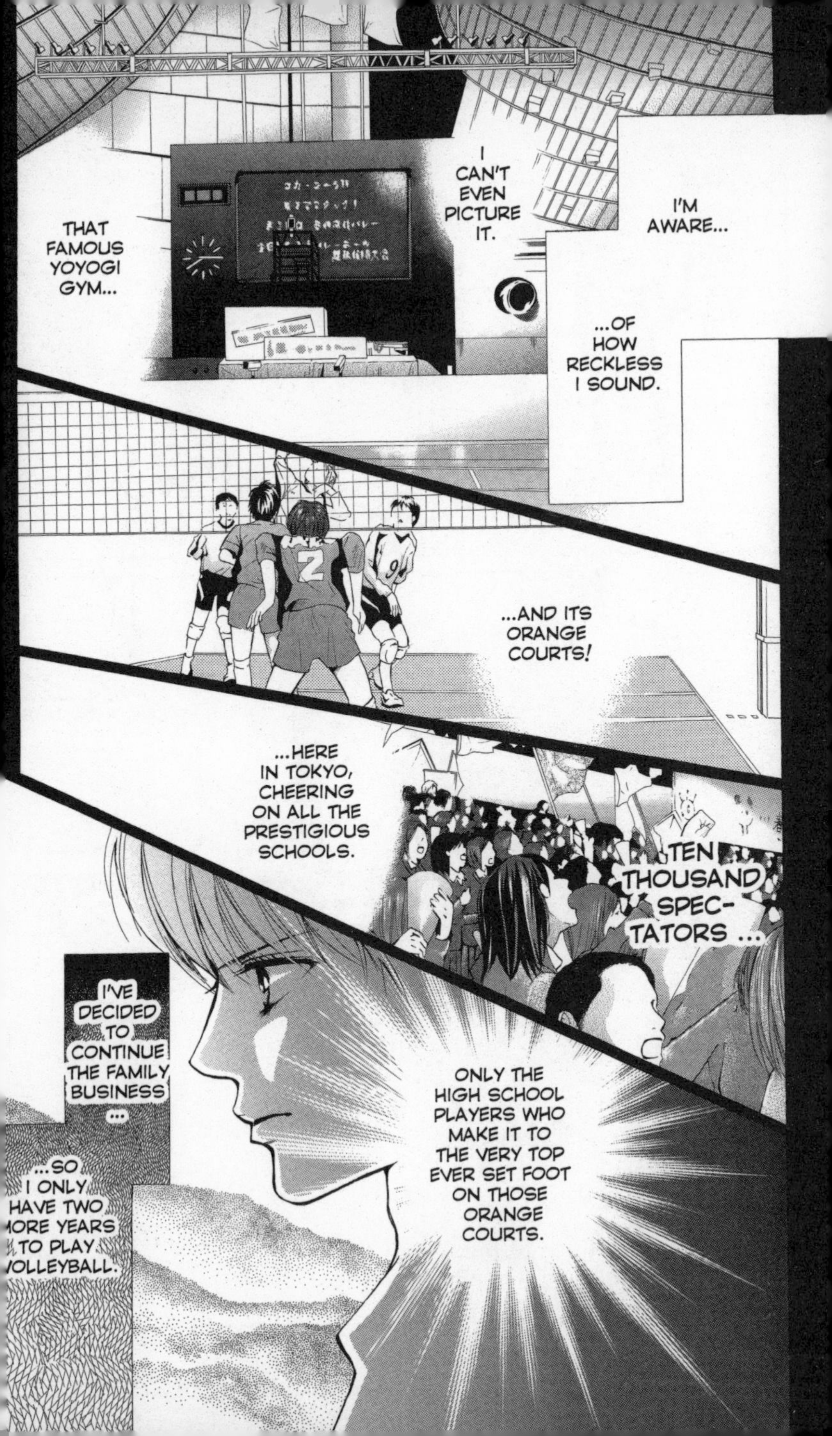
I'M AWARE...
...OF HOW RECKLESS I SOUND.
I CAN'T EVEN PICTURE IT.
THAT FAMOUS YOYOGI GYM...
...AND ITS ORANGE COURTS!
TEN THOUSAND SPECTATORS ...
...HERE IN TOKYO, CHEERING ON ALL THE PRESTIGIOUS SCHOOLS.
ONLY THE HIGH SCHOOL PLAYERS WHO MAKE IT TO THE VERY TOP EVER SET FOOT ON THOSE ORANGE COURTS.
I'VE DECIDED TO CONTINUE THE FAMILY BUSINESS ...
...SO I ONLY HAVE TWO MORE YEARS TO PLAY VOLLEYBALL.

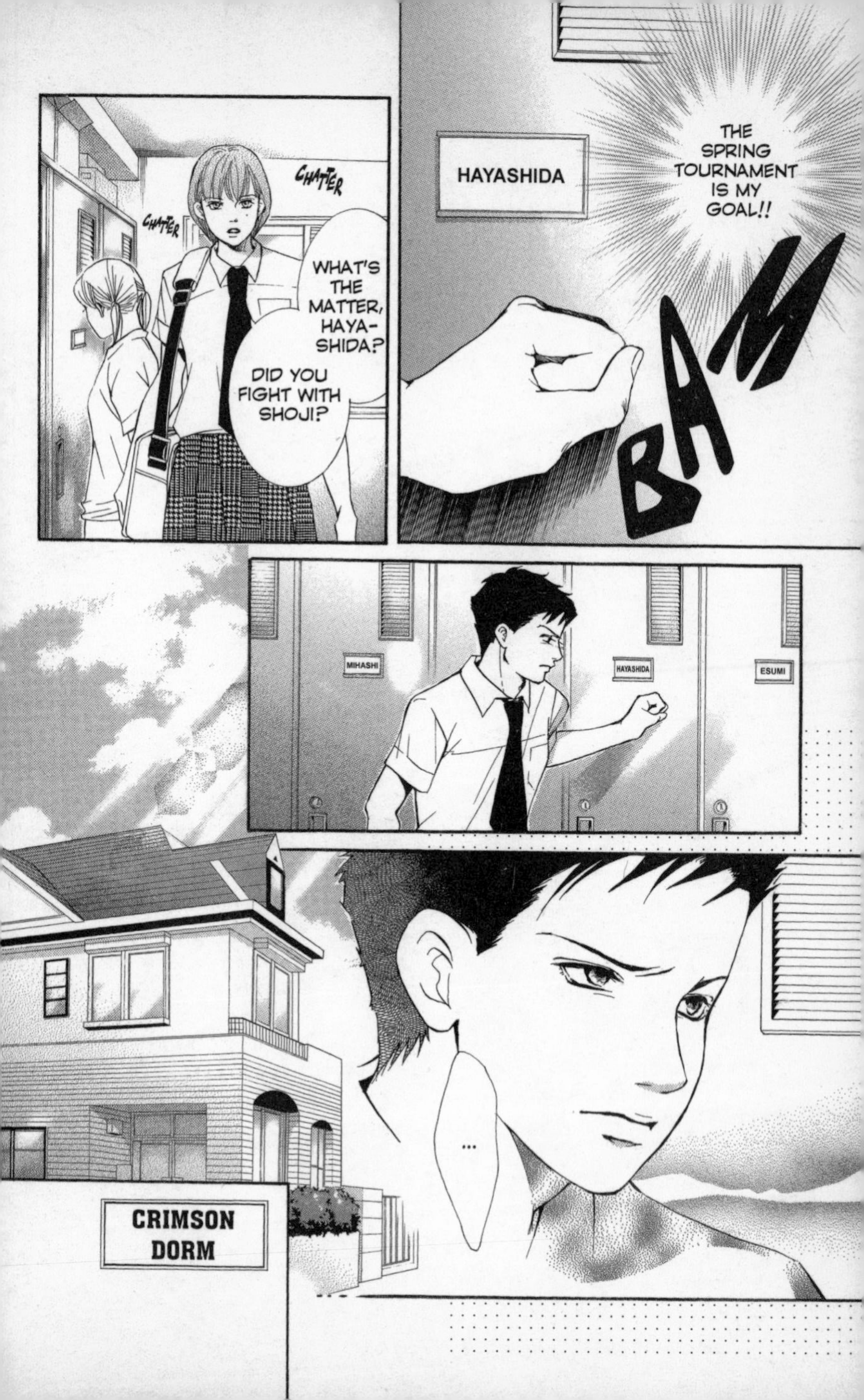
HAYASHIDA
THE SPRING TOURNAMENT IS MY GOAL!!
BAM
CHATTER
CHATTER
WHAT'S THE MATTER, HAYA-SHIDA?
DID YOU FIGHT WITH SHOJI?
MIHASHI
HAYASHIDA
ESUMI
...
CRIMSON DORM

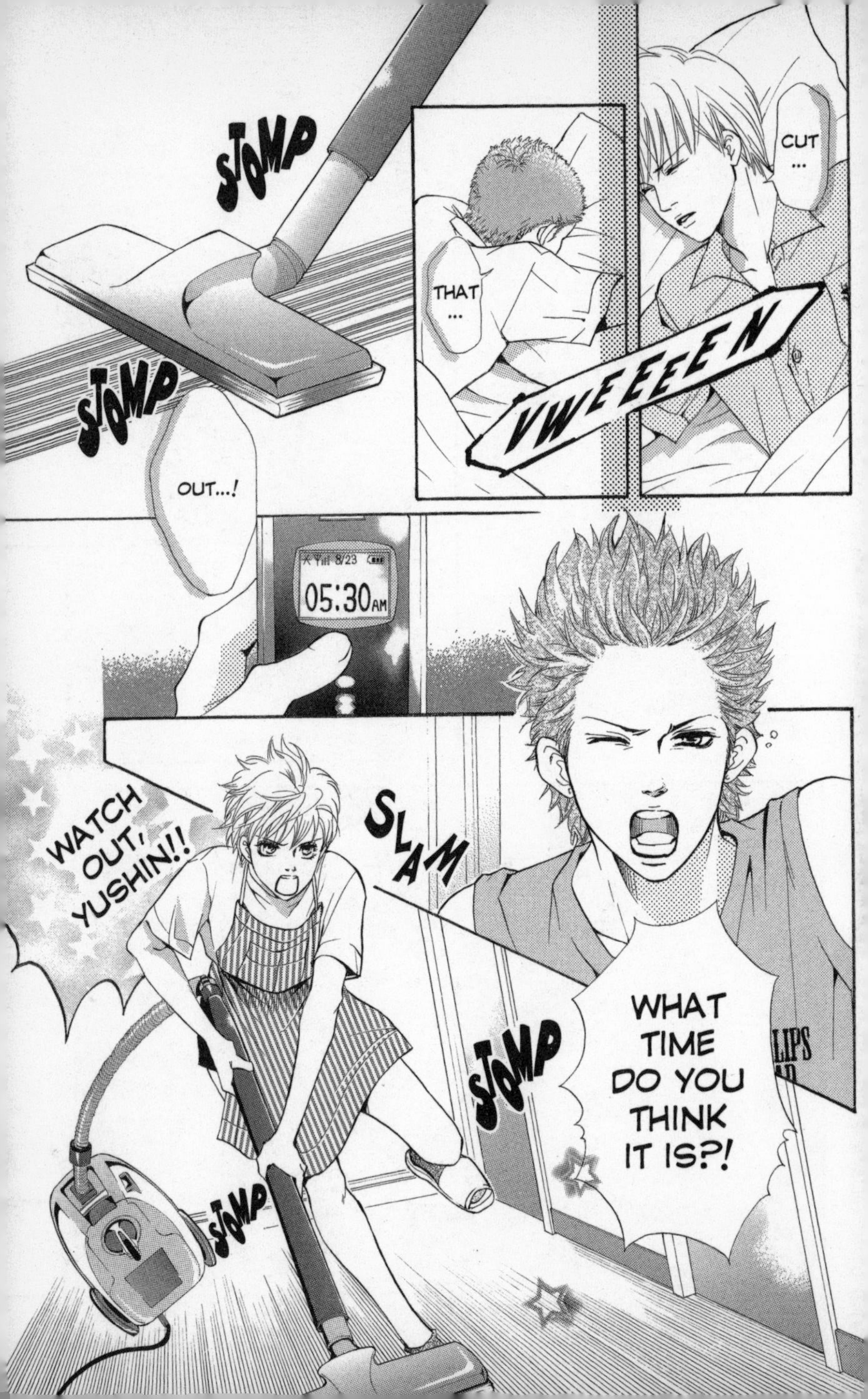
CUT ...
VWEEEEEN
THAT ...
STOMP
STOMP
OUT...!
05:30AM
SLAM
WHAT TIME DO YOU THINK IT IS?!
STOMP
WATCH OUT, YUSHIN!!
STOMP

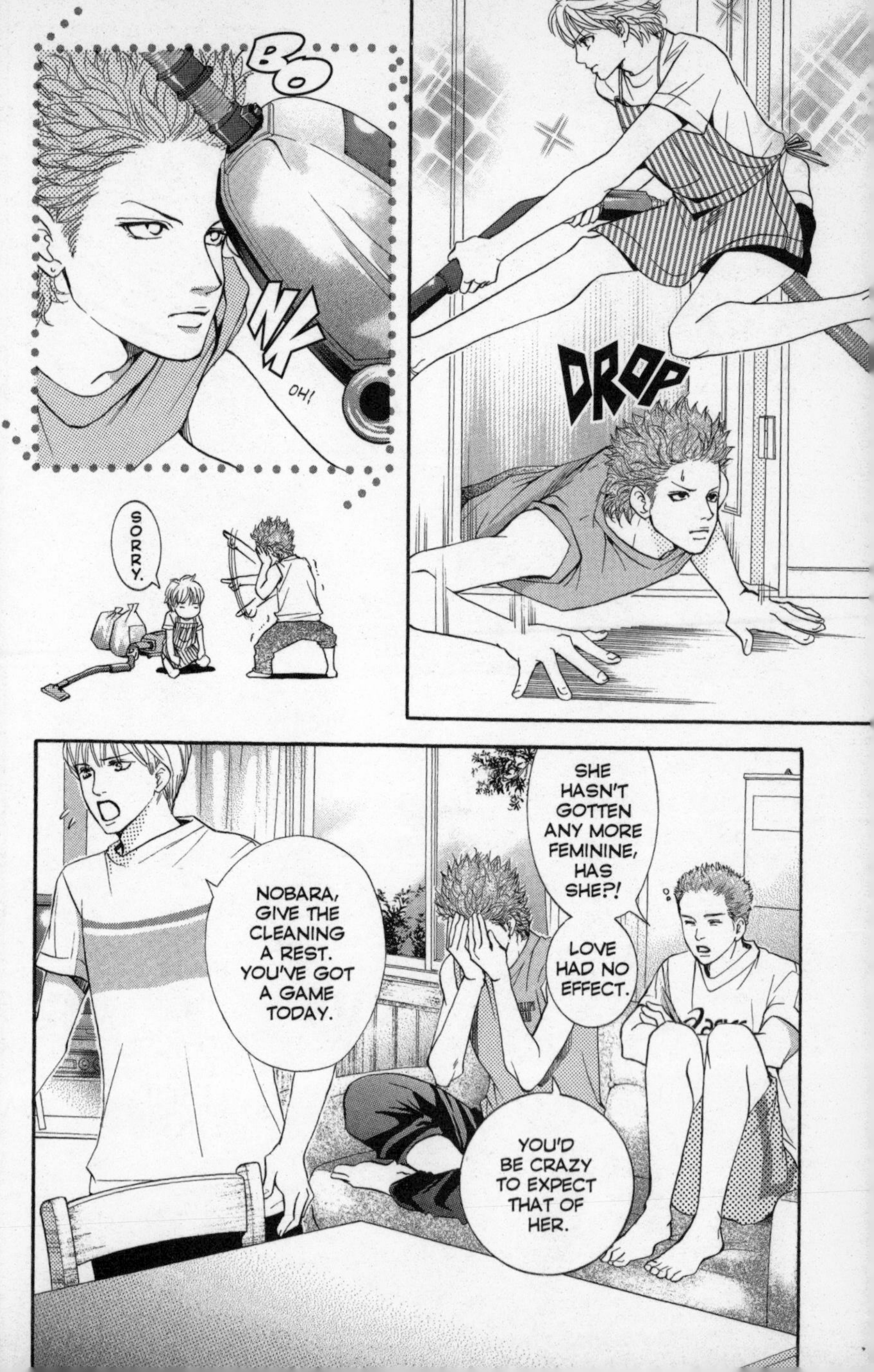
DROP
BONK
OH!
SORRY.
SHE HASN'T GOTTEN ANY MORE FEMININE, HAS SHE?!
LOVE HAD NO EFFECT.
NOBARA, GIVE THE CLEANING A REST. YOU'VE GOT A GAME TODAY.
YOU'D BE CRAZY TO EXPECT THAT OF HER.

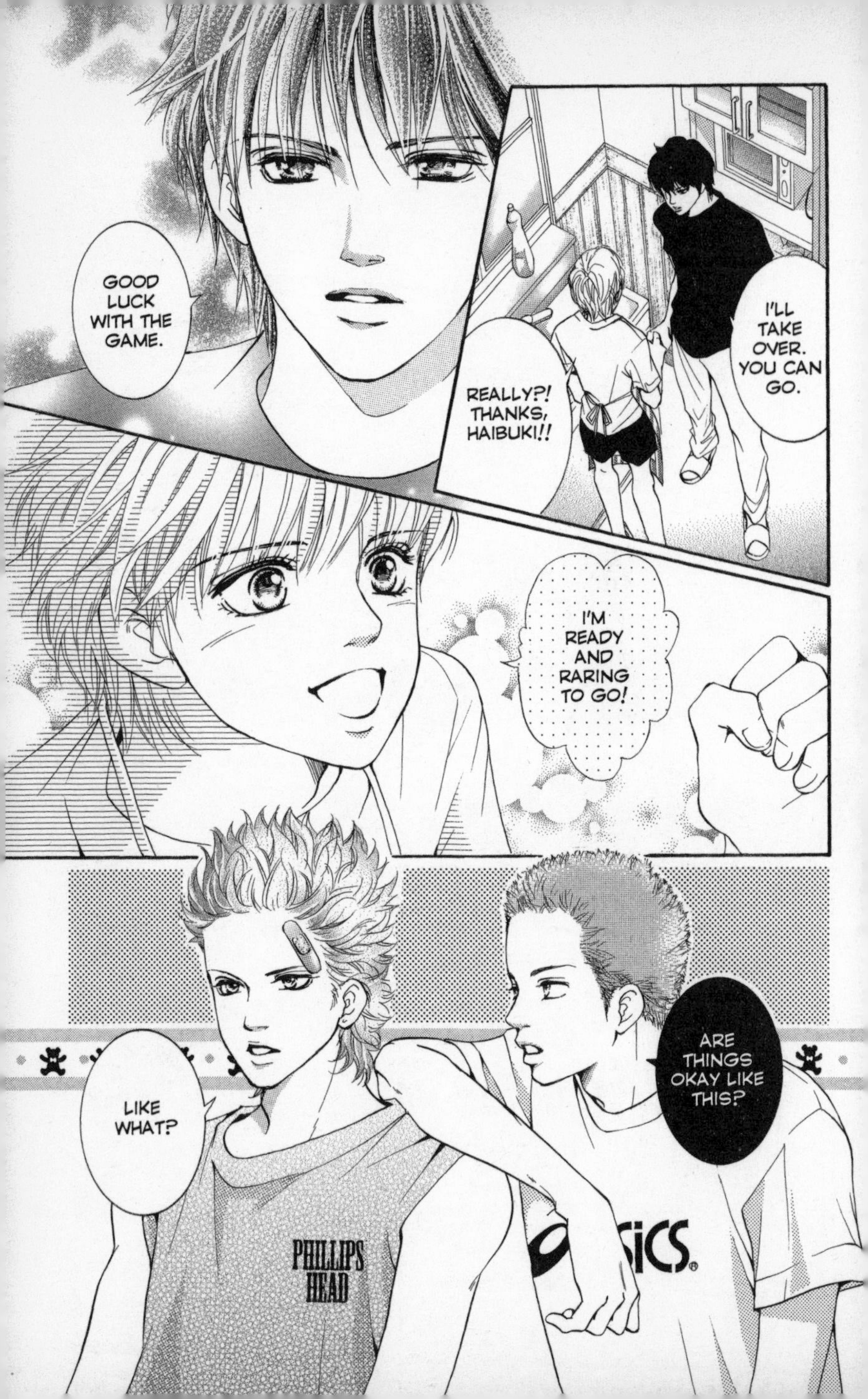
I'LL TAKE OVER. YOU CAN GO.
REALLY?! THANKS, HAIBUKI!!
GOOD LUCK WITH THE GAME.
I'M READY AND RARING TO GO!
ARE THINGS OKAY LIKE THIS?
LIKE WHAT?
PHILLIPS HEAD

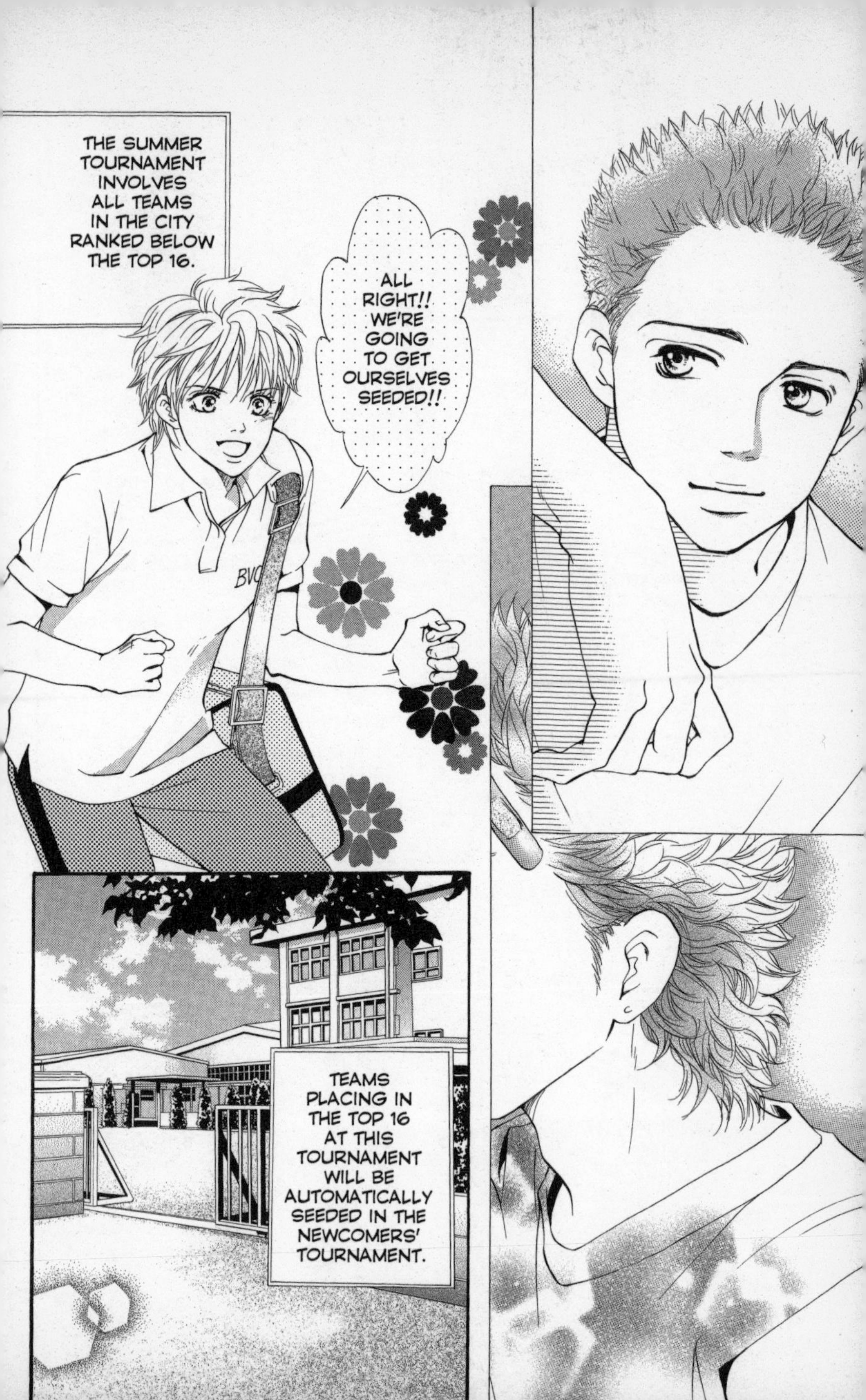
THE SUMMER TOURNAMENT INVOLVES ALL TEAMS IN THE CITY RANKED BELOW THE TOP 16.
ALL RIGHT!! WE'RE GOING TO GET OURSELVES SEEDED!!
BVC
TEAMS PLACING IN THE TOP 16 AT THIS TOURNAMENT WILL BE AUTOMATICALLY SEEDED IN THE NEWCOMERS' TOURNAMENT.

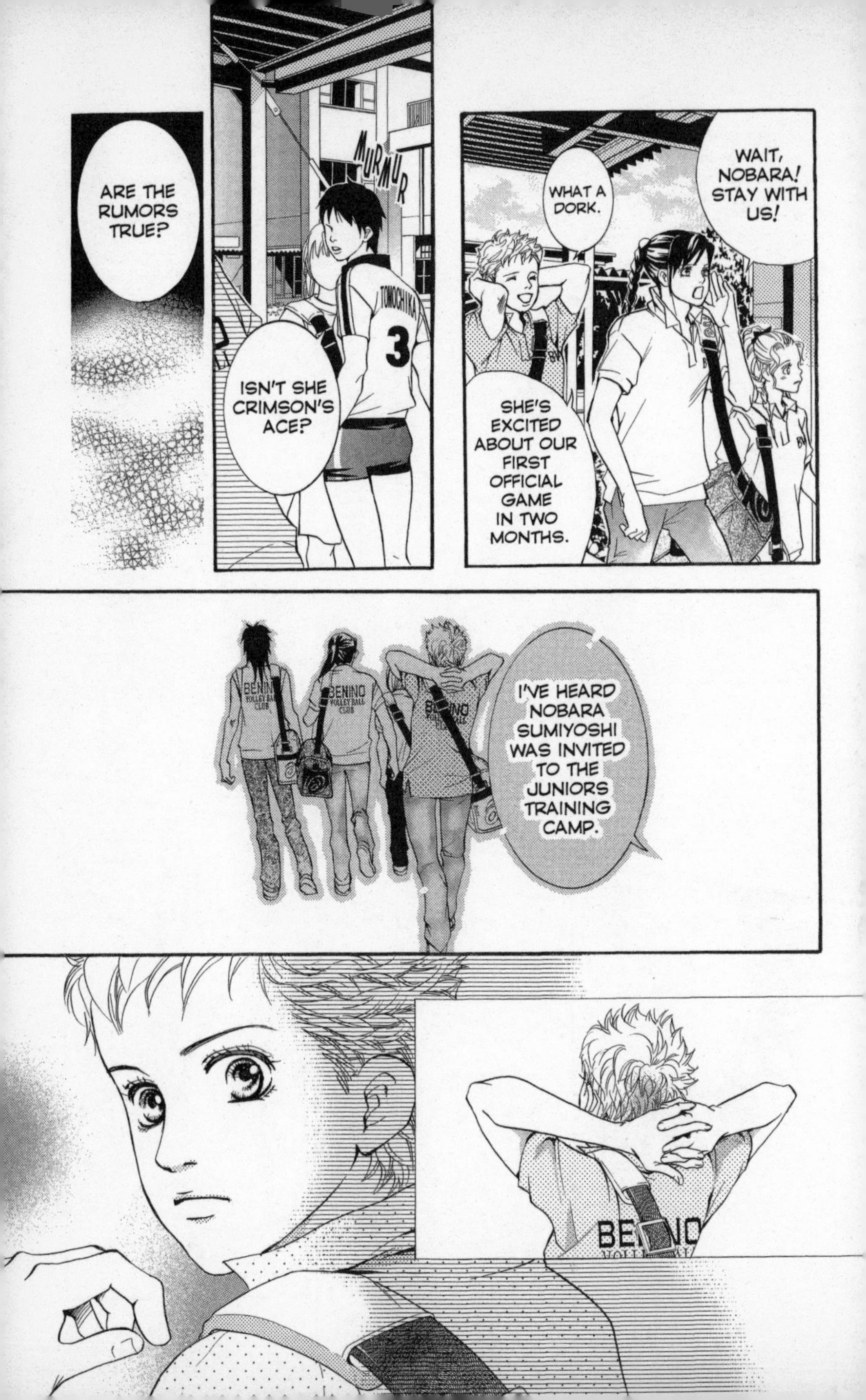
WAIT, NOBARA! STAY WITH US!
WHAT A DORK.
SHE'S EXCITED ABOUT OUR FIRST OFFICIAL GAME IN TWO MONTHS.
MURMUR
TOMOCHIKA
3
ISN'T SHE CRIMSON'S ACE?
ARE THE RUMORS TRUE?
I'VE HEARD NOBARA SUMIYOSHI WAS INVITED TO THE JUNIORS TRAINING CAMP.
BENINO VOLLEY BALL CLUB
BENINO

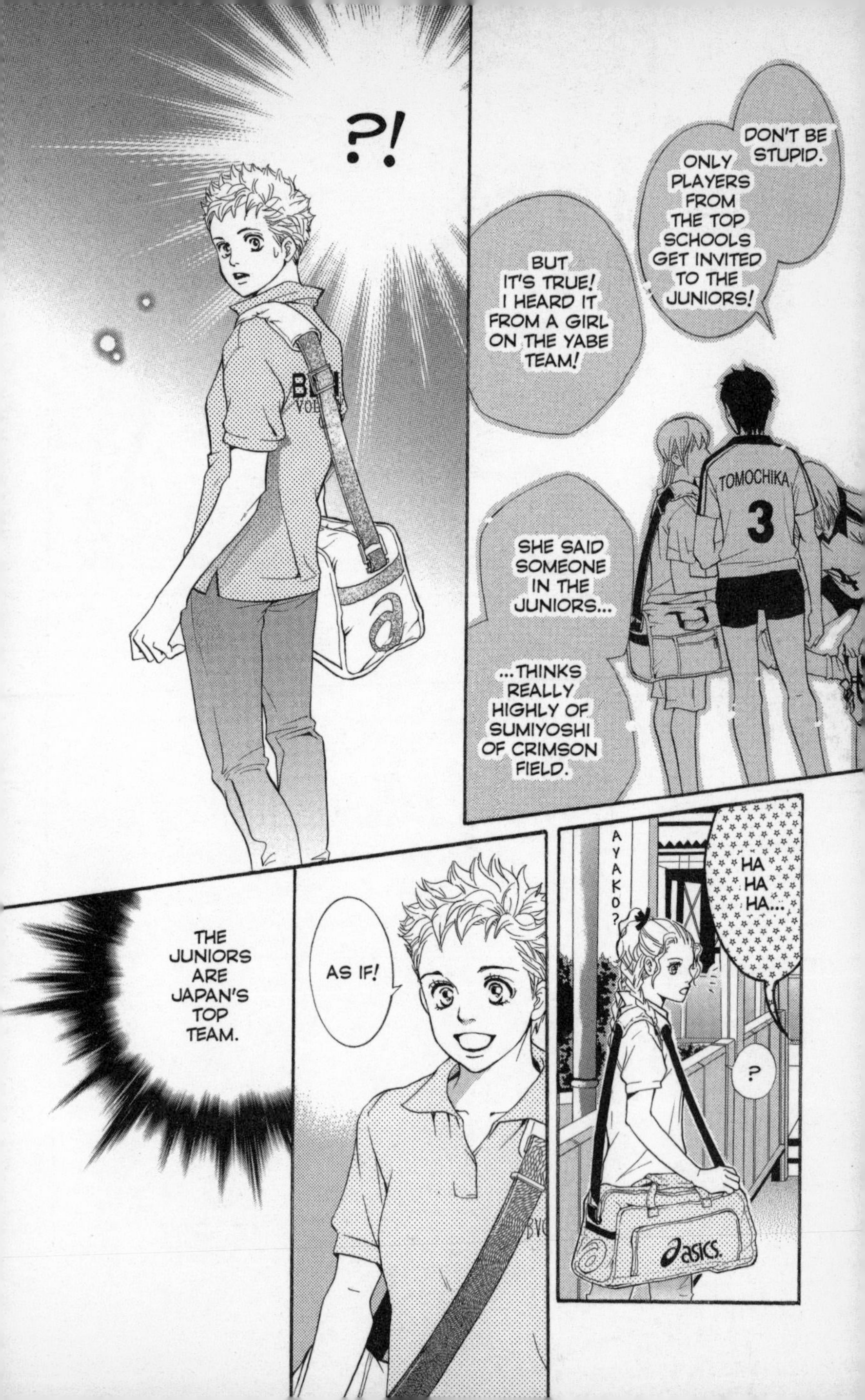
DON'T BE STUPID.
ONLY PLAYERS FROM THE TOP SCHOOLS GET INVITED TO THE JUNIORS!
BUT IT'S TRUE! I HEARD IT FROM A GIRL ON THE YABE TEAM!
TOMOCHIKA 3
SHE SAID SOMEONE IN THE JUNIORS...
...THINKS REALLY HIGHLY OF SUMIYOSHI OF CRIMSON FIELD.
?!
HA HA HA...
AYAKO?
?
AS IF!
THE JUNIORS ARE JAPAN'S TOP TEAM.

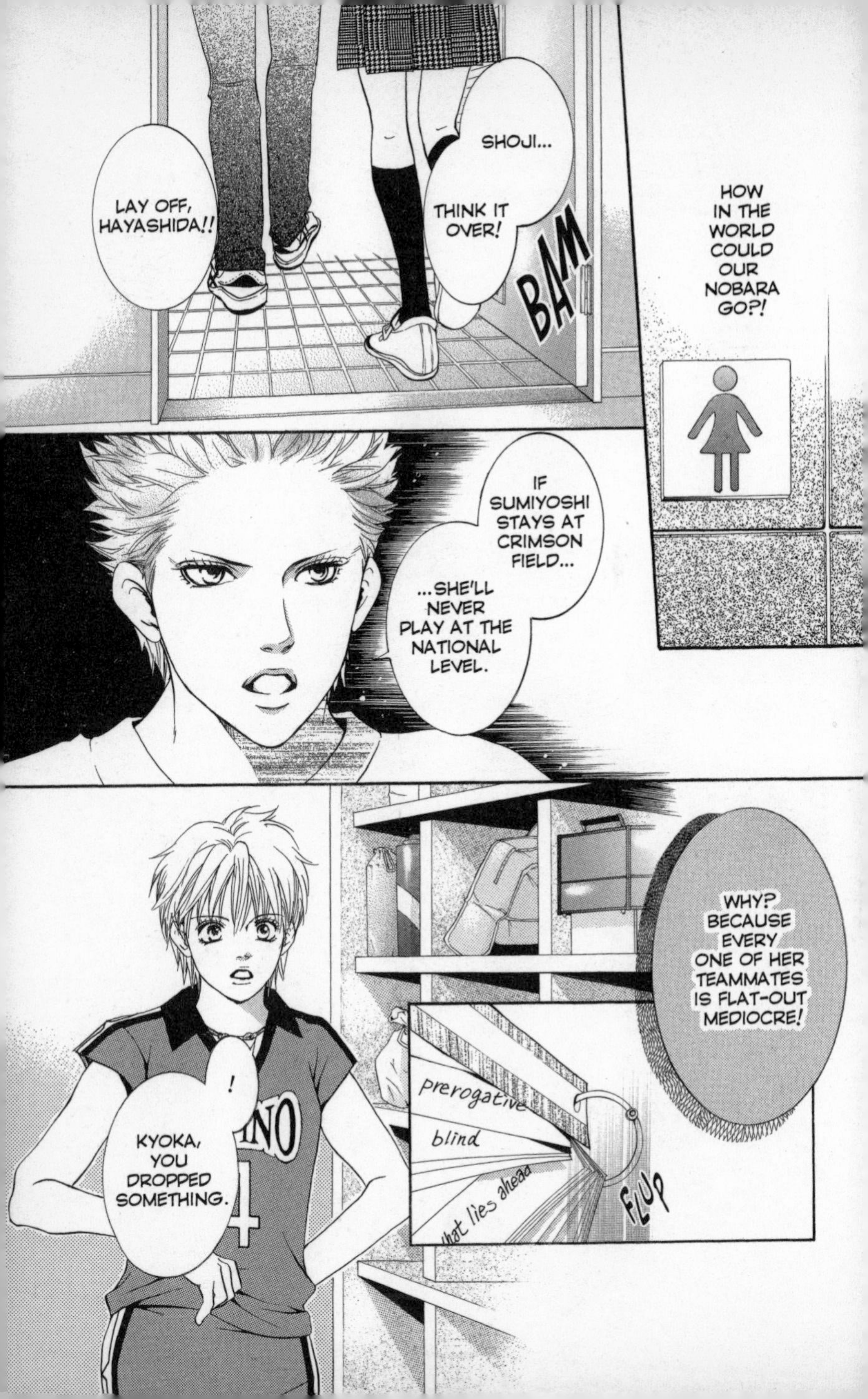

HOW IN THE WORLD COULD OUR NOBARA GO?!
SHOJI...
THINK IT OVER!
BAM
LAY OFF, HAYASHIDA!!
IF SUMIYOSHI STAYS AT CRIMSON FIELD...
...SHE'LL NEVER PLAY AT THE NATIONAL LEVEL.
WHY? BECAUSE EVERY ONE OF HER TEAMMATES IS FLAT-OUT MEDIOCRE!
prerogative
blind
what lies ahead
FLUP
!
KYOKA, YOU DROPPED SOMETHING.

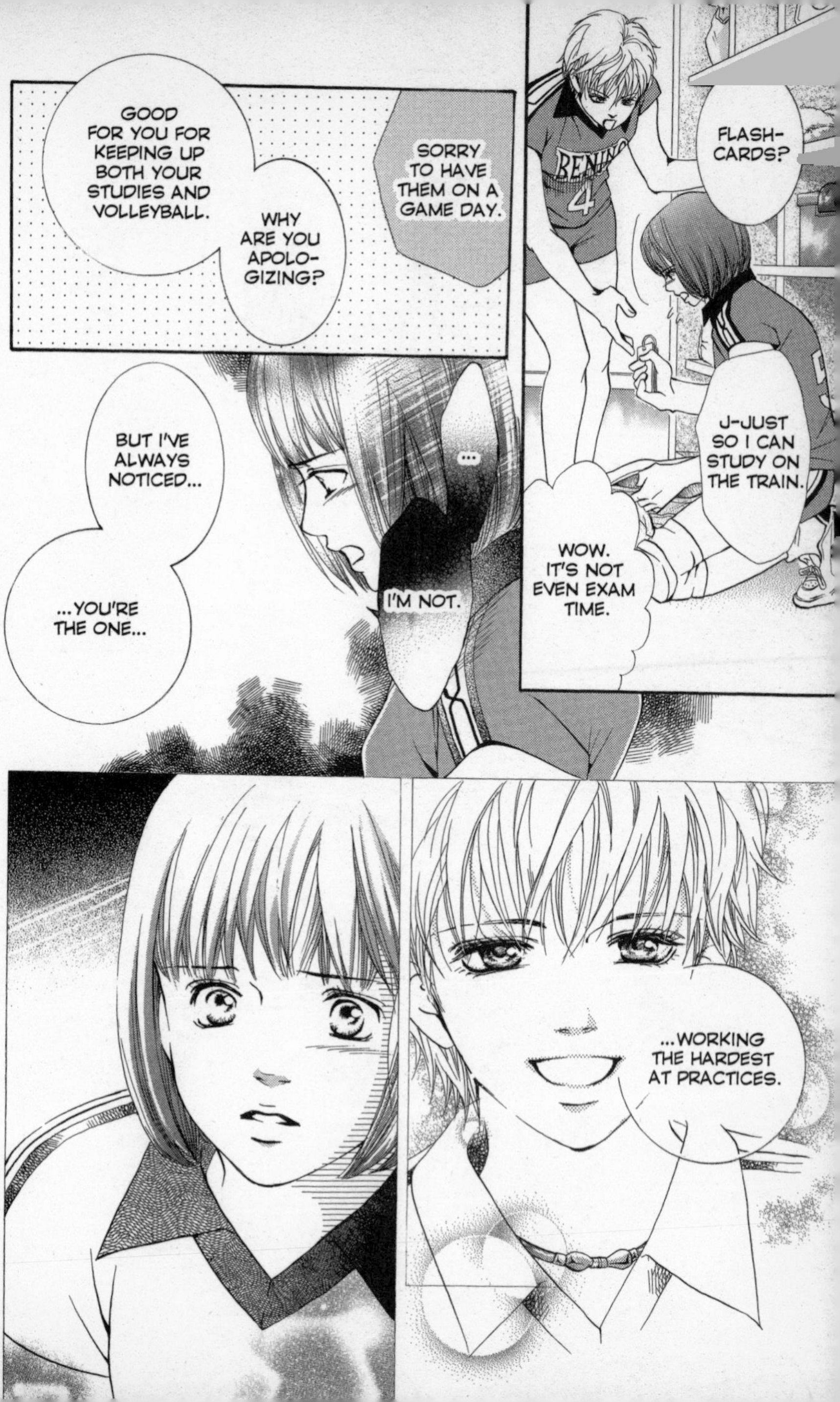
FLASH-CARDS?
J-JUST SO I CAN STUDY ON THE TRAIN.
WOW. IT'S NOT EVEN EXAM TIME.
SORRY TO HAVE THEM ON A GAME DAY.
GOOD FOR YOU FOR KEEPING UP BOTH YOUR STUDIES AND VOLLEYBALL.
WHY ARE YOU APOLOGIZING?
...
I'M NOT.
BUT I'VE ALWAYS NOTICED...
...YOU'RE THE ONE...
...WORKING THE HARDEST AT PRACTICES.

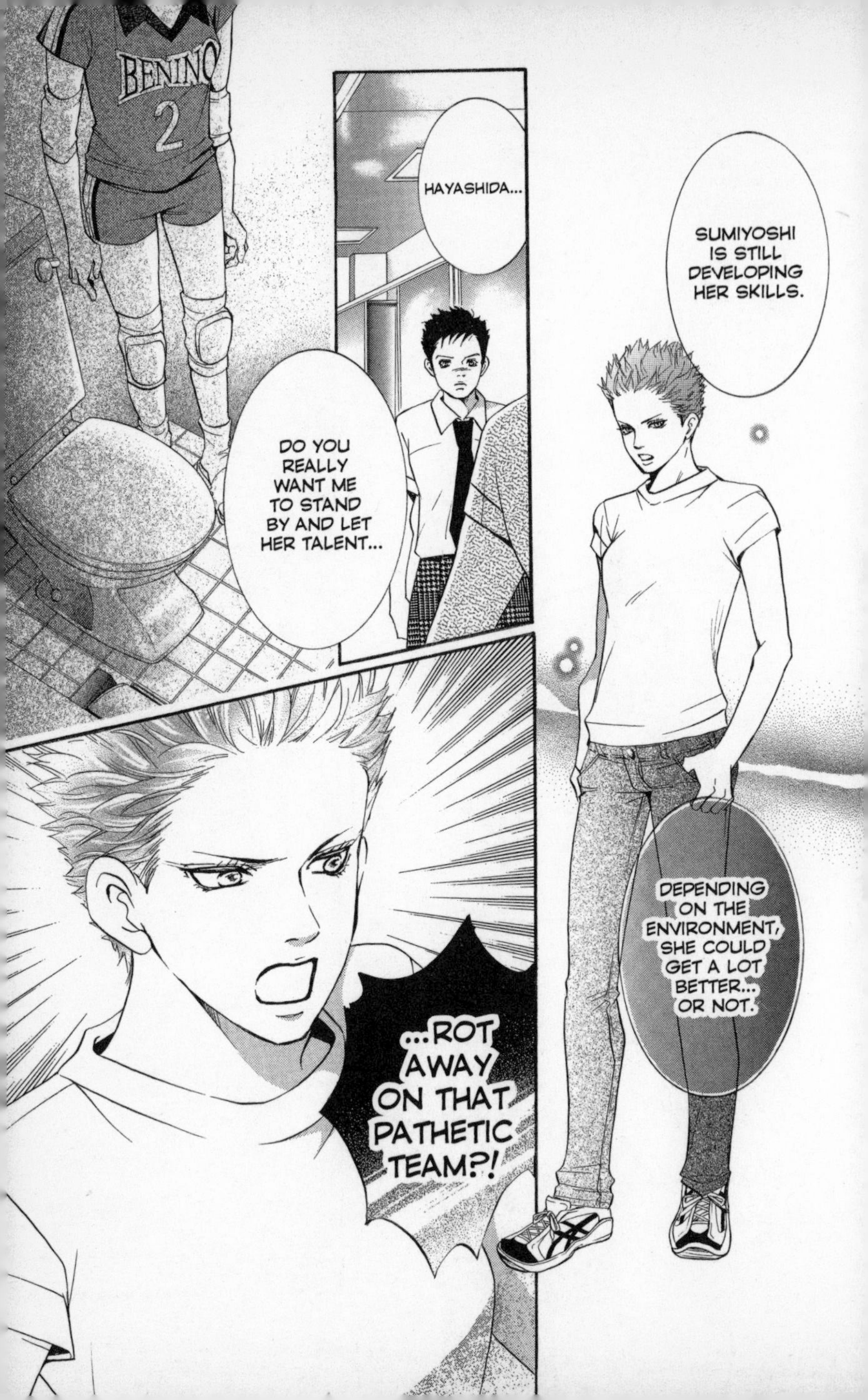
SUMIYOSHI IS STILL DEVELOPING HER SKILLS.
DEPENDING ON THE ENVIRONMENT, SHE COULD GET A LOT BETTER... OR NOT.
HAYASHIDA...
DO YOU REALLY WANT ME TO STAND BY AND LET HER TALENT...
...ROT AWAY ON THAT PATHETIC TEAM?!

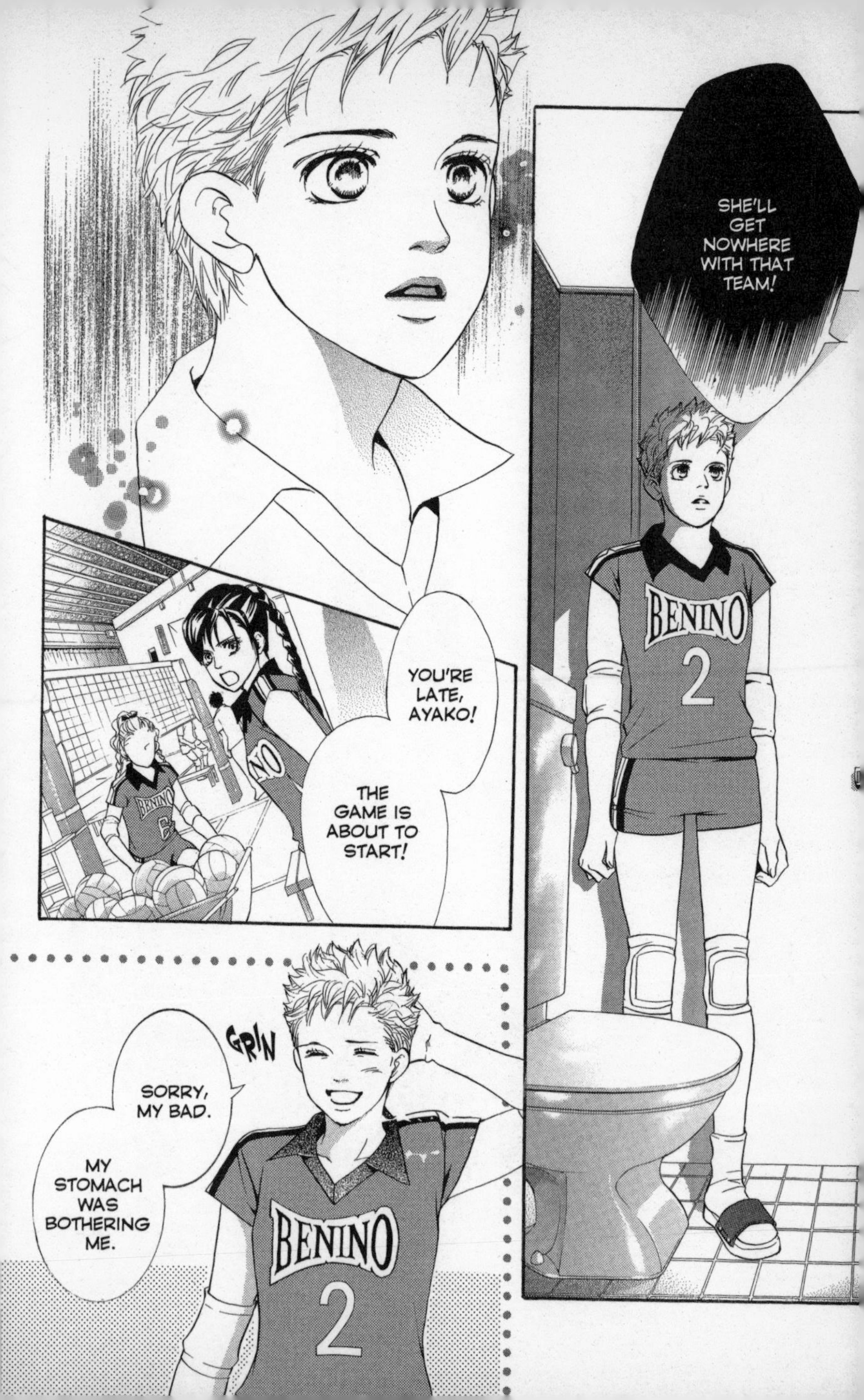
SHE'LL GET NOWHERE WITH THAT TEAM!
YOU'RE LATE, AYAKO!
THE GAME IS ABOUT TO START!
GRIN
SORRY, MY BAD.
MY STOMACH WAS BOTHERING ME.

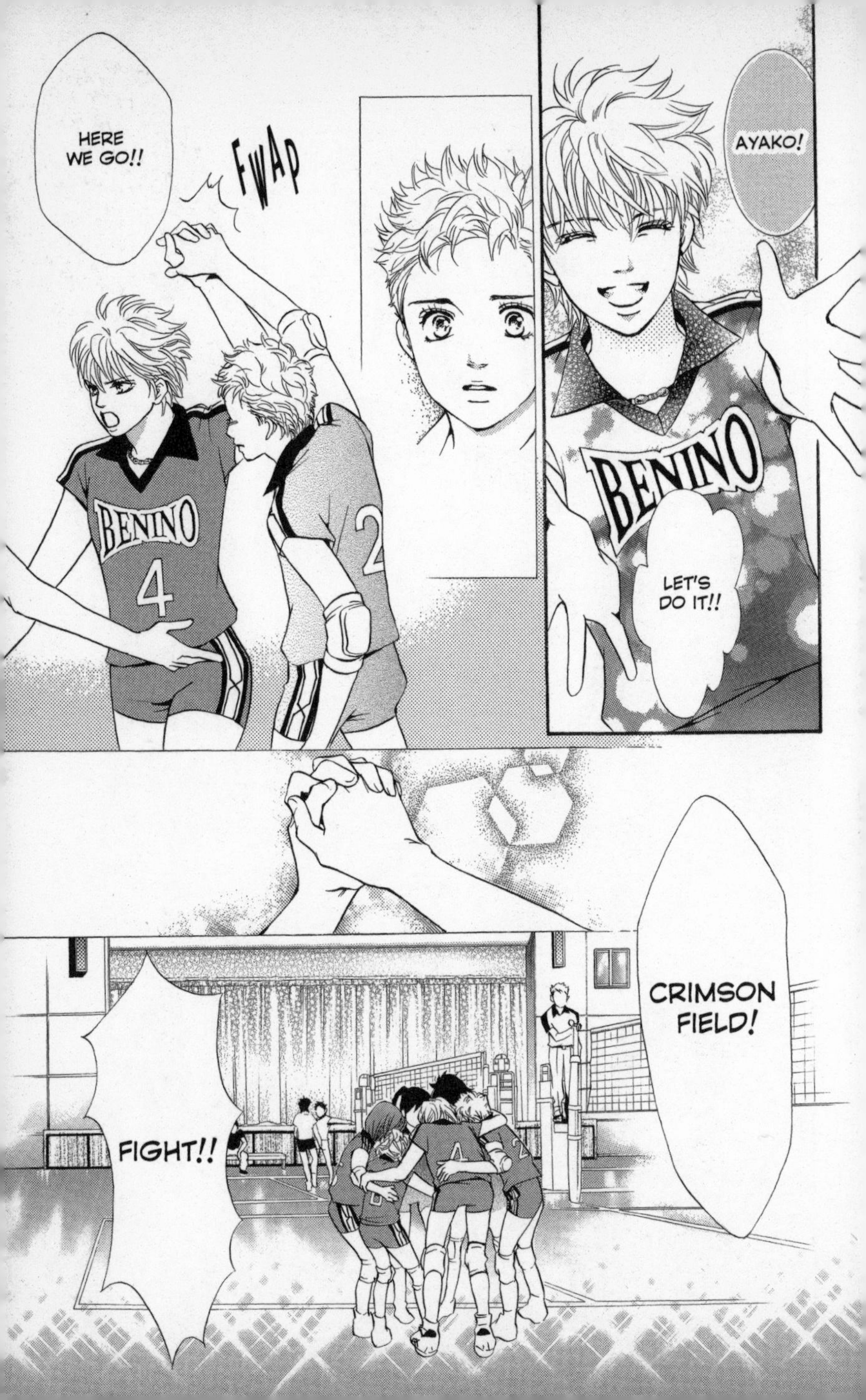
AYAKO!
LET'S DO IT!!
HERE WE GO!!
FWAP
CRIMSON FIELD!
FIGHT!!

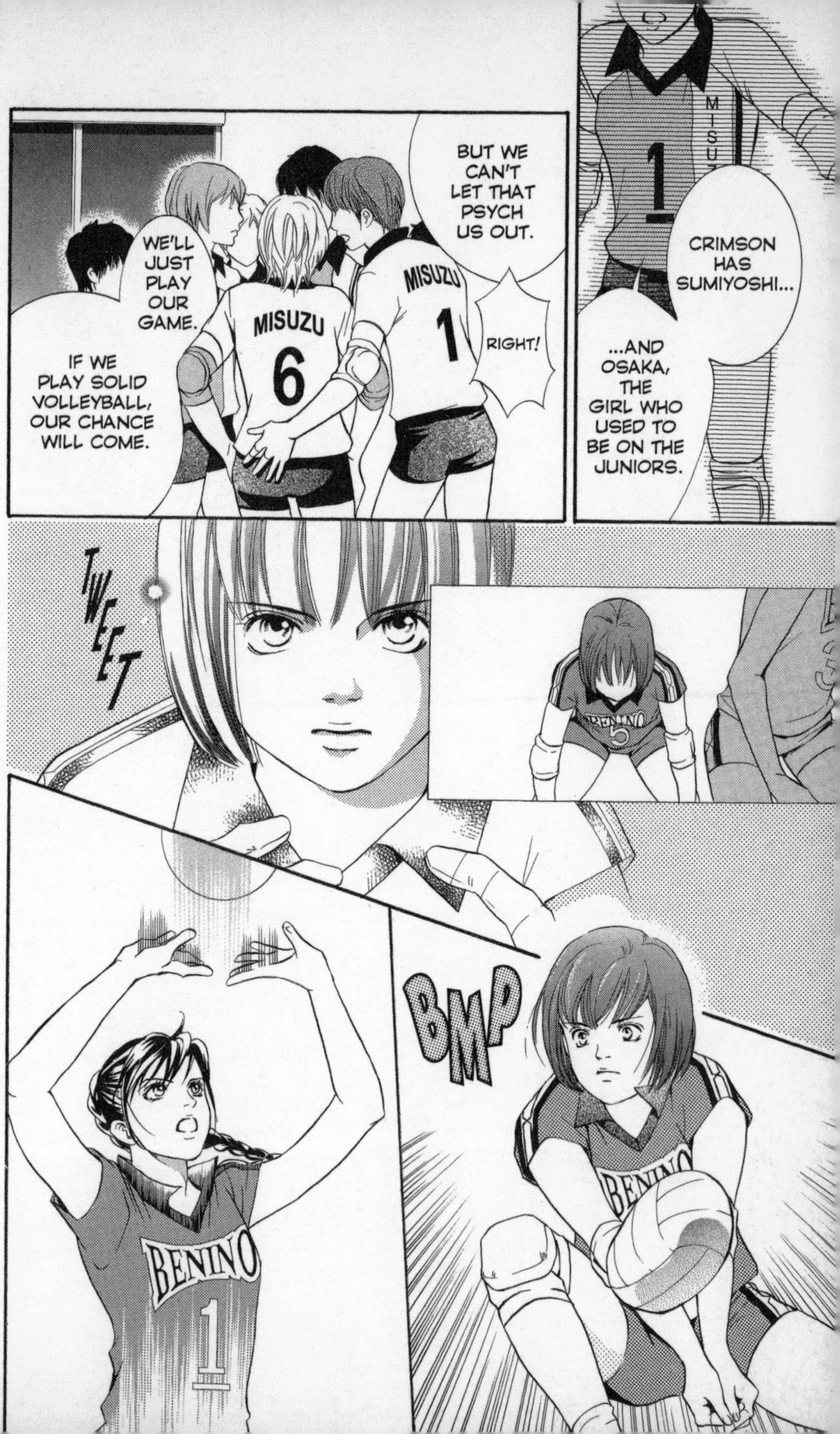
CRIMSON HAS SUMIYOSHI...
...AND OSAKA, THE GIRL WHO USED TO BE ON THE JUNIORS.
BUT WE CAN'T LET THAT PSYCH US OUT.
RIGHT!
WE'LL JUST PLAY OUR GAME.
IF WE PLAY SOLID VOLLEYBALL, OUR CHANCE WILL COME.
TWEET
BMP

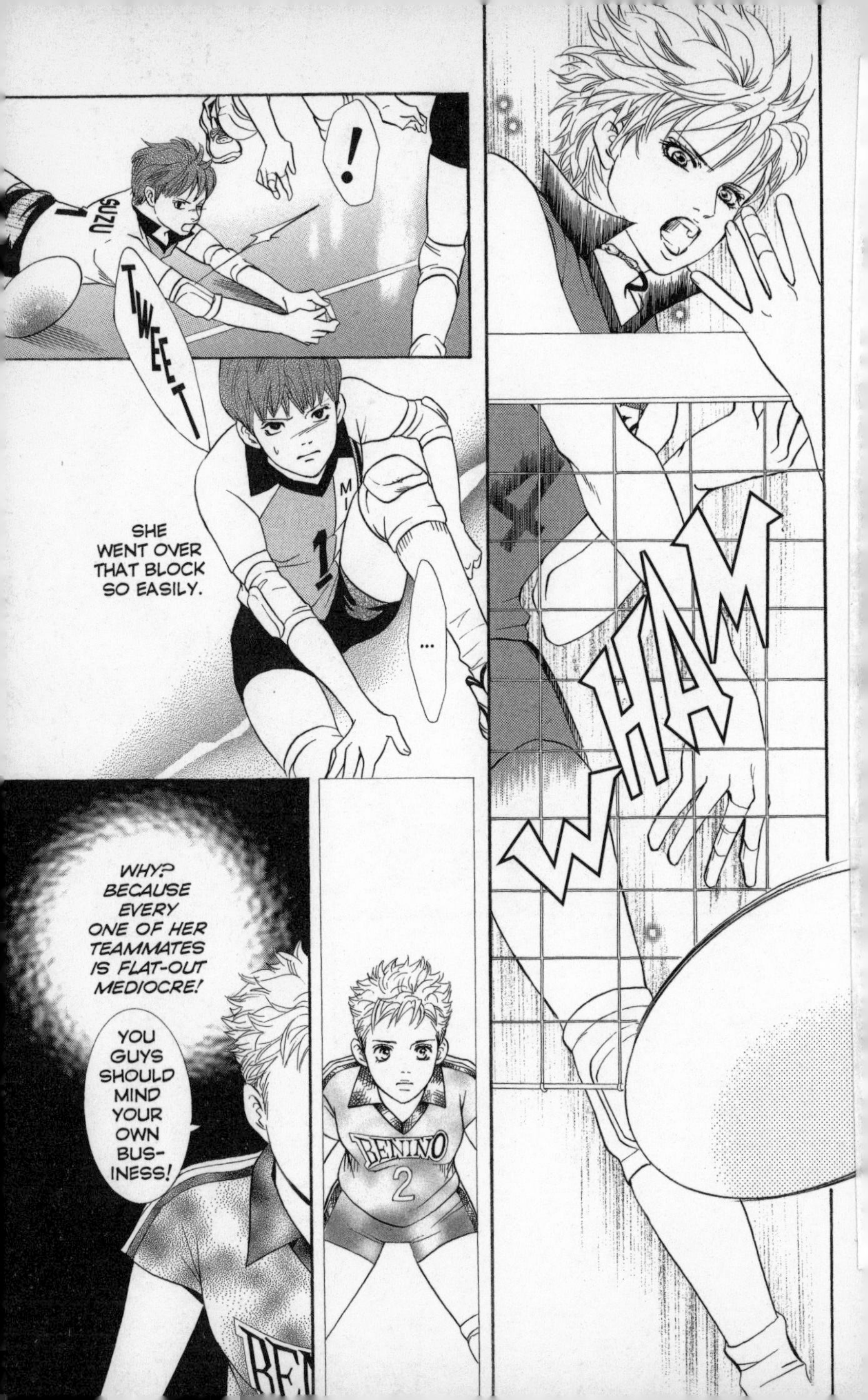
WHAM
!
TWEET
...
SHE WENT OVER THAT BLOCK SO EASILY.
WHY? BECAUSE EVERY ONE OF HER TEAMMATES IS FLAT-OUT MEDIOCRE!
YOU GUYS SHOULD MIND YOUR OWN BUS-INESS!

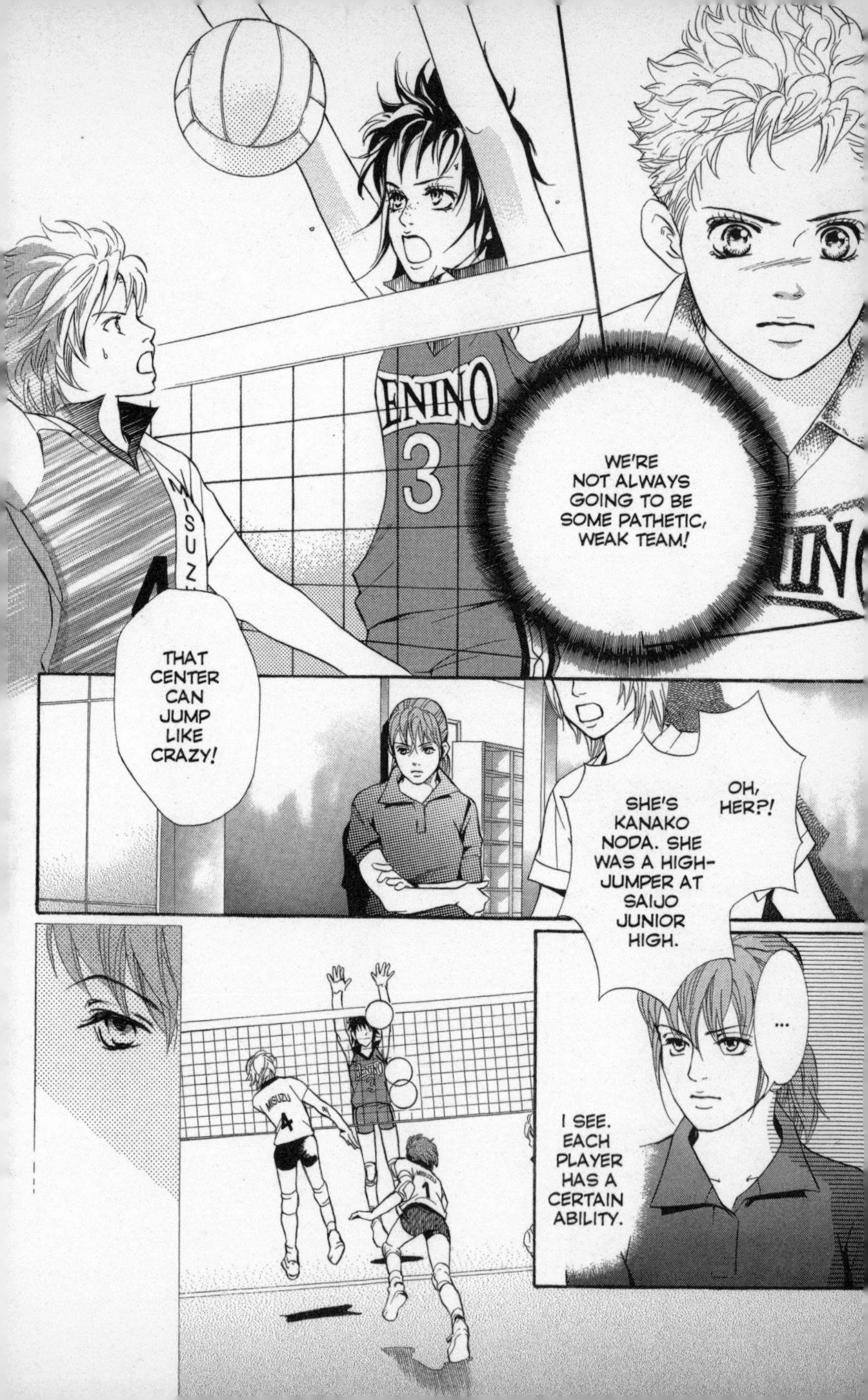
WE'RE NOT ALWAYS GOING TO BE SOME PATHETIC, WEAK TEAM!
THAT CENTER CAN JUMP LIKE CRAZY!
OH, HER?!
SHE'S KANAKO NODA. SHE WAS A HIGH-JUMPER AT SAIJO JUNIOR HIGH.
...
I SEE. EACH PLAYER HAS A CERTAIN ABILITY.

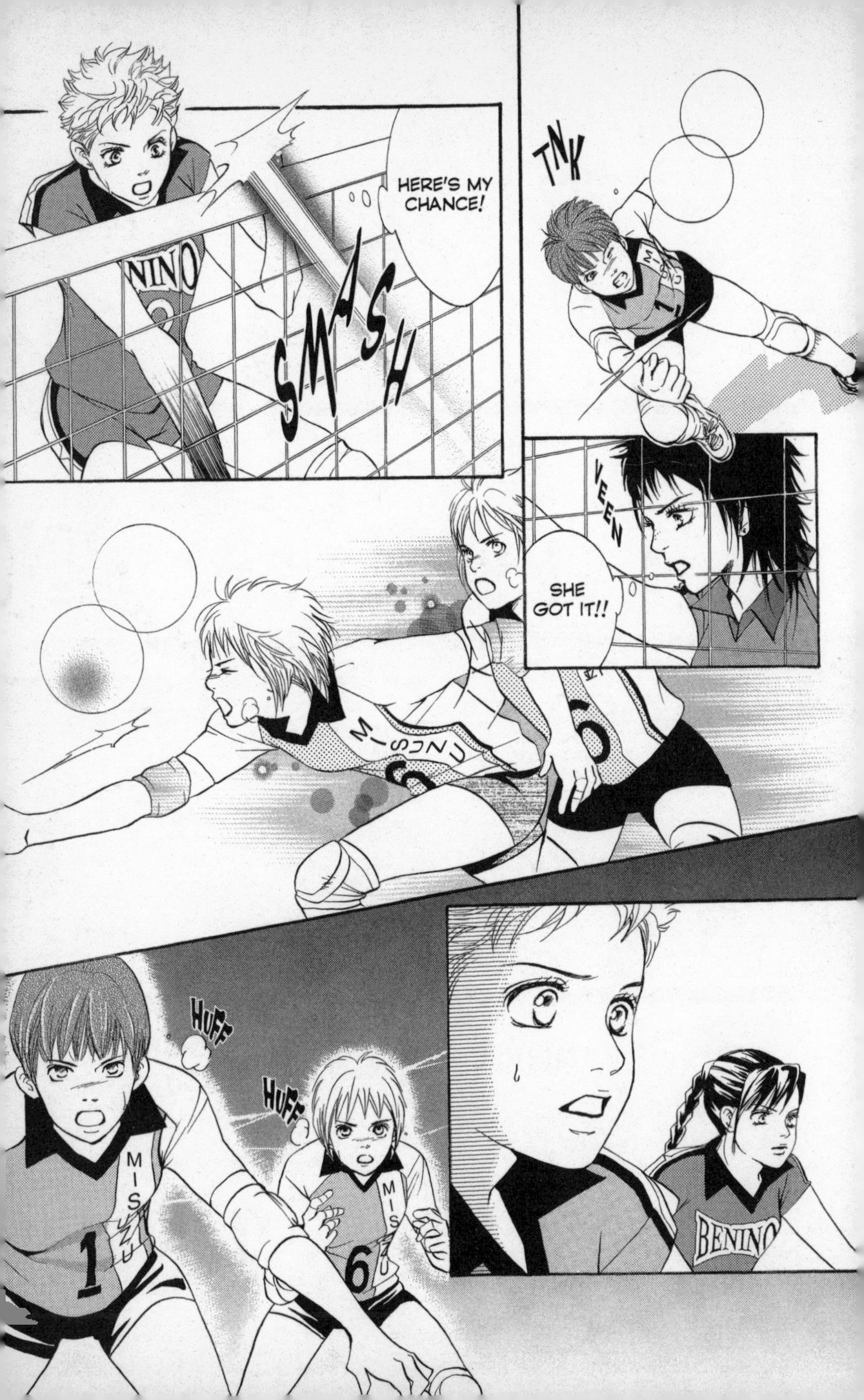

TNK
VEEN
SHE GOT IT!!
HERE'S MY CHANCE!
SMASH
HUFF
HUFF

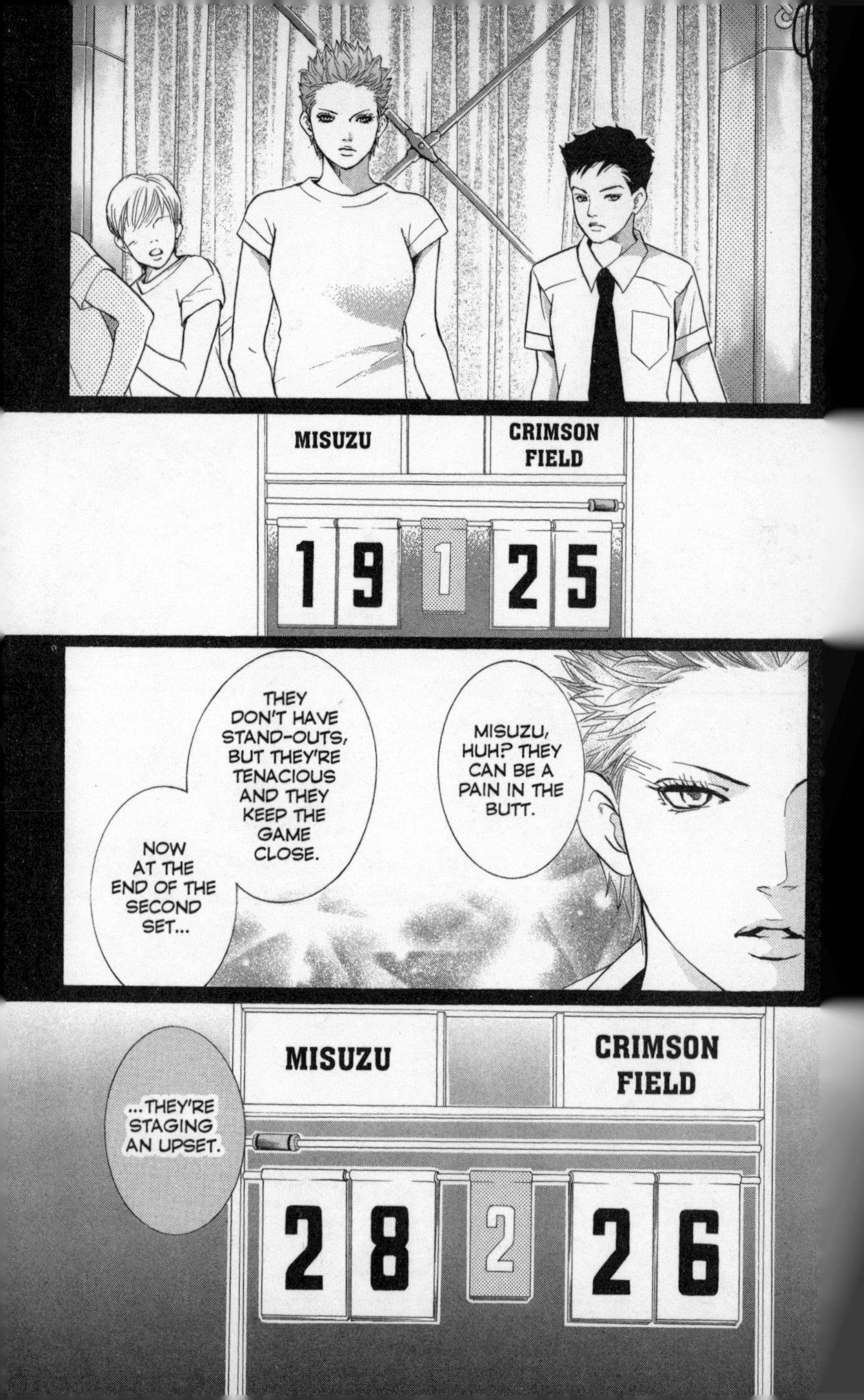
MISUZU
CRIMSON FIELD
19 1 25
MISUZU, HUH? THEY CAN BE A PAIN IN THE BUTT.
THEY DON'T HAVE STAND-OUTS, BUT THEY'RE TENACIOUS AND THEY KEEP THE GAME CLOSE.
NOW AT THE END OF THE SECOND SET...
MISUZU
CRIMSON FIELD
28 2 26
...THEY'RE STAGING AN UPSET.

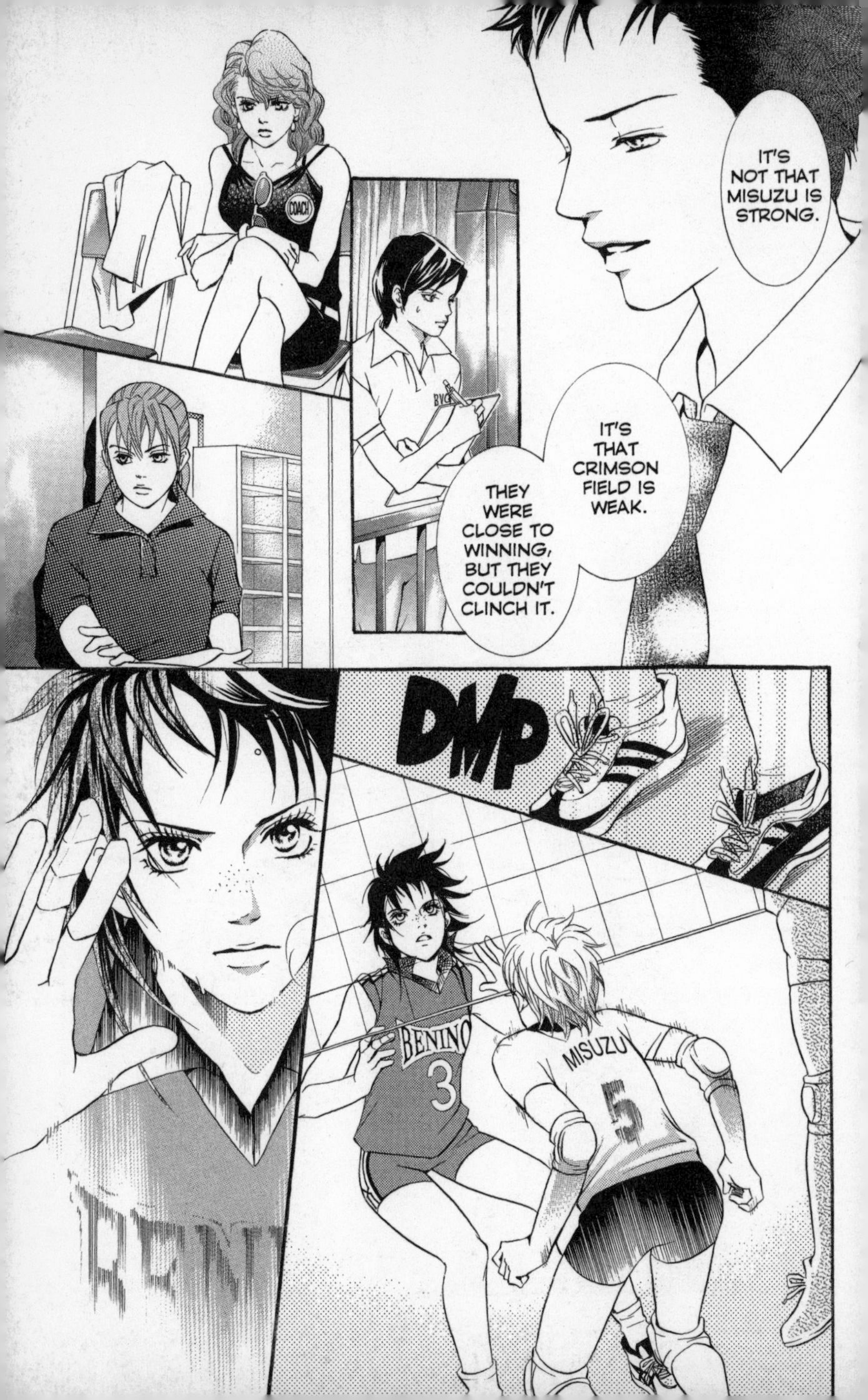
IT'S NOT THAT MISUZU IS STRONG.
IT'S THAT CRIMSON FIELD IS WEAK.
THEY WERE CLOSE TO WINNING, BUT THEY COULDN'T CLINCH IT.
DMP
MISUZU
5
BENINO
3

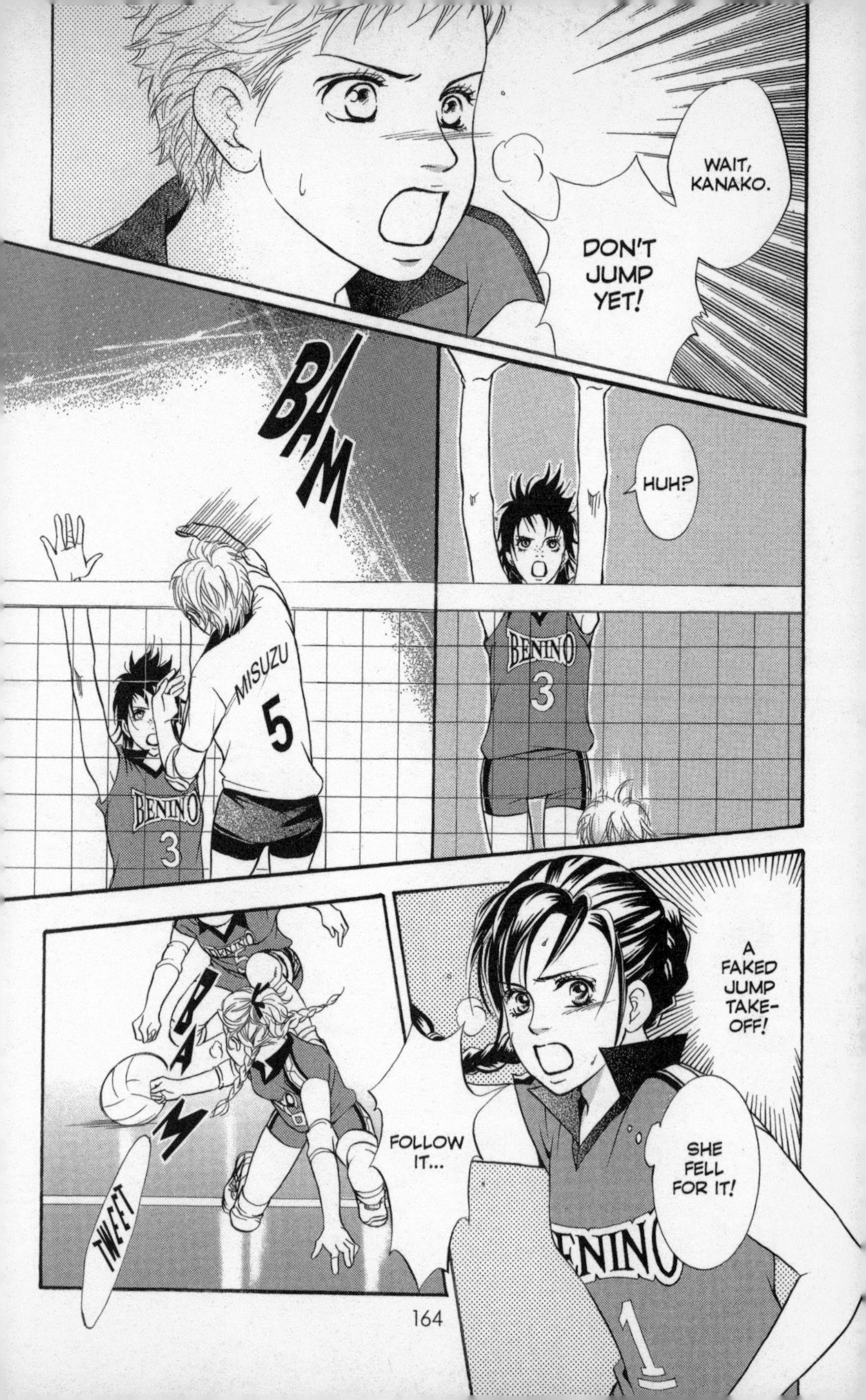
WAIT, KANAKO.
DON'T JUMP YET!
HUH?
BAM
A FAKED JUMP TAKE-OFF!
SHE FELL FOR IT!
FOLLOW IT...
BAM
TWEET

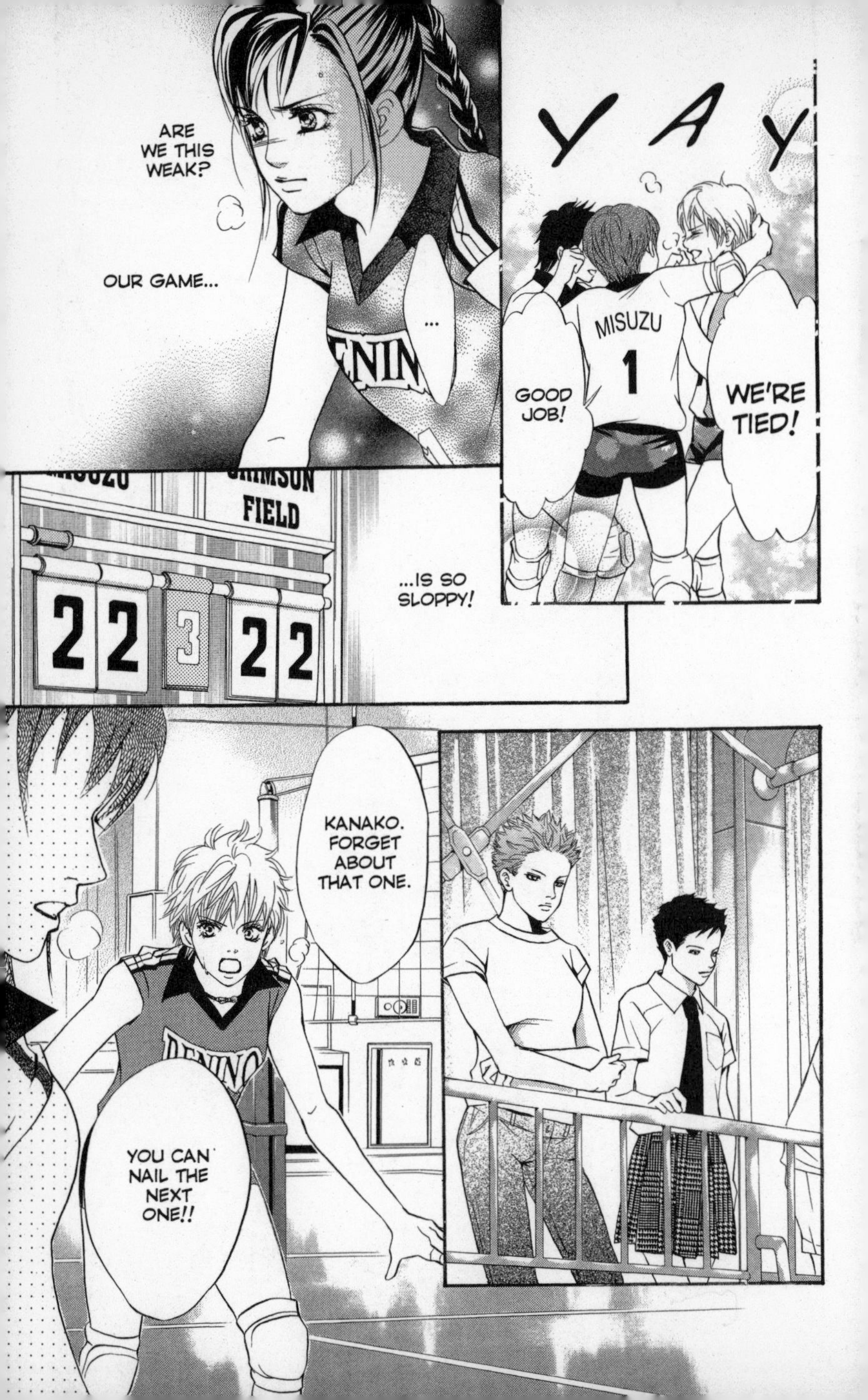
YAY
WE'RE TIED!
GOOD JOB!
MISUZU
1
ARE WE THIS WEAK?
OUR GAME...
...
...IS SO SLOPPY!
FIELD
22 3 22
KANAKO. FORGET ABOUT THAT ONE.
YOU CAN NAIL THE NEXT ONE!!

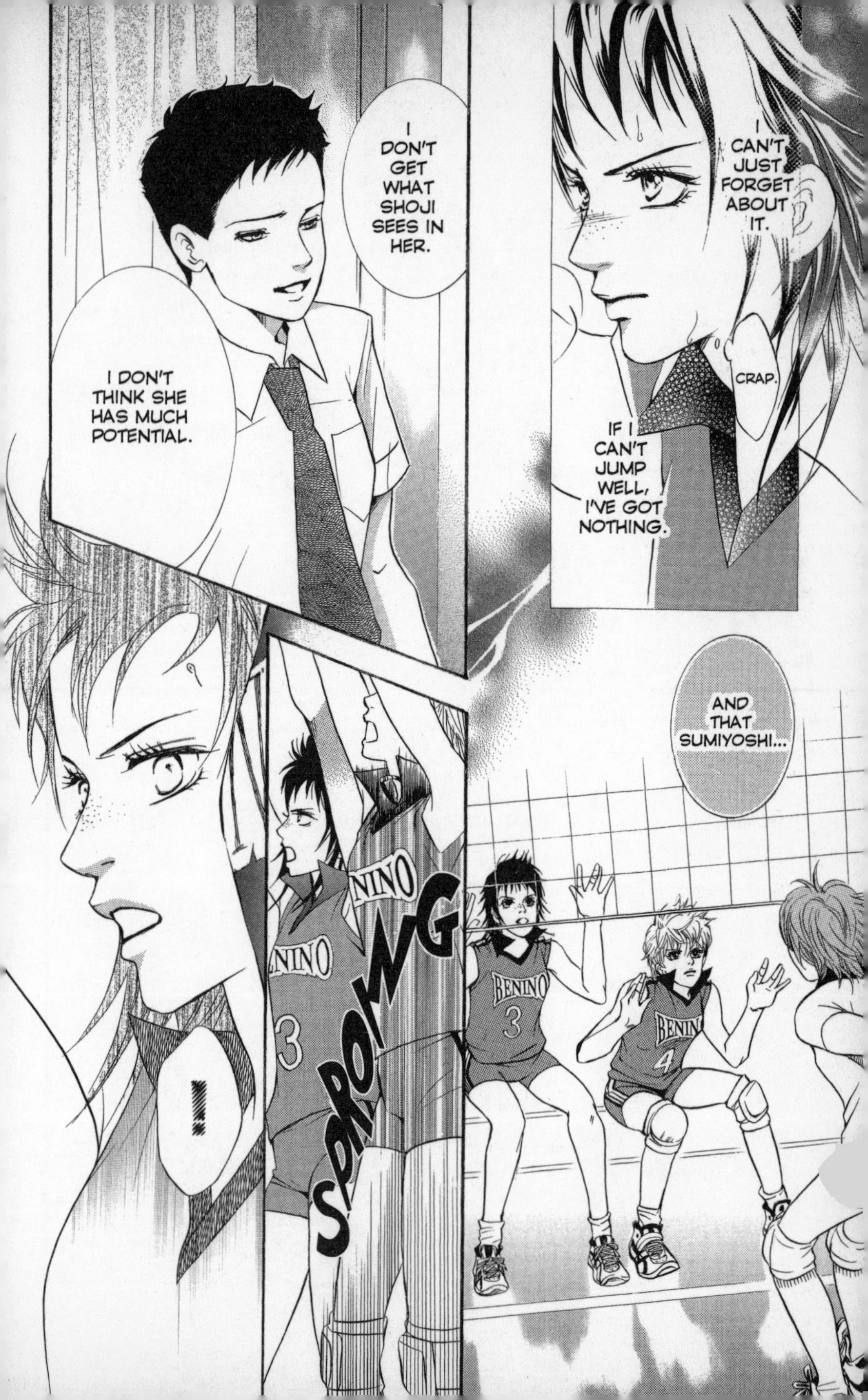
I CAN'T JUST FORGET ABOUT IT.
CRAP.
IF I CAN'T JUMP WELL, I'VE GOT NOTHING.
I DON'T GET WHAT SHOJI SEES IN HER.
I DON'T THINK SHE HAS MUCH POTENTIAL.
AND THAT SUMIYOSHI...
BENINO
3
BENINO
3
BENINO
4
NINO
BENINO
3
SPROING
!!

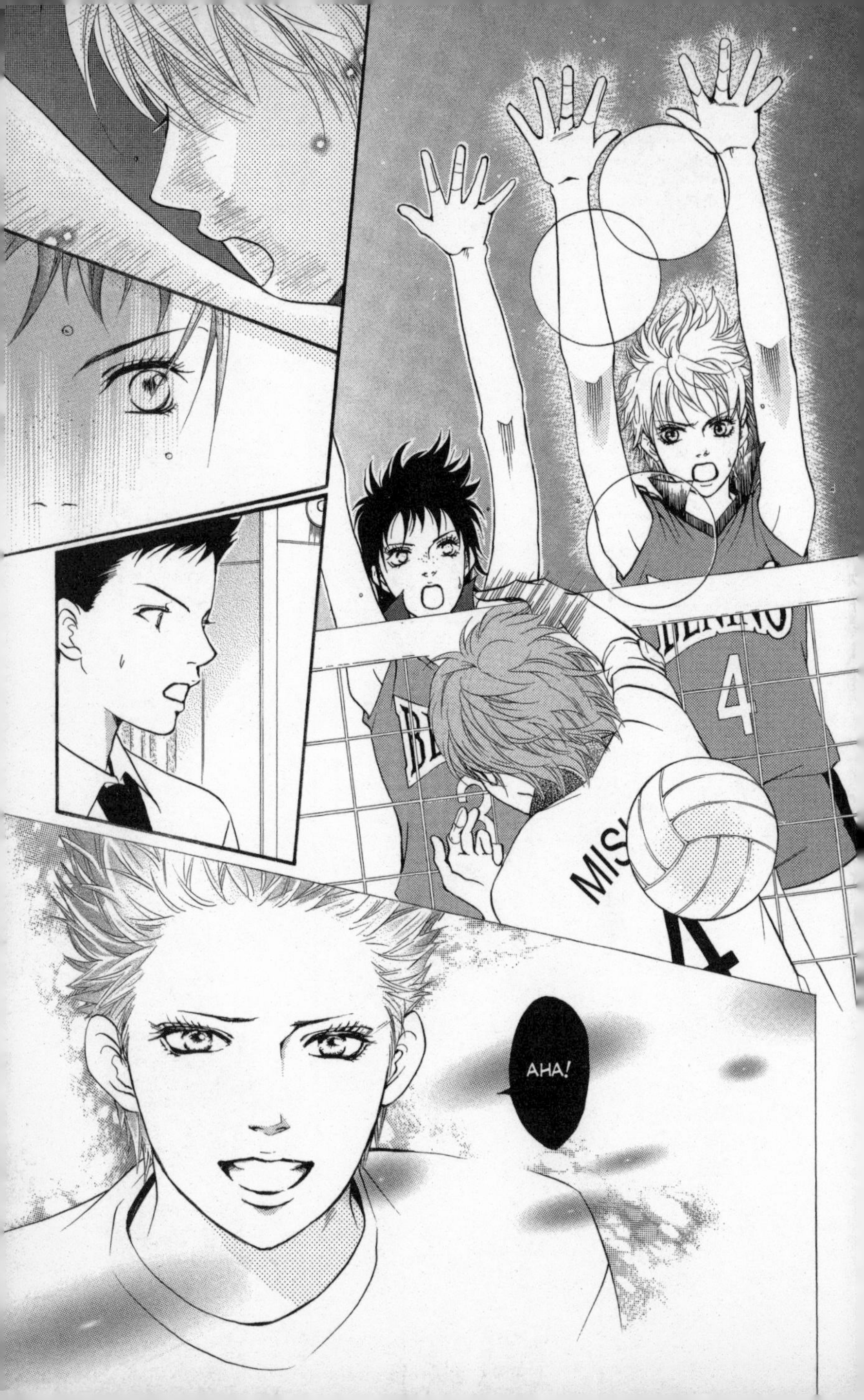
AHA!

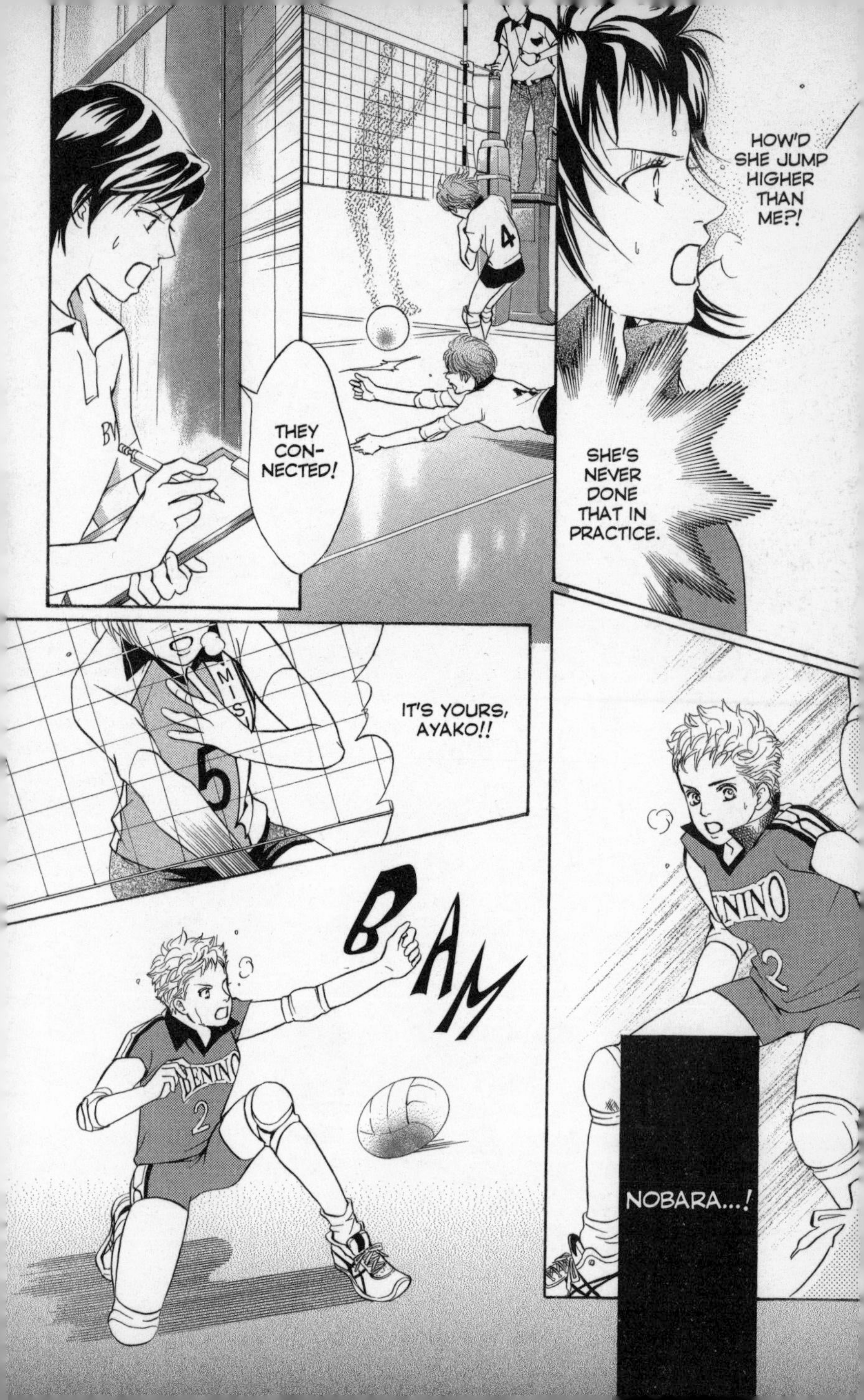
HOW'D SHE JUMP HIGHER THAN ME?!
SHE'S NEVER DONE THAT IN PRACTICE.
THEY CON-NECTED!
NOBARA...!
IT'S YOURS, AYAKO!!
BAM

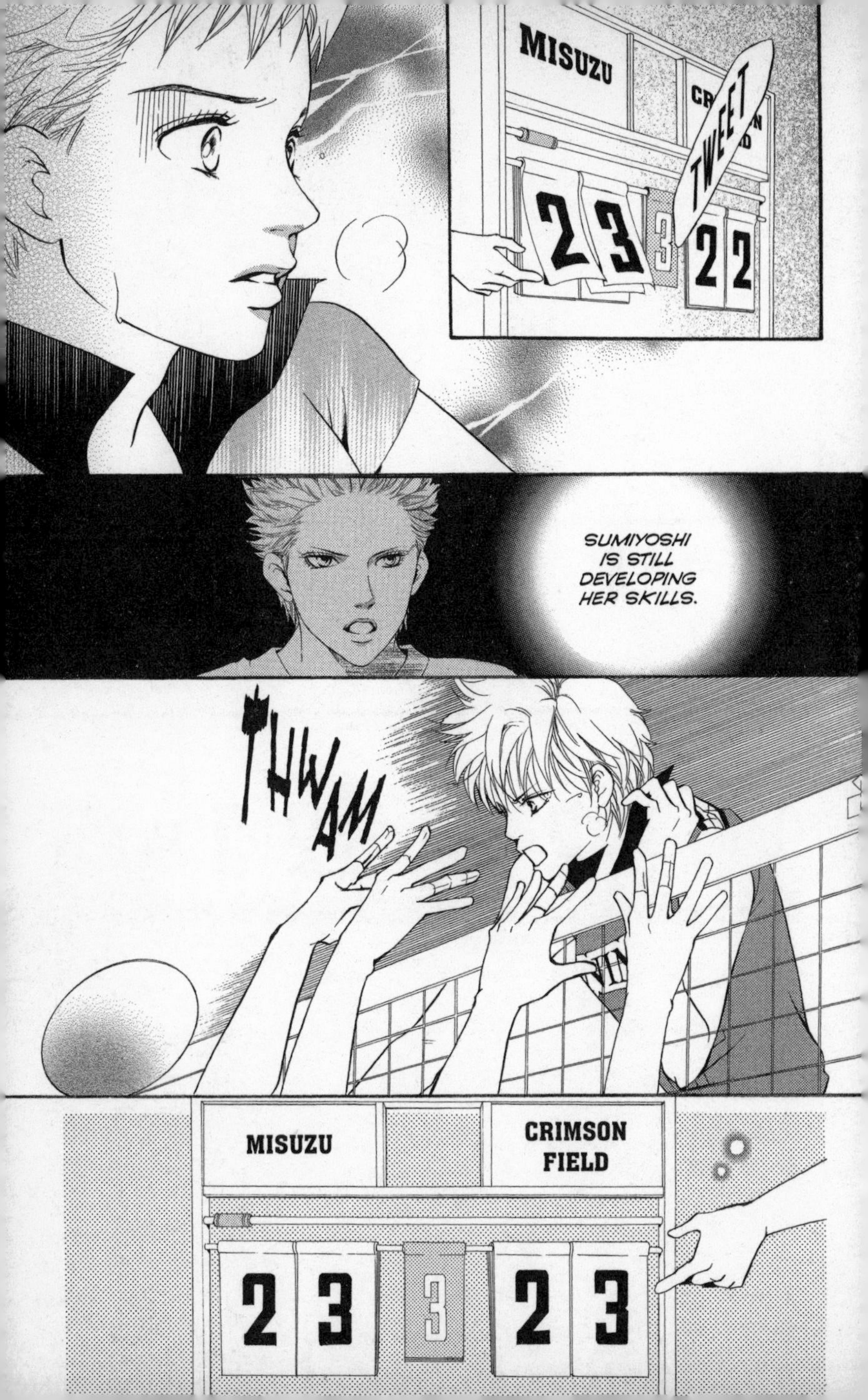
MISUZU
TWEET
23
3
22
SUMIYOSHI IS STILL DEVELOPING HER SKILLS.
THWAM
MISUZU
CRIMSON FIELD
23
3
23

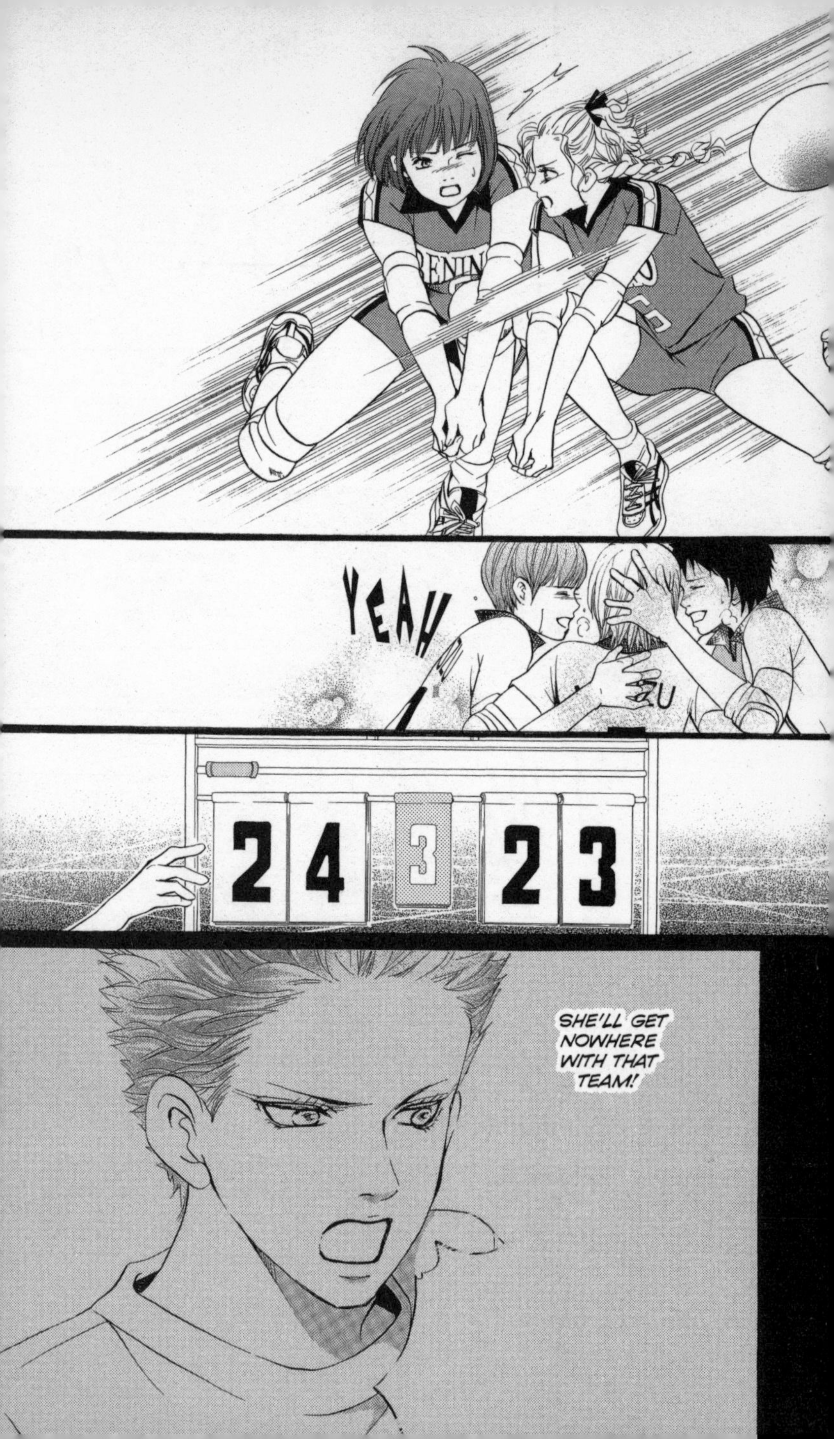
YEAH
24 3 23
SHE'LL GET NOWHERE WITH THAT TEAM!

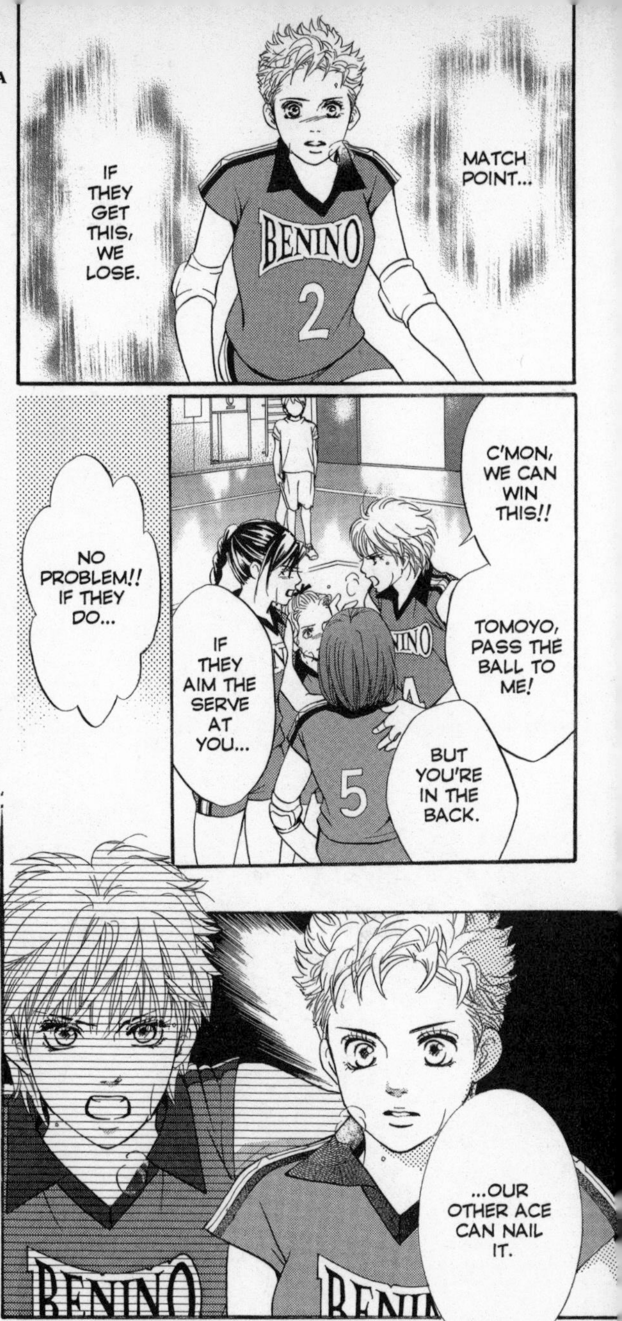
MATCH POINT...
IF THEY GET THIS, WE LOSE.
BENINO
C'MON, WE CAN WIN THIS!!
TOMOYO, PASS THE BALL TO ME!
BUT YOU'RE IN THE BACK.
IF THEY AIM THE SERVE AT YOU...
NO PROBLEM!! IF THEY DO...
...OUR OTHER ACE CAN NAIL IT.
BENINO
BENINO

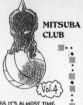

MITSUBA CLUB

Vol.4

I GUESS IT'S ALMOST TIME FOR US TO PART. RECENTLY I'VE BEEN LISTENING A LOT TO SAMBOMASTER. THEY'RE SO GOOD IT BRINGS TEARS TO MY EYES. IT WRINGS MY HEART.

MITSUBA TAKANASHI
C/O CRIMSON HERO EDITOR
VIZ MEDIA
P.O. BOX 77010
SAN FRANCISCO, CA 94107

ADDRESS YOUR LETTERS THERE. THANK YOU FOR YOUR CONTINUED CORRESPONDENCE. I READ EVERYTHING. PLEASE GIVE ME YOUR FEEDBACK. ALSO, YOU CAN SEND EMAIL THROUGH BETSUMA'S WEBPAGE [JAPANESE ONLY].

AND TO ALL MY STAFF MEMBERS...

Special Thanks
Nina
Chie . Abe
Ayako . Shitoh
Tamati san
Naomi . Minamoto
Kanon . Ozawa
Noriko . Ohtani
Aiji . Yamakawa
Haru . Kudoh
+
S. imai
+
Ryo
and
You

WELL THEN, IT MIGHT BE A LITTLE BIT UNTIL VOLUME 7 GOES ON SALE, SO THANK YOU FOR YOUR PATIENCE. I HOPE TO SEE YOU ALL AGAIN IN VOLUME 7!

MITSUBA TAKANASHI

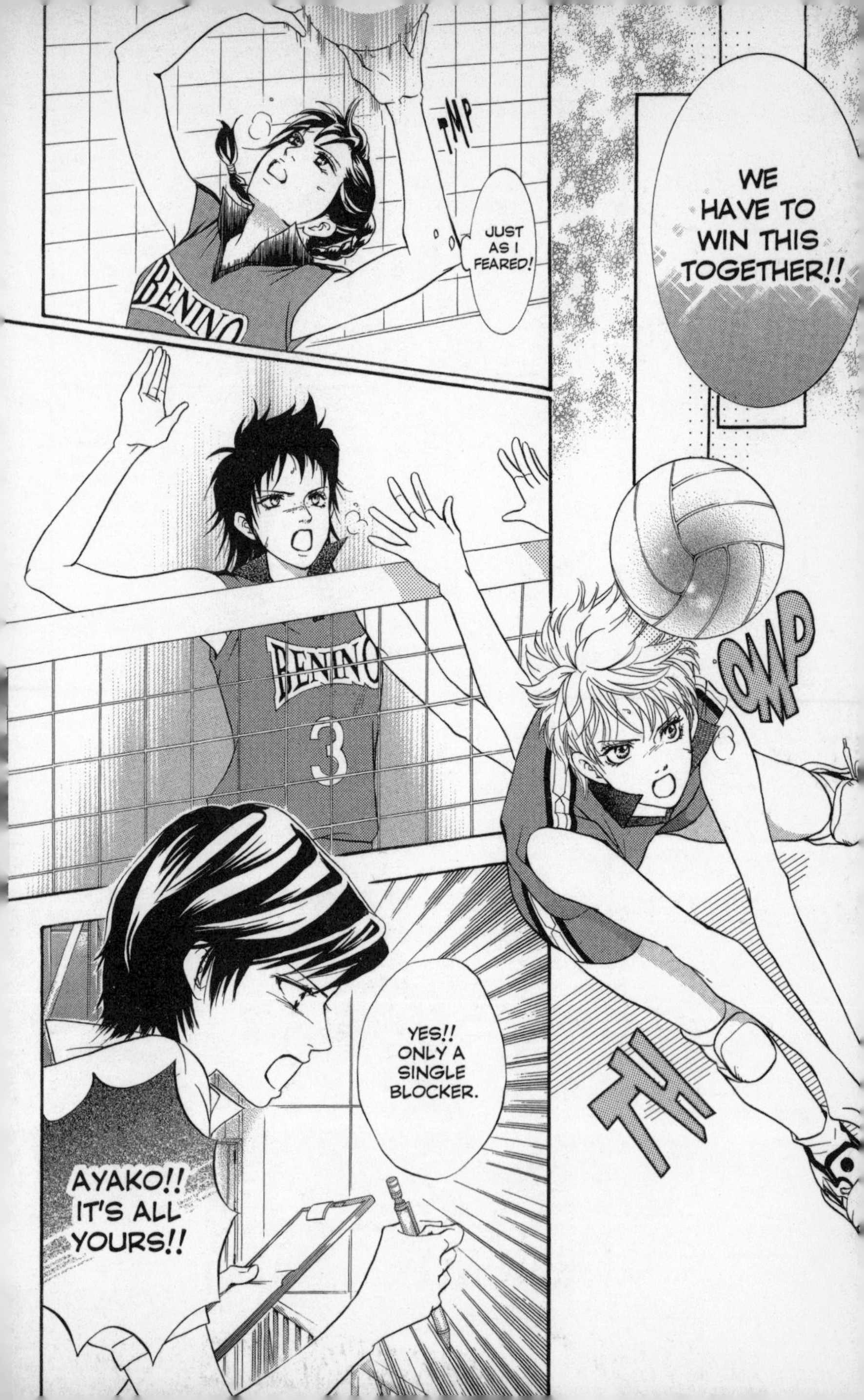
WE HAVE TO WIN THIS TOGETHER!!
OMP
TH
TMP
JUST AS I FEARED!
YES!! ONLY A SINGLE BLOCKER.
AYAKO!! IT'S ALL YOURS!!

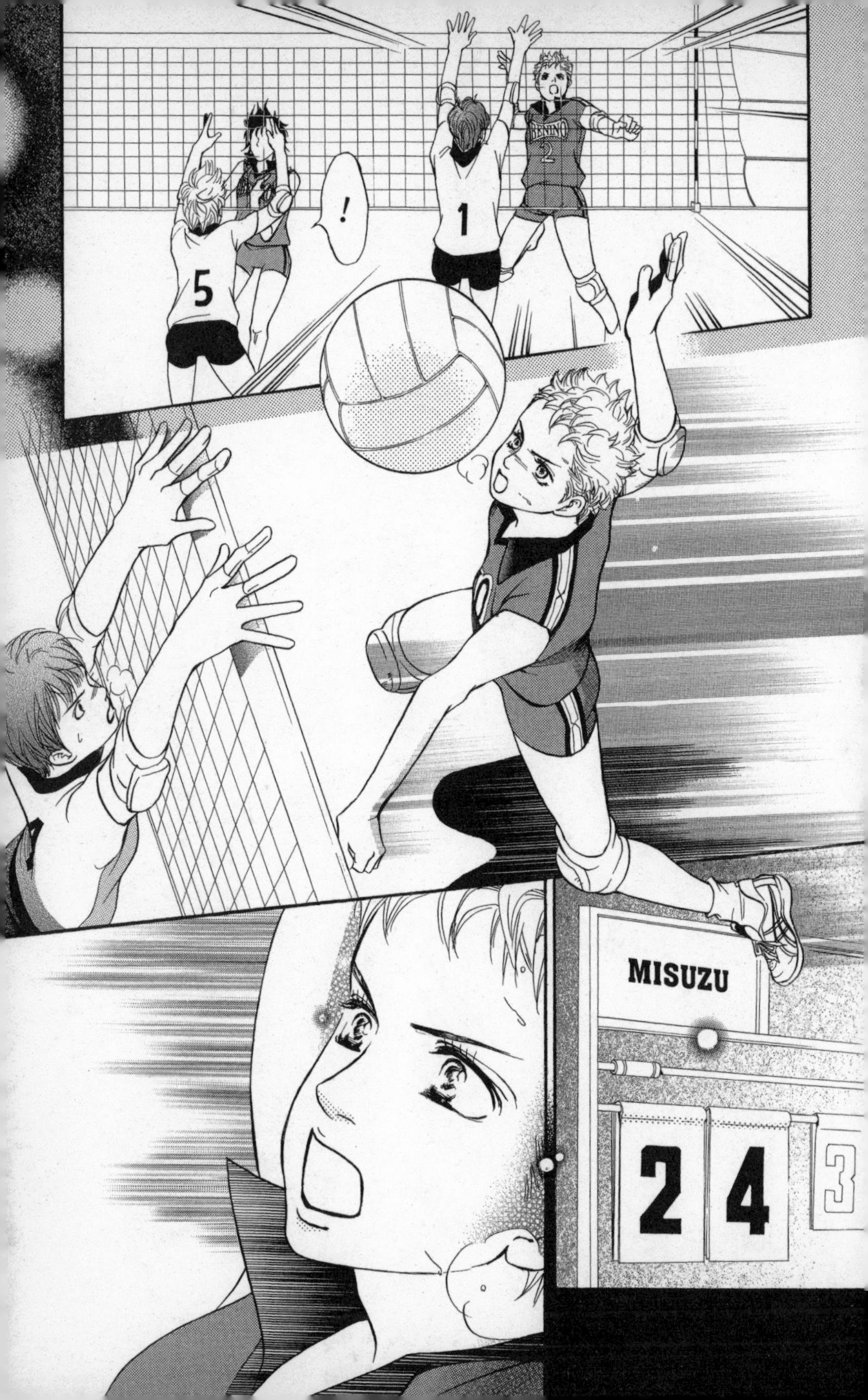
!
MISUZU
24
3

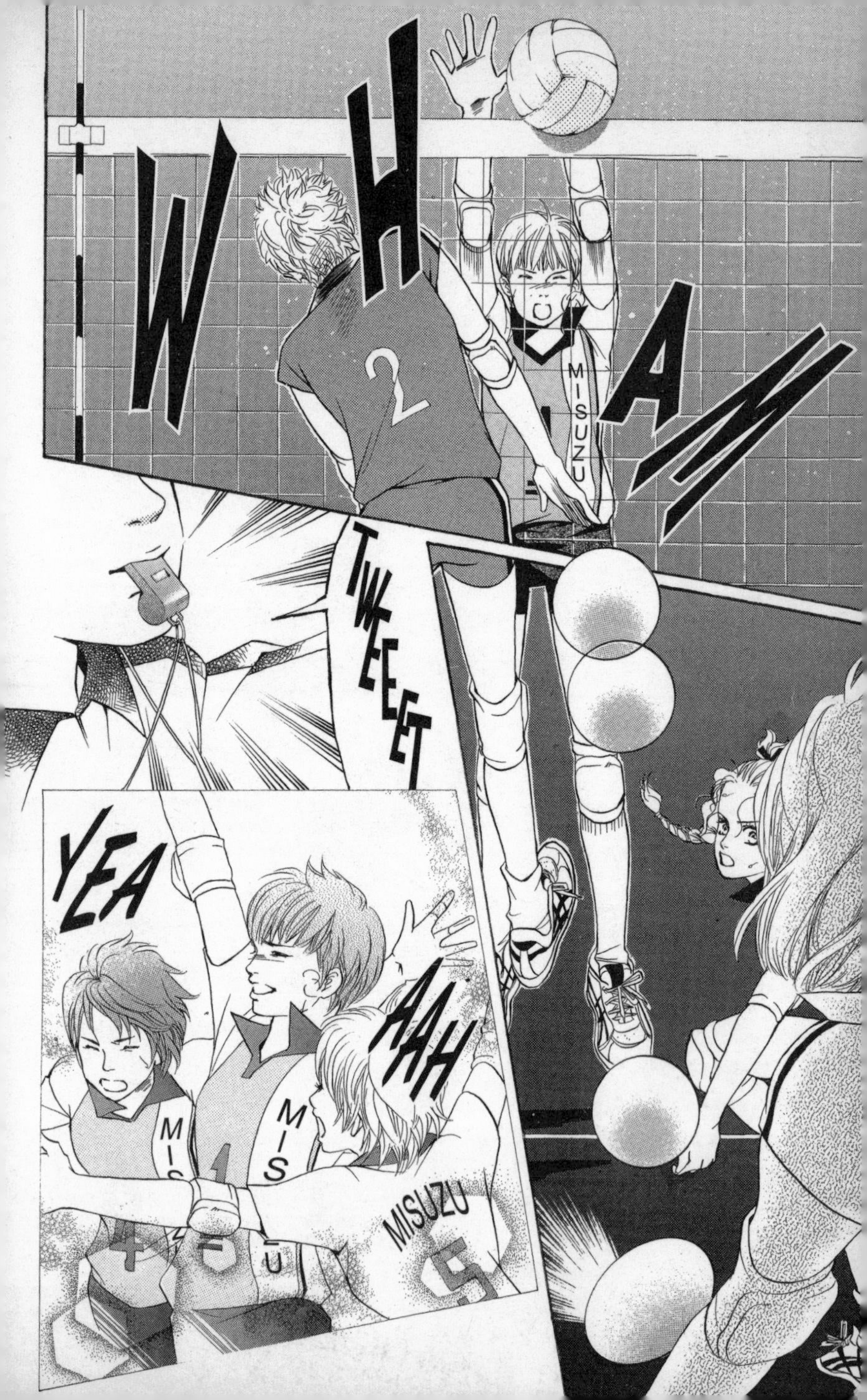
WHAM
MISUZU
TWEEEET
YEA
AAH
MIS
MIS
MISUZU

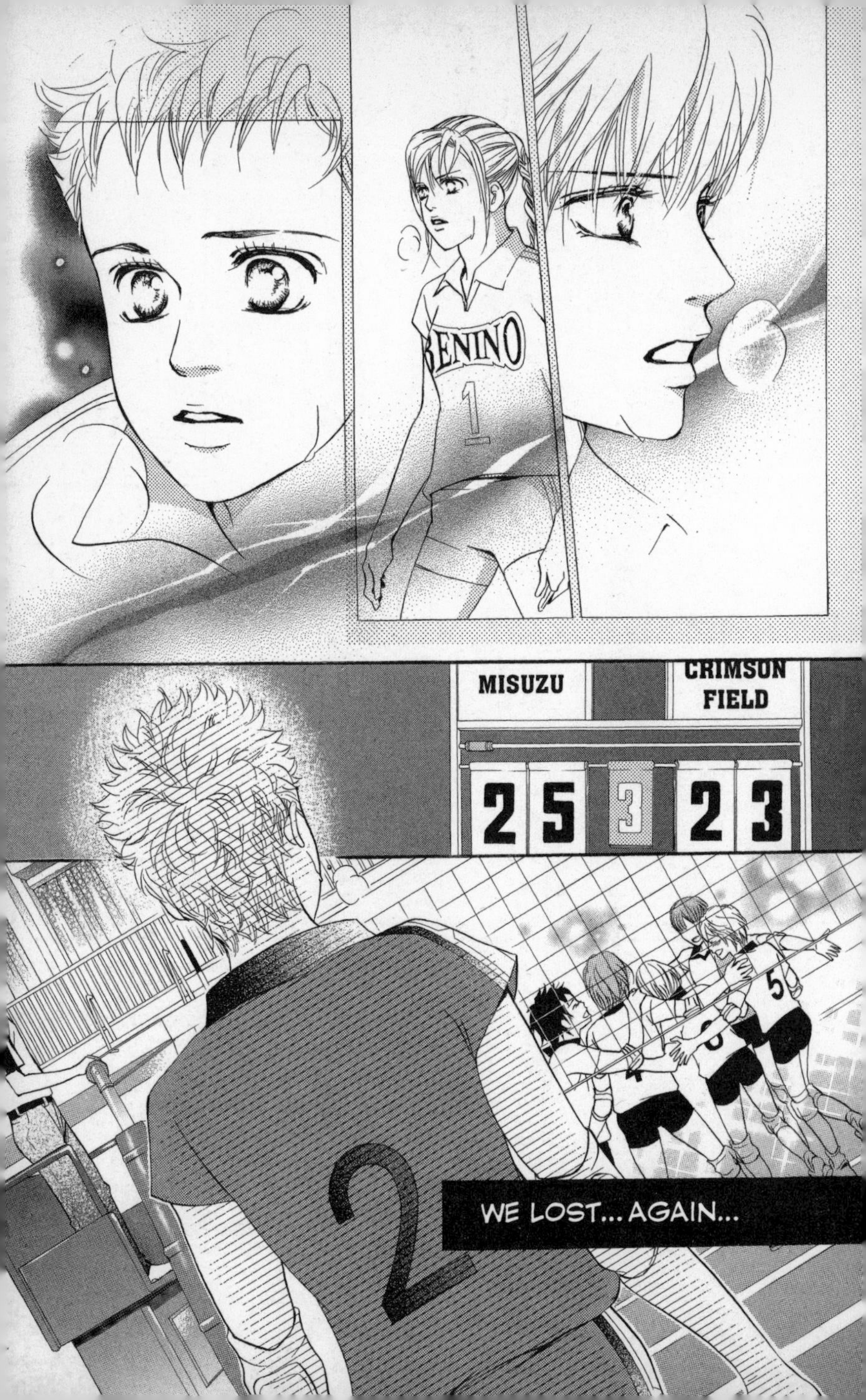
BENINO
1
MISUZU
CRIMSON FIELD
25 3 23
WE LOST... AGAIN...

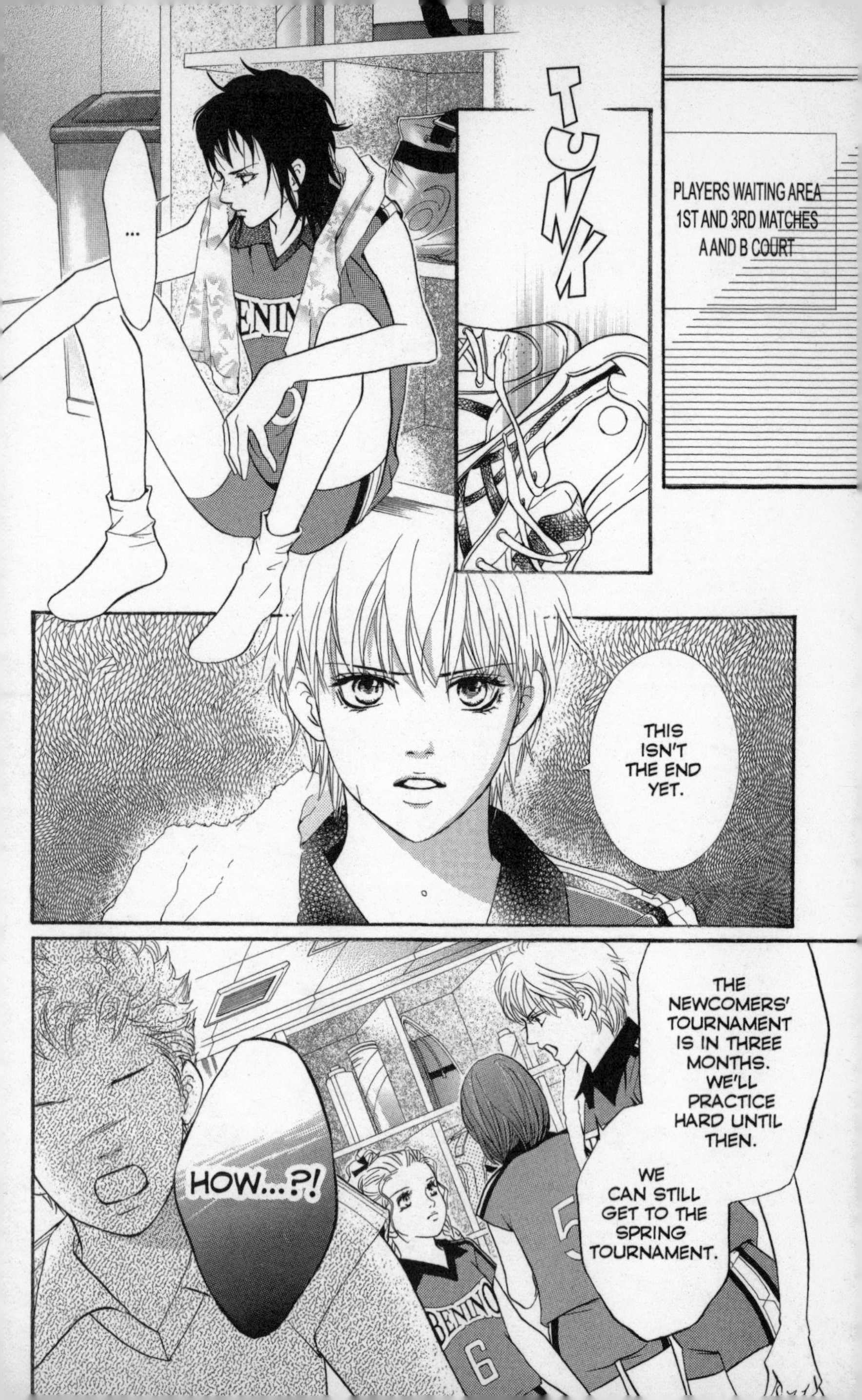
PLAYERS WAITING AREA
1ST AND 3RD MATCHES
A AND B COURT
TUNK
...
THIS ISN'T THE END YET.
THE NEWCOMERS' TOURNAMENT IS IN THREE MONTHS. WE'LL PRACTICE HARD UNTIL THEN.
WE CAN STILL GET TO THE SPRING TOURNAMENT.
HOW...?!

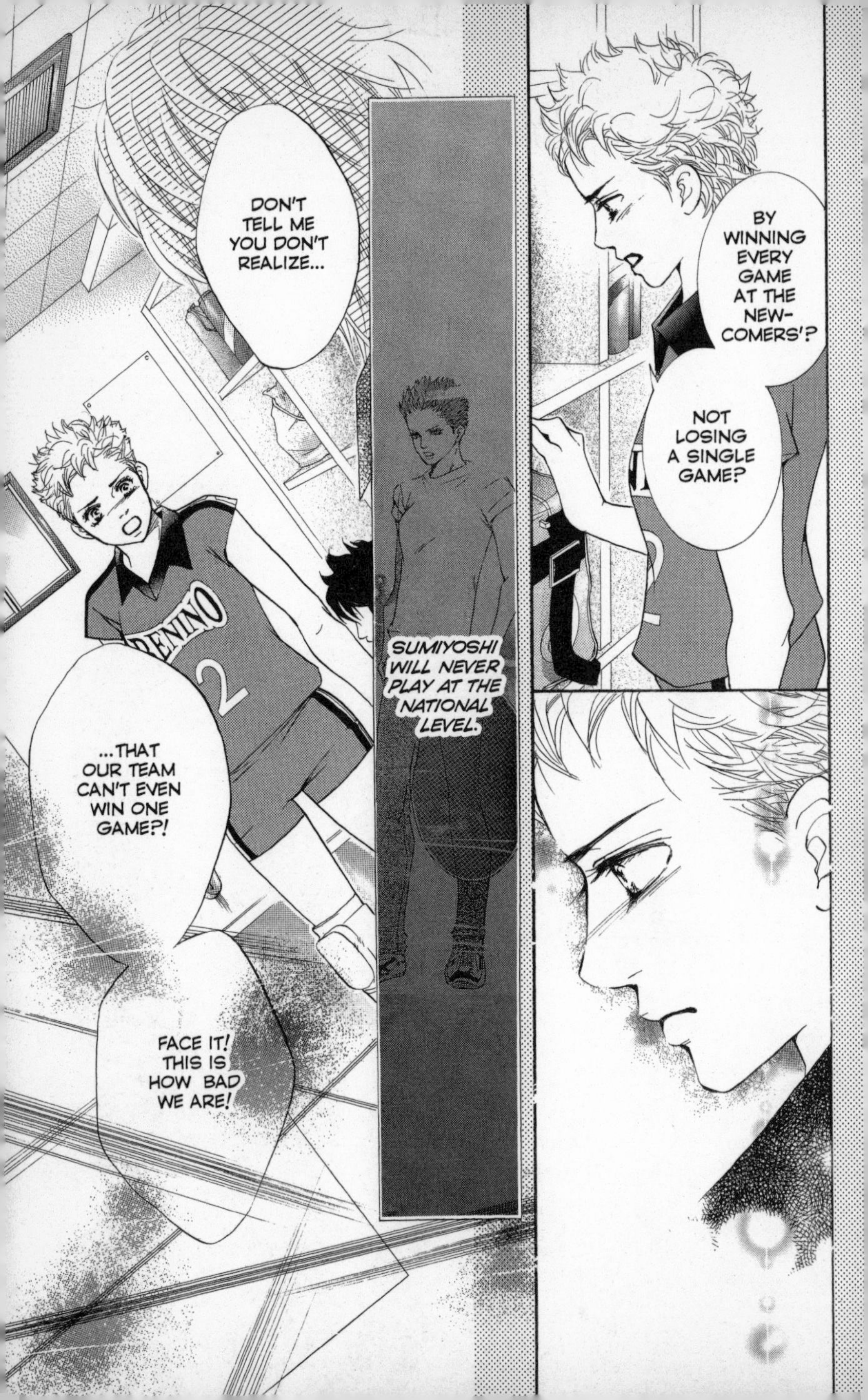
BY WINNING EVERY GAME AT THE NEW-COMERS'?
NOT LOSING A SINGLE GAME?
SUMIYOSHI WILL NEVER PLAY AT THE NATIONAL LEVEL.
DON'T TELL ME YOU DON'T REALIZE...
...THAT OUR TEAM CAN'T EVEN WIN ONE GAME?!
FACE IT! THIS IS HOW BAD WE ARE!

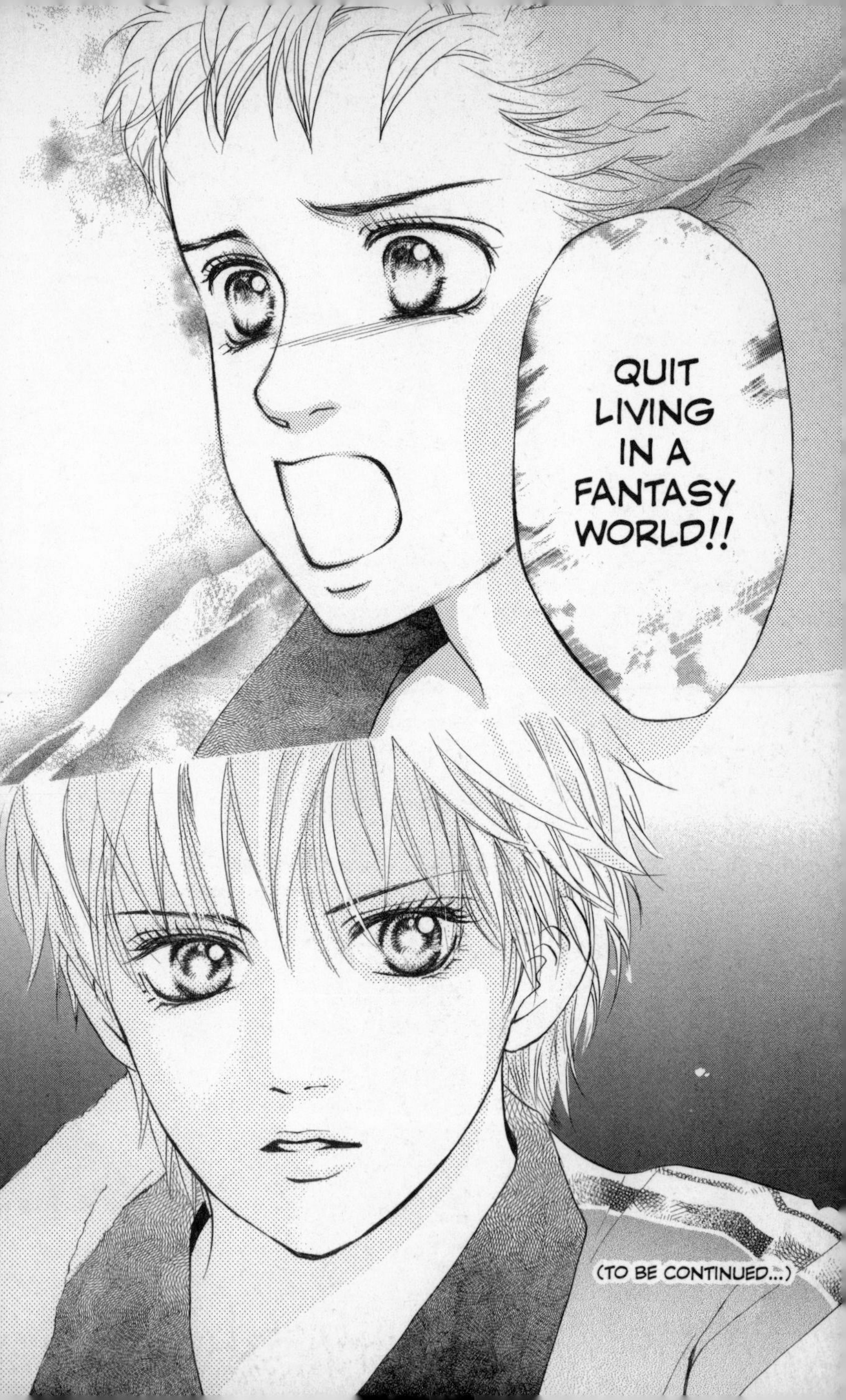
QUIT LIVING IN A FANTASY WORLD!!
(TO BE CONTINUED...)

♥Having been granted a little break, I took the opportunity to re-read *Crimson Hero* and found that there are a huge number of characters. Personally, I'm too scared to actually count how many. And I plan to introduce more. Part II will be starting soon in *Betsuma* magazine. If you'd like, please take a look at the magazine too.

—Mitsuba Takanashi, 2004

At age 17, Mitsuba Takanashi debuted her first short story, *Mou Koi Nante Shinai* (Never Fall in Love Again), in 1992 in *Bessatsu Margaret* magazine and now has several major titles under her belt.

Born in the Shimane Prefecture of Japan, Takanashi now lives in Tokyo, where she enjoys taking walks, watching videos, shopping, and going to the hair salon. Takanashi has a soft spot for the Japanese pop acts Yellow Monkey and Hide, and is good at playing ping-pong.

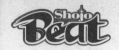

CRIMSON HERO

VOL. 6
The Shojo Beat Manga Edition

This manga volume contains material that was originally published in English in *Shojo Beat* magazine, March–June 2007 issues.

STORY AND ART BY
MITSUBA TAKANASHI

Translation & English Adaptation/Naoko Amemiya
Touch-up Art & Lettering/Mark Griffin
Graphics & Cover Design/Courtney Utt
Editor/Nancy Thistlethwaite

Editor in Chief, Books/Alvin Lu
Editor in Chief, Magazines/Marc Weidenbaum
VP of Publishing Licensing/Rika Inouye
VP of Sales/Gonzalo Ferreyra
Sr. VP of Marketing/Liza Coppola
Publisher/Hyoe Narita

Printed in Canada

Published by VIZ Media, LLC
P.O. Box 77010
San Francisco, CA 94107

Shojo Beat Manga Edition
10 9 8 7 6 5 4 3 2
First printing, August 2007
Second printing, October 2007

www.viz.com
store.viz.com

PARENTAL ADVISORY
CRIMSON HERO is rated T for Teen and is recommended for ages 13 and up. This volume contains suggestive themes.

ratings.viz.com